SEMANTICS AND COMMUNICATION

SEMANTICS AND COMMUNICATION

Proceedings of the

3rd Colloquium

of the

Institute for Communications Research and Phonetics

University of Bonn

February, 17th - 19th, 1972

edited by

Carl H. Heidrich

1974

North-Holland Publishing Company – Amsterdam • London
American Elsevier Publishing Company, Inc. – New York

©NORTH-HOLLAND PUBLISHING COMPANY – AMSTERDAM – 1974

Library of Congress Catalog Card Number 73–93561
ISBN North-Holland 0 7204 2801 7
ISBN American Elsevier 0 444 10634 0

PUBLISHERS:

NORTH-HOLLAND PUBLISHING COMPANY – AMSTERDAM
NORTH-HOLLAND PUBLISHING COMPANY, LTD. – LONDON

SOLE DISTRIBUTORS FOR THE U.S.A. AND CANADA:

AMERICAN ELSEVIER PUBLISHING COMPANY, INC.
52 VANDERBILT AVENUE
NEW YORK, N.Y. 10017

PRINTED IN THE NETHERLANDS

CONTENTS

PREFACE

The original title of the 3rd colloquium of the Institut for
Communications Research and Phonetics, IKP, was "Probleme einer
Kommunikationssemantik". At the time when this concept was chosen
people from the institute tried to establish new directions in the
main research area of the institute, verbal interpersonal
communication. We now call the objects of interpersonal
communications 'interactions', borrowing a well known term from
Sociology or Psychology. It seemed clear to us that 'interpersonal
communication' being a relational concept has to be interpreted
apriori as a pragmatic concept. The crucial problem that arises is
to characterize interactions by linguistic objects that occur in
interpersonal communication and to relate "contents" or "meaning"
to them. This view of the problem, I think, justifies an analogous
use of the concept 'semantics' and it was the origin of introducing
the compound noun "Kommunikationssemantik".
As we tried to characterize interactions by constructing models for
communication processes, we noticed that methodes for analyses were
either lacking or insufficient. This was the reason for us to make
procedures of analysis the main topic of our 3rd IKP colloquium.
When I began to organize the colloquium, I thought it would be
fruitful for us to invite scholars from different fields. The list
and grouping of the participants shows that we have selected some
aspects from Philosophy of Language, Philosophy of Pragmatics,
Sociology, Psychoanalysis, Modal Logic, and Formal Linguistics.
I want to express my thanks to the institutions, to the invited
speakers and chairmen, and to the colleagues who helped me to
realize the colloquium: The IKP is indebted to the Deutsche
Forschungsgemeinschaft (DFG) and to the International Union of
History and Philosophy of Science, Division of Logic, Methodology
and Philosophy of Science for their financial support; my thanks
are especially due to Dr. Briegel and Dr. Buntfuß of the DFG, and
to Prof. Rescher.
The spontaneous agreement of all speakers and chairmen to the plan
of the colloquium I suggested and their cooperation in the panels
and in the discussions contributed very much to the success of the
meeting.

VIII

Preface

My colleague, Mrs. Dr. A. Weidmann, helped me by doing a lot of
practical arrangements of the meeting.
The DFG also supported the preparation of the publication: the
students L. Biewer, S. Doenhoff, G. Liehr, J. Maurer, E. Preuschoft,
and H. Sievert transcribed the tape recordings of the meeting, and
G. Busch, M. Michels, W. Nothdurft did the typing of the
manuscripts, which were corrected by B. Haag.
The procedure of editing the material was as follows: Each speaker
who presented a paper in a panel has edited his paper and his
contributions to the discussion of the panel which he had been a
member of. I am responsible for the presentation of the rest of the
discussion. In exception to this procedure the contributions of the
discussion in Panel 1 of Prof. Staal, who was on vacation, was
edited by myself, M. Böttner helped me to correct the English
version.
I thank Mr. E. Fredriksson from the North-Holland Publishing Company
for his encouragement to publish the material.
My special thanks are due to Prof. Ungeheuer, the director of the
IKP, who generously gave me the opportunity to organize the
colloqium according to my intentions.

Carl H. Heidrich

PROBLEMS OF LINGUISTIC SEMANTICS FROM THE STANDPOINT OF THE
PHILOSOPHY AND METHODOLOGY OF LANGUAGE

Panel: Y.Bar-Hillel, The Hebrew University of Jerusalem
        H.Hiż, University of Pennsylvania, Philadelphia
        J.F.Staal, University of California, Berkeley
Chairman: H.Schnelle, Technische Universität Berlin

February, 17th, morning session.

SCHNELLE:

Ladies and Gentlemen.
This session is concerned with methodological and philosophical
problems emerging in the developement of linguistic semantics. In
view of preparing this session I put the following problem areas to
the attention of the panelists:
1. How do you understand the concept "linguistic semantics"? Do you
think that there is a set of defining properties on which all
linguists could agree? What is the relation between linguistic
semantics and the description of processes of language
communication?
2. What are the advantages or disadvantages of systems or theories
of linguistic semantics, in particular those proposed by the
panelists?
3. Can you present examples illustrating the proposed theory of
linguistic semantics?
I think that the panelists will expose directly or indirectly their
views on these problem areas. The first contribution will be that of
Prof.Y.Bar-Hillel. It will be followed by that of Prof.H.Hiż and
Prof.Staal.

BAR-HILLEL:

The same as many of my colleagues, I was and am accustomed to make
rather free use of the nominal strings "logical semantics" and
"linguistic semantics", without giving much thought to the question:
what lies behind the difference between them? - although we were
probably always aware of its importance. When in 1934 Rudolf Carnap
introduced the term "logical syntax", he was fully conscious of the
fact that this adjective "logical" gave rise to a mode of speech
which sharply deviated from the current use made by linguists at
that time of the word "syntax", even though he himself did not use
the complementary term 'linguistic syntax'. Neither do I know who
was the first to use the string "logical semantics" and in which
language. And this, of course, is of a certain systematic importance.
When in 1954 I published my essay "Logical syntax and semantics" in
the American journal L a n g u a g e, I used the string "logical
semantics" neither in the title nor in the text; although the
principal aim of the essay was to draw the attention of my fellow-
linguists to the fact that logicians such as Carnap and Tarski had
developed methods for dealing with artificial languages without
themselves applying them to natural languages, but which the
linguists could disregard only to their own loss. Carnap used the
adjective "logical" with "syntax" in two different senses:
(1) more or less synonymous with "formal", i.e., expressed
negatively, without any reference to meaning and use, and, expressed
positively, with sole reference to the kind and sequence of the
signs of which the larger strings are composed,
(2) to charakterize a conception of syntax which would enable us to
deal with the logical properties of sentences and with the logical
relations between them, something that for the linguists had until
then been absolutely unusual and strange.
The first-mentioned sense, both contextually and historically, is
not particulary apposite, and it is not worth while going into it.
The second one, too, has since become obsolete, especially through
Carnap's own later works. Instead, another pair of concepts has
emerged in recent decades. This opposes a "syntactic" to a
"semantic" treatment of logic, whether it is a matter of constructed
or natural languages, and in which such highly interesting problems
as the possibilities and limitations of the replacement of semantic
methods of dealing with logic by syntactic ones have been formulated
and partly solved, with such pertiment theorems as those of Gödel
and Tarski.

In 1933 Carnap still strove for a s y n t a c t i z a t i o n o f
l o g i c a l s e m a n t i c s, to put it in slogan terms, with
all the dangers connected with such simplifying formulations.
Shortly afterwards, however, he realized that this endeavour was
superfluous, after he had learned from Tarski that semantics can be
treated in a metaphysics- and in particular ontology-free manner.
Nowadays logicians are concerned with the problem to what purpose,
and how far, semantic logic is replaceable by a syntactic logic,
again in slogans: with the purposes and limitations of a
s y n t a c t i z a t i o n o f s e m a n t i c l o g i c rather
than of logical semantics.
What, then, is logical semantics? It will surprise nobody when,
after brief reflection, he will discover that the nominal string is
equivocal. I believe the contrary would surprise us nowadays. In one
sense, logical semantics is nothing else than semantics, whether of
artificial or natural languages, as it is practised by logicians;
linguistic semantics, correspondingly, is semantics as practised by
linguists; and philosophical semantics - the third element in this
triad and which I do not whish to go into today - is, of course,
semantics as practised by philosophers. This is an important, though
not very instructive, analysis, for as such it does not say much
about the methods of treatment.
When, sitting at my desk, I contemplated in what way the logical
treatment of semantics could be distinguished from the linguistic
treatment of semantics, as to its contents, I soon was led to the
following five dichotomies: The first is "normative" versus
"descriptive"; the 2nd "artificial" vs. "natural"; the 3rd "universal" vs. "particular"; the 4th "pure" vs. "applied"; and the 5th
"with particular regard to logical relations" versus "without
particular regard to logical relations". The first element of each
pair seemed to have something to do with "logical" and the second
with "linguistic". Here my imagination gave out.
I am, of course,unable to undertake a serious analysis of these
dichotomies within the limited time at my disposal. Such an analysis
will be carried out with some thoroughness in a chapter entitled
"Logic and theoretical linguistics" in vol.XII of C u r r e n t
T r e n d s i n L i n g u i s t i c s (J.A. Seboek, ed.), to be
published in 1973. I would like to devote the reminder of my time to
a short exploration of the last-mentioned dichotomy, i.e., "with
particular regard to logical relations" versus "without particular
regard to logical relations". This dichotomy is discussed much less

frequently than the other four. On my panel you see Professor Staal
who, in 1967, participated in a symposium on "Formal logic and
linguistics" which I prepared and introduced within the framework of
the 3rd International Congress on Logic, Methodology and Philosophy
of Sciences, and who subsequently published an excellent report on
this symposium in F o u n d a t i o n s   o f   L a n g u a g e, 5
(1969), pp. 256-284. I presume that some of those present here have
attended that symposium. There it was already clear that many
linguists - at first in America, but soon also in Europe - had come
to realize that no serious description of natural languages is
feasible without somehow dealing with the logical form of the
sentences in those languages, after which the logical properties and
relations of these sentences can be formulated. The fifth dichotomy
was recognized already at that time as a pseudo-dichotomy, though I
would not claim that all linguists share this view. Neither do I
have the time to go into the interesting historical developments
which led to this realization. In place of this pseudo-question
there arose another, much more serious, question which from the very
beginning transcended the borderlines between logicians and
linguists. The question now was whether logical form, which
determines the logical properties of and the relations between the
sentences, should be attributed to the sentences as such in their
surface structure -as was the current term already at that time - or
to the deep structures underlying them; perhaps even whether logical
form should be identified with deep structure. At the outset, not
every linguist was aware of the fact that this same differentiation,
though not in exactly the same terminology, had already been made by
Russell and Wittgenstein, both philosophical logicians or logical
philosophers, half a century earlier. One of the numerous questions
I asked those gathered at the Amsterdam symposium was whether this
taking into account of the logical properties and relations of the
sentences in natural languages should be direct or indirect, meaning
by this pair of adjectives precisely the opposition just formulated
- though I did not then formulate it in this way and, therefore
was not properly understood by all the participants in the
discussion - and right ly   so. Of course, you will see at once that
this dichotomy overlaps several of the previously mentioned
dichotomies so that, for instance, one can be of the opinion that
the deep structure of sentences in natural languages should best be
represented in a suitable artificial language, that this artificial
language, then, should be the same for all natural languages, i.e.

that it should be universal that this artificial language could be
discovered by transcendental reflexion and that, in this sense, it
would be both normative and pure, etc. Those of you who were in
Amsterdam will recall that Montague (of whom only few people knew
until then that he had been exploring for years, very intensively,
the logic, semantics, and pragmatics of natural languages) pleaded
in favour of the direct method and gave the first hints of his
researches which, shortly thereafter, started to appear in print in
quick succession and which are about to influence decisively the
attitudes of many professional mathematical logicians towards the
logic of natural languages and the attitudes of many linguists
towards the use of the sophisticated methods of mathematical
logicians and model theorists for their own purposes. But the mode
of expression I just employed is not sufficiently precise. Montague
objected to the deep structure syndrome only, or mainly, because it
originated from the M.I.T. school of linguistics (the so-called MIT-
niks) whose work appeared to him as lacking in precision to such a
degree as to be ruled out of serious competition. But in his own
semantics, Montague by no means dealt with sentences of natural
languages as such but rather with ordered pairs of such sentences
and so-called indexes, which themselves were ordered quadruples of
points of reference indicating the speaker, the audience, the time,
and the place of the various utterances - in short, describing the
situation of the utterance, and all this relative to possible
worlds. In addition, he had no objections to representing these
constructs in a language of intensional logic, i.e. to a typically
indirect treatment. Among others, Katz was in favour of the direct
method at that time, pleading for the method of semantic representations in his own specific sense. I am mentioning all this only in
order to deal finally with the decisive question: How does all this
look five years after Amsterdam? Although the chaos in linguistic
semantics has rather increased since then and will probably increase
even more over the coming years, and dozens of new systems, or at
least of new variants of old systems, are making and will make their
debut each year - some of which might even show up during this panel
discussion and perhaps also in the other discussions - this much
seems to be clear to me : The opposition between logical and
linguistic methods of dealing with the semantics of natural
languages is progressively evaporating. And when one reads two
contributions by unknown authors to the problem of, say, the
presuppositions, the number of logical inaccuracies on the one hand

and of naive sounding remarks on linguistic usage on the other, this
might provide a clue to their different backgrounds; but this can
hardly be deduced from the contents of their remarks.

With regard to the subject of deep structures, surprisingly enough
hardly anything decisive has happened in the course of the past four
years. Whereas Montague officially declined to work with
transformations, though he did, of course, work with other means
which perform some of their functions, David Lewis, for instance, no
longer has any scruples of this sort. The variety of opinions as to
how the deep structures should look, which types of transformations
are strong enough but not too strong, has even increased, and it is
anything but clear whether something like deep structures are at all
necessary for the logical form, although, as far as I know, no
seriously competitive conception has been put forth as yet. Neither
has anything definitely new been said about the best form of
semantic rules. Today it ought to be rather generally recognized
that dictionaries and rules of projection are far from sufficient
(though Katz, in his new book S e m a n t i c   T h e o r y (1972),
continues to make do with such means); but it cannot be said that
there has been a consensus or even a rapprochement on the question
of the format of the needed additional rules. Likewise, there has
been rather a sharpening of the differences of opinions as to which
·type of logic should form the basis of the semantics of natural
languages, whether this is the correct mode of expression at all,
and if so, where the line should be drawn between semantics and the
basic logic, and whether, e.g., logic can be identified with
universal semantics in any serious sense - as I once proposed -
which would then also require an explication of the term "universal
semantics" which has not been seriously undertaken so far. This
task, by the way, is very urgent anyway, since the prefix
"universal" has come into general use lately, not only in connection
with universal languages and universal grammars, but also with
universal syntax and recently even with universal pragmatics.
Chomsky has already pointed out the double meaning of "universal" in
this context, viz., firstly, as c o m m o n   t o   a l l
l a n g u a g e s - in which case one could further differentiate
between "universal" as necessarily common and "general" as
accidentilly common if this suits the author's philosophical
position. as I also tentatively hinted at the time: and secondly, as
d e t e r m i n i n g   t h e   c o n d i t i o n s that any adequate
semantics must fulfil, thus t r a n s c e n d e n t a l in a

quasi-Kantian sense. It ought to be clear what a hornets' nest one
would thereby stir up, and this is probably the main reason why I
have not yet seen any further elaboration of Chomsky's ideas in this
connection although I am convinced that we shall hear more about
this in the course of our meeting. Another reason for this neglect
may lie in the fact that the expression "semantic universals" is
much more attractive than "universal semantics" since the former
expression evokes associations with profound perennial philosophical
problems, whereas the latter reminds us, at most, of Leibniz'
c h a r a c t e r i s t i c a   u n i v e r s a l i s which, since
the early 19th century, was no longer able to stir up the interest
of linguists, at least not until the publication of Chomsky's
C a r t e s i a n   L i n g u i s t i c s.
I hope that what I have said will suffice to indicate that I am not
prepared to recognize substantive barriers of any kind though I
would not go so far as to accept the formula of Montague and many
others to the effect that there are no differences whatsoever
between natural and constructed languages - as this formula seems to
me far too extreme and only liable to revive unnecessary
controversies.
The breach of the last psychological barriers between logicians and
linguists with regard to the treatment of the semantics of natural
languages came from a quite unexpected direction, namely from syntax
syntax. An interesting development emerged in recent years, of which
I am not sure whether it is known to all interested linguists,
although we have amongst us some active participants in this
development. What I mean is the renaissance of the c a t e g o r-
i c a l   g r a m m a r s. It is assumed by many that Chomsky's
phrase structure grammars (regular, simple, context-free, linear,
context-sensitive, etc.) are adequate at least for the basis of the
natural languages, perhaps even for the generation of the set of
a l l sentences of natural languages as well, but at least for the
generation of the sentences needed in computer languages; thus an
immense literature has appeared within a short period, dealing with
these and similar grammars in their innumerable axiomatic details,
examining the scope of their application, ascertaining their weak
and strong equivalences and non-equivalences, etc. I myself have
been occupied with such things for some years. However, it is known
to a minority only that the first attempts at an algebraic
linguistics were concerned with grammars of an at least
superficially different structure, that is, with the categorial

grammars developed mostly by Ajdukiewicz on the basis of beginnings
made by Kotarbiński and Leśniewski, and developed some more by
myself and my collaborators. These grammars have considerable
pedagogical, but not less substantive advantages of the phrase
structure grammars, as was recently pointed out by, for instance,
Mr. Potts here and by Mr. Lehrberger who is a pupil of Mr. Hiż
here though not yet published. Therefore it is rather a pity that
I myself interrupted the development of these grammars at the time,
i.e. in 1953 (although I still published something about them from
time to time), for reasons of which I already gave a hint elsewhere
but which I now wish to describe at some greater length since they
seem to me important for the revival of these grammars. Apart from
the banal fact that in that year I returned from the United States
to Israel and my new academic duties occupied me fully over that
period, leaving no time for further serious reseach, the principal
reason was that I had come up against barriers which, in 1953, I did
not know how to overcome in a simple manner although I had some
ideas. Of these numerous barriers I shall mention, for the sake of
brevity, only two: 1. D i s c o n t i n u o u s   e x p r e s-
s i o n s, such as "called...up" as in <u>John called his girl friend</u>
<u>up</u> where the length and sometimes also the syntactic structure of
the strings between the parts are indeterminate, or at least
appeared thus to me then, and could not, therefore, be dealt with
by means of the classical categorial grammars nor, for that matter,
of the classical phrase structure grammars. 2. The fact that certain
expressions, as for instance ad-sentences (sentential adverbs) like
"unfortunately" can be interpolated in simple sentences in almost
any place, which again could not be dealt with by the means current
at that time. I was not clever enough to notice that all this, and
much nore, could be done by means of Chomskyan transformations, for
the simple reason that at that time there existed no transformation
grammars. When Chomsky discovered or invented them in the following
year, he unfortunately based them on phrase structure grammars,
probably because this type of grammar was closely related to the
constituent grammars which were common in America at the time so
that he could avoid introducing two essential innovations
simultaneously and could save his strength for the one revolutionary
innovation.

Mr. Hiż here is doubtlessly acquainted with the categorial grammars
since his student years in Poland, and he is still working on their
further development with important results. I have just mentioned

a new Technical Report by one of his students. Montague probably
heard of these categorial grammars from his teacher Tarski, who
being a pupil of Leśniewski and Kotarbiński, knew of them as a
matter of course though he did not himself engage in their
development. Then David Lewis probably heard about categorial
grammars from Montague. Peter Geach, who is not with us, knows
Polish, was always interested in Polish logic, and probably became
interested in the categorial grammars through this source. I presume
that my colleague, Mr.Potts here, got interested through him. I am
not saying all this because the biographical details are of
particular importance, but only in order to emphasize my belief
that the revival of the interest of eminent philosophical logicians
in categorial grammars would probably have died down again had not
men like David Lewis, Potts and others, independently from each oth
other and from me (though I made occasional mention thereof in
lectures and seminars, I had not published anything important on the
subject in years), hit upon the decisive, though almost obvious,
idea to develop a c a t e g o r i a l - t r a n s f o r m a -
t i o n a l g r a m m a r, analogous to the phrase-structure-
transformational grammar, but superior to the latter in essential
points. For us it might be of decisive importance that there is
every indication that it will be feasible to create for categorial
grammars a semantics which would be adequate for logical purposes,
by means of rules with a clearer structure than for other grammars
current today. Should it turn out that, additionally, one can make
do with transformations which do not alter the semantic contents
of the transformands (and, despite Chomsky, there is a certain
chance for this although it is not yet possible to predict what
price will have to be paid for this extremely useful property), then
I foresee that categorial grammars will gain in popularity, both
with logicians and with linguists - and this, as already adumbrated,
would eliminate the last barriers to an understanding between them.
And since the elimination of these barriers is the L e i t -
m o t i v of my crusade of nearly twenty years' duration, let me
close my discourse on this optimistic note.

HIŻ:

I would like, first of all, to make some comments about the
relationship between linguistics and semantics because that is the
title of our panel. It is quite clear that semantics has always been
part of linguistics and that there is really no dualism between the
two. Rather the question is to what extent semantical facts enter
various parts of linguistics and in what way.

The distinction usually made is not between linguistics and
semantics but between semantics and syntax, for instance. But when
one thinks how linguists work, it seems clear that semantical facts
enter every facet of linguistic work, even in phonology. In
phonology, when we establish that two utterances contrast or that
they do not contrast, we say that the two utterances do not count
as repetitions of each other, or that they do, and the judgement is
a semantical judgment. This point was noted by Harris, in his
M e t h o d s   i n   S t r u c t u r a l   L i n g u i s t i c s
(1951), but not noted by many of his reviewers.

Similarly, in syntax we take semantical facts into account. It is
clear that when we speak about a structure (in anyone of many
senses of "structure" and in any theory of syntactic structure of a
sentence or of a longer utterance), we speak of the structure which
is imposed on utterances by semantical considerations.

And it is not different in mathematics. This point should be
stressed. It is a well known fact that in a mathematical language,
say in propositional calculus, one can give a purely syntactic
generation of all and only well-formed formulas, and one often
concludes that this is a purely syntactic characterization of the
language. However, this is a gross misrepresentation of what
actually happens. The set of well-formed formulas can be generated
in a purely syntactical fashion in many different ways. But we
choose one, namely the one which will be called for by the rules of
inference. We state rules of inference, for example, that for a
variable you can substitute expressions of a particular kind, and
therefore, if our syntactic description of the structure of a
formula does not specifically indicate variables, then such a
description would be useless for stating or for using the rules of
inference. Similarly if one gives some generation of the set of
well-formed formulas of the propositional calculus which does not
take into account the fact that an implication has an
antecedent and a consequent, then one would never be able to use

m o d u s   p o n e n s. It is m o d u s   p o n e n s, the rule of
detachment, which imposes on formulas of the propositional calculus
the proper structure. In arithmetic when you have a formula
'2 + 3 = 5', you consider that there are two sides of the equation,
that the main functor is the equal sign, and that to the left of it
is a numerical phrase and to the right of it is a numerical phrase,
and you do so because otherwise you would not be able to operate
with a semantic rule: that to both sides of the equation you may
add the same quantity, preserving the truth of the equation. This
rule of inference is semantically valued. One may multiply examples
to show that in mathematics, in chemical formulas, and similarly in
all sience and in ordinary language, one has semantic rules and one
looks at the structure of utterances from the point of view of
those rules.
Of course, one states the rules by means of some technical apparatus.
apparatus. The technical apparatus may be some grammatical
categories, it may be sequences of some abstract concepts, it may be
trees, it may be sequences of trees, it may be a combination of
these, or still other trickery, and the very same apparatus in which
you formulate your rules of inference will apply to the description
of the structure of the utterances to which the rules apply.
I would like to give an example of how semantic considerations enter
syntactic work. Let us take a very simple two sentence text:
        I did my graduate work.   So may Jane.
First, this text may be considered ambiguous. But what does it mean
that it is ambiguous. The judgement is already a semantic one. More
exactly: What is ambiguity? We characterize this ambiguity by
saying that in one sense this text implies, or gives as a
consequence, the following statement:
        Jane may do her graduate work.
In the other sense this text gives a consequence:
        Jane may do my graduate work.
Therefore, if I am saying that this text is ambiguous, I am saying
that there is a sentence, for instance:
        Jane may do my graduate work,
which is a consequence of this text in one sense and not a
consequence of it in another sense. In addition, there is a
sentence, namely
        Jane may do her graduate work,
which is a consequence of this text in the second sense, and not a
consequence of it in the first sense. Therefore ambiguity here boils

down to two different statements about the field of consequences of
this text. No syntactician ever intends to eliminate the discussion
about consequences from linguistics, just as no logician ever
intends or intended to eliminate the concept of conseqence from
logic. Even if sometimes logicians and linguists try to syntacticize
a given semantic concept to give a complete syntactical characterization of it to show that there is a syntactical concept which is
of the same extension, semantic concepts are a subject of main study
by logicians and linguists. For very simple logical systems the
concept of consequence has been syntacticized, has been described
completely in syntactical terms. This has not eliminated semantics;
it has only described it in syntactical terms. For a natural language, of course, the concept of consequence is much too rich to
hope to be completely syntacticized, but we still want to state some
rules of consenquence, and one can look at the development of transformational grammmars for the last twenty years exactly as an
attempt at stating various consequences, paraphrase , and other
semantic rules.
To show a little bit more about the text which serves as an example,
let me write here a little bit of grammar, or syntactic characterization, of it. I will claim that the syntactic characterization
will be exactly the one which will be used for stating, for instance
instance, the fact about consequences which I stated a moment ago.
Graduate work is an interesting creature linguistically because it
looks as if it were a nominalization. Work is a nominalization,
graduate work is not; you do not work graduately. The modifier makes
work not a nominalization any more. And therefore graduate work has
to be treated as one expression which is a noun. Our example is
composed of two grammatically interwoven sentences. In the formula
below they are S and S. This formula shows a structure with which
one can take ^{7} the ^{16} text.

```
        I   do                        past        my
        N   (   (S; N N); Tp/M)      ( Tp; N)    ( Poss; N)
        1   2   67  [1][10]  [8]      3  8  [1]   4   9   [1]

        graduate work.  So
        (  N; Det)      (  (  S; Tp/M N); ((S; NN); Tp/M)
        5  10  [9]      11 15 16  [14]  [13]

                        may          Jane.
        (Poss;N) (N;Det))    ( Tp/M; N)   N
                            12   14       13
```

In the notation used $\underline{N}$ is a noun phrase, $\underline{Tp}$ is a tense-person
morpheme, $\underline{M}$ is a modal, α / β is either α or β, $\underline{P\ o\ s\ s}$ is a
possessive, $\underline{D\ e\ t}$ is a determiner (a $\underline{P\ o\ s\ s}$ is a $\underline{D\ e\ t}$),
$(\alpha; \beta_1, \ldots, \beta_k)$ is a phrase which forms a phrase of category
together with phrases of categories $\beta_1, \ldots, \beta_k$ respectively. For
instance, graduate work is considered (N;Det), that is a phrase
which together with a determiner forms a noun phrase. The determiner
required is the possessive 9. The Poss is formed by the word $\underset{4}{\underline{my}}$

(or it may be spelled $\underset{4}{\underline{one's}}$) which is in agreement with a noun

phrase. The noun phrase here is N. So that N in 4 indicates that N
$\qquad\qquad\qquad\qquad\qquad\qquad\qquad\qquad\quad 1 \qquad\qquad\qquad 1$
does not occur in $\underline{my}$, but only that the phrase $\underline{my}$ uses N for its
$\qquad\qquad\qquad\qquad\qquad\qquad\qquad\qquad\qquad\qquad\qquad 1$
agreement. Similarly, the square brackets around 9 in $\underset{5\quad\ \ 10\quad [9]}{\underset{(\quad N;\quad Det)}{\underline{graduate\ work}}}$

show that in the phrase 5, that is in graduate work, the determiner

does not occur but that it is required to occur somewhere else and

that Det is taken as satisfying this requirement. Incidentally, $\underline{so}$
$\qquad\qquad\qquad\qquad\qquad\qquad\qquad\qquad\qquad\qquad\qquad\qquad\qquad\qquad\ \ 9$
is a referential to a part of the previous sentence S. And what $\underset{7}{S}$ $\qquad^7$

contributes to S is, firstly, the verb $\underline{to\ do}$, but without its
$\qquad\qquad\qquad\ \ 16$
tense, secondly, graduate work, and thirdly, the possessive $\underline{one's}$.

This is indicated by the assignment of grammatical   category to $\underline{so}$.

$\underline{So}$ is considered a functor which forms a phrase of grammatical
category (S; Tp/M N) together with three phrases of the grammatical
categories of $\underline{do}$, $\underline{my}$, and graduate work respectively, namely
((S; NN); Tp/M), (Poss; N) and (N; Det). Note that no such phrases
actually occur in S. $\underline{So}$ is only a referential to such phrases in S.
$\qquad\qquad\qquad\qquad\ \ 16 \qquad\qquad\qquad\qquad\qquad\qquad\qquad\qquad\qquad\qquad\qquad\qquad 7$
These phrases in S therefore play a double role: whatever role each
$\qquad\qquad\qquad\quad 7$
of them plays in S and the role of arguments to the functor 15 in
$\qquad\qquad\qquad\quad 7$
S. Similarly, N is used as an argument to three different functors
16
in S. A categorial grammar in which an occurence of a phrase can be
$\ 7$
used as an argument to more than one functor or as a functor more
than one set of arguments was elaborated by John Lehrberger in his
doctoral dissertation (University of Pennsylvania, 1971). In this
spirit a referential is a functor which takes its referend as an
argument. In the case of $\underline{so}$ the referend is discontiguous; it
appears in three segments.

The grammatical structure shown by the formula can be, of course,
written using a more common way of writing using trees and
transformations. The difference would be mainly in "spelling". Here
is a fragment:

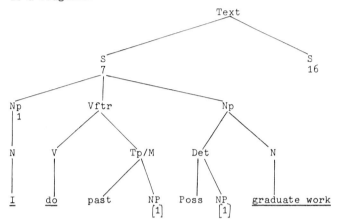

Vftr is a finite transitive verb. It is more complicated to write
the structure of S. But in any case it is the rule of consequence
                  16
which will really show the use of the structure not this or
another notation. S   takes do Poss graduate work in the structure
                   16
of S as its functor and may and Jane as arguments.
   7

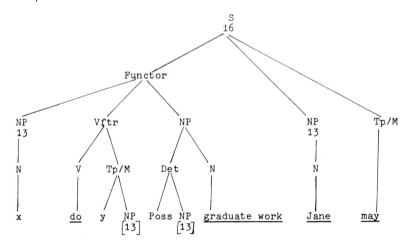

The rule must state that 'x' and 'y' of the functor are to be
replaced by Jane and may respectively to get a correct consequence
of the text.
To end with I would like to say that it is important that in the
text I did my graduate work. So may Jane, when we characterize
this as an ambiguous text, we are saying that there is a sentence
which is a consequence of it in one sense and not a consequence of
it in another. And perhaps this is in practice one of the very
important differences between the work of a linguist and the work
of a logician. But only in practice; that is, we take negative
information, a negative datum, in linguistics much more extensively
than we do in mathematics. In mathematics a logician is interested
in independent proof, but in linguistics every linguist works all
the time with negative data. Something does not exist, something is
not transformed in such and such a way, something is not negated in
the way something else is; all such observations are very important
material for a linguist. Just as in phonology, from the very
beginning of modern linguistics, negative information of contrast
or lack of contrast was used, so now whether something is a
consequence or is not a consequence enters into every phase of
linguistics.
Finally, there are certainly semantical concepts which are only
barely relevant for the actual work of a linguist. One of them is
the concept of truth. It is hopeless to try to make even slight
progress in the syntactization of the concept of truth. However,
this does not mean that we cannot say some reasonable things about
truth. But this extends beyond the usual work of a linguist. This
is rather work of metalinguistics, another theory of language,
and a much stronger one, where much stronger semantical relations
occur than those of consequence, paraphrase, negation or inquiry.
Truth, falsehood, meaning are such stronger concepts. A linguist
deals rather with preservation of truth, preservation or difference
of meaning than with truth and meaning by themselves. It is
therefore important to realize that linguistics, as practiced now,
does not exhaust semantical problems and that there may be plenty
of semantical problems which are not helpful immediately for a
syntactician and which a syntactician cannot attack very well
because they are too rich.

STAAL:

Let me start with some remarks in reaction to the questions that our chairman, Professor Schnelle, raised and then continue with a few special cases that seem to present some interest within this context.

Professor Schnelle asked what linguistic semantics is. Is there a set of properties defining that notion? In my opinion, there is at present no set of properties which defines linguistic semantics. Linguistic semantics might be something like the following: a proper part of the grammer of a natural language, that is to say, of a system that will relate sound and meaning of all sentences of a natural language to each other. Now, whether that system will consist of, say, phonology, syntax, semantics and pragmatics, or whether it will consist of more or fewer components, or whether there will be some kind of continuum between those parts, or whether there will be some mixture, I do not know. One might be tempted to say that linguistic semantics would be that part of that system (if there i s a seperate part of that system) which deals more directly with meaning. But it might be better to say that, if we have found that it pays to postulate linguistic semantics as a separate one, we are in a position to evolve a meaningful manner of talking about meaning.

This point of view implies that linguistic semantics, if found to exist as a separate domain, would have to be developed within a theory of grammar. Therefore the important work that has been done by logicians, philosophers, and methodologists of language has to be studied by linguists and then, I think, it has to be done all over again within the framework of linguistics.

This would seem to imply particularly such systems as have been proposed by Montague and Davidson.

This point of view implies that there i s a distinction between these logical systems and the parts of linguistics that may be constructed to incorporate them. I tend to stress that when in the company of logicians and philosophers. But when talking to linguists, I tend to agree with Montague or Bar-Hillel who say that there is no distinction between natural and artificial languages. But when I am by myself, or not thinking of any particular audience or company, I think that this problem is a) not so very important, b) it is anyway to early to settle it. Let me say a little bit more about the distinction before I go into some kind of detail. Linguists in the footsteps of Chomsky, even if

they are not transformationalists, try to give a universal - and
universal is here what Bar-Hillel called what is "notwendig
gemeinsam" -, a general unified theory of natural languages which,
however, covers only the phenomena of natural languages. Chomsky's
basic intuition about language seems to be that there is something
"innate" about its structure. That has led to much confusion and to
an enormous amont of discussions. Chomsky means, among other things,
that languages in a way that is not "natural", "necessary",
"obvious" or "logical" relate sound and meaning to each other.
Rather they do this in very particular ways and these are
characteristic of human beings as users of languages. In support of
these views, Chomsky generally discusses some examples with which
you may or may not agree, examples, for instance, exemplifying the
cycle of transformations, something that seems extremely far
fetched to people not user to this kind of linguistics. Once you
work with it and start to think about it, it seems to have a certain
naturalness - but then many things become natural when you get used
to them though at first sight they might have seemed strange and
weird. Why should sound and meaning in language not be related in
such a way as to incorporate a system of transformations that work
cyclically? And why shouldn't there be some transformations that
are precyclical and others that are postcyclical?
You may not like this theory or you may not believe in it and after
ten years, that theory may have disappeared; but what is important
is the idea which is behind it: namely that there is something
specific about language, just like there is something specific
about the number of teeth which we have, or the number of legs. It
is quite understandable that we have two legs: you can do a lot of
things on two legs. But one might also have three legs, or one leg,
or wheels.
So, there is a difference between natural languages and artificial
languages. One would expect that the languages logicians study are
the most general possible systems of relation between writing
systems and meaning. But since human languages have rather specific
properties, they would constitute a proper subset of the languages
logicians study. So you would expect there to be an additional
constraint that has to be put on these general systems before they
would happen to coincide with the structures that characterize
natural languages.
Now it should be obvious that we have not by any means reached a
general theory of languages, from which we can derive natural as

well as artificial languages by imposing certain constraints, by
imposing certain additional conditions. Moreover, there is a
difference between at least some logicians and some linguists with
respect to these constraints. Most linguists feel that not only the
correct grammatical sentences of natural languages have to be
derived, but that they have to be derived in the correct way. This
seems to be one of the points that irritates Quine as may be seen
in the discussions of the Stanford colloquium published in
S y n t h e s e, Vol.21/22. Quine either does not understand or he
does not like that one has not only to derive correct results, but
that one has also to derive them in the correct fashion. Listening
to Professor Hiż, I feel that he would basically agree with the
linguists, but still there is a kind of dangerous use of
terminology. For instance, when speaking about rules, trees, sequences of trees and so on he says "and such trickery". But at other
times he clearly contrasts different approaches, namely those with
transformations and those without, by saying: "well, this is not
merely a difference in spelling, which would be like trickery,
which would be like deriving the correct result without paying any
attention to the way in which it should be derived".
Next I want to give a few illustrations of the kind of problems
that linguists are puzzled by, and that, - I think it is always
good to remind logicians and philosophers of, otherwise they tend
to repeat themselves -. This is not precisely what our chairman
called "Analysen linguistischer Fragestellungen", it is rather a
couple of odd things for which I do not think it is easy to give
any kind of analysis.
Let me first take an example discussed by Robin Lakoff, which comes
close to pragmatics (if that is a separate domain), or at any rate
involves the s i t u a t i o n and the c o n t e x t, that is to
say, it makes different utterances of sentences in different
contexts. I should like to know whether it has a counter-part in
German since I only have it in English: A customer comes into a
store to buy some apples and he points at them and he asks: What
is their price? The storekeeper might reply Those will be three
for a dollar. Why does the storekeeper use the form will be? What
one could say is If you buy them then you w i l l h a v e t o
p a y a dollar for three. But why it is so is unclear.
Another fact which I quote from Jespersen, the "P h i l o s o p h y
o f G r a m m a r", but which you find in a number of books,
is on sequences of tenses. Let me read what Jespersen says about it:

"Corresponding to

(1)   I am ill

(2)   I saw her today

(3)   I have not yet seen her

and he goes on for some time, "indirect discourse has the shifted
tenses in

(1')   he said that he was ill

(2')   he said that he had seen her the other day

(3')   he said that he had not seen her yet."

So the corresponding members are:

       I am ill
       he said that he was ill

       I saw her the other day
       he said he had seen her the other day

       I have not yet seen her
       he said that he had not seen her yet

       I shall have finished by noon
       he said that he should have finished by noon

and so on.

What is going on here could be described in transformational terms.
Treating tenses as something like modal operators, I prefix the
tenses to sentences as some kind of pre-sentence. If tenses are
written as T_1, T_2, ... and sentences incorporating these tenses as
$T_1(S)$, $T_2(S)$, ..., where 'S' is some kind of sentence radical, we
can embed such structures in higher sentences which have the
structure 'O': I saw that Z. Now, given a sentence $T_1(S)$, embedding
it in such a higher structure yields $O(T_2(S))$, when T_2 depends on T_1
in a systematic way. But though it is a systematic and obviously
rule-governed dependency, it is not at all obvious how it should be
treated.

Another example is taken from Sanskrit, as described by the Sanskrit
grammarians beginning with Pāṇini. In Sanskrit, and only in
Sanskrit, we have the following fact: If someone asks Have you made
the mat? and you want to answer Yes, I have made it, then in
Sanskrit you answer with the present indicative, i.e., you say:
Yes, I make it, using the present indicative. However, when you use
the negation or when you use a certain particle which hardly has
any meaning by itself, there is option in: You can either use the
present or you can answer in some past tense. For instance, if the

question is Have you made the mat? , then you can either answer:
No, I have not made the mat or you can answer No, I do not make the
mat. And if you want to use this particular particle which is n u,
and the question is Have you made the mat? , then you can either
answer N u, I have made the mat or n u, I am making the mat.
A similarly curious use of indexes mentioned for instance by Geach
and by Robin Lakoff is the use of tenses in letter writing in Latin.
In Latin, when a person writes a letter, he uses the past tense,
when referring to what he is doing now, that is to say, he adopts
the view of the person who receives the letter. In English, you
could write: While I write this, I am aware of such and such, but in
Latin one writes: While I wrote this, I was aware of..... That is to
say, one does something like the following: When you read this,you
will learn that when I wrote this I was aware..., from which all
the higher clauses are subsequently deleted. This may be achieved
by a whole lot of deletion transformations which omit all those
parts, so that you are left with the right result. But whether this
is actually the right way to handle it, I do not know.
The last example I want to give is again from Sanskrit and
concerns the use of the perfect tense. In English has been, has
alone etc. are sometimes described as expressing an action in the
past which has present relevance, whatever that is. In Sanskrit,
both as described by the grammarians and as found in actual usage,
the situation is different. The Sanskrit grammarians have arrived at
an abstract formulation which covers all the cases of actual usage
and which is intuitively quite clear, but which seems to be
exceedingly difficult to formalize, or even clearly write down. The
definition of the grammarians as you find it in Pānini is the
following: The perfect denotes or expresses what is out of sight -
"paroksa" - that is to say, something that from the point of view
of the speaker is entirely out of sight of the speaker, that has
happened for instance a long time ago and that he has forgotten.
This is explained in a grammatical commentary, which may be
paraphrased in the following terms: What is out-of-sight? Since we
are dealing with words, how can a word be i n - s i g h t or
o u t - o f - s i g h t? The answer is that it means the meaning
expressed by the word. What is the meaning? The action expressed by
it. But in that case one would expect the perfect in He cooked a
meal yesterday where in fact the imperfect is used since the
action is not seen. But notice that actions are never seen. It is
the instruments that bring the action about that may or may not be

seen. For example, if one sees water in which rice has been cooked,
one might say He cooked, using the imperfect. But if not, if one
does not see the water in which the rice has been cooked, but there
are other circumstances which imply that rice has been cooked, then
one says: he has cooked, using the perfect.
This analysis has other implications which are supported by the
facts. When can the perfect be used for the first person? Very
rarely, only when a person has been asleep, or drunk, of fully
absent-minded. For instance: Being asleep I have (or: I seem to
have) chattered. When I was intoxicated, I seem to have talked to
a lot in front of him. Here Sanskrit uses for what I translated as
I seem to have talked, I seem to have chattered, or chattered, or
talked, the perfect because intoxication or being asleep you do not
quite know what exactly you were doing. For instance: The grammarian
Sakatayana who was sitting on a road (which is not uncommon in
India) was so absorbed in grammatical problems that he did not
notice that a caravan was passing by. And when he later described
that event to a colleague, he said: I seem to have seen... using
the perfect. What happened is that he did not really see the
caravan, for he was fully absorbed in his problems. But someone else
told him that the caravan had passed by.
This use of the perfect also occurs with negatives, in the following
way. Did you stay in the country of the Kaliṅgas? Answer: I did not
so much as go to the Kaliṅgas, using the perfect: I have not gone
there at all. And in question it may also be used, for instance,:
Did you perform a sacrifice? Here one can use the perfect or the
imperfect because the questioner does not know whether the person
did or did not perform a sacrifice. Only when the answer has been
given you know which tense you ought to have used.
The pragmatics of such a usage seems to me to be extremely puzzling.
All I can do is to submit it to the consideration of logicians and
linguists.

DISCUSSION:

Schnelle: As already initially announced, we shall now have a
discussion between the panelists. Let me initiate the discussion
by putting the question about the relationsbetween logical semantics
and linguistic semantics. The evaluation of this relation seems to
be controversial among the panelists. More specifically:
Could there be a collaboration of logicians and linguists or not? As
I understand Mr. Staal, he says: "Well, the logicians may have given
us some suggestions; but that may be the most. The actual work
which should be done must be done by linguists themselves and they
will have to do what logicians have done all over again for those
parts where they find it worth while."
The other panelists hold quite different views on that, I think.
We should give them just the opportunity to attack Mr.Staal. Mr.Bar-
Hillel said, if I remember correctly, that there is no adequate
description of natural language, which does not take account of
the logical form of sentences, and Mr.Hiż on the other hand said
that the semantic problems which may be treated by logicians or
which are of interest for logicians cannot be exhausted by a
linguistic treatment and what the syntactitian can do nevertheless
he can solve many problems within this field. He would therefore
say that the difference between what the logician does in his
logical syntax and what the linguist would do is not so much
different. So I should like to ask Mr.Bar-Hillel and Mr.Hiż to
comment on the statements of Mr.Staal and then he should give a
reply.
Bar-Hillel: Well, I'll try to do my best. I don't really see any
basic differences between the views of the three of us, which is
a shame and a pity. I hope that the audience at least will raise
some basic disagreements.
I have, however, two comments, one on Hiż's presentation and one on
Staal's. Hiż's statement that linguists are not interested in
truth, I take it, was not a purely descriptive statement but was
probably also meant to be normative. That is not really the
business of linguists to be interested in truth. This negative
remark should be supplemented by the positive statement to the
effect that linguists should be and are indeed beginning to be
interested in t r u t h   c o n d i t i o n s, which is a different
matter. We don't have to accept the position of Davidson and others
that truth conditions completely determine the meaning of

expressions of natural languages or adopt a somewhat more liberal
attitude to it, the treatment of truth conditions is something which
linguists cannot avoid dealing with. I hope that Henry would agree
to this truth. Though, then, reference, extension and truth are
outside of the linguists interests, sense, intention, and truth
conditions are certainly things linguists have a vital interest in
no less than logicians.

Second a historical remark with regard to the claim that logicians
deal with general grammar and linguists with particular grammars.
As a historical aspect let me remind you of chapter 4 of Carnap's
"Logical Syntax of Language" (1934, the German edition; 1937,
English edition) was called: "General Syntax", which seems to
support your claim. But on the second page of this particular
chapter, it turnes out that Carnap's "General Syntax" is anything
but "general". He says there very explicitly and very casefully
(though not in this terminology) that he is not going to deal in the
"General Syntax" with the syntax of context or cotext dependent
languages, he leaves aside. Therefore one cannot say that linguists
deal with special cases of the languages dealt with in "General
Syntax". Before 1965, approximately, no mathematical logician of any
stature dealt with context or cotext dependency, not to mention all
the other aspects of pragmatics. They were just left aside as a hot
potato. That this has changed in the last years, mainly through the
work of Montague, is another matter. I regard the question whether
there exists an autonomous semantics not as a question of empirical
fact, as Chomsky is in the habit to formulate it, but rather as
something to be decided upon "transcendentally", the empirical part
lying in the comparison between the prices to be payed for each
decision.

Hiż: Well, I would like to give the following comment about truth
and the place of truth in the study of language. The study of
language does not mean just linguistic study. Linguistics is a very
particular kind of study of language. For instance linguistics, as
such, is not interested in, or linguists, as such, do not duty for
what occasions you use which kind of politeness, etc. These are
ethnographic considerations, or ethnolinguistics or linguistic
ethnology,but not pure linguistic problems. Now, all the divisions
between sciences are, of course, artificial and provisional. One
can do all sorts of things; one can join the competence of a
logician or a linguist or a philosopher or a Sankritist. Also, one

can study the strong semantics of a natural language. Many attempts
have been made at a full, strong semantics of natural languages. So
far as I can see there is no chance of defining truth for a natural
language as we can define truth for a formal language in a
substantially richer language. There are at least two reasons for
this. First, a natural language includes its own metalanguage
(a point stressed both by Tarski and by Harris), and therefore it is
hard to think of a substantially richer language in which such a
definition could be carried. Secondly, it is doubtful whether well-
formedness for natural language can be defined without using truth.
It is doubtful whether the set of sentences for a natural language
is recursively enumerable by means of pure syntax. Such a definition
or enumeration seems to be a prerequisite for a definition of truth.
There is, however, another way of dealing with truth for a language.
Instead of defining it, we can use truth as a primitive concept and
try to define other concepts, for instance, the concept of meaning,
by means of it. An attempt of constructing such a semantic theory
based on truth as a primitive concept is shown in my paper "Aletheic
Semantic Theory", P h i l o s o p h i c a l   F o r u m   1   (1969).
It is not a serious question whether the aletheic semantics belongs
to linguistics or not. We can fix and change the boundaries of a
science depending how attractive candidates for inclusion there are.
A more substantial problem is that the aletheic semantics or a
semantics of equal strength requires methods which far exceed the
usual methods used by a linguist. It calls for an abstractive theory
based on principles far removed from empirical justification. And it
requires that for every text closed with respect to referentials
truth or falsehood should be predicable. If we do not know whether a
given closed text is true, we cannot study the meaning of phrases
occurring in this text. Linguists, usually, do not try to
characterize the set of true texts of the language. Rather they try
to study the set of grammatical texts of the language. And instead
of asking which texts are true, they ask which texts are true
provided that some other texts are supposed to be true. They study
the rules of consequence. They also study the rules preserving some
other semantic property (e.g. topic preserving rules) or rules
changing a semantic property always in the same manner (e.g.
negation, stress).

Staal: If one says that linguists are not interested in truth, it
would not mean that they are interested in falsehood. To say that

they are interested in truth conditions is describing something
which they do automatically, even if they are not aware of certain
work that has been done on truth conditions. On the other hand, it
is also well-known that one can talk about, say,
i m p l i c a t i o n in terms of truth conditions with reference
to truth. False sentences or statements but not with reference to
modalities, imperatives and so on. About the collaboration of
linguists and logicians: I feel there is a lot of collaboration that
should be done because I expect something from it. But the
collaboration is very largely, I would think, of the following kind:
Linguists tell logicians about their latest headaches. Logicians
come with all kinds of proposals for solutions. Linguists study
those proposals very carefully, they try to understand them, and
then they do their own work. Concerning categorial grammars I have
only a few things to say and I can make the point best again by
giving an illustration. My feeling is that it is really quite
premature to decide on the pragmatic attractiveness of categorial
grammars over phrase-structure grammars at this stage. But one can
not evaluate both grammars at all in isolation. One can only
evaluate whether it is better to use categorial grammars than
phrase-structure grammars if one has really worked out a much larger
portion of syntax even for a single natural language than has now
been done. I want to give you an example of a sentence that has to
be handled with transformations and which exemplifies these
"Splitterausdrücke" - discontinuous elements - which Bar-Hillel
talked about. There is a problem here because this fact of English
undoubtedly can only be handled in using transformations in a way in
which they are used differently from being used in the cycle. You
may relate the problem to the buse of the grammar, that is to say,
whether you have a categorial or whether you have a phrase-structure
grammar. The fact of English is the following one. I am going to
talk about certain interrogative questions, they are generally
derived from positive statements.

(1)   Mary talked to someone
can be made into a question by questioning the different parts of
the sentence. I want to consider those questions that can be
derived, for instance,

(2)   To whom did Mary talk?
or
(3)   Whom did Mary talk to?

The occurrence of <u>to</u> can be described by transformations in a very simple fashion. But now look what happens if you embed this sentence in a bigger sentence. For instance:

(4)   Mike heard that Mary talked to someone.

We know for a great vanity of facts that (1) is an embedded sentence in (4).

Now, with respect to (2), (3), the transformation which moves <u>whom</u> together with this <u>to</u> or without <u>to</u> is needed in a lot of languages. Now the question is: When you have an embedding like (4) does it move <u>whom</u> to the form of (2), (3) or does it move to the front of the entire sentence (4)? Well, the cyclical concept of the transformation means that you first apply all the transformations in the lowest embedded sentence; having done that, then you apply it in the whole sentence - and this is quite natural when you get used to it. If you apply this procedure to (1) and an embedding like (4) either with <u>to</u> or without <u>to</u>, you get something that is entire rubbish:

(5)   Mike heard that to whom did Mary talk.

You have to put <u>to whom</u> in the beginning:

(6)   To whom did Mike hear that Mary talked?

or

(7)   Whom did Mike hear that Mary did talk to?

And similarly for examples like

(8)   John believed that Mike heard that Mary talked to someone.

(9)   To whom did John believe that Mike heard that Mary talked?

That kind of fact is not generally talked about when one talks about the distinction between phrase-structure grammars and categorial grammars, but that is the kind of fact that has to be considered immediately on top of those phrase-structure or categorial grammars as soon as you are going to do a little bit more. Only in that kind of context you can evaluate which one is better.

Schnelle: Would someone of you like to add something or comment on this last question?

Bar-Hillel: When I was talking about "better", I had exclusively one particular sense in mind. I meant "better" in the sense of "clearer". My claim - which will probably turn out to be wrong - was, then, that in a transformational grammar with a categorial base the semantic rules will become clearer, simpler, easier intelligible, and the like.

Staal: Well, only to support it to a large extent: You added that

this is the more significant the more it is likely that
transformations do not change meaning. And you added also that,
even though Chomsky seems to be unhappy about it, it is still quite
possible that transformations do not change meaning. But since the
whole thing is uncertain, of course, the evaluation becomes the more
difficult. Because, if transformations do effect meaning, then the
fact that categorial grammars give us a more direct representation
of meaning than phrase-structure grammars may give, does not show
very much. We do not know how complicated it will be to state the
meaning-transformation that accompany transformations.

Bar-Hillel: Just one short remark. When I talked about categorial
grammars, I, of course, had in mind not only Lewis but also more
recent works which have not jet been published, as I mentioned
before, namely the works by Pòtts and Lehrberger, for instance.
I tend to believe that these new investigations will show that if
transformation can be formulated in such a way that they are meaning
preserving, it might turn out that categorial grammars will in thus
sense be simpler.

Hiż: The tedency which Prof.Staal represents seems to imply that
there is a natural way of studying a natural language, and I have,
of course, great doubts about it. I do not see that in our minds
there are any trees, I do not see that in our way of looking at a
language there must be this or something else, and, in particular,
I do not think that we have necessarily any mechanism for generating
sentences. All this is black magic for me, like any talk of
innateness. These things represent a religous element in modern
science. These ornaments can be discarded easily. On the other hand,
transformations themselves, independent of any theory of
transformations, are linguistic facts. It is a linguistic fact that
people paraphrase, draw consequences, negate, and put stress. Some
of these are generalizable. General rules of paraphrases are some of
the transformations. Whatever is a good theory of language must take
account of these facts. And therefore if one speaks about a
categorial grammar, or any other grammar, one should ask whether it
gives a good description of the facts: among others, the relations
between sentences, and such relations which are intuitively well-
founded in peoples' semantics, in peoples' semantic behaviour. There
is no opposition between categorial grammar and transformational
grammar: at most, you may say that the facts of transformations can
be explained or described within one theory better than within the

other.

Staal: Now there is something coming up that is more like a
difference of opinion. I disagree to some extent with what you said.
First a matter of pure fact. It is not easier to work with a system
that you are used to. I am not used to work with categorial
grammars, I am used to work with phrase-structure grammars. I have a
hell of a job to give a semantic interpretation of my phrase-
structures. Whether I would find it easier when I were equally
competent to work with categorial grammars to give a semantic
interpretation of those fragments of categorial grammars, I just do
not know.

I disagree with Prof.Hiż, in the following sense, even taking into
account the difference between a linguistic description of the
generation of a sentence and the process by which sentences are
generated when we speak. Even though Prof.Hiż talks not only as if
we had no direct access to what was going on inside the brain when
we produce languages - with which I agree - but he also speaks as
if it did not matter what was inside the brain. I think it does
matter. At one stage we might know something more about the brain,
and we might see why a certain explanation is more natural than the
other one. We only know the most general things about that now. And
in particular, we cannot experiment very well in the brain while
people are talking, that is the pity.

Schnelle: Thank you. Now I premised you that we should try to
relate what was said on logical and linguistic semantics to the
general problem of language communication and to a general theory of
communication. I should like to start with a citation from Staal's
paper. I am not quite sure whether he has said it this morning, but
it was in the written version of his paper. There he accuses the
logicians that they sometimes tend to become dull and barren in
their descriptions unless they are provided with challenges taken
from real life and that is to say natural language. But one may have
some doubts whether the concept of a natural language, say English,
is as assumed by linguists "real life" or whether it is not also a
construct. Certainly, this construct is by several orders more
complicated than what logicians take account of, but still it is a
construct. Accordingly, the subject matter of linguistic semantics
as it is usually presented and as it was presented on the panel
treats is as an abstraction relative to the actual data. The
semantics of speech acts is embedded in a large system of other

acts, situations, knowledges, intentions, and so on. The question I
want to put to the panelists is the following: Is it clear how we
shall find our way back from describing these abstractions to the
explanations of the actual processes of speech communication in
context, or, in short, from linguistic semantics to a theory of
communication? If this is too complicated, is it possible, at least,
to justify the abstractions we are making?
Now, in order to give you some idea what kind of abstractions are
made by someone who says "I am describing English", I want to refer
to the following list:
Abstraction in Linguistics
1. Action-rule abstraction
2. Structure-of-means abstraction
3. Abstraction from simultaneous context
4. Abstraction from the larger context (e.g. of the plan of action)
5. Abstraction from the variability of languages
6. Component abstraction.
Let me briefly comment on it. Well, I think that these six
abstractions are usually made by linguistics and sometimes, there
may be even more. By action-rule abstraction, I understand the
abstraction from the placement of speech act in space and time. This
is the abstraction leading from events of speech acts to speech act
types or -designs, and further to speech act rules , that is to say,
the rules organizing the system of types which in turn are related
to speech act events. So on a certain level of description you will
rather treat rules, but not rules in the grammatical sense, but in
the sense of psychology or sociology.
Let me turn to the second abstraction. In applying the structure-of-
means abstraction instead of describing the acts themselves, you
describe the means - or even the structure of the means used in the
acts. With respect to communication with language, for instance, you
describe the structure of the utterances of phrases and sentences,
that is to say, the structure of sentences, phrases and so on. This
is generally done in grammar and it is supposed that the
description of the means has implications for the speech acts
themselves in which these means are used. The result of this
abstraction is to consider the treatment of syntax and semantics of
languages as the genuine tasks of linguistics.
Third point: I think that there is an abstraction from the contexts
simultaneous to utterances of words and sentences. You may, for

instance, abstract from the situation, the knowledge about the
participants, their immediate intentions, and so on.
The fourth point refers to abstraction from the role of the context.
That is to say from the fact that a linguistic action is part of a
larger plan of action, being executed by the persons. By this fact,
the acts get a particular intentional or teleological aspect which
is abstracted from when applying the abstraction under point four.
Point five: Abstraction from the variability of languages. When
somebody is saying "I describe English", he abstracts from the fact
that the English he describes is just one level of the English
language. But the English language has historical, sociological,
and geographical parameters or differences and has, moreover, a
number of registers determined by rhetoric and stylistic factors.
In linguistic descriptions one frequently abstracts from these
aspects of variability.
Then the sixth point mentions component abstraction. You may take,
for instance, the position illustrated by Hiż: "Well, let us treat
as many aspects as possible in syntax. That is what the
l i n g u i s t qua linguist should do. Though there are certain
aspects connected with these linguistic aspects, there is a certain
component that provides the basis for all aspects to be taken
account of and this component is syntax. Let us abstract from the
other aspects; they may, at most, serve as a heuristic function."
Now, I think, in making these abstractions, linguistics and
linguistic semantics moves away from a number of problems, which
will have to be treated in a complete theory of linguistic
communication. I want to confront you now with the following
question: What can be said on the ways in which results of
linguistic semantics can be embedded into a less abstract theory of
linguistic communication? Or is it at least possible to justify the
abstractions presently made in linguistics?
Bar-Hillel: First of all I would like to stress strongly that the
slogan that linguistics deals with sound-meaning-relation is a very
misleading one. I think that it should be perfectly clear that ab
initio linguistics deals with a relation between sounds-in-context
and meaning. And this "in-context" should by no means be eliminated
ab initio. This is what you had, of course, in mind by raising the
question of abstraction. To what degree, and when, under what
conditions one may abstract from the context to move from this
linguistically basic relation between sound-in-context and meaning

to the binary relation between sound and meaning is the probably
most serious question of contemporary linguistics altogether , but
its answer should not be biassed by the fact that in the first
sentence of many textbooks one finds that linguistics deal with the
relation between sound and meaning.
So, what the organizers of this conference had in mind, I guess,
when they talked of communicative semantics (or, rather,
K o m m u n i k a t i o n s s e m a n t i k) was to stress the
relation between sound-in-context and meaning. Now, when can
abstractions be justified? Any of the five mentioned by the chairman
or all of them together? What I'm going to say will perhaps sound
facitious, but I have a minute or so at my disposal. There are two
kinds of justifications. First, by abstracting you increase the
number of useful theorems where, of course, this answer is question-
begging, because the term "useful" contains everything that is in
the original question; secondly, when you thereby impress research
foundations. If by abstraction you get a nice paper which contains
definitions 1-7 and then theorems 1-16, then certain research
foundations will be impressed and perhaps continue to provide
further fonds for your research which might be rather useful.
Hiż: I am not quite clear about some points, but I am clear that
there is a difference in understanding what a language is, and what
a linguist, therefore, describes. I take the following attitude
towards this: linguists, on the whole, contrary to Bar-Hillel, do
not consider pragmatics. Why? Because linguistics has a very
particular kind of problem of its own, namely, it grew out of the
question of how to write a grammar. You have to teach people a
foreign language. When you teach people a foreign language, you do
not teach them truth-conditions, you do not teach them pragmatic
situations, and you do not teach them what is true. You can lie in
a language equally well if you know the language. And it is not up
to the linguist to teach whether to tell the truth or not.
Bar-Hillel: According to the Berlitz School method this is exactly
what you do: teaching by giving truth-conditions.
Hiż: On the whole this is not writing a grammar. Linguistics grew
out of techniques of teaching foreign languages. These are very
particular techniques. For instance, the concept of a phoneme and
the entire phonemic structure of a language give a transparent view
of the phonological structure of a language. It is a good
instrument for teaching. Certainly there may be other insights into

the structures of a language which linguists have not discovered at
all. And there may be other approaches to teaching a language
besides giving its structures. It is also the case that linguistics
has often departed far from the goal of providing a pedagogical
instrument.

Staal: I would like to comment on two points: I think what Henry
says is historically incorrect in as far as the oldest grammars
which we have are the Hindu-Grammars and they were not written to
teach anyone a foreign language. In fact they were only intelligible
to people who knew the language already and who want to describe it
perfectly. But this does not really affect your argument.
I was very much interested in what Bar-Hillel said about this common
fallacy of saying that language relates sound and meaning. He says,
rather, it relates sound-in-context and meaning. I like that
improvement, but I would like to improve it further and say: It
relates sound-in-context to meaning-in-context. Because that is
exactly what it does. I think that the distinction which Bar-Hillel
made reflects something that is very pervading in a lot of
linguistics and a lot of philosophy that may have some roots in some
kind of positivism. It is some kind of feeling like the following:
Sounds are clear. Meanings are mysterious. I do not think that this
is the fact at all. I think this was the basic motivation behind
structural linguistics, it is still extremely strong in all later
forms of linguistics we are now dealing with. But there is
absolutely no justification for that kind of feeling because it is
a certain development of science or the fact that linguists were
impressed by physics, which they misinterpreted for in fact physics
had more theories and more abstraction than almost any other science
at the time and may be even now. Bar-Hillel refines this
distinction in a way which, I think, is very correct, but he does it
only half way and the reason might be this old prejudice.

Schnelle: Thank you very much. Because the time is almost up, there
is time for only one question.

Kummer: I have a question to Bar-Hillel about the distinction
between semantics and pragmatics which regard to the examples of
Staal concerning tenses and the uses of tenses. My question is: Whi
Which parameters for points of reference would you incline for rules
of truth, or would you accept that you need other types of rules
like rules of adequate usage?

Bar-Hillel: Many of my colleagues from Konstanz and students who are

sitting around here now, that I dedicated to this question a good
part of my course in the last semester, in slogan terms, what you a
are asking is: What are the limits of the semanticization of
pragmatics? I have indeed grave doubts as to the possibility of
semanticizing a l l of pragmatics. Nowadays logicians are used to
talk about truth in a model, truth in a possible world, and truth
relative to certain indices. Now, whether we are going to a truth-
concept which is relative to a set of indices and includes indices
referring to the speaker, the hearer, the kind of utterance, the
location of the utterance, etc., a pragmatic or semantic concept I
do not care.

Schnelle: Coming to the end, I want to thank the panelists and I
hope that they did not only give you a specimen of the deplorable
stage of linguistic methodology, but also that there is still some
hope and that confidence is not quite ill-founded, so that progress
may still be expected from that field. Tank you.

THE INTEGRATION OF SEMANTIC EXPLORATIONS INTO THE
PSYCHOANALYTIC PROCESS

Panel: A.Lorenzer, Universität Bremen
       K.Lorenz, Universität Hamburg
       P.Watzlawick, Mental Research Institute, Palo Alto
Chairman: E.K.Specht, Universität Bonn

February, 17th, afternoon session.

LORENZER:
Herr Bar-Hillel hat heute früh die Zweiteilung des Tagungsthemas
Semantik in logische und linguistische Semantik benannt. Mein
Beitrag fällt weder unter das eine noch unter das andere, und das
bringt gewiß eine Zäsur in die Thematik. Wer in Kenntnis meines
Firmenschildes Psychoanalyse freilich erwartet, es ginge nun um
eine sprachpsychologische Annäherung ans Thema, muß enttäuscht
werden. Ich werde mein Bestes tun, klarzustellen, daß die psychoanalytische Beschäftigung mit Sprache keine Psychologie ist. -
Sollten Psychologen hier sein, so werden sie das möglicherweise mit
Befriedigung vernehmen. Diese Befriedigung wäre verfrüht, denn
natürlich reklamiere ich einen Teil des herkömmlichen psychologischen Themenbereichs - so zum Beispiel die Frage nach der Bildung
von Sprache in Individuen, nun aber nicht aufgefaßt als Frage nach
den Invarianten der Sätze, des Sprachverhaltens im Sinne einer
Entwicklungspsychologie, sondern als Frage nach der lebensgeschichtlichen und das heißt auch vor allem gesellschaftlichen Bestimmtheit
von Sprache in den Subjekten. Dies geschieht in der Perspektive
einer kritischen Sozialwissenschaft. Wenn man diese Perspektive
einschlägt, wird man freilich vorweg ein Selbst-Mißverständnis der
Psychoanalyse korrigieren müssen, weil es, wie Sie gleich aus einem
Zitat, das ich dem Buch von Herrn Watzlawick und seinen Koautoren
entnehme, sehen können, genau das systematisch verstellt, worum es
in der Psychoanalyse geht, nämlich um die Klarlegung der Problematik
von Interaktionsstrukturen. Das Zitat lautet:
"Die Psychoanalyse postuliert, daß Verhalten weitgehend durch ein
hypothetisches Zusammenspiel intrapsychischer Kräfte bedingt ist.
Diese Kräfte folgen denselben Gesetzen der Erhaltung und Umwandlung
von Energien wie in der Physik. In diesem Sinne belegt die klassische Psychoanalyse primär eine Theorie intrapsychischer Energetik.
Und im wesentlichen blieb die wechselseitige Abhängigkeit des
Individuums und seiner Umwelt ein vernachlässigtes Gebiet der
Psychoanalyse. Und gerade auf diesem Gebiet ist es unerläßlich, den
Begriff des Informationsaustausches als Kommunikation zu berücksichtigen."
Zwischen dem psychodynamischen - sprich psychoanalytischen - Denk-
modell und jener begrifflichen Formulierung der Wechselbeziehung
zwischen Organismus und Umwelt besteht ein grundsätzlicher Unter-
schied. Nochmals, so zutreffend das Zitat das Selbstverständnis von
Psychoanalyse als einer Naturwissenschaft des Seelischen - im
herkömmlichen Verständnis der Psychoanalytiker - wiedergibt, so

falsch ist seine Aussage.

Meine Grundthese ist demgegenüber: Die psychoanalytische Theorie
ist keine Theorie der intrapsychischen Energetik, sondern ist - und
da greife ich die Formulierung von Herrn Watzlawick im umgekehrten
Sinne nun auf - eine begriffliche Formulierung der Wechselbeziehung
zwischen Organismus und Umwelt. Gegenstand der Psychoanalyse sind
nicht psychische Funktionen, sondern sind Interaktionsentwürfe und
ihre geglückte beziehungsweise mißglückte Realisierung in zwischen-
menschlichen Beziehungen. Dementsprechend läßt sich die psychoanalytische Theorie auch als Sozialisationstheorie bezeichnen, und
zwar unter Berücksichtigung ihrer Methode als kritisch-hermeneu-
tische Sozialisationstheorie.

Ausgehend von der Grundthese, daß psychoanalytische Theorie als
Sozialisationstheorie anzusehen ist, möchte ich kurz noch den
Rahmen dieser Theorie umreißen. Es geht um den Zusammenhang der
Auseinandersetzung von innerer Natur und Interaktionsformen im
Beziehungsgefüge einerseits und um den Zusammenhang von Interaktion
und objektiven gesellschaftlichen Verhältnissen andererseits.
Beides wird in den Subjekten in Interaktionsmustern vermittelt, die,
und das zielt auf unser Thema hier, in Sprache eingelassen sind.
In dieser Perspektive stellen sich zwei Probleme, die zu erörtern
sind, bevor wir zum Thema des psychoanalytischen Prozesses kommen
können. Der Kürze halber präsentiere ich diese Probleme in Thesen-
form:

These 1: Die Interaktionsmuster werden vom ersten Moment des Lebens
an eingeübt in einer Interaktion zwischen Mutter und Kind. Diese
Einübung beginnt vorsprachlich, ist aber niemals außersprachlich,
da die Mutter ja in eine bestehende Sprachgemeinschaft, und das
heißt, in eine bestimmte gesamtgesellschaftliche Praxis eingefügt
ist. Die Einübung ist als Einigung zwischen Mutter und Kind
anzusehen in dem Sinne, daß das Verhalten der Mutter die Antwort
auf drängende Körperbedürfnisse des Kindes ist, die auf diesem Wege
sich darstellen und bilden.

These 2: Der Sprachaufbau erwächst aus der eingeübten Praxis, das
heißt, er erwächst aus konkreter Interaktion. Nur wenn man an einem
derart strikten Aufbau festhält,lassen sich die psychoanalytisch
zentralen Aussagen über Bewußtsein und Unbewußtes sprachtheoretisch
formulieren, ohne nicht entweder Sprachgemeinschaft biologistisch
zu deuten oder umgekehrt Interaktion und Interaktionsstrukturen
sprachidealistisch von materiell-historischer Praxis abzulösen.
Ich hoffe, ich habe mit dieser Vorrede zur allgemeinen Lage in der

Psychoanalyse etwas abseits des umschriebenen Tagungsthemas Ihre
Geduld nicht überfordert. Worauf ich hinauswollte, ist, eine Frage
vorzubereiten, die ich nicht nur für besonders angemessen für dieses
Panel in seiner Zusammensetzung halte, sondern die meines Erachtens
auch der Angelpunkt ist, an dem ein Zusammenhang von psychoanalytischen Erkenntnissen und Sprachtheorie überhaupt hängt, nämlich:
Wie wächst Sprache aus den vorsprachlich eingeübten Interaktions-
mustern?
Besonders wichtig erscheint mir dabei die Verknüpfung psychoanaly-
tischer Überlegungen mit den vom Konstruktivismus herkommenden
Annahmen, deren Grundintention - ich zitiere Herrn Lorenz aus
"Elemente der Sprachkritik" - lautet:" Den üblichen von der Syntax
über die Semantik zur Pragmatik der Rede fortschreitenden Gang
sprachphilosophischer Überlegungen konsequent umzukehren." Diese
Fundierung der Sprachproblematik in der Pragmatik erlaubt es, eine
Brücke zu den sozialisationstheoretischen Fragestellungen der
Psychoanalyse zu schlagen. Nun bewegen sich die Lorenzschen
Annahmen ausdrücklich nicht im Rahmen einer Sozialisationstheorie.
Wenn wir in diesen Rahmen überwechseln, stellen sich einige Fragen,
zunächst: Die elementare Sprachhandlung, nämlich die Prädikation,
das heißt, die Zuordnung von Wörtern oder, im weiteren Sinne, von
signifikanten Gesten zu Gegenständen und Handlungen, setzt zwar
keinen Vorrat von abgegrenzten Gegenständen voraus, wohl aber eine
Distanzierung von Subjekt und Objekt und von Subjekt zu Subjekt,
denn es wird ja dem Lernenden der Prädikator vermittelt, indem auf
etwas gezeigt wird.
Würde man beim Überwechseln in den sozialisationstheoretischen
Rahmen diese Annahme unbesehen als Aussage über den Sprachbildungs-
verlauf übernehmen, so würde das heißen, daß auf die Interaktionsstrukturen, die fertig gebildet sind, nach Abschluß der entscheiden-
den Differenzierung zwischen Subjekt und Objekt dann gleichsam Sprache erst draufgesetzt wird. Damit würde die Prädikation aber ihre
bewußtseinskonstitutive Bedeutung vorweg einbüßen, weil sie erst
sekundär dann zur Dialektik von Körperbedürfnissen und gesellschaftlichen Normen hinzutreten würde. Wenn aber die Sprachkonstruktion
in die Subjekt-Objekt-Differenzierung selbst eingelassen ist, dann
müssen wir uns doch wohl die Prädikation von Handlungen und die
Prädikation von Gegenständen in einer ontogenetischen Sequenz
denken, derart, daß die Prädikation von Handlungen der Prädikation
von Gegenständen vorausgeht. Diese Sequenz entspräche der psychoanalytischen Erfahrung eines Herauswachsens objektlibidinöser

Beziehungen aus dem primären Narzißmus. Wir müssen darüber hinaus
diese Sequenz noch verlängert denken in folgender Weise, nämlich
als Ansatz der Prädikation in noch ungeschiedener szenischer
Interaktion; das soll heißen: Das, worauf im allerersten Ansatz
gezeigt wird und nur gezeigt werden kann, ist nicht ein Gegenstand
und auch keine separierte Handlung, sondern ein eingeübtes
szenisches Arrangement zwischen Kind und Umwelt, ein szenisches Arrangement, das noch nicht in differente Positionen von Ich und Nicht-
Ich auseinandergefallen ist. Um an einem Beispiel zu illustrieren:
das Wort Mama kennzeichnet, wenn meine These richtig ist, nicht einen
umschriebenen Gegenstand, sondern ein szenisches Verhältnis, das sich
im weiteren Aufgliederungsprozeß erst allmählich vergegenständlicht.

Vergleicht man nun diese Annahmen mit dem von Herrn Watzlawick
gezogenen Vergleich analoger und digitaler Kommunikation mit
Konnotation und Denotation, dann werden Übereinstimmungen deutlich,
gerade auch hinsichtlich der entwicklungsgeschichtlichen, nicht nur
phylogenetischen, sondern auch ontogenetisch denkbaren Schichtung.
Die Konnotation, die auf szenische Verhältnisse verweist, ist
archaisch. Meiner These zufolge entspricht dem eine ontogenetische
Stufenordnung, genauer gesagt: eine lebensgeschichtliche Abfolge.
Die umschriebene Denotation erwächst aus den umfänglicheren
konnotativen Benennungen von Szenen. Trifft meine These zu, dann
wäre auch eine Hierarchie semantischer Strukturen gegeben als
Verästelung von Subjekt- wie Objektsymbolen, die dann als zunehmend
aufgegliederte Vergegenständlichungen anzusehen wären. Der Prozeß
der Sozialisation verläuft danach in folgender Reihe:

1. Stufe: Einübung in Interaktion als Einigung zwischen materiellen
Bedürfnissen des Kindes und den Angeboten der Mutter, wobei diese
Angebote vorsprachlich, aber, wie gesagt, nicht außersprachlich
sind.

2. Stufe: Die Einigungsformel wird benannt, so zum Beispiel mit
dem Namen Mama.

3. Stufe: Eine Stufenfolge semantischer Differenzierungen setzt ein,
wobei die Elemente der Aufgliederung jeweils gezeigt werden;
konsistente Verweisungen erzeugen dabei idealiter konsistente
semantische Strukturen.

4. Stufe: Selbst wenn man annehmen wollte, die Entwicklung verliefe
bis zu diesem Moment ideal, so wäre hier doch eine Fallgrube
anzunehmen, die wir aus der Erfahrung über Neurosen kennen, nämlich

die neurotische Brechung der Entwicklung in folgender Weise:
Unter den Bedingungen des neurotischen Konfliktes kommt es zur
Exkommunikation, das heißt, zur Verstoßung der Interaktionsformeln
aus der Sprachkommunikation, und damit zur Verstoßung in ontogenetisch ältere, nämlich sprachlose Interaktionsstrukturen. An
Stelle des der Reflexion zugänglichen symbolvermittelten Handelns
tritt dann ein von szenischen Interaktionszwängen bestimmtes
sprachlos bewußtloses Agieren.

LORENZ:

SINN UND GELTUNG. ZUR UNTERSCHEIDUNG DER EBENEN DES VERSTEHENS
UND DES ANERKENNENS.

Ich möchte in meinem Versuch zur Klärung des Unterschieds von Sinn
und Geltung, wie er in den Publikationen von Lorenzer auftritt,
zugleich einige Bemerkungen zu dem vorangegangenen Beitrag machen,
weil so noch deutlicher wird, was unter der "Ebene des Verstehens"
und der "Ebene des Anerkennens" verstanden werden muß.
Ich rekapituliere zunächst ein paar Dinge, die in Lorenzers Beitrag
nicht ausdrücklich vorgekommen waren. Es werden von ihm drei Stufen
des Verstehens unterschieden, die 'logisches Verstehen', 'psychologisches Verstehen' und 'seelisches Verstehen' genannt werden,
mit dem Ziel, die dritte Stufe des seelischen Verstehens als den
"Hauptweg des psychoanalytischen Verstehens" (Lorenzer,
S p r a c h z e r s t ö r u n g ..., S. 114) auszuweisen. Der Grund
sei darin zu suchen, daß an dieser Stelle weder der Sinn von Sätzen
noch die Bedeutung dramatischer Handlungen, von Gesten etwa,
sondern das Interaktionsmuster, also die Beziehungen des Subjekts
mit den anderen Subjekten und mit seiner übrigen Umwelt, infrage
stehe. Der 'sachbezogen' genannte Sinn von Sätzen hingegen sei
durch das logische Verstehen zu ermitteln, und die 'subjektbezogen'
genannte Bedeutung dramatischer Handlungen durch das psychologische
Verstehen oder Nacherleben. Auf allen drei Stufen aber wird
ausdrücklich die Sinnfrage von der Geltungsfrage abgehoben, zunächst
jedenfalls. Es wird also nicht gefragt: gilt der geäußerte Satz des
zu verstehenden Gegenübers, ist die fragliche gestische Äußerung
aufrichtig, ist das Interaktionsmuster durch die Praxis des Subjekts
gedeckt, verhält es sich dementsprechend? Deshalb wird so nicht
gefragt, weil die Störungen der gemeinsamen Verständigung auf jeder
dieser Stufen sichtbar gemacht werden sollen, die darin bestehen,
daß auf der sachbezogenen Stufe Wörter privatsprachliche Bedeutung
haben können, daß auf der subjektbezogenen Stufe Gesten theatrali-
sche Bedeutung zukommen kann und daß auf der kommunikativen Stufe
Interaktionen von der Umgebung als unverständlich, nicht dem
allgemein anerkannten Muster entsprechend, abgewiesen werden können.
Zur Aufhebung der Störung soll die Rekonstruktion eines historischen
Originalvorfalls dienen, bei dem die Verdrängung ursprünglich
sprachlich vermittelter Interaktionsformen einsetzt; diese
Verdrängung äußert sich durch 'Desymbolisierung' und damit Klischee-
bildung. Die dem szenischen Verstehen eigentümliche Verschmelzung
von Sache und Person, von Sachverhalt   - durch einen Satz

dargestellt - und demjenigen, der den Sachverhalt äußert als seine
Sicht der Sache, diese Verschmelzung weist darauf hin, daß der
entscheidende Ansatzpunkt für die Bedeutungsbestimmung der Wörter,
Zeichen und anderen Ausdrücke im situativen, also praktischen
Kontext des Zeichenverwenders zu suchen ist. Und nur von dort her
können dann auch Verfahren zur möglichen Aufhebung von
Kommunikationsstörungen gelingen.

An dieser Stelle möchte ich eine Bemerkung zu der Diskussion heute
morgen einfügen, in der das Problem der Bedeutungsbestimmung als
unerheblich abgetan wurde, so, als dürfe die Rede von Bedeutungen
mittlerweile als geklärt gelten; ich glaube, genau das Gegenteil ist
der Fall. Störung und Wiederherstellung von Kommunikation haben
gerade damit zu tun: die Bedeutung der jeweils verwendeten Zeichen
muß bestimmt werden. Darin besteht das hier anstehende 'Sinn-
problem'.

Ich möchte jetzt darauf hinaus, daß die drei genannten Stufen auf
der Sinnebene, insbesondere die für die dritte Stufe charakteristische Verschmelzung von Sachbezug und Personbezug, ihre Entsprechung auf der Geltungsebene haben, also bei der Erörterung des
sogenannten Wahrheitsproblems wiederkehren. Sachbezogen spricht man
ja bekanntlich von der Geltung oder Wahrheit eines Satzes, wenn er
der in ihm bloß fingierten oder vorgestellten Wirklichkeit
korrespondiert; personbezogen hingegen spricht man von der Geltung
eines Satzes, wenn ihm alle Menschen zustimmen, der Möglichkeit
nach wenigstens. Terminologisch stehen sich eine Korrespondenztheorie und eine Konsenstheorie der Wahrheit gegenüber, obwohl es
sich eigentlich nur um zwei verschiedene Aspekte des Wahrheits-
begriffes handelt. Durch die gesamte Geschichte des Wahrheitsproblems ist stattdessen ein Streit zwischen einem, wie ich sagen
möchte, s e m a n t i s c h e n und einem p r a g m a t i s c h e n
Wahrheitsbegriff ausgetragen worden, der genau diese unnötige
Konfrontation der beiden Aspekte 'Sachbezug' und 'Personbezug' bei
der Äußerung von Sätzen widerspiegelt. Will man diesen Disput
auflösen und auf der Geltungsebene die Verschmelzung von Sachbezug
und Personbezug wiederholen, die für die dritte Stufe auf der
Sinnebene charakteristisch war, so muß eine Verschmelzung des
semantischen Verfahrens der Wahrheitseinführung (Korrespondenz) mit
dem pragmatischen Verfahren der Wahrheitseinführung (Konsens)
herbeigeführt werden, die bekannte Schwierigkeiten nach sich zieht,
wenn zugleich die Schwächen der beiden Positionen vermieden werden

sollen. Es genügt, an dieser Stelle mit Stichworten auf diese
Schwächen hinzuweisen, da darüber in der Literatur längst ausführlich berichtet ist. Die Schwäche der Korrespondenztheorie besteht
darin, kein intersubjektives Kriterium für das Vorliegen einer
Korrespondenz angeben zu können, weil 'Welt' nicht sprachfrei zur
Verfügung steht; die Schwäche der Konsenstheorie hingegen besteht
darin, kein subjektunabhängiges Sachkriterium für die Unterscheidung eines bloß vorgetäuschten oder fingierten Konsens von einem
"wirklichen", also berechtigten Konsens zur Verfügung zu haben.
Um aus diesem Dilemma herauszukommen, schlage ich vor, mit einer
pragmatischen Basis für die nachkonstruierende Einführung von
Sprache zu beginnen, und das heißt speziell mit der Zeicheneinfü-
führung. Sie wird in einem für den systematischen Zweck der
Rekonstruktion des Sinnes und der Geltung sprachlicher Äußerungen
stilisiert konzipierten Lehr- und Lernprozeß für die Verwendung
der Zeichen angesiedelt, von dem nicht behauptet wird, an dieser
Stelle irgendeine empirische Adäquatheit zu besitzen, etwa für
pädagogische oder gar für psychotherapeutische Zwecke schon
angemessen zu sein. Ehe solche zusätzlichen Fragen beantwortbar
werden, muß das Verfahren der Zeicheneinführung, speziell der
Worteinführung, gleichsam als Maßstab schon zur Verfügung stehen,
und das heißt als eine Rekonstruktion angesichts faktisch bereits
vorliegender Zeichenverwendung, in der wir uns in der Alltagswelt
befinden.(vgl. Lorenz, Der dialogische Wahrheitsbegriff, in:
N e u e   H e f t e   f ü r   P h i l o s o p h i e   2 / 3 , S. 119)
An dieser Stelle würde ich daher gegen den Vorschlag der
Sozialisationstheorie folgendes einwenden: Es geht an dieser Stelle
noch nicht darum, den möglichen Gang vom Kleinkind zum Erwachsenen
zu rekonstruieren, sondern zunächst , die Mittel bereitzustellen,
mit denen ein Erwachsener, speziell ein Wissenschaftler, für sein
eigenes Sprechen Maßstäbe zur Verfügung bekommt, die dann für eine
solche Sozialisationstheorie taugen mögen. Ein solcher Zwischen-
schritt wäre einzufügen. Mit dessen Hilfe kann man zeigen, daß das
Verfahren, welches für die Auflösung des Geltungsproblems gedacht
war, auch auf der Sinnebene das Verständnis leitet, und in der Tat
dort die dritte Stufe des szenischen Verstehens der Ausgangspunkt
der Zeicheneinführung wird und nicht die Stufen des logischen oder
des psychologischen Verstehens. Die Zeicheneinführung geschieht,
ganz in der von Lorenzer betonten Charakterisierung, in der szenisch
noch ungeschiedenen Situation, die durch die ersten Prädikationen
erst gegliedert wird. Dabei ist wichtig, daß in den Einführungs-

situationen für Zeichen, also auch für Wörter, noch kein Geltungsproblem besteht. Die Zeichen repräsentieren die Weltumgebung der
Beteiligten 'hic et nunc'; es hat noch keinen Sinn, zwischen Sinn
und Geltung einen Unterschied zu machen. Die Zeichen stellen
allererst die von da an verwendeten Gliederungen dar; ich würde
aber gleichwohl nur ungern von einer Entsprechung (Korrespondenz)
von Gegenständen und Wörtern sprechen, vielmehr lieber von einer
Entsprechung der Wörter und der Unterscheidungen, um mögliche Mißverständnisse darüber auszuschließen, daß hier eine Annahme über
schon bestehende natürliche Gliederungen gemacht werden müsse.
Ich möchte jetzt sagen: Es liegen W ö r t e r vor (genauer:
B e g r i f f s w ö r t e r oder P r ä d i k a t o r e n), die in
den Einführungssituationen als Ein-Wort-Sätze verwendet sind und so
auch eingeführt werden - durch gemeinsames Essen, Spielen, Singen,
Turnen usw. Es ist vollkommen angemessen, dafür 'Szenenarrange-
ments' zu nehmen, mit und in denen sich eine solche Einführung
darstellt. Aus diesem Grunde haben die so gewonnenen Wörter bloß
einen S i n n , und das soll heißen: Ihre Einführung ist von den
am zugehörigen Lehr- und Lernprozeß Beteiligten erfolgreich
vorgenommen worden, sie beherrschen die Verwendung dieser Wörter,
die Wörter haben einen Sinn. Der Sinn ist also auf Grund dieser
Konstruktion den Beteiligten gemeinsam, anders kommt Sinn gar nicht
vor. Das braucht für die Wörter in beliebigen Verwendungssituationen
bekanntlich nicht der Fall zu sein, Mißverständnisse sind
Dokumente dafür.
Zugleich aber, und das ist nun der entscheidende Schritt, gewinnen
die Wörter mit und nach dieser Einführung ein Eigenleben, da sie ja
selber Handlungen darstellen, graphische oder phonische Handlungen,
kraft dessen sie zur bloßen Vorstellung von Situationen taugen, die
mit der Redeverwendungssituation, in der sie geäußert werden, nichts
mehr zu tun haben brauchen; Wörter werden zu Symbolen. Der Ausdruck
'Symbole' wird verwendet, um anzudeuten, daß zugleich mit der
Einführung der Wörter die kraft der Wörter mögliche Distanzierung
von der Situation, die sie repräsentieren, auftritt. Diese
Distanzierungsmöglichkeit geht, wenn ich es recht verstanden habe,
im Prozeß der Verdrängung an bestimmten Stellen offenbar gerade
verloren und führt im Klischee dann zu der gleichsam automatischen
Abfolge von Situation und sprachlichen oder nichtsprachlichen
Reaktionen darauf.
Der jetzt folgende Schritt ist die Einführung von Verwendungs-
weisen für diese Symbole, also die in der philosophischen Tradition

so genannte 'Vorstellungen' und damit für jede separate Verwendung
von Wörtern. Diese neuen Einführungsmöglichkeiten, nämlich von
Verwendungsweisen, konstituieren eine sekundäre Praxis, mit der
sich zum ersten Mal das Geltungsproblem stellt.
Diese sekundäre Praxis wieder generell möglich zu machen, also die
durch Desymbolisierung verloren gegangene Möglichkeit zur
Distanzierung gegenüber der Situation, in der man gerade lebt,
wiederzugewinnen, ist der psychoanalytische Heilungsprozeß. Daraus
folgt, daß die Fehldeutung des Patienten gegenüber seiner eigenen
Situation von dem Versagen herrührt, Sinn und Geltung von Zeichen
an bestimmten Stellen auseinanderzuhalten. Damit ist zudem die
Maxime gerechtfertigt, in der psychoanalytischen Exploration die
Geltungsfrage zunächst nicht zu stellen und so die scheinbare
Inkohärenz in der Selbstdarstellung des Patienten nicht anzuerkennen.
Das sei stichwortartig, etwa am Beispiel Rauchen, noch kurz
erläutert.

Zunächst das Wort rauchen, bloß eingeführt im Zusammenhang mit den
hier am Orte leider - oder glücklicherweise - nicht erlaubten
Handlungen; sodann dieses selbe Wort verwendet, um zu verbieten,
aufzufordern, zu warnen, festzustellen usw., das heißt: Situationen
- wir sind jetzt bei dem Schritt in die sekundäre Praxis - , die
der Einführungssituation "gleichen" (in diesem "gleichen" steckt
ein Problem, das ich hier nicht erörtern kann),sollen hergestellt
werden, vermieden werden, bestätigt werden, beseitigt werden usw.
Ich beschränke mich aus Zeitgründen auf die Feststellungsverwendung,
oder auch Behauptung, etwa: r a u c h e n . Ergänzen Sie bitte das
sprachlich nicht repräsentierte hier ist gerade ..., also: hier ist
gerade rauchen, oder auch noch mit der zusätzlichen Spezialisierung
des Herrn Meier, also: rauchen des Herrn Meier. Eine solche Feststellungsverwendung, auf der Basis schon stattgehabter Einführung
von rauchen (und gegebenenfalls seiner Spezialisierung zu rauchen
des Herrn Meier) fordert zum Vergleich mit der Einführung des
gleichen Wortes heraus, bei der dann zu überprüfen ist, ob diese
Feststellung korrekt ist oder nicht, gilt oder nicht, wahr ist oder
nicht; die Sinnfrage zieht die Geltungsfrage nach sich. Dieses
Verfahren des Vergleichs der Verwendung mit der Einführung muß
durch besondere, für Feststellungen, also für Behauptungen erst
eigens einzuführende Weise durch Verwendungsregeln für das Behaupten
(die zum Beispiel von den Regeln für das Erzählen verschieden wären)

festgelegt sein: Zum Beispiel sind Argumentationsregeln für bestimmte Kontexte wissenschaftlichen Gebrauchs von Behauptungen die
Verwendungsverfahren für Feststellungen .

Jetzt aber entsteht eine Reihe von Problemen, unter denen ich nur
zwei herausgreifen möchte.
Das erste Problem entsteht, wenn nach der Einführung von semantischen Verbindungen von Wörtern zu neuen Wörtern oder prädikativen
Ausdrücken gefragt wird; von der Lösung dieses Problems habe ich
Gebrauch gemacht, als ich rauchen zu rauchen des Herrn Meier
spezialisierte. Diese semantischen Verknüpfungsverfahren müssen
ihrerseits auf einer pragmatischen Basis eingeführt werden und
hätten den Grundstock einer linguistischen Semantik bereitzustellen.
Das zweite Problem, im Beitrag von Herrn Lorenzer bereits genannt,
ist das Problem der Stabilisierung von Gegenständen, oder, in
traditionell philosophischer Terminologie, das Konstitutionsproblem
der Gegenstände. Solange ich nämlich rauchen, hier ist gerade
rauchen oder rauchen des Herrn Meier äußere, kommt kein Gegenstand
vor,es sei denn, die ganze Situation als raumzeitliche Umgebung des
Sprechenden wird als Gegenstand genommen, nämlich im Sinne der
Benennung durch hier ist gerade .

Damit aber wäre die Verwendungsmöglichkeit von Rede sehr beschränkt.
Es geht jetzt darum, die Stabilisierung von Gegenständen über die
jeweilige Redesituation hinaus zu ermöglichen, den allgemeinen
Bezugsrahmen von Rede (einer natürlichen Sprache), ihren "frame of
reference" zu bestimmen.
Ich habe dafür in "Elemente der Sprachkritik" einen Vorschlag
gemacht, der darauf hinausläuft, die Benennung im Rahmen der
Prädikation zu behandeln. Das hat für unser Beispiel die Konsequenz, aus dem situationsgebundenen Satz rauchen des Herrn Meier
hier den Satz Herr Meier raucht zu ergänzen: dort, wo er sich
gerade befindet, nicht notwendigerweise hier, zu machen.

Auf diese Weise wird der Situationsbezug des Wortes sprachlich
explizit gemacht und nicht mit der Äußerung des Wortes mitgeführt.
Diesen Kunstgriff möchte ich den Übergang vom Wort
zum Satz nennen. Der Satz in seiner behauptenden Verwendung
als Assertion natürlich tritt dabei mit der zusätzlichen Behauptung
auf, daß alle anderen Verwendungsweisen dieses Satzes den behauptenden Satz als Kern enthalten, ganz im Sinne der Regel R. M. hares
(vgl. Hare, The Language of Morals), da der

neustische Anteil eines Satzes in jeder Phrastik (Frage, Wunsch,
etc.) enthalten ist.

WATZLAWICK:

A GAME ANALOGY OF COMMUNICATION

My contribution to the subject matter of this meeting comes, so to
speak, through the backdoor: I am by training a clinical psycho-
therapist and my interest in the phenomena of communication and
their systematization arose only secondarily, that is, within the
frame of therapy. Only thus, and not as my primary concern, did I
get involved in semiotics and especially the one of its three
sub-areas which is of the greatest interest to the study of human
behaviour, namely pragmatics - the theory of the effect of signs
and symbols on their users. As you know, pragmatics is the least
explored and systematized part of semiotics, especially in the
sense in which behaviour research would like to conceive of it:
not merely as the study of the relation between sender and sign,
or sign and receiver, but rather as the interaction between two
organisms which mutually influence each other through the use of
signs. In this perspective, the triad sender-sign-receiver becomes
the smallest unit of all pragmatic research. But even this smallest
unit can be studied meaningfully only in the context of the
preceding and the subsequent units. Peirce already pointed out
that signs are not entities which independently from one another
somehow hang in the air, but that the use of the sign produces a
reaction in its receiver, which reaction then triggers off another
sign-reaction in the original sender, and so on. We are thus faced
with sequences which have their own structure and lawfulness.

Let me present a simple thought model by which the rule-governed
nature of these pragmatic sequences may be illustrated:
Suppose that somebody who does not know the game of chess is in a
foreign country whose language he does not speak and comes across
two people who are obviously engaged in a symbolic activity: they
are moving figures on a board. While he cannot ask them for an
explanation of their behaviour, it is not difficult to imagine
that he will be able to deduce the rules of the game, including its
end point (the check mate), merely from the observation of a
sufficient number of plays. It should be borne in mind:
1. The hypothetical observer could not ask the players for an
explanation of their behaviour; he deduced the rules exclusively
from the redundancy of their game behaviour (an approach,
incidentally, which the students of animal behaviour have
increasingly used since they began to liberate themselves from the

restraints imposed by such ill-defined concepts as instincts,
drives, needs, and the like).
2. There is no necessity for the observer to explore and understand
the personalities of the players, their past, and the experiences
determining their outlooks on life; he arrives at an understanding
of their behavioural rules by watching what is going on here and
now on the board.
3. In this perspective it is likewise unnecessary to attribute to
the game itself any deeper or symbolic meaning. As you know, there
exist very poetic explanations for what chess "really" symbolizes -
but these explanations contribute to the understanding of the game
as little as astrology contributes to astronomy.- What all this
boils down to is simple: The observer asked himself w h a t the
players are doing, not w h y they are doing it.
As members of a given culture, subculture, tradition, family etc.,
we are born into a complex system of very specific behavioural
(pragmatic) rules. On the one hand, we are mostly unaware of their
existence (in fact, any attempt to make them conscious may violate
a taboo) but, on the other hand, we are therefore likely to follow
them all the more precisely. Any violation of such a rule is
considered by the others as upsetting or embarrassing behaviour,
in more serious cases even as evidence of madness or badness. In
any case, these violations of pragmatic rules are much more
flamboyant and socially disturbing than syntactic or semantic ones,
which can usually be shrugged off as a person's educational shortcomings.
Let me illustrate this fact with a somewhat more concrete example
than the chess analogy: There is in every culture a rule about the
"right" distance to be taken up when facing a stranger. In Western
Europe and North America this distance happens to be the proverbial
arm's length; a fact that can easily be verified with two naive
subjects. In Mediterranean countries and in Latin America this
distance is different: two strangers walking up to each other stop
face to face at a much shorter distance. Please remember that the
question w h y   this should be so is irrelevant for our
considerations. For whatever reasons, in their respective cultural
contexts these distances are considered the "right" ones and as
long as this particular behavioural rule is not broken, no conflict
will arise. But if, say, a North and a South American find themselves in this situation, a very specific sequence of behaviours
is bound to occur: the South American will take up the distance

which for him is the right one; the North American will have the
vague, uncomfortable feeling of excessive physical closeness and
will step back to establish what by his (unconscious) cultural
rule is the right distance; the Southerner will then feel that
something is wrong and will move closer; and so on until the
Northerner may find himself with his back against a wall and go
into a homosexual panic.

Trivial as it may be, this example does provide a valid model of a
particular human conflict situation, of a pathology which arises
out of the interaction between the two partners and which cannot,
therefore, be reduced to the one or the other individually. It is
the result of the interference of two incompatible behavioural
rules which are outside the awareness of either participant. What
rises into awareness is only the vague feeling: "The o t h e r is
behaving inappropriately."

This view of the pathology of human relationship was originally
proposed by the mentor of the so-called Palo Alto group, the
anthropologist Gregory Bateson, as one of the results of his study
of communication patterns in the family of schizophrenics.
Instead of examining the situation in the traditional psychiatric
way (i.e. by paying exclusive attention to the behaviour of the
most disturbed family member and trying to find out w h y he is
behaving in this way), Bateson used the anthropological approach
and - very much like our chess observer - observed w h a t was
going on in these families. This afforded the Palo Alto group
basically new insights into the communication patterns existing in
these families and made it possible to avoid the otherwise
inevitable unprovability and self-reflexiveness of all intra-
psychic assertions and their vague metaphysical implications.
Of course, this procedure was not entirely new. As early as in his
"Logischer Aufbau der Welt", Carnap already pointed to the important difference between the object and the relationship
properties of all statements and cautioned against the logical
consequences of any confusion of these two spheres. We could also
have learned from Tarski that any research into communicational
patterns must take into account the hierarchical level structure of
all language systems, i.e. the ascending order of object language,
metalanguage, metametalanguage, etc., and the fact that valid
assertions about any of these levels can only be made from the
next-higher level.

On the other hand, the Palo Alto group had realized from the very

beginning that Whitehead and Russell's Theory of Logical Types is
of decisive importance for the understanding of disturbed communication. I am here referring above all to the pragmatic effects of
the antinomies, that is, of patterns of paradoxical communication.
Important groundwork has already been done in this area, too, for
instance by Wittgenstein who in his investigations of "language
games" has already recognized the pragmatic importance of paradox.
Since the frame of my presentation does not permit me to deal with
this area of communication in greater detail, I should like to
illustrate the psychopathological effects of paradox with at least
one simple example. It is the frequent interpersonal dilemma that
arises when one partner in a relationship demands of the other a
behaviour which by its very nature can only be spontaneous, but
cannot now occur spontaneously because it has been demanded.
Following Ronald Laing we call this impasse a ' "Be spontaneous!"-
paradox', or in Bateson's terms a 'Double Bind'. Structurally it is
identical with the famous paradoxes in classical logics; e.g. the
statement by Epimenides of Crete that all Cretans are liars.
A more concrete example of such a double bind is supplied by a
mother who wants her child to do his homework, but wants that he
should w a n t to do it. Thus, it is not enough for her that he
study because he has to; according to her he should study spontaneously but, of course, in the way she wants him to.
The conflicts arising out of these paradoxes in human communication
are of a purely i n t e r personal nature. While it is undoubtedly
true that expectations (like that of the mother just mentioned) are
acquired in the past, these past reasons (the w h y of this
behaviour) are irrelevant when it comes to solving the present
conflict produced by this type of communication. What a successful
solution presupposes is an adequate understanding of w h a t is
going on here and now, so that this w h a t can then be influenced
metacommunicatively. As will be appreciated, this approach to human
problems provides new tools for their solution; solutions which are
based on the introduction of semiotic - especially pragmatic -
principles into therapy.
Let me conclude my very sketchy presentation here; I have no doubt
that in the forthcoming discussion I shall be able to eliminate any
remaining clarity.

DISKUSSION

<u>Specht</u>: Wir beginnen mit der Diskussion im Panel und schließen die
Diskussion mit dem Auditorium an.- Herr Watzlawick hat eine Frage
an Herrn Lorenz.

<u>Watzlawick</u>: Ja, ich habe eine Frage: ich bin mir nicht darüber klar,
wie Sie sich zum Problem der Zuschreibung von Bedeutung stellen.
Es ist ja so, daß wir speziell in der Psychiatrie und in der Psycho-
pathologie den Fehler begehen, von der Wirklichkeitsanpassung eines
Patienten zu sprechen und damit meinen, ob er die Welt adäquat
sieht oder nicht. Wir fallen da meines Erachtens in einen ziemlich
banalen Fehler, nämlich, anzunehmen, daß es eben eine Wirklichkeit
gibt, über die sich sogenannte normale Menschen klarer sind als
Psychotiker. Ich wollte nun fragen, ob in ihren Ausführungen die
Frage der Zuweisung, der Zuschreibung von Wert und von Bedeutung an
ein Objekt gemeint war, das heißt, während es ohne weiteres klar
ist, daß dies zum Beispiel eine Brille ist, ist es keineswegs
sicher, ob Menschen, die in einer Kommunikationssituation stehen,
demselben Objekt dieselbe Bedeutung und denselben Wert zuweisen.
Aller Wert und alle Bedeutung ist ja interpersönliche Konvention.
Der Wert einer Banknote besteht nicht darin, daß es ein verschieden-
farbig bedruckter Papierzettel ist, sondern darin, daß es sich um
einen Wert handelt, der sozusagen durch Konvention festgelegt ist.
Vielleicht könnten Sie darüber etwas sagen.

<u>Lorenz</u> : Über den Wert, den Gegenstände,bzw. den Unterscheidungen
für die betroffenen Individuen haben, habe ich gar nicht gesprochen.
Die Werte müssen natürlich erörtert werden, wenn es um die
Hierarchien in der Reihenfolge dessen, was wichtig ist und was
nicht, geht. Auch kam 'Bedeutung' bei mir nicht im Zusammenhang der
Bedeutung von Gegenständen vor, sondern nur als Bedeutung von
Zeichen, also spezieller Gegenstände, in diesem Falle der Wörter,
und dann kraft der Einführungssituation auch nicht so, daß etwa
die Brille gleich als Ding auftritt - ich möchte gern 'Dinge' von
den 'Gegenständen' unterscheiden und sie "spezielle Gegenstände"
nennen; 'Gegenstände' verwende ich im logischen Sinne, also univer-
sell, so wie es zum Beispiel auch Carnap tut - ; vielmehr gehört
zur Einführungssituation von <u>Brille</u> natürlich das Brillenaufsetzen,
gegebenenfalls sogar das Brillebeschaffen und so weiter, dazu; die
Einführungssituation geschieht nicht bloß in einem Verweis auf ein
Ding; solche Reduktionen finden erst an einer ganz späten Stelle
dieser Sprachrekonstruktion statt. An der primären Stelle der

ungeschiedenen szenischen Situation würde mit <u>Brille</u> der gesamte
Komplex einschlägigen Umgangs mit Brillen genannt sein, der damit
sprachlich vertreten ist, aber natürlich in unserer faktischen
deutschen Umgangssprache mit dem Wort <u>Brille</u> allein nicht repräsentiert wird. Das Wort <u>Brille</u> ist längst schon als Nomen Vertreter
für spezielle Gegenstandsbereiche, die überhaupt nicht mehr
auf dem Wege ungeschiedener szenischer Situationen repräsentierbar
sind, und die auch nicht mit diesem Rekonstruktionsverfahren, etwa
individueller Geschichte, eingeholt werden können, und zwar aus dem
ganz einfachen Grunde nicht, weil wir uns in einer historisch
gewordenen natürlichen Sprache bewegen, in der zum Beispiel die
syntaktischen Kategorien schon gelernt sind, ehe sie begriffen
werden, so   daß die Herstellung der syntaktischen Kategorien zum
Beispiel bei dem Rekonstruktionsprozeß noch mitzuleisten ist.
Wenn ich vorhin das Beispiel der Spezialisierung <u>rauchen</u> - <u>rauchen</u>
<u>des Herrn Meier</u> als ganz einfaches Beispiel einer semantischen
Zusammenfügung nannte, dann ist diese Relativierung wohl noch
vergleichsweise einfach zu verstehen, die Unterscheidung von <u>Rauch</u>
und <u>rauchen</u> hingegen schon ganz sicher nicht mehr. Das würde also
durch ein derart einfaches Unterfangen nicht einzufangen sein,weil es
nämlich auf die Frage der Handlung-Ding-Unterscheidung und damit der
Nomen-Verbum-Unterscheidung führte, die somit zu einer Grundsatz-
überlegung über die Differenzierung der Wörter zu Wortarten heraus-
fordert, einem Problem, auf das ich nicht zu sprechen kam.
<u>Lorenzer</u>: Ich wollte also noch etwas zu dem sagen, was Herr
Watzlawick vorgetragen hat. Zunächst eine, wenn Sie so wollen,
persönliche Vorbemerkung: Ich habe ein etwas schlechtes Gewissen
gehabt, weil ich das Selbstmißverständnis der Psychoanalyse nun
ausgerechnet mit einem Zitat aus Ihrem Buch belegt habe. Ich habe es
dann aber doch sehr sorgfältig überlegt, das scheint mir wichtig zu
sein, von vornherein in einer Auseinandersetzung klarzumachen,wie
sie zwischen Ihrem Standpunkt und dem meinen stattfinden könnte, daß
wir in der Tat den gleichen Bereich reklamieren, zugegeben mit ganz
anderen Perspektiven. Es wäre jetzt eigentlich für eine fruchtbare
Diskussion noch zu leisten anzudeuten, worin der Unterschied
besteht; lassen Sie mich also aus meiner Sicht formulieren. Dann
glaube ich, gerade Ihr Beispiel des Schachspiels zeigt sehr klar,
wie Sie vergleichbare Sachverhalte in einer ganz anderen Weise
ansehen, als es die Psychoanalyse macht, nämlich: schon die Auswahl
des Schachspielbeispiels verdeutlicht das sehr klar. Sie haben bei
Ihrem Schachspielbeispiel eine Szene ausgesucht, bei der ein

Beobachter ein ihm fremdes Verhalten von außen untersucht; das ist
ganz ohne Zweifel schon in der Anlage eine Anordnung, die auch jeder
naturwissenschaftlichen B e o b a c h t u n g entspricht, jeden-
falls in der D i s t a n z i e r u n g zwischen Beobachter und dem
zu Beobachtenden. Nun haben Sie zweitens bei dem Schachspiel ein
Beispiel benutzt, das meines Erachtens nicht von ungefähr der
Vorgang einer instrumentellen Handlung ist, einer Verfügung über
Figuren und eines Spiels nach Regeln, wobei es sich dabei um ein
Spiel handelt, das in seiner Entwicklung von der emotionalen
Situation, von der lebensgeschichtlichen wie der geschichtlichen
Situation der Betreffenden völlig neutralisiert ist. Wir wissen ja,
daß das Schachspiel in Spanien vor fünfhundert Jahren ebenso
gespielt worden ist, wie Sie sich vorstellen können, daß es in drei-
hundert Jahren noch gespielt wird. Die Regeln wie auch der Vorgang
sind lebensgeschichtlich und geschichtlich neutral. Man muß gerade
in Gegenüberstellung zu dem Modell Schachspiel sich vergegenwärtigen,
daß die psychoanalytische Situation nicht die eines Beobachters an
einem ihm äußerlichen Vorgang ist, sondern die eines Mitspielers in
einem Spiel, in dessen Regeln er einbezogen ist, ohne sie genau und
vollständig zu kennen. Anders ausgedrückt: Ich meine, daß es sehr
wichtig ist, die psychoanalytische Situation als Teilnahme an einem
Sprachspiel zu verstehen, bei dem die Regeln den Beteiligten nicht
voll ausweisbar bekannt sind, und auch nicht erkennbar werden in
Distanzierung. Der zweite Punkt ist vielleicht noch der wichtigere:
Ihr Schachspielbeispiel ist ja das eines gelungenen und ungestörten
Vorgangs: Die Spieler, wer immer auch verliert, spielen nach klaren,
ungebrochenen, auslegbaren Regeln. Wenn wir das auf die Interaktion
in der Psychoanalyse übertragen, so ist der Ansatzpunkt eben nicht
die ungestörte Interaktion, sondern die gestörte Interaktion, und
zwar nicht die gestörte Interaktion, die bei Ihnen von außen her
betrachtet wird, sondern eine , an welcher der Analytiker teilnimmt,
indem er in einem Verfahren der inneren Interpretation , der inneren
Adaptation dieses Vorgehens versucht, die Störung ausfindig zu machen. Wenn man es zusammenfaßt, könnte man in ein paar Worten sagen:
Ihr Verfahren ist ein naturwissenschaftliches, nach dem Modus der
Naturwissenschaften aufgebautes Beobachtungsverfahren. Demgegenüber
ist der Zugang der Psychoanalyse zu der Gestörtheit hermeneutisch
zu nennen, weil sich ja erst im Prozeß der Verständigung das heraus-
holen und begreifen läßt, worum es geht. Er ist zugleich auch
kritisch zu nennen, weil er nun nicht in der Anlage einer experimentellen oder quasi-experimentellen Situation vor sich geht,

sondern in der Destruktion von Annahmen, die zwischen den Beteiligten bestehen und die destruiert werden müssen, damit aus ihnen das
lebensgeschichtlich wie geschichtlich Besondere herausgeholt wird.
Watzlawick: Ja, ich bin durchaus Ihrer Meinung, daß wir über dieselben Dinge sprechen, nur eben von verschiedenen Gesichtspunkten
her. Indem ich jetzt versuche, auf Ihre Einwände einzugehen, frage
ich mich, wie weit ich Gefahr laufe, diese Diskussion in eine
Diskussion zwischen Angehörigen zweier verschiedener therapeutischer Auffassungen degenerieren zu lassen, die für das Publikum, das
aus einem ganz anderen Grund hier ist, wahrscheinlich weniger
Interesse hätte. Es ist aber kaum möglich, nicht doch gewisse Bezüge
zu nehmen auf die Frage des Vorgehens in den beiden Schulen; vor
allem aber möchte ich darauf verweisen, daß es sich meines Erachtens
bei Freud wohl um Interaktion handelt, aber nicht um eine Interaktion zwischen den eigentlichen Personen, sondern darum, wie der
Patient sich mit den Introjekten jener Personen auseinandersetzt,
und zwar intrapsychisch. Ich bin der Meinung, daß diese Grundformen
geprägt werden durch die Erlebnisse mit den eigentlichen, tatsächlichen, physischen Personen, daß dann aber in psychoanalytischer
Sicht diese Tatsache sehr rasch in den Hintergrund rückt und man
sich in psychoanalytischer Theorie und Praxis hauptsächlich damit
befaßt, was der Patient aus diesen Personen dann intrapsychisch
gemacht hat. Ich möchte darauf verweisen, daß Freud, als er mit
Breuer seine Studien über Hysterie abschloß, erstaunt war, in dem
doch recht puritanischen Wien mit, wie er sagte, monotoner Regel-
mäßigkeit auf die Tatsache stieß, daß in dem Vorleben seiner
hysterischen Patientinnen immer die sexuelle Verführung durch den
Vater eine ganz wesentliche Rolle spielte, bis es Freud eben klar
wurde, daß das nicht ein Erlebnis mit der tatsächlichen Person war,
sondern ein Phantasieerlebnis mit dem Introjekt des Vaters.
Soviel zur Auffassung, daß man in der Psychoanalyse auch mit
Interaktion arbeitet. Ich würde dem zustimmen, aber dazufügen, daß
es eben doch nur strikt i n der Seele stattfindet. Aus diesem
Grunde - und ich fürchte, jetzt abzugleiten in rein therapeutische
Überlegungen - haben wir uns dann sehr bald entschlossen, Patienten
nicht mehr allein zu sehen, sondern in dem natürlichen Kontext
ihrer Familie. Dann wird es nämlich offensichtlich, wo die Interaktionen wirklich verlaufen; es ist dann ganz etwas anderes, man
muß als Therapeut dann auch nicht mehr sich mühsam fragen und
mühsam feststellen: Wie kann ich das Verhalten des Patienten mir
gegenüber nun übertragen, übersetzen in ein Verhalten, das er mit

einer Schlüsselperson seines eigenen Lebens hat? Die Interaktionsmuster spielen sich ja dann vor unseren Augen ab und nicht auf dem
Umweg über die Übertragung. Der zweite Punkt, den Sie erwähnten, und
zwar die Tatsache, daß man ein Schachspiel zwar als sozusagen
"detachierter" Beobachter anschauen kann, daß aber in der therapeutischen Situation diese Absonderung und dieses Detachement nicht
möglich wäre, steht zweifellos fest; ich stoße mich nur etwas an der
impliziten Auffassung - ich weiß, ich gehe da über Ihre Ausführung
hinaus - das Menschliche sei sowieso dem Menschlichen zugänglich:
nichts Menschliches ist mir fremd, im Goetheschen Sinne ungefähr.
Auch das klingt zwar plausibel, aber praktisch ist dem doch nicht
so, denn wenn immer wir an ein menschliches System herangehen, das
in irgendeinem gestörten Kommunikationsspiel begriffen ist, so ist
es nicht a priori klar, daß uns das Spiel und seine Regeln von
vorneherein (qua Mensch zu Mensch) klar sein müßten. Es geht jeder
therapeutischen Intervention unweigerlich eine Zeit voraus, in der
man als Beobachter sich ganz einfach fragt: Welches Spiel spielt
nun diese Familie oder dieses Ehepaar? , und das führt dann zum
nächsten Punkt; daß in der menschlichen Pragmatik eine enorme, fast
erschreckende Regelgebundenheit besteht.
Wenn wir in den anderen beiden Gebieten der Semiotik, also in der
Syntaktik und der Semantik von Regelgebundenheit sprechen, und
davon, daß wir fast unbewußt diesen Regeln folgen, daß Menschen ihre
Sprache korrekt und fließend sprechen können, ohne die leiseste
Ahnung zu haben, welches die grammatischen und syntaktischen Regeln
dieser Sprache sind, so gilt das auch vollinhaltlich für die
Pragmatik: Menschliches Verhalten ist nun einmal immer an Regeln
gebunden, und es ist daher meines Erachtens zulässig, vom Schachspiel als Analogie, wenngleich als vielleicht übertriebene und
etwas zu einfache Analogie, auszugehen.
Wenn wir uns fragen, welches Kommunikationsspiel einem bestimmten
menschlichen System zugrunde liegt, dann kommen wir nicht umhin, uns
ähnlich zu verhalten wie dieser hypothetische Beobachter des Schachspiels, das heißt, uns zunächst einmal zu fragen: Wie funktioniert
dieses System, welches sind seine Regeln, und welche Folgen ergeben
sich, wenn Regeln gebrochen werden?; in anderen Worten: Welche
Rückkoppelungsmechanismen treten dann in Funktion und stellen die
Stabilität des Systems wieder her?
Lorenz: Ja, ich würde gern gerade zu dem letzten Punkt etwas sagen,
weil diese Verteidigung des Beobachters impliziert, das Verfahren,
das zunächst mal bloß vor Augen liegende Verhalten aufzufassen und

dabei nicht nach den Gründen oder Zielen dieses Verhaltens zu
fragen, sei leichter, also die beobachtende Haltung insbesondere
von vornherein unvoreingenommener als zum Beispiel die teilneh-
mende. Das ist zwar, sagen wir, gut belegte Tradition, und gleichwohl deswegen nicht richtig - meine ich. Denn gerade das eigene
Verhalten des Beobachters, seine Sprachverfassung zum Beispiel, ist
ja relevant für die Auswahl dessen, was er beobachtet; es ist doch
nicht wirklich so, daß mit dem Weglassen der Redundanzen des
Verhaltens sozusagen die charakteristischen Strukturen aufgefunden
werden können; das geht nur auf der Basis schon unterstellten
gemeinsamen Verhaltens, das eben nicht mehr als bloße Beobachtung
interpretiert werden kann, sondern bei dem wir vereinbaren können,
" das sind jedenfalls auch Menschen", "die bestimmten Tätigkeiten
entsprechen den unseren", so daß also allenfalls für einen gewissen
Bereich Beobachtung und diese erst auf der Basis einer Teinahme
zulässig ist. Es stellt sich sofort die nächste Frage: Von welcher
Art sind die pragmatischen Regeln, wenn sie tauglich sein sollen?
Für den Gesamtkontext unserer Überlegung einer Kommunikationssemantik ist doch gefordert, daß sie schließlich Theoriestatus
bekommen sollen, wie haben sie dann auszusehen, in welcher Form
werden sie notiert zum Beispiel, da ja doch eine Notation bloß mit
Wörtern ersichtlich nicht ausreicht? Wir haben heute morgen einige
Hinweise bekommen, wie das auszusehen hätte; bei all diesen Vor-
schlägen und auch dem, was Sie am Anfang gesagt haben, scheint aber
unterstellt zu sein, daß ein solches Regelsystem die Struktur eines
mathematischen Formalismus haben müsse, dessen Voraussetzungen
natürlich ein vorgegebener Gegenstandsbereich, Prädikatbereich usw.
ist, den an dieser Stelle bereitzustellen aber ja gerade das Problem
darstellt. Dieser theoretische Ansatz stellt daher, meine ich, eine
petitio principii dar für den Theoriestatus der hier zu erstellenden
Wissenschaft. Denn, wie ich ganz am Ende meines Exposés klarzustellen versuchte, ist die Frage der Bereitstellung der Gegenstände
der Rede das große Problem. Also verlangt in diesem Zusammenhang
etwa das Problem der allmählichen Ausgliederung aus <u>Mama</u>, verstanden
zunächst als szenische Arrangements, die verschiedene Personen
betreffen können, schließlich die individuelle Person, und damit
eine Abfolge von Individualisierungen unter demselben Wort, das
ganze Problem der Gegenstandskonstitution jetzt unter dem Titel
'Individuation' abzuhandeln. Das kann ja nicht dadurch gelöst
werden, daß man etwa einen Bereich von Variablen für die gegebenen

Gegenstandsbereiche zur Verfügung stellen kann, mit denen dann die
Theorie arbeitet. Gerade das ist ja das Problem, und, um mein
Beispiel noch einmal zu verwenden, der Zusammenhang, der jetzt
syntaktisch-semantisch zwischen Rauch, rauchen, Raucher besteht,
verlangt ja, wenn Sie nicht mit bloßen unverbundenen Gegenstands-
bereichen im Sinne von Dingen, Menschen, Handlungen arbeiten wollen,
Verbindungen herzustellen, die das eine aus dem anderen zu ent-
wickeln erlauben, genauer gesagt: den einen Gegenstand aus dem
anderen herzustellen erlauben durch geeignete, ersichtlich nicht
bloß semantische Operationen. Pragmatische Konstruktionen sind schon
allein deswegen notwendig, weil etwa der Übergang von rauchen zu
Rauch eine Unterscheidung von Handlungen und Dingen verlangt, die
auf der Basis bloßer Bedeutungsanalyse garantiert nicht zu leisten
ist. Soviel zu dem Status einer solchen Theorie, die von vorneherein
jedenfalls nicht gleich die Gestalt eines Formalismus haben kann.
Specht: Herr Watzlawick, ich habe in dem Zusammenhang auch eine
Verständnisfrage: Meinen Sie, dieser Beobachter würde das wie ein
Naturwissenschaftler registrieren? Der würde doch nie verstehen,
warum der Spieler den Königsbauern vorzieht, weil er ja nicht die
Absichten verstehen kann. Der Witz des Schachspiels ist doch, daß
Absichten verfolgt werden, und das kann ein Naturwissenschaftler
als Beobachter doch gar nicht feststellen. Er ist doch von vorne-
herein in einem Sinn-Zweck-Zusammenhang, und, so meine ich, auch die
Kreisprozesse oder die Rückkoppelungsprozesse haben einen Sinn, eine
Absicht. Es ist doch nicht nur ein Formalismus, der abläuft, sondern
da verfolgen Menschen Zwecke. Oder habe ich das falsch verstanden?
Watzlawick: Die Absicht des Schachspiels oder der Zweck all dieser
Züge würde sich ebenfalls aus der Beobachtung ergeben. Wenn der
Beobachter feststellt, daß sich das Schachmatt, oder unter Umständen
die Remise, jeweils am Ende des Spieles ergibt, daß die Spieler
dann aufstehen oder eine neue Partie beginnen, so glaube ich, ließe
sich daraus - ich spreche jetzt nur in Zusammenhang mit dem Schachspiel - doch immerhin der Zweck des Spiels oder die Absicht der
Spieler ableiten.
Lorenz: Wie unterscheiden Sie Gewinn und Verlust?
Watzlawick: Im Augenblick bin ich nicht sicher, ob diese Unterscheidung notwendig wäre zu dem von mir postulierten, sehr begrenz-
ten Zweck des Verständnisses der Regeln und daher der relativen
Voraussagbarkeit des Verhaltens der Spieler. Die Frage des Gewinns
oder des Verlustes ist meines Erachtens hier von sekundärer, wenn

nicht irrelevanter Bedeutung.

Lorenzer: Gerade Ihr Einwand, Herr Specht, macht es mir deutlicher.
Natürlich ist in diesem Schachspielbeispiel nicht ein Beispiel
naturwissenschaftlicher Experimental-Situation gegeben, natürlich
habe ich auch vorher beiseite gelassen, daß das Problem des
Verständigtseins auch in Ihrem Schachspielbeispiel, Herr Watzlawick,
noch vorhanden ist, denn irgendwo muß der Beobachter ja verstehen,
was dieses Tun für die beiden Spieler bedeutet. Nur ist es deutlich,
daß in Ihrem Beispiel dieses Problem s t i l l g e s t e l l t
ist, das ist gleichsam als unwesentlich ausgeklammert, es ist
unproblematisch; und wenn man es weiter verfolgt, ist natürlich auch
die Frage nach den I n h a l t e n , nach der lebensgeschichtlichen
Besonderheit dieser Inhalte wie auch der geschichtlichen Bestimmtheit dieser Inhalte, methodisch ausgeklammert, denn der Blick geht
auf das Spiel, der Blick geht auf die beobachtbare Interaktion.
Er geht nicht auf die Besonderheit der subjektiven Interaktionsstrukturen, sondern auf das beobachtbare Spiel. Da würde ich doch
sagen, daß Ihr Durchblick auch durch die Kommunikationsprozesse
ähnlich ist wie bei einer gruppendynamischen Untersuchung, bei der
die Dynamik der Spielformen untersucht wird, dabei aber abgesehen
wird von der Problematik gestörter Bedeutungen. Dem wird nicht
weiter nachgegangen, es wird nur r e g i s t r i e r t , daß es
Störungselemente gibt, die in diesem Spiel zum Vorschein kommen.
Watzlawick: Die Problematik gestörter Abläufe ergibt sich natürlich
nicht mehr aus der Schachanalogie, sie ergibt sich sehr wohl aus der
Beobachtung vor unseren Augen ablaufender menschlicher Interaktionen. Vielleicht wird die Sache etwas klarer, wenn ich darauf
verweise, daß der Anthropologe oder der Sprachwissenschaftler, der
sich einer ihm unbekannten Zivilisation oder einer ihm unbekannten
Sprache exponiert, einen sehr ähnlichen Prozeß durchläuft.
Zweifellos weiß er, daß die Menschen, deren Sprache er nun zu
studieren hat, in dieselben physischen Gegebenheiten eingespannt
sind wie er; die existentielle Tatsache, daß sie einen Körper haben,
der Schwerkraft unterworfen sind, Alterungserscheinungen, Krank-
heiten usw. ausgeliefert sind, all diese Dinge sind ja von vorneherein klar. In diesem Sinne besteht zweifellos eine Basis des
Menschseins, die er unweigerlich einbeziehen wird, darüber hinaus
aber wird er wahrscheinlich so unvoreingenommen wie nur möglich an
die zu studierenden Phänomene heranzutreten haben. Ich glaube,
diesen Unterschied müssen wir machen; auch als Therapeut ist man
natürlich jeweils mit drinnen; das ist ja gar keine Frage, aber man

hält sich auch wieder heraus, denn man versucht auch, nicht zum
Beispiel von dem phantastischen Absorptionsvermögen einer schizo-
phrenen Familie eingefangen zu werden. Aber das sind vielleicht
nebensächliche Punkte. Vergegenwärtigen wir uns, daß die
architektonische Darstellung des Grundrisses eines Hauses eine
kodifizierte Darstellung ist, deren Regeln man verstehen muß. Wenn
man sie verstanden hat, ist man dann in der Lage, auch andere
Grundrisse zu verstehen. Es ist damit aber nicht gesagt, daß daher
irgendeine wesentliche Ähnlichkeit zwischen verschiedenen Häusern
besteht; man hat nur verstanden, daß sie sich in einer ganz
bestimmten Weise darstellen lassen, darüber hinaus aber ist dann das
"So-sein" eines Hauses eine Sache für sich.

Lorenzer: Man kann deutlich sehen, wie Sie versuchen, sowohl
'Interaktion' wie 'Kommunikation' in einem Netz ahistorischer
Kategorien einzufangen, innerhalb derer dann dieses "So-sein"
bestimmt wird. In Ihrem Kategoriengerüst ist das geschichtliche
Moment zum Verschwinden gebracht, wobei Sie nachträglich versuchen,
die Geschichte dann noch in dieses Netz einzufangen.

Watzlawick: Ich will nicht leugnen, daß menschliche Haltungen
natürlich die Resultate von Erfahrungen in der Vergangenheit sind,
und daß Erwartungen, die Verhalten beeinflussen, zweifellos
präformiert und ausgebildet werden in der Vergangenheit. Ich möchte
nur darauf verweisen, daß es in pragmatischer Sicht, wie ich das zu
definieren versucht habe, unnotwendig ist, in die Vergangenheit zu
gehen - allein schon deswegen, weil die Vergangenheit uns niemals
offensteht. Wir haben nur die Selbstberichte des Betreffenden, und
die sind notorisch unzuverlässig. Ich bin mir vollkommen darüber
klar, daß es scheinbar eine fast amputierende Selbstbeschränkung
ist, wenn man auf das Historische verzichtet; ich möchte aber darauf
verweisen, daß sich eben aus dieser Amputierung heraus dann ganz
wesentliche heuristische Möglichkeiten ergeben.

Lorenz: Und der ganze Witz ist ja, daß diese Unzuverlässigkeit ja
zunächst keine Rolle spielt.

Specht: In der Psychoanalyse...?

Lorenz: Genau!

Watzlawick: ...in der Psychoanalyse nicht.

Lorenz: Aus dieser Zusammenstellung wird erst ganz allmählich über
bestimmte Rekonstruktionsverfahren die Möglichkeit für die
Geltungsfrage wieder geschaffen und damit auch für Kontrollver-
fahren.

Specht: Herr Watzlawick, als Beispiel der Film "Spiel mir das Lied
vom Tod". Da wird drei Stunden ein immenses Interaktionsgeschehen
gezeigt, und das bleibt völlig unverständlich, wenn nicht in letzter
Minute das historische Ereignis gegeben wird, das überhaupt den
Handlungsablauf verständlich macht. Nicht bei allen Aktionen, aber
bei gewissen, müssen Sie auf das historische zurückgreifen.
Watzlawick: Jaja, ich bin sicher, daß das Kinopublikum wahrscheinlich enttäuscht wäre, wenn letzten Endes die Gebrauchsanweisung
nicht mitgeliefert würde. Und wiederum habe ich die Angst, in das
rein Therapeutische abzurutschen. Die Frage ist eben doch, ob das
in therapeutischer Hinsicht irgendwie wesentlich ist. Man kann die
unerhört reiche Geschichte eines Menschen ununterbrochen immer
weiter zurückverfolgen. Die Psychoanalyse, oder meinetwegen Systeme
wie die Christian Science oder der Marxismus, haben ja diese
phantastische Fähigkeit, sich jeweils selbst zu bestätigen. Zum
Beispiel, wenn der Zustand des Patienten sich noch nicht gebessert
hat, so ist es deswegen, weil die tieferen Ursachen dieses Problems
noch nicht genügend erleuchtet wurden, was wiederum die Richtigkeit
der Annahme beweist, daß seelische Störungen in sehr tiefen
Schichten des Unbewußten liegen. In infinitem Regreß geht die
Therapie also dahin; aber, wiederum, ich rutsche ins Therapeutische
ab.
Lorenzer: Lassen Sie mich eine Bemerkung dazu machen, daß bei Ihnen,
Herr Watzlawick, nicht nur der Durchblick auf Lebensgeschichte
unwichtig wird, sondern über die Lebensgeschichte hinaus der
Durchblick auf Geschichte entfällt und bedeutungslos wird. Da ist
es nicht von ungefähr, daß Sie Psychoanalyse, Christian Science
und den Marxismus in einen Topf geworfen haben. Lassen wir mal die
Christian Science beiseite, so ist natürlich in der Tat der
Psychoanalyse und dem Marxismus mindestens dieses Problem gemeinsam: die Frage nach der geschichtlichen Entwicklung von Strukturen.
Genau das ist die Frage, die bei der Analyse von Spielformen oder
Zusammenspiel von vorneherein ausgeschieden ist.
Watzlawick: Ich möchte lediglich die tendenziöse Bemerkung machen,
daß wir, glaube ich, einen Punkt der menschlichen Geschichte
erreicht haben, an dem wir uns von dem Gruftdeckel des geschichtlichen Bewußtseins befreien müssen, wenn wir Lösungen finden
wollen; die Geschichte liefert sie uns nicht.
Specht: Darf ich den Vorschlag machen - ich glaube, das Publikum
will nachher noch diskutieren - noch ein anderes Thema anzuschneiden ?

Lorenz: In Ihrem Exposé, Herr Lorenzer, kam das Votum, daß im
Sozialisationsprozeß den Beginn 'Handlungen' einnehmen müssen und
danach erst 'Gegenstände'; Sie sagen jedesmal gleich 'Dinge'. Das
ist ja ganz unabhängig davon eine alte sprachphilosophische
Streitfrage gewesen über den Primat der Dinge vor den Handlungen,
und es sieht ja so aus, als würden diese jetzt von mir vorgeschlage-
nen Einführungssituationen für Wörter notwendigerweise auf
Handlungen als Beginn angewiesen sein. Das würde ich für ein
Mißverständnis ansehen, daß nämlich am Beginn solcher Einführungssituationen solche Klassifikationen, die in der beschreibenden Rede
auftreten, schon zur Verfügung stünden. Gerade das muß abgewiesen
werden, das ist das Dilemma in dieser beschreibenden Sprache,
Deutsch oder eine andere zu verwenden, die keine Wörter zur
Verfügung hat, die Unterscheidungen noch nicht mitmachen, die in der
Sprache gemacht sind, also etwa von Handlungen zu sprechen, wenn man
davon noch nicht reden will. Ganz deutlich läßt es sich wieder an
dem Mama-Beispiel machen, wo eben ein ganzes szenisches Arrangement
den Beginn bildet und dieses gar nicht erlaubt, hier schon einen
Unterschied von Handlungen und Dingen einzuführen.
Und wieder ist es das Problem, ausgehend von dieser Unterscheidung
an solchen Komplexen - das ist auch nicht korrekt, es liegen
ungeschiedene Situationen vor, was heißt da "komplex", komplex
sind sie erst im nachhinein, rückschauend, aufgrund der späteren
Strukturierung, es wäre ein Mißverständnis, vorher von 'komplexer
Situation' zu sprechen - diese, jetzt sage ich, Komplifizierung,
Schritt für Schritt einzuführen und sie in diskutierbare Regeln
zu verwandeln. Das, meine ich, scheint mir der Punkt zu sein, auf
dem zu insistieren lohnt.
Lorenzer: Was ich sagen will, ist eigentlich nur eine kleine
ergänzende Bemerkung. Ich möchte bei der Einführungssituation noch
auf die Besonderheit der Einführungssituationen in der Kindheit
hinweisen. Dort liegt ein noch nicht entfaltetes System von Sprache
vor. Bei einer sehr drängenden Spannung zwischen den eigenen
Körperbedürfnissen und den von der Gesellschaft vermittelten Formen
ist eine andere Situation gegeben als beim Erwachsenen, bei dem
eingeführt wird in ein reich entfaltetes System von Symbolen und
Zeichen. Und zwar nicht mehr in dieser drängenden Lage etwas
artikulieren zu müssen, wie das die frühkindliche Situation aus-
zeichnet.
Watzlawick: Ja, akzeptiert. Ich habe nur von der systematischen
Rekonstruktion, nicht von der empirischen Kindheits-Einführungs-

situation sprechen wollen und können.

Specht: Wir gehen jetzt über zur Diskussion mit dem Publikum.

Zenz: Ich bitte, zu folgenden Statements Stellung zu nehmen:

1. Logische Paradoxien in sozialen Handlungen zu erkennen, bedarf
es keiner historischen Forschung; ihr Funktionieren zu verstehen
aber bedarf es historischer Forschung.

2. Das zweite richtet sich insbesondere an Herrn Lorenzer: kann
man wirklich davon ausgehen, daß durch pure Einfühlung neurotisches
Handeln verstehbar ist? Ist nicht gerade aus der Laien-Analyse
bekannt, daß das unmittelbare Verstehen fehlläuft, daß tatsächlich
Kenntnisse und die Beobachtung von Bedingungen notwendig sind, so
daß doch ein Doppelschritt-Vorgehen notwendig ist: ein sozusagen
"naturwissenschaftliches Erklären" und ein "einfühlendes Verstehen"?

Specht: Die erste Frage richtete sich wohl an Herrn Watzlawick.

Watzlawick: Ich bin Ihnen für Ihren Einwand dankbar. Ich gebe gern
zu, daß zum Verständnis der Zwecklosigkeit oder der Verfahrenheit
von Paradoxien die geschichtliche Perspektive notwendig ist.
Ich möchte meine frühere Bemerkung dahingehend korrigieren, daß die
Geschichte uns etwas lehren kann, nämlich das, was wir nicht tun
sollen. Das ist mehr als nur ein bon mot. In der Therapie fragen
wir nämlich ganz spezifisch danach, was hat der Betreffende oder
was hat das betreffende menschliche System bisher versucht, um der
Lage Herr zu werden?, und wir werden dann sorgfältig vermeiden,
diese selbe Lösung anzustreben; also in dieser Hinsicht: ja, die
Notwendigkeit des Verstehens, des geschichtlichen Verstehens, aber
eben, wie Sie das ja, glaube ich, meinten, im Sinne seiner negativen
Bedeutung.

Lorenzer: Ja, das ist völlig richtig, daß der analytische Prozeß
nicht auf schlicht umgangssprachliches Verstehen allein reduziert
werden kann. Immerhin gibt es die Möglichkeit, sich vorzustellen,
daß es ein Verstehen mit einem Minimum an Annahmen gibt, wie zum
Beispiel bei den Balintschen Ärztegruppen, bei denen in der Tat mit
einem Minimum an neurosenpsychologischen Annahmen gearbeitet wird.
Das ist aber nur ein Randfall, der auch zeigt, wie wenig tragfähig
das ist. Meine Behauptung ist, kurz zusammengefaßt, die, daß
für den einzelnen Schritt bis zur Aufklärung, bis zum
"Auf-den-Begriff-Bringen", kein Zwischenglied notwendig ist, daß
danach aber sehr wohl die Einfügung in eine Theorie erforderlich
ist. Dabei ist zu sagen, "danach" heißt jetzt nicht : nach Abschluß
einer Analyse oder nach fünf Monaten oder zwischendurch, sondern
das kann heißen: nach einem kurzen nur über einige Stunden,

vielleicht nur über zehn Minuten laufenden - um es einmal ganz
extrem zu nehmen - Aufklärungsprozeß wird "danach" etwas eingefügt.
Das ist ein Stück der Theoriebildung, die sehr genau dem entspricht,
was bei den Schlüssen im Rahmen einer kritischen Theorie entwickelt
wird. Jedenfalls ist es ganz klar, daß ich hier keineswegs die
Rolle der Theoriebildung unterschätzen will; sie hat vielmehr einen
systematischen Platz, der im einzelnen noch genauer zu diskutieren
wäre.

Apel: Ich möchte gerne zwei Bemerkungen machen, die ich natürlich
auch als Fragen aufgefaßt haben möchte: eine richtet sich in erster
Linie an Herrn Lorenz, und eine betrifft die wissenschaftstheore-
tische Debatte zwischen Herrn Watzlawick und den anderen Herren.
Die erste Frage liefert den Ertrag des Statements von Herrn Lorenz
für eine Pragmatik. Wir haben heute morgen gesehen, wie die
Pragmatik ins Spiel kommt, wenn man mit Syntax und Semantik anfängt
und dann zu den Restproblemen kommt; und jetzt haben wir ein
Beispiel, wie es aussieht, wenn man mit der Pragmatik anfängt, und
zwar genetisch aus dem Sozialisierungsprozeß heraus, aus der
Situation der Einführung dieser Ein-Wort-Sätze in ungeschiedenen
szenischen Einführungssituationen der Prädikatoren, etwa beim Kind.
Sie haben gerade rauchen benutzt, das Beispiel ist natürlich für
das Kind nicht geeignet. Sie haben unabhängig von der psychoanalytischen Problematik eine ideale Erlanger Rekonstruktion von
rauchen gegeben, vom Rauchen des Herrn Meier bis zu dem Satz
Herr Meier raucht, wobei zu ergänzen ist hier oder an irgendeiner
Stelle. Nun, was mich hier interessiert, ist: das Ganze kann ja als
Einführung in folgendes Phänomen genommen werden: daß man nämlich
von einer situationsabhängigen Pragmatik der Rede vorstößt bis zu
dem Punkt, wo wir das Wort-Satz-System haben, das situationsunabhängig ist. Das war wohl in dem oben zitierten Satz repräsentiert. Worauf ich hinweisen wollte, ist die Gefahr, daß man von
einer genetisch erzeugten Pragmatik zur Konstitution des Wort-Satz-
Systems gekommen ist und so zu einem Satz im Sinne der Sprache, der
situationsunabhängig angewendet werden kann. Man vergißt dann, daß
trotzdem alle Sätze der Sprache doch wieder an der Situation
festgemacht werden müssen. Diese Entwicklung, von der Sie, Herr
Lorenz, in der Rekonstruktion gezeigt haben, daß sie gewissermaßen
kompensiert werden muß, wird kompensiert durch das, was die Sprache
in deiktischen Wörtern, in Referentials etc. hat. Sie müssen
außerdem noch hinzufügen, was alles an Wörtern entwickelt wird, um
alles das zu artikulieren, was vorher unartikuliert in den

Ein-Wort-Sätzen, die im szenischen Hintereinander auftreten,
enthalten ist. Es ist doch sehr interessant, was alles ausgefüllt
werden muß, um die Situationsbezüge wieder herzustellen, denn ohne
das "Hier und Jetzt", ohne die deiktische Festmachung an Situationen
sind diese Sätze gar nicht verwendbar. Das ist das erste.
Das zweite zu der wissenschafttheoretischen Diskussion. Ich will
sagen, hier war folgende Konfusion im Spiel: Es wurden zwei
Schritte dauernd miteinander verwechselt: einmal die wissenschaftlichen Verfahren, in denen man wirklich nur beobachtet, von externer
Beobachtung zu externen Gesetzeshypothesen vorgeht, und die
Regelphänomene. Alle Regelphänomene können nicht durch solche
Beobachtung erfaßt werden, sie unterscheiden sich fundamental von
Gesetzesphänomenen. Deswegen kommt man nie dahin, überhaupt zu
wissen, daß da ein Spiel gespielt wird, daß die Leute sich nach
Regeln richten, daß es richtige und falsche Züge gibt. Ich würde
natürlich alles das bestätigen, was schon von Herrn Lorenz und auch
von Herrn Specht gesagt worden ist.
Der andere Schritt, den offenbar Herr Lorenzer im Auge hatte, das
ist der zwischen solchen Regelphänomenen, die immerhin noch
formalisiert werden können und deshalb eine gewisse Verwandtschaft
mit den Naturwissenschaften haben, und den geschichtlichen, bei
denen eine Abstraktion nicht durchzuführen ist. Ich möchte ganz
gerne wissen, ob Sie das als Klärung ansehen.
Lorenz: Ja, ich möchte nur bestätigen, daß mein Mini-Schritt von
rauchen, Rauchen des Herrn Meier bis zu Herr Meier raucht natürlich
nicht das Ende der Geschichte ist, in der Tat, nicht die alten
Bezüge müssen dann wieder eingebracht werden, das Unabhängig-Machen
war ja gerade der Witz dieser Konstruktion. Aber dieser Satz wird
jetzt in komplexere eingebettet - es kommen zum Beispiel adverbiale
Bestimmungen hinzu - , alles das muß jetzt durch eigene Konstruktion
geleistet werden, und da spielen dann auch die deiktischen Bezüge
wieder eine Rolle, die gerade in diesem speziellen Satz - das war
auch Absicht - herausgefallen sind. Nur um diese Möglichkeit
anzudeuten, sage ich das, weil diese dann etwa für wissenschaftliche
Sprachen konstitutiv ist. In der Wissenschaft handelt es sich um
spezielle wissenschaftliche Kommunikationen, die sich von alltäg-
lichen sehr wohl zu unterscheiden haben, und für derlei Zwecke
sind eine ganze Menge weiterer Konstruktionen erforderlich, genau
in dem Sinne, wie Sie es angedeutet haben. Dem würde ich also
völlig beipflichten, das ist jetzt eine ganze Theorie.

<u>Watzlawick</u>: Nur ganz kurz, ja, Ihre Ausführungen über die beiden
Schritte, herr Apel, haben mir geholfen, wir sind hier anscheinend
in dieses Dilemma gekommen. Das einzige, was ich hinzufügen wollte,
wäre, daß eben eine nur externe Beobachtung doch meines Erachtens
letzten Endes auch die Ableitung oder ein Verständnis ermöglicht, aus
dem sich dann - und hier spreche ich wiederum nur von meinem Gebiet
her - eine Intervention, also eine Änderung der bestehenden
Situation ermöglicht. Um auf das Schachspiel nochmal zurückzukommen,
es ergibt sich nicht nur, daß man einfach nun das Spiel versteht,
sondern es ergeben sich daraus wesentliche Korrelate, eben zum
Beispiel die Möglichkeit, das Verhalten der Spieler weitgehend
vorauszusagen.

<u>Lorenzer</u>: Ja, ich wollte eigentlich zu dem Hinweis auf die Deixis
noch sagen, daß das doch ein wichtiger Punkt ist. Wenn wir hier
also ganz abgekürzt das psychoanalytische Verfahren etwa unter dem
Gesichtspunkt einer Analyse von unverträglichen Bedeutungen, einer
kritischen Aufarbeitung dieser Bedeutungen auf dem Weg der lebensgeschichtlichen Aufhellung beschreiben und dabei dann den Unterschied gegen das von herrn Watzlawick Vertretene daran festmachen,
daß es hier um die kritische Aufarbeitung von subjektiven
I n t e r a k t i o n s s t r u k t u r e n geht, dann wäre das
natürlich sehr irreführend, wollte man dabei nicht noch etwas im
Auge behalten, was unbedingt dazugehört, nämlich die unablässige
Bewährung der einzelnen Schritte in einer realen Interaktion. Daß
das dazugehört, läßt sich auch empirisch sehr leicht aus einem
Phänomen nachweisen, das in seiner Bedeutung zweifellos noch nicht
genügend ausgeschöpft worden ist: daß es nämlich bestimmte Grenzen
etwa auch für einen psychoanalytischen Prozeß gibt: Patienten, die
aus irgendwelchen Gründen draußen keine realen Beziehungen haben
oder haben können, erweisen sich als unbehandelbar. Wenn wir davon
ausgehen, daß etwa eine Analyse eine Stunde am Tag dauert, so sind
die übrigen dreiundzwanzig Stunden von nicht geringer Bedeutung.
Sie gehören dazu, und das ist ein bislang sicher noch unter-
schlagenes Kapitel der Aufklärung der therapeutischen Wirksamkeit.
Es wäre also in der Tat recht falsch, wollte man nur auf die
Aufarbeitung von inneren, von subjektiven Strukturen abheben und
nicht auch die lebensgeschichtliche Aufklärung wie auch den - ich
möchte es noch einmal sagen - Durchblick auf Geschichte immer im
Zusammenhang mit einer Veränderung der Praxis sehen. Das ist natürlich der entscheidende Punkt.

Schneider: Ich wollte nochmal auf die Hauptthese dieses Gesprächs
zurückkommen, nämlich die Parallelisierung der Untersuchung von
Herrn Lorenzer mit den Untersuchungen zur Einführung sprachlicher
Ausdrücke von Herrn Lorenz, und insofern richtet sich meine Frage
an beide Herren.
Es wurde unterschieden einerseits ein 'logisches Verstehen', was
von Herrn Lorenz parallel gesetzt wurde zur Gegenstandskonstitution,
andererseits ein 'psychologisches Verstehen', die Parallele dazu
wären alle Handlungen, die durch Auffordern, Bitten etc. - man kann
sagen: durch 'speech acts' - verwirklicht werden. Es bleibt
schließlich das szenische Verstehen. Ich frage nun, ob im szenischen
Verstehen dann nicht zusammen mit einem speech act auch die
Verwendung der Wörter gegeben sein muß, um von szenischem Verstehen,
vom Verstehen einer Handlung reden zu können? Im Minimalfall
könnte das das Spiel sein, ein Wort nachzusprechen. Aber unter
einem 'ungeschiedenen szenischen Verstehen' kann ich mir, wenn es
um die Verwendung von Wörtern geht, nichts vorstellen.
Lorenz: Also, zunächst einmal entsprach dem 'logischen Verstehen'
nicht die Gegenstandskonstitution und so weiter, sondern die
Rekonstruktion der Einführung war ein Versuch, dieselbe Vermittlung
zwischen Sachbezug und Personbezug, die das szenische Verstehen,
relativ zum logischen und psychologischen Verstehen, auf der
Sinnebene leisten soll, für die Geltungsebene ebenfalls herzustellen, und dabei geschah es sozusagen für die Sinnebene gleich
mit: auf der Stufe der Wörter der Sinn und auf der Stufe der Sätze
die Geltung. Natürlich bleibt die Sinnfrage erhalten. Daß das
szenische Verstehen, mit anderen Worten die Einführungssituationen,
wenn sie komplex sind, gegebenenfalls schon als strukturiert
verstanden werden, das würde dann in der Tat andere Einführungen
voraussetzen. So war das nicht gemeint, jedenfalls nicht in allen
Beispielen, gerade das Beispiel, mit Mama bei dem kleinen Kind,
eines szenischen Arrangements, soll deutlich machen, daß hier keine
anderen sprachlichen Hilfsmittel mehr vorausgehen, daß das als ein
Anfang gemeint ist. Nachträgliche Beschreibungen dieser Szene
gelten nicht offiziell, sondern sind höchstens zur gegenseitigen
Verständigung gedacht. Das besagt nicht, daß man nicht später
komplexe Situationen als Ausgangspunkt verwenden kann auf der Basis
einer schon gelieferten Strukturierung mit Hilfe anderer, also etwa
daß man einen ökonomischen Prozeß, Kaufen - Verkaufen, auf der
Basis schon eingeführter Strukturen an einer derartigen Szene,
einführen kann, das ist aber dann ein weiterer Fall, das war bisher

nicht unterschieden worden.

Lorenzer: Ich möchte vielleicht noch eine Unterscheidung bringen:
Es ist eigentlich vom 'Szenischen' hier in zweierlei Sinn gesprochen
worden. Ich habe diesen Begriff des szenischen Verstehens ja
zunächst in einem bestimmten Zusammenhang vorgebracht, nämlich in
der lebensgeschichtlichen Rekonstruktion bestimmter Szenen, die
nicht mit den Einführungssituationen identisch sind, sondern Szenen,
die "Originalvorfälle" sind, in denen eine bestehende Verständigung
zerbricht. Das heißt, diese Szenen verweisen nicht auf frühkindliche
- oder wie immer auch spätere - Einführungssituationen, sondern auf
jene Situationen, wo das schon Eingeführte wieder exkommuniziert
wird. Das berührt den Komplex der Neurose, den wir hier jetzt wohl
schwer aufrollen können. Jedenfalls geht das szenische Verstehen auf
diese Exkommunikationssituation aus. Zweitens ist - und das gehört
jetzt immer noch zum Verständnis von Szene - dazu zu sagen, daß im
analytischen Prozeß das szenische Verstehen nicht ansetzt bei
formulierbaren Szenen, sondern den Versuch des Aufgreifens und
Formulierens darstellt, also ein Vorgang, der, wenn er auf den
Begriff gebracht ist, dann in der Tat zwar eine Szenerie beschreibt,
aber nicht mit jener Ungeschiedenheit verwechselt werden kann, die
sowohl die Situation des sprachlich Exkommunizierten ausmacht, wie
auch die Situation jener frühen Einführungssituation kennzeichnet,
in der sich diese Differenzierung ausbildet. Ich stimme jedenfalls
durchaus zu, daß dort, wo etwas wirklich auf den Begriff gebracht
ist, dann jene Ungeschiedenheit nicht mehr vorliegt, sondern schon
eine Differenzierung besteht. Wohlverstanden, nur die Originalvorfälle, die diese Exkommunikationssituationen betreffen, lassen
sich rekonstruieren. Jene anderen Einführungssituationen lassen sich
lebensgeschichtlich nicht rekonstruieren.

N.N.: Ich habe zu dem Beitrag von Herrn Apel eine Frage. Habe ich
Sie richtig verstanden, daß dem externen Beobachter sich die Regel-
Folgen der beobachteten Gruppe entziehen?

Apel: Noch viel radikaler: Durch rein externe Beobachtung werden Sie
niemals ausmachen können, ob da wirklich eine Regel befolgt wird.
Eine Regel, die jemand falsch oder richtig befolgt, ist ein vollkommen anderes Phänomen, wenn es auch die meisten Leute abstreiten
wie ein Gesetz, das eben nicht durchbrochen werden kann.

Specht: So sagt Meister Wittgenstein.

N.N.: Ich hätte eine Frage an Herrn Watzlawick. Wenn es stimmt, daß
der externe Beobachter nicht feststellen könnte, nach welchen Regeln

Personen spielen, dann könnte er das Spiel der Personen nicht
verstehen.

Apel: Doch, er kann verstehen.

N.N.: Ich verstehe doch ein Spiel nur dann, wenn ich die Regeln des
Spiels kenne.

Apel: Wenn ein Stein fällt, dann geben Sie das Verstehen von vorneherein auf und suchen nach Gesetzeshypothesen, die Sie extern heran-
tragen. Sie suchen überhaupt nicht danach, hier in ein Spiel hinein-
zukommen. Sie versuchen gar keine Kommunikation, wenn es sich um das
Fallen eines Steines handelt. Wenn es sich vermutlich um ein Spiel
nach Regeln handelt, dann müssen Sie versuchen, mindestens virtuell
teilzunehmen, so daß Sie mit einer gewissen Verfremdung mitspielen
wie jemand, der eine Theorie über das Spiel aufstellen will.

Specht: Wir sollten Herrn Watzlawick dazu fragen.

Watzlawick: Ich nahm an, zumindest bis jetzt, daß das Wahrnehmen
von Redundanzen im wesentlichen die Basis naturwissenschaftlichen
Verständnisses ist; bekanntlich besteht kein Beweis dafür, daß diese
Feder, wenn ich sie jetzt auslasse, zufällig einmal nicht nach oben
fallen wird; dieses Dilemma teilen wir mit den Naturwissenschaft-
lern.

Brekle: Ich möchte noch einmal zu dem für mich noch immer problematisch gebliebenen Verhältnis zwischen einem szenisch Ungeschiedenen
und dem dann ja vollständigen Satz wie Mama komm her und dem Ausdruck Mama zurückkommen. Ich glaube, darauf haben auch schon die
Herren Apel und Schneider vorher angespielt, und meine Bemerkung
richtet sich insbesondere an Herrn Lorenz. Mir ist nicht ganz klar
geworden, ob es sich um denselben Ausdruckswillen handelt, wenn das
Kind Mama sagt und wenn es Mama komm her sagt. Mein Problem ist nun:
würden Sie zustimmen, daß ein wissenschaftlicher Beobachter dem
szenisch Ungeschiedenen dieselbe Struktur zuordnen kann wie den
elaborierten Sätzen?

Lorenz: In der Tat für das Verfahren eine zentrale Frage. Ich wüßte
nicht, auf welche Weise kontrolliert werden soll, ob eine spätere
strukturierte Darstellung der Situation als dieselbe wie die ursprünglich unstrukturierte vertreten werden kann. Zunächst mal doch
nur soviel, um bei dem Mama-Beispiel zu bleiben, der Gegenstand
Mama dieses Ein-Wort-Satzes - und es spielt jetzt keine Rolle, ob
das empirisch zutreffend ist, wir können das auch fingieren - tritt
in späteren Situationen nicht mehr auf; diesen Gegenstand gibt es
nicht mehr. Sie können ihn natürlich später wieder einführen.

Aber es hat keinen Sinn, sozusagen von einem Substrat zu sprechen,
das beibehalten bleibt, sich durch die verschiedenen Strukturie-
rungen durchhält. Ich wüßte nicht, was das heißen soll. Ich kann
die früheren komplexen sprachlichen Fassungen, etwa diese Ein-Wort-
Sätze, beibehalten, auch dann, wenn sie faktisch aufgrund der
differenzierenden Möglichkeiten aufgegeben werden, die es dann etwa
erlauben würden, solche Möglichkeiten durch syntaktische Zusammen-
setzungen adäquat zu repräsentieren, obwohl gerade dieses Beispiel
beweisen würde, daß es mit den Mitteln der deutschen Syntax nicht
gelingt, gerade dieses frühkindliche Mama adäquat zu repräsentieren,
das müßte noch zusätzlich eingeführt werden. Die Antwort ist etwas
unbefriedigend, ich weiß es, aber es sind noch einige zusätzliche
Probleme dort verborgen.

Schmidt: Ich habe eine Frage an Herrn Watzlawick. Sie haben vorhin
Furcht geäußert, bei der Behandlung des Therapieproblems in
professionelles Analytikergespräch abzugleiten, aber eigentlich ist
doch das Therapieproblem der Kern, denn dort muß sich die Tragfähig-
keit Ihres Konzeptes erweisen. Die Psychoanalyse ist doch in der
Lage des Beobachters, der ein Schachspiel beobachtet, in dem die
beiden Spieler Fehler machen, das heißt: der Beobachter kennt einen
Katalog von Bestandteilen dessen, was die beiden Leute tun, und hat
Vorstellungen darüber, was sie weiterhin tun müssen. Was soll er
weiter machen? Er kann ihnen sagen, wie dieses Spiel eigentlich
geht, denn sie bringen dieses Spiel nicht richtig zu Ende, sie
bringen es nicht fertig, wirklich miteinander zu spielen. Wenn er
ihnen aber einfach sagt, wie die Regeln wirklich lauten, dann wird
vielleicht jeder der beiden Spieler, die verschiedene Fehler
machen, auf seiner Vorstellung der Regeln beharren. Die einzige
Möglichkeit besteht darin, daß der Beobachter sich wenigstens an die
Stelle e i n e s Spielers setzt und versucht, ihm im Spiel die
Unstimmigkeit seiner Vorstellung über Regeln zu zeigen. Meine Frage
an Sie ist: Wo in Ihrem Konzept ist der Anfang der Metakommunikation
begründet, die notwendig ist, um Störungen überhaupt zu behandeln,
zu verbalisieren?

Watzlawick: Ich glaube, Sie haben das psychoanalytische Vorgehen
recht gut beschrieben: ein wichtiger Teil der psychoanalytischen
Methode besteht ja eben darin, daß man den anderen in der einen
oder der anderen Form, natürlich nicht direkt durch einfaches
Zureden, auf die Unzulänglichkeit seines Verhaltens hinweist. Man
kann das tun, indem man ihn frei assoziieren läßt, man kann Träume

deuten, man kann ihn konfrontieren mit gewissen Tatsachen. Ich würde
persönlich heute diese Auffassung nicht mehr teilen, und zwar deswegen, weil ich glaube, daß die Probleme der Pathologie doch wesentlich komplizierter sind: es handelt sich nicht darum, daß es ein
richtiges Verhalten gibt, das der Gestörte, sei er Neurotiker oder
sei er Psychotiker, eben noch nicht richtig mitbekommen hat, dessen
Regeln er nicht versteht, und daß es sich also nur darum handelt,
ihm nun die Regeln klarzulegen, worauf er sie befolgt, und alles ist
in Ordnung. Es ist wohl vielmehr so, und das ist meine derzeitige
Auffassung von der Pathologie, daß die menschlichen Systeme, in
denen diese Kommunikationsspiele stattfinden - sehr oft gerade die
gestörtesten Familien - das starrste, unnachgiebigste und vielleicht
am ehesten verständliche Repertoire von Regeln aufweisen (obgleich
die Soziologen behaupten, daß solche Systeme chaotisch und nicht
regelgebunden seien: sie sind es nur an dem Berührungspunkt mit
der Außenwelt, aber in sich sind diese Systeme überaus starr).
Meine derzeitige Auffassung von der Pathologie ist also die, daß in
diesen starren, regelgebundenen Systemen etwas fehlt, das man in
Anlehnung an die Semiotik die 'Meta-Regeln' nennen könnte: das heißt,
das System hat Regeln, und es befolgt diese Regeln auch, aber
diese Regeln selbst bringen das System immer wiederum in denselben
circulus vitiosus. Aufgabe der Therapie ist es daher, in dieses
System von außen her die nötigen Meta-Regeln, das heißt, die
Regeln für die Änderung der eigenen Regeln, einzuführen.
Da nun beginnt meines Erachtens die Aufgabe der Therapie. Das
System kann aus sich heraus die Meta-Regeln nicht erzeugen, die
notwendig wären, eine Änderung seiner leidenschaffenden patholo-
gischen Regeln selbst durchzuführen. Nehmen wir das einfache Beispiel, das wir schon einmal erwähnten: Die Verfassung eines Landes
sieht unbeschränkte parlamentarische Debatte vor. Es ist natürlich
klar, daß die Gegenpartei diese Regel dazu verwenden kann, das
Parlament vollkommen handlungsunfähig zu machen: die Gegenpartei
braucht nur, wie das ja auch sehr oft versucht wird, ganz einfach
in endlosen Debatten die ganze Regierungsmaschinerie zu paraly-
sieren. Es wird für dieses Land dann notwendig sein, in seine Verfassung eine Änderung dieser Regel einzuführen. Diese Änderung
aber, die notwendig wäre, und die von allen als notwendig verstanden
wird, kann deswegen nicht eingeführt werden, weil die Einführung
der Regel s e l b s t wiederum der Pathologie unterliegt, die
sie beheben soll: das heißt, die Einführung der Regel, daß die

parlamentarische Debatte irgendwie beschränkt werden muß, kann
ihrerseits durch unbegrenztes Debattieren unmöglich gemacht werden.
Wenn wir das auf krankhafte menschliche Systeme anwenden, so sehen
wir, daß sehr viele Familien oder andere menschliche Systeme wie
zum Beispiel Ehen, große Organisationen, Universitäten, sehr
richtig, das Militär, die Politik im weitesten Sinne, auch die
internationalen Beziehungen, in diesem "Spiel ohne Ende", wie ich
das zu nennen vorgeschlagen habe, gefangen sind. Und um noch einmal
auf eine frühere Bemerkung zurückzukommen; gerade da wird die
Anwendung des gesunden Menschenverstandes dann zur Katastrophe, denn
der gesunde Menschenverstand kann diese Fragen nicht lösen.
Lorenzer: Ich habe den Eindruck, Sie haben es anders gemeint. Sie
haben jedenfalls, so wie ich es verstanden habe, die psychoanalytische Situation richtig beschrieben, als Sie sagten, der Beobachter
nehme zumindest die Position e i n e s Schachspielers ein. Und
genau das möchte ich noch etwas radikalisieren: Der Psychoanalytiker
muß nicht nur in die Rolle des einen Schachspielers eintreten,
sondern befindet sich bei diesem Eintritt in der Situation, daß
überhaupt nicht Schach gespielt wird, sondern ein v o m
P a t i e n t e n e r f u n d e n e s S p i e l gespielt wird.
Oder, um es noch schärfer auszudrücken: es geht nicht nur um ein
vom Patienten erfundenes Spiel, sondern es geht um ein vom Patienten
produziertes, falsch dargestelltes und unbefriedigendes Spiel
anstelle eines befriedigenden Spieles, und erst die Destruktion des
gefundenen, die kritische Aufarbeitung des vorgefundenen Spieles
erlaubt es, zu jenem eigentlich befriedigenden Spiel durchzudringen.
Das ist der Zweck der lebensgeschichtlichen Aufarbeitung. Nun haben
Sie natürlich ganz recht, der entscheidende Punkt ist: Wenn die
Aufarbeitung erfolgt ist, wenn also jenes befriedigende Spiel
hergestellt ist, dann muß der Punkt kommen, wo das Spiel in der
Realität funktioniert. Das meinte ich ja auch vorher mit den
dreiundzwanzig Stunden; es muß also dann der Punkt kommen, wo sich
zeigt, daß es sich um ein in der Realität befriedigendes Spiel
handelt, daß also die Interaktion sich draußen real abspielt. Dieser
Prozeß des kritischen "die-Regel-in-Frage-Stellens" unterscheidet
sich sehr deutlich von dem, was Herr Watzlawick vorschlägt, der ja
im Grunde genommen auf ein vorgegebenes Regelsystem, auf ein von
einem Beobachter oder Außenstehenden vorgegebenes Regelsystem
rekurriert. Das möchte ich in aller Kürze als eine positive
Anthropologie in ihrer positivistischen Wendung kennzeichnen.

Watzlawick: Ich verstehe nicht, was Sie meinen, wenn Sie sagen, daß
ich auf ein vorgegebenes Regelsystem rekurriere. Im Gegenteil!
In der individuellen Psychotherapie, natürlich nicht in der Ehe
oder in der Familienpsychotherapie, aber in der individuellen
Psychotherapie, kommt der Patient und versucht, dem Therapeuten
sein Spiel aufzuzwingen. Er wiederholt damit das Verhalten, das er
auch in der Außenwelt an den Tag legt und auf diese Weise in
Schwierigkeiten kommt. Nun, zweierlei ergibt sich daraus: erstens,
daß der Therapeut dieses Spiel zunächst einmal verstehen muß; er
muß wissen, welches Spiel der Patient ihm aufdrängen will, und
zweitens wird er dann versuchen, dieses Spiel eben nicht zu spielen
und im Nicht-Spielen des Spieles dem Patienten die Möglichkeit,
die Einsicht in das Vorhandensein anderer Möglichkeiten zu eröffnen.
Lorenzer: Darf ich ganz kurz etwas dazu sagen? Der Unterschied wird
natürlich schon deutlich; erstens, ich bin ganz mit Ihnen einverstanden, wenn man sagt, der Patient will dem Analytiker ein Spiel
aufzwingen; aber schon der nächste Schritt ist different: der
Analytiker läßt sich dieses Spiel in der Tat aufzwingen, er tritt
in dieses Spiel ein, aber nur, um dieses Spiel von innen her zu
destruieren und , um aus der Destruktion jenes Vorhergehende zu
gewinnen, das dann die befriedigende Situation ist, während bei
Ihnen die Distanz, die Sie von vornherein festhalten, auf einer
Kenntnis nicht des individuellen Spieles, sondern formaler Spiel-
möglichkeiten, Spielregeln, basiert, die Innen gestatten, sich
vorzustellen, wie so ein Spiel unabhängig vom Inhalt besser
funktionieren könnte. Der Unterschied liegt in der anderen Behandlung der Inhaltsproblematik.
Watzlawick: Ja, wenn Sie es als ein Zurückgreifen auf einen
bestehenden Katalog von Möglichkeiten sehen. Und die zweite
Bemerkung, die ich machen würde, wäre die, daß das Annehmen des
Spieles, um es dann von innen her ad absurdum zu führen - da bin ich
vollkommen Ihrer Meinung - meines Erachtens nur eine Frage der
Taktik und nicht der Strategie ist. In manchen Fällen mag es durchaus möglich sein, von vornherein das Spiel nicht zu akzeptieren.
Ob man darauf zunächst eingeht und es dann zu Fall bringt oder von
vornherein opponiert, ist nur eine taktische Frage.
N.N.: Eine Frage an Herrn Lorenz: Sie müssen erstens bei der
Rekonstruktion der Sprachzeichen davon ausgehen, daß das Szenarium,
das Sie etablieren, adäquat ist. Zweitens folgt aus der Äußerung
des Wortes nicht das Verständnis. Sie müssen ja immer feststellen,
ob der Hörer tatsächlich verstanden hat, was die exemplarische

Einführung besagt. Drittens ist mir nicht ganz klar, ob Sie nur mit
außersprachlichen Mitteln arbeiten. Wenn Sie das tun, dann würde ich
gern wissen, wie Sie Imperative und Fragen exemplarisch einführen.
Lorenz: Zum ersten: Das Geltungsproblem stellt sich deswegen nicht,
weil dort die Wörter eingeführt werden. Wenn Sie aber zugleich die
Frage beantwortet wissen möchten, daß es dieselben Wörter doch
schon im Sprachbestand gibt, für die Sie die Frage der Adäquatheit
überprüfen, so ist das ein Sonderfall, den ich hier nicht erörtert
habe. Das würde ich auch nicht unter dem Geltungsproblem abhandeln,
sondern unter dem Titel "Adäquatheit" oder ähnlich. Zur zweiten
Frage: Das Verständnis muß ich einüben, das gehört zur Einführungssituation. Was 'einüben' heißt, ist durch eine bestimmte Praxis
gesichert, so wie Sie in der Tat Regeln lernen können, wenn Sie
Regeln hinreichend oft benutzen.
N.N.: Wie stellt man denn fest, daß jemand etwas verstanden hat, um
mit Wittgenstein zu fragen, oder, wann hat jemand eine Regel verstanden? Was für Kriterien haben Sie?
Lorenz: Das kann ich Ihnen auseinandersetzen; es ist aber eine
komplizierte Geschichte, man muß nämlich auf die Wittgensteinsche
Pointe eingehen, daß auf der ersten Stufe in der Tat keine Kriterien
zur Verfügung stehen, und daß die Kriterien selber sprachliche
Mittel sind, die sich erst auf einer komplizierten Stufe einführen
lassen, daß dann erst die Frage nach Kriterien sinnvoll wird, auf
der elementaren Stufe in der Tat nichts als Kontrollinstanz zur
Verfügung steht.
Specht: Wittgenstein würde sagen: " Sicher bist du nicht, daß er es
verstanden hat."
Lorenz: Und das Dritte: Der Imperativ ist natürlich auch eine
Zusammensetzung; ich muß in diesem Falle, also etwa , wenn rauchen
wieder zur Debatte steht, einen solchen Imperativ es soll geraucht
werden, dann nur begrifflich zerlegen; in der praktischen Einführung natürlich nicht. Begrifflich zerlegt wird er in die
Einführung der sprachlich repräsentierten Handlung und einen zusätzlichen Funktor, der die Aufforderung repräsentiert, der eigens
einzuführen ist und über das Herstellen dieser Handlung kontrolliert
werden kann. Das ist dann ein eigener, zusätzlicher Prozeß, aber
natürlich nur in der Rekonstruktion; in den faktischen Handlungen
ist das ungeschieden.
Specht: In der Diskussion sind ja offenbar zwei Stränge nebeneinan-
der hergelaufen, und ich habe den Eindruck, daß es nicht ganz

gelungen ist, die beiden Stränge zu synthetisieren. Ich sehe auch
nicht, wie das möglich ist.

ON THE THEORETIZABILITY OF SOCIAL INVARIANTS FROM THE
STANDPOINT OF SEMANTICS

Panel: K.O.Apel, Universität Frankfurt
       W.K.Essler, Universität München
       Y.Bar-Hillel, The Hebrew University of Jerusalem
Chairman: G.Ungeheuer, Universität Bonn

February, 18th, morning session.

APEL:
EINFÜHRENDE BEMERKUNGEN ZUR IDEE EINER "TRANSZENDENTALEN SPRACH-
PRAGMATIK"

I. D a s   P o s t u l a t   e i n e r   t r a n s z e n d e n t a -
l e n   P r a g m a t i k   a l s   V e r m i t t l u n g
z w i s c h e n   s p r a c h a n a l y t i s c h e r
P h i l o s o p h i e   u n d   K a n t i a n i s m u s
Ich möchte im Folgenden zu zeigen versuchen, daß man die
s p r a c h l i c h e   K o m m u n i k a t i o n   zum Thema einer
t r a n s z e n d e n t a l p h i l o s o p h i s c h e n
R e f l e x i o n   machen kann und muß. Damit ist eine an Kant
anknüpfende Fragestellung und methodische Blickeinstellung
angedeutet, die zunächst einmal von der modernen Problematik einer
entweder   e m p i r i s c h e n   oder   l o g i s c h -
k o n s t r u k t i v e n   Analyse sprachlicher Tatbestände
wegzuführen scheint.
Die Hauptschwierigkeit, der unser Ansatz angesichts dieser - im
Sinne des Logischen Empirismus vollständigen - Methodendisjunktion
begegnet, scheint in der Rechtfertigung der   t r a n s z e n d e n -
t a l e n   R e f l e x i o n   als philosophischer Methode zu liegen.
Die moderne Diskussion ist seit der Russellschen Typentheorie und
ihrer logisch-semantischen Verallgemeinerung in der Unterscheidung
von Objektsprache und Metasprache von der Vorstellung geprägt, daß
eine Reflexion des aktuellen Sprachgebrauchs im Sinne der Selbstrückbezüglichkeit der natürlichen Sprache als wissenschaftliche oder
auch philosophisch-wissenschaftstheoretische Methode nicht
zugelassen werden kann.[1] Eine   t r a n s z e n d e n t a l e
R e f l e x i o n   auf den Sprachgebrauch als Bedingung der Möglichkeit und Gültigkeit von Wissenschaft und Philosophie muß demgegenüber als   R e f l e x i o n   i n   d e r   n a t ü r l i c h e n
S p r a c h e   durchgeführt werden.[2] Soviel vorab über das Befremd-
liche unseres Unternehmens unter den Diskussionsbedingungen der
Gegenwart.
Unsere Fragestellung scheint aber auch von der philosophischen
Tradition wegzuführen: denn Kants   t r a n s z e n d e n t a l e
R e f l e x i o n   führte bekanntlich nicht auf so etwas wie
Sprache oder gar Sprach-Gebrauch als Bedingung der Möglichkeit und
Gültigkeit von Wissenschaft zurück, sondern auf transzendentale
Funktionen   p s y c h i s c h e r   V e r m ö g e n   eines unter-
stellten "Bewußtseins überhaupt" - auf die synthetischen Funktio-
nen von "Anschauung", "Verstand" und "Vernunft". Die Sprache kam bei

Kant nicht in der "Kritik der reinen Vernunft", sondern in der
"Anthropologie in pragmatischer Hinsicht" vor[3] und war damit - wie
in der Okhamistischen Tradition der neuzeitlichen Philosophie über-
haupt - als bloßes Instrument der Bezeichnung und Mitteilung der
Resultate vorsprachlichen Denkens und Erkennens vorgestellt. Die
Versuche einer sprachphilosophisch orientierten Meta-Kritik an der
Kantschen "Kritik der reinen Vernunft", wie sie Hamann und Herder
schon zu Lebzeiten Kants unternahmen, konnten der herrschenden
Tradition gegenüber nicht durchdringen, d.h., sie konnten den
Begriff der Sprache bzw. des Sprachgebrauchs nicht so radikal neu
begründen, daß die Möglichkeit einer Transformation des Kantschen
Ansatzes sichtbar geworden wäre. Dasselbe gilt in je verschiedener
Weise auch von Hegel und W.v.Humboldt, bei denen sich wichtige
Teilansätze einer sprachphilosophischen Transformation der Transzendentalphilosophie finden lassen.
Der von uns ins Auge gefaßte Ansatz einer Transzendentalphilosophie
der Sprache, oder genauer: des kommunikativen Sprachgebrauchs
scheint nach dieser ersten historischen Orientierung wenig Aussich-
ten auf positive Problemanknüpfungen zu besitzen: die moderne
Diskussion sperrt sich - so scheint es - gegen die transzendental-
philosophische Reflexionsmethode; diese selbst aber in ihrer
traditionellen Gestalt scheint der modernen Diskussion recht zu
geben, indem sie die transzendentale Reflexion auf das Bewußtsein
einschränkt und die Thematik der Sprache oder gar des Sprachgebrauchs nur als Gegenstand und nicht als Bedingung der Möglichkeit
der Erfahrung zuläßt.
Dieser Situation gegenüber möchte ich jedoch die These vertreten,
daß gerade die moderne Diskussion der sprachanalytischen Philosophie die Denkmittel bereitgestellt hat, die Hamann und Herder bei
ihrem Versuch einer sprachphilosophischen Meta-Kritik der Kantschen
Vernunftkritik fehlten. Eine kritische Rekonstruktion der "Entfaltung der s p r a c h a n a l y t i s c h e n Philosophie"[4] unseres
Jahrhunderts führt m.E. mit innerer Notwendigkeit zu einer Wieder-
aufnahme der transzendentalphilosophischen Problematik in Begriffen
der Sprache und des kommunikativen Sprachgebrauchs. Soweit ich sehe,
lassen sich in Anknüpfung an die geschichtlichen Ursprünge der
sprachanalytischen Philosophie vier Wege unterscheiden bzw.
beschreiten, um die Richtigkeit dieser These zu erweisen.
1. Der erste Weg eröffnet sich im Ausgang von der p r a g m a t i -
s c h e n S e m i o t i k, die durch Ch.S.Peirce begründet und von
Ch.Morris als d r e i d i m e n s i o n a l e S e m i o t i k mit

der von R.Carnap begründeten s y n t a k t i s c h - s e m a n t i-
s c h e n   S p r a c h k o n s t r u k t i o n verknüpft wurde.
Dieser Weg ist deshalb als erster zu beschreiten, weil er geeignet
ist, den Terminus "Zeichen-Pragmatik" bzw. "Sprach-Pragmatik" einzuführen und im Sinne einer "transzendentalen Pragmatik" mit dem
Kantischen Problem einer "t r a n s z e n d e n t a l e n   R e-
f l e x i o n"   a u f   d i e   B e d i n g u n g e n   d e r
M ö g l i c h k e i t   u n d   G ü l t i g k e i t   d e r
E r k e n n t n i s zu verknüpfen.

2. Der zweite Weg eröffnet sich bei der kritischen Rekonstruktion
der **verschwiegenen** transzendentalen Voraussetzungen der von Carnap
begründeten s y n t a k t i s c h - s e m a n t i s c h e n
W i s s e n s c h a f t s l o g i k. Er hängt mit dem ersten Weg
insofern zusammen, als gerade und **erst** der Umstand, daß Carnap die
d r e i d i m e n s i o n a l e   S e m i o t i k von Morris als
Grundlage der logischen Sprachkonstruktion akzeptiert hat, den
t r a n s z e n d e n t a l p r a g m a t i s c h e n Charakter der
verschwiegenen Voraussetzungen der analytischen Wissenschaftslogik
sichtbar macht.

3. Der dritte Weg in die transzendentale Sprach-Pragmatik eröffnet
sich - zwar nicht dem Terminus nach, wohl aber im Sinne der gemein-
ten Sachproblematik - von der Sprachspiel-Analyse des späten
Wittgenstein und von der sg. "Ordinary Language Philosophy" her. Der
t r a n s z e n d e n t a l p r a g m a t i s c h e Charakter
dieser Sprachanalyse liegt einerseits in der Voraussetzung der
"Verwobenheit" des kommunikativen Sprachgebrauchs mit Tätigkeiten
in einem Situationskontext, zum anderen in der quasi transzendentalen Funktion der "Sprachspiele" als Bedingungen der Möglichkeit und
intersubjektiven Gültigkeit von G e g e n s t a n d s i d e n t i-
f i k a t i o n (Referenz) und p r ä d i k a t i v e r   W e l t-
i n t e r p r e t a t i o n. (Es fragt sich darüber hinaus, ob nicht
in allen faktischen Sprachspielen ein t r a n s z e n d e n t a-
l e s   S p r a c h s p i e l[5] vorausgesetzt werden muß, das in
einer universalpragmatischen, kommunikativen Kompetenz[6] der Menschen
qua Menschen gegründet ist und die Kommunikation zwischen verschiedenen Sprachspielen - z.B. die Übersetzung zwischen verschiedenen
Sprachen und das hermeneutische Verstehen fremder Lebensformen -
prinzipiell möglich macht.)

4. Der vierte Weg eröffnet sich in jüngster Zeit auf der Linie einer
Ergänzung der - dem System der "langue" (F.de Saussure) korrespon-

dierenden - Idee der "linguistischen Kompetenz" im Sinne der von
N.Chomsky begründeten g e n e r a t i v e n T r a n s f o r m a -
t i o n s g r a m m a t i k durch die Idee einer u n i v e r -
s a l p r a g m a t i s c h e n, k o m m u n i k a t i v e n
K o m p e t e n z.[7] Während die linguistische Kompetenz die
Menschen - unabhängig von der Interaktionssituation des Dialogs -
in den Stand setzt, syntaktisch wohlgeformte Sätze zu bilden (und
sie eventuell noch im Sinne eines Sprach-Systems semantisch richtig
zu interpretieren), befähigt die kommunikative Kompetenz sie
darüber hinaus dazu, sprachliche Ausdrücke (die eventuell unvoll-
ständig, deformiert, aus verschiedenen Sprachen zusammengesetzt,
bewußt ungrammatisch im Sinne einer syntaktischen oder semantisch-
metaphorischen Intention gebildet, durch Schweigen oder extra-
verbale Gestik ergänzt sein können) durch adäquate Situierung zur
Herstellung sozialer Beziehungen und zur Verständigung über diese
und die erfahrbare Gegenstandswelt zu benutzen.
Der vierte Weg hängt mit dem ersten Weg durch den Terminus
"Pragmatik", mit dem dritten durch den Ausgang von der "Sprechakt-
Theorie" (Austin, Grice, Searle) zusammen. Er hat bereits durch die
Konfrontation von "Ordinary Language Philosophy" und moderner
Linguistik zu einer, den wissenschaftstheoretischen Status der
transzendentalen Sprachpragmatik implizit thematisierenden,
Diskussion des Verhältnisses von linguistischer und philosophischer
Methode geführt.[8]
Ich werde im Folgenden nur den ersten und zweiten Weg in die
Problematik einer t r a n s z e n d e n t a l e n P r a g m a -
t i k zu skizzieren versuchen: eine Ergänzung dieser einführenden
Bemerkungen im Sinne des dritten und vierten Weges hoffe ich dem-
nächst vorlegen zu können.[9]

II. D e r s e m i o t i s c h e P r a g m a t i s m u s v o n
Ch. S. P e i r c e u n d s e i n e e m p i r i s t i s c h e
R e d u k t i o n b e i Ch. M o r r i s u n d R. C a r n a p
Der erste Weg in eine transzendentale Pragmatik wurde m.E. bereits
durch das philosophische Lebenswerk von Ch.S.Peirce eröffnet, der
seine semiotisch begründete pragmatistische Forschungslogik zeit-
lebens als Transformation der Kantschen Vernunftkritik verstand.
Peirce hat seine Semiotik - sehr im Gegensatz zu Ch.Morris - nicht
als primär empirisch-behavioristische Disziplin konzipiert, sondern
als n o r m a t i v e Grundlage einer philosophischen S i n n -
K r i t i k und S i n n - E x p l i k a t i o n der Wissen-

schaftssprache. Die Grundpostulate seiner pragmatischen Semiotik
gewann **Peirce** durch Reflexion auf die Voraussetzungen sinnvoller
Argumentation in der Experimentier-Gemeinschaft der Wissenschaftler.
Ich kann im gegenwärtigen Zusammenhang nicht auf die äußerst
komplizierten Details der Peirceschen Philosophie[10] eingehen,
sondern möchte nur einen Punkt herausheben, der als Voraussetzung
und als Kontrastfolie für Morris' und Carnaps Konzeption einer dreidimensionalen Semiotik beachtet werden sollte.
Peirce hat - insbesondere im Rahmen seiner Untersuchungen zur Logik
der Relationen - die nicht reduzierbare D r e i s t e l l i g -
k e i t der Zeichenrelation herausgestellt und die Konsequenzen
dieser Tatsache für eine philosophische Theorie zeichenvermittelter
Erkenntnis entwickelt.
Die prinzipielle Dreistelligkeit der Zeichenrelation liegt nach
Peirce in dem Umstand, daß e i n Z e i c h e n f ü r e i n e n
I n t e r p r e t e n e t w a s b e z e i c h n e t (genauer:
etwas in einer Hinsicht - als etwas -, die durch den sg. "logischen
Interpretanten" festgelegt ist, welcher als normative Interpreta-
tionsregel das richtige Zeichenverständnis und zugleich das daraus
resultierende praktische Verhalten unter allen denkbaren Bedingungen
regulieren soll). Jedes der drei Glieder der Zeichen-Relation setzt
demnach in seiner Funktion die beiden anderen schon voraus, und eine
Nichtberücksichtigung dieser Voraussetzung bei der methodischen Abstraktion innerhalb der Semiotik hat unweigerlich eine "abstractive
fallacy" zur Folge. Für die Erkenntnis- und Wissenschaftstheorie
ergibt sich daraus eine Klassifikation möglicher Reduktionismen, die
vom Peirceschen Standpunkt aus abzulehnen sind.
So wäre z.B. ein - sensualistischer oder aprioristischer -
B e w u ß t s e i n s i d e a l i s m u s abzulehnen, weil in ihm
das interpretierende Bewußtsein ohne die Voraussetzung der zu interpretierenden Zeichen und der zu bezeichnenden Realität (bloße
Fiktionen setzen diese immer schon voraus!) gedacht werden soll. Ein
n a t u r a l i s t i s c h e r R e a l i s m u s (Materialismus)
andererseits, in dem das Reale ohne die epistemologische Voraussetzung der Zeichen und der Zeichen-Interpretation gedacht werden soll,
ist ebenso abzulehnen wie ein e r k e n n t n i s t h e o r e t i -
s c h e r R e a l i s m u s, in dem die Erkenntnis im Sinne einer
bloß zweistelligen Subjekt-Objekt-Relation als Kausal-Affizierung
der Sinne durch eine bewußtseinsunabhängige Realität gedacht wäre.
In der letzteren Konzeption kann nach **Peirce** allenfalls die in der
Erkenntnis involvierte Begegnung des Ich mit dem Nicht-Ich ,

insbesondere die Erfahrung des Willenswiderstandes, nicht aber die
notwendigerweise zeichenvermittelte, begriffliche Interpretation des
Realen als etwas gedacht werden. Das Reale muß zwar einerseits - als
Willenswiderstand im Sinne einer zweistelligen Ich-Nichtich-Relation
als unabhängig von den faktischen Erkenntnisbemühungen und Erkennt-
nisresultaten unterstellt werden: als sinnvoll Meinbares aber kann
das Reale nach Peirce nicht unabhängig von seiner zeichenvermittelten Interpretierbarkeit und - insofern Erkennbarkeit - gedacht
werden. Dieser Gedanke transformiert den   e r k e n n t n i s -
t h e o r e t i s c h e n   R e a l i s m u s   in den   s i n n -
k r i t i s c h e n   R e a l i s m u s. - Ebensowenig wie die
Erkenntnisrelation als zweistellige Subjekt-Objekt-Relation ohne
Zeichen- und damit Begriffsvermittlung gedacht werden kann, darf
sie andererseits unter Abstraktion vom interpretierenden Subjekt auf
die zweistellige Relation zwischen Zeichen bzw. zeichengetragenen
Propositionen und Dingen bzw. Sachverhalten reduziert werden. Damit
wäre z.B. die antike Ontologie, sofern sie auf eine   K o r r e s -
p o n d e n z - Theorie der Wahrheit ohne Ergänzung durch   E v i -
d e n z - und   K o n s e n s - Theorie sich stützt, und ihre moderne
sprachanalytische Rekonstruktion im Sinne einer   O n t o -
S e m a n t i k ebenfalls als unzulänglich charakterisiert.
Schließlich kann selbstverständlich auch das Zeichen (bzw. die
Sprache als Zeichensystem) nicht als Medium von Erkenntnis gedacht
werden, ohne dabei eine als etwas zu bezeichnende Realität und ein
interpretierendes Bewußtsein vorauszusetzen.
Vergleicht man im Licht des soeben skizzierten semiotischen und
epistemologischen Prinzips der   D r e i s t e l l i g k e i t   die
K a n t i s c h e   E r k e n n t n i s t h e o r i e   mit der modernen   a n a l y t i s c h e n   W i s s e n s c h a f t s l o g i k,
so kann man m.E. eine frappierende Einsicht gewinnen: Beide Positionen enthalten in ihrer Grundlage eine "abstractive fallacy", die
d e r   T e n d e n z   n a c h auf eine   R e d u k t i o n   d e r
d r e i s t e l l i g e n   E r k e n n t n i s - R e l a t i o n
a u f   e i n e   z w e i s t e l l i g e   R e l a t i o n   hinausläuft. Freilich bezieht sich die illegitime Abstraktion in beiden
Fällen auf verschiedene Stellen der dreistelligen Relation, so daß
eine wechselseitige Kritik beider Grundpositionen möglich ist: im
Falle Kants liegt eine illegitime Abstraktion von der Zeichen- bzw.
Sprachvermitteltheit der Erkenntnis vor[11] - ein Umstand, den wir
eingangs schon - mit Hamann, Herder und Humboldt - bemerkt haben.
Im Falle der analytischen Wissenschaftlogik aber liegt, wie noch zu

zeigen ist, eine illegitime Abstraktion von der interpretativen
Funktion des Erkenntnissubjekts vor. Streng genommen kann hier nicht
mehr von philosophischer Erkenntnistheorie die Rede sein: diese wird
vielmehr, soweit sie nicht auf logische Semantik reduziert werden
kann, in die empirische Psychologie abgeschoben.
Die "abstractive fallacy", die bei Kant vorliegt, wurde im Neu-
kantianismus durch Ernst Cassirers "Philosophie der symbolischen
Formen" ansatzweise korrigiert. Cassirer dachte aber nicht daran,
daß der Einbau der an materielle Zeichenträger gebundenen "Symbol-
funktion" in die Subjekt-Objekt-Relation der Erkenntnis auch für die
Konzeption der beiden übrigen Relata Konsequenzen haben muß -
Konsequenzen, die mit dem n e u k a n t i s c h e n B e w u ß t -
s e i n s i d e a l i s m u s unverträglich sind. Peirce hat in
seinem lebenslangen Versuch einer s e m i o t i s c h -
p r a g m a t i s c h e n T r a n s f o r m a t i o n d e r
t r a n s z e n d e n t a l e n E r k e n n t n i s - L o g i k
alle diese Konsequenzen zu ziehen versucht. Hier seien nur die auf
die D r e i s t e l l i g k e i t der Zeichen-Relation bezogenen
Aspekte dieser Transformation angedeutet.
1. Das nach Kant unerkennbare "Ding-an-sich" wurde von Peirce
transformiert in das e r k e n n b a r e Reale, das zwar von allem
f a k t i s c h E r k a n n t e n prinzipiell unterschieden,
gleichwohl aber von uns als q u a l i t a t i v e r l e b b a r
und insofern "ikonisch" prädizierbar, d e i k t i s c h (durch die
sg. "indices" der Sprache) identifizierbar und "in the long run"
b e g r i f f l i c h i n t e r p r e t i e r b a r gedacht werden
muß, wenn das Wort "real" einen Sinn haben soll. Hierin liegt m.E.
die Transformation des ersten Gliedes der zeichenvermittelten
Erkenntnisrelation auf der Linie eines s i n n k r i t i s c h e n
R e a l i s m u s.
2. Die Kantische Problematik der S y n t h e s i s von
Empfindungsdaten durch Anschauungsformen und Verstandesformen bzw.
Kategorien wurde von Peirce transformiert im Sinne einer L o g i k
d e r s y n t h e t i s c h e n S c h l u ß v e r f a h r e n
(I n d u k t i o n u n d A b d u k t i o n). Diese stützen sich,
im Unterschied zur Deduktion, nicht nur auf Begriffs-"Symbole",
sondern darüber hinaus auf sg. "indices" zur Identifikation von
Gegenständen in Raum und Zeit und auf "ikonische" Zeichenfunktionen,
durch die der qualitative Eindruck der Erscheinungswelt in unsere
symbolischen Prädizierungen - insbesondere in die kreative "Hypothe-
senbildung" der Wissenschaft - eingehen soll. In Anknüpfung an Kant

läßt sich dieser ebenso dunkle wie faszinierende Aspekt der
Peirceschen Transformation, in dem das Zusammenwirken von drei
Zeichentypen bzw. Zeichenfunktionen als Medium der Erkenntnis
begriffen werden soll, unter dem folgenden Prinzip zusammenzufassen:
"symbol"-gestützte Deduktionen ohne "indices"-gestützte Induktionen
und "ikon"-gestützte Abduktionen (Erkenntnis-Hypothesen) wären leer;
"ikon"-gestützte Abduktionen und "indices"-gestützte Induktionen
ohne "symbol"-gestützte Deduktionen wären blind.

3. Am wichtigsten in unserem Problemzusammenhang ist zweifellos die
Peircesche T r a n s f o r m a t i o n   d e s   E r k e n n t n i s-
s u b j e k t s qua Subjekt der Z e i c h e n - I n t e r p r e-
t a t i o n : Hier läßt sich die transzendental-pragmatische Pointe
der Peirceschen Kant-Transformation verdeutlichen, indem man sich
auf den von Kant so genannten "höchsten Punkt" der transzendentalen
Deduktion der Kategorien bezieht. Um die notwendigen subjektiven Bedingungen der Möglichkeit und Gültigkeit der Erkenntnis als Funk-
tionsbestimmungen im System der Erkenntnis deduzieren zu können, muß
man nach Kant von der "transzendentalen Synthesis der Apperzeption"
ausgehen, d.h. von der in jeder Erfahrung zu erreichenden Einheit
der Vorstellungen im Sinne der Einheit des Gegenstandsbewußtseins
und des Selbstbewußtseins. Nach Peirce kann diese, vom G e w i ß-
h e i t s - oder E v i d e n z -begriff des m e t h o d i-
s c h e n S o l i p s i s m u s her begründete Idee des Erkennt-
nis-Ziel nicht genügen, wenn es um i n t e r s u b j e k t i v
g ü l t i g e Erkenntnis geht, die in einem Prozess der Zeicheninterpretation vermittelt werden muß. Vor allem kann durch die metho-
disch-solipsistische Zielvorstellung der Einheit des Bewußtseins
nicht verständlich gemacht werden, daß die Erkenntnis als Schluß-
und Interpretationsprozess i n t h e l o n g r u n der Realität
als dem Erkennbaren (d.h. unendlich Interpretierbaren) gewachsen
sein kann, wie das nach Peirce in der Idee des Realen von uns immer
schon vorausgesetzt wird. Peirce postuliert daher anstelle der
"transzendentalen Synthesis der Apperzeption" eine, in der "unbegrenzten Gemeinschaft" der Wissenschaftler in einem unbegrenzten
Zeichen-Interpretationsprozess zu erreichende, E i n h e i t d e r
I n t e r p r e t a t i o n des Realen und definiert das Reale als
Gegenstand der letzten, übereinstimmenden Überzeugung, zu der die
unbegrenzte Interpretationsgemeinschaft nach einem hinreichend lan-
gen, experimentelle Evidenzen integrierenden Interpretationsprozess
gelangen würde bzw. müßte.[12] Die hiermit begründete transzendental-
pragmatische "Community"-Philosophie des sg. "Logischen

Sozialismus"[13] wurde in Amerika durch J.Royce im Sinne einer
geisteswissenschaftlichen Sozialphilosophie der "Community of Interpretation" ergänzt und weiterentwickelt,[14] und ohne sie ist auch der
"symbolische Interaktionismus" des Neubegründers der Sozialpsychologie, G.H.Mead, nicht zu begreifen, wie das folgende Zitat zeigt:

"Universal discourse is the formal ideal of communication. If
communication can be carried through and made perfect, then
there would exist the kind of democracy..., in which each
individual would carry just the response in himself that he
knows he calls out in the community. That is what makes
communication in the significant sense the organizing process
in the community."[15]

Integriert man auf der Linie von J.Royce and G.H.Mead die bei Peirce
noch szientistisch beschränkte Konzeption des Subjekts der Zeichenrelation, so erweist sich als Thema einer   t r a n s z e n d e n -
t a l e n   Z e i c h e n - bzw.   S p r a c h p r a g m a t i k   die
- von uns in aller Argumentation schon immer als Bedingung der
Möglichkeit und Gültigkeit kontrafaktisch vorausgesetzte -
i d e a l e   K o m m u n i k a t i o n s g e m e i n s c h a f t,
die in der realen Kommunikationsgemeinschaft - der menschlichen
Gesellschaft - immer noch erst zu realisieren ist. Diese, in der
realen antizipierte, ideale Kommunikationsgemeinschaft bildet m.E.
das transzendentale Subjekt einer semiotisch transformierten
Wissenschaftstheorie, Sozialphilosophie und Ethik.[16]

Es ist nun das Verdienst von Ch.Morris, durch seine "Grundlegung der
Zeichentheorie" von 1938[17] die semiotischen Ideen von Peirce und
Mead in die moderne Diskussion - genauer: in die Diskussion der
sprach-analytischen Philosophie - eingebracht zu haben. Morris er-
gänzte in seinem epochemachenden kleinen Buch (das bezeichnenderweise in der "Encyclopedia of Unified Science" erscheinen sollte)
die vom logischen Empirismus, insbesondere von R.Carnap, in der
Sprachkonstruktion thematisierte Dimension der Zeichen- bzw. Sprachfunktion - die   s y n t a k t i s c h e   Beziehung der Zeichen
untereinander und die   s e m a n t i s c h e   Beziehung der Zeichen
zu den als etwas bezeichneten Sachen - durch die sg.   p r a g m a -
t i s c h e   Dimension der Zeicheninterpretation im Situationskontext der Verhaltenspraxis (s. Figur I). Entsprechend postulierte
er drei Teildisziplinen der Semiotik: S y n t a k t i k,
S e m a n t i k,   P r a g m a t i k, von denen jede sowohl als
empirische wie als formalkonstruktive Wissenschaft zu betreiben sei.
Dabei schärft er ein, daß die Teildisziplinen sich jederzeit der für

ihren Gegenstand konstitutiven Abstraktion von der dreidimensionalen
Zeichen- bzw. Sprachfunktion bewußt bleiben müßten.

Auf diese Weise hat Morris, wie es zunächst scheinen kann, sowohl
der D r e i s t e l l i g k e i t der Zeichenrelation im Sinne
Peirces wie auch der wissenschaftstheoretischen Methoden-Disjunktion
des Logischen Empirismus (im Sinne der Alternative von
E m p i r i e und l o g i s c h f o r m a l i s i e r e n d e r
K o n s t r u k t i o n) Rechnung getragen. Und auf diesen Umstand
gründet sich zweifellos der durchschlagende Erfolg des triadischen
Schemas von Morris in der analytischen Wissenschaftslogik, der mit
der Rezeption des Schemas durch R.Carnap einsetzte. (Zahlreiche
Lehr- und Handbücher bringen seitdem einen kurzen Abriß des Morris-
schemas, als ob es sich dabei um eine nicht weiter problematisier-
bare Selbstverständlichkeit handelte.) Bei näherem Zusehen muß man
jedoch feststellen, daß die von Morris intendierte Synthese von
L o g i s c h e m E m p i r i s m u s u n d p r a g m a t i -
s c h e r S e m i o t i k im Sinne von Peirce keiner von beiden
Positionen ohne problematischen Rest angepaßt werden kann. Bereits
die Rezeptionsgeschichte gibt einige Hinweise auf die bis heute
ungelösten Probleme.

Von vornherein fällt auf, daß die D r e i d i m e n s i o n a l i -
t ä t des Morrisschen Schemas die Dimension des kommunikativen
Sprachgebrauchs nicht eigentlich als pragmatische Integration und
kommunikative Begründung der synthetischen und semantischen Regeln
erscheinen läßt, sondern als bloße Ergänzung derselben - gewissermaßen als Dimension der Inbetriebnahme eines schon vorausgesetzten
syntaktisch-semantischen Sprachsystems. J.Dewey hat darin ein dem
Pragmatismus widersprechendes Zugeständnis an die idealsprachlich-
systemorientierte Sprachkonzeption des Logischen Positivismus gesehen.[18] Ich komme darauf noch zurück.

R.Carnap andererseits hat bezeichnenderweise nicht sofort den von
Morris vorgesehenen Parallelismus der drei empirischen und der drei
formalen semiotischen Disziplinen akzeptiert, sondern die
P r a g m a t i k zunächst nur als e m p i r i s c h -
b e h a v i o r i s t i s c h e Ergänzungsdisziplin der logischen
S y n t a x u n d S e m a n t i k aufgefaßt.[19] Der aporetische
Hinweis, der in dieser verkürzten bzw. modifizierten Primärrezeption
liegt, wird auch durch die spätere Inangriffnahme des Programms
einer "formalen Pragmatik"[20] nicht rückgängig gemacht; denn erstens
ist bis heute nicht erwiesen, daß sich die wesentlichen Aspekte der
pragmatischen Zeichen-Dimension - z.B. die "Deixis" und die damit

eng zusammenhängenden "performativen" und zugleich "reflexiven"
Leistungen der kommunikationskonstitutiven Sprechakte - überhaupt
formalisieren lassen;[21] und zweitens war schon Carnap klar, daß bei
einer k o n s t r u k t i v e n   P r a g m a t i k genauso wie
bei der konstruktiven Semantik eine Restproblematik der Interpretation und Verifikation bestehen bleibt: Diesen Rest muß Carnap gemäß
der Methoden-Disjunktion des Logischen Empirismus in jedem Fall
einer e m p i r i s c h e n   P r a g m a t i k übertragen. Praktisch ist jedenfalls die Situation in der analytischen Wissenschafts-
schaftslogik bis heute durch den Umstand gekennzeichnet, daß die
"pragmatische Dimension" als sg. "paper-basket" für alle nicht (oder
noch nicht) formalisierbaren Hintergrundsprobleme der Erkenntnis-
systematisierung behandelt wird - z.B. einerseits für den sg.
"context of discovery" und in diesem Zusammenhang für die Problematik des Vorwissens bzw. des Vorverständnisses, der leitenden Erkenntnisinteressen und Problemstellungen usw., und andererseits für
den "context of interpretation and verification". Dabei ist entscheidend, daß die nicht formalisierbaren Probleme der "Pragmatik"
grundsätzlich als solche einer empirischen Disziplin - gewöhnlich
der Psychologie - angesehen werden.[22]
Genau hierin kommt nun, wie ich zeigen möchte, die im vorigen schon
behauptete i l l e g i t i m e   A b s t r a k t i o n   v o n   d e r
t r a n s z e n d e n t a l p r a g m a t i s c h e n   D i m e n-
s i o n des Erkenntnissubjekts zum Ausdruck; denn die in den
pragmatischen "paper-basket" verwiesenen Probleme stellen zum
großen Teil gar keine empirischen Probleme dar, sondern solche einer
transzendentalpragmatischen Reflexion auf die Bedingungen der
Möglichkeit und Gültigkeit zeichenvermittelter Erkenntnis. Von einer
pragmatischen Integration der syntaktischen und semantischen Regeln
kann jedenfalls auch dann keine Rede sein, wenn die formale Syntaktik und Semantik, wie Morris gefordert hatte, durch eine formale
Pragmatik ergänzt wird; denn die Sprache der philosophischen
Semiotik, in der die empirischen und formalen Disziplinen unterschieden und ihre Ergebnisse aufeinander bezogen werden, kann in
dieser Einteilung grundsätzlich nicht berücksichtigt werden. Um
diese Sprache, in welcher der Logische Empirismus seine philosophische Position expliziert und Argumente für sie vorbringt, in einer
pragmatisch integrierten Semiotik rechtfertigen zu können, müßte es
erlaubt sein, jene implizit selbstrückbezüglichen universalen Sätze
über die Struktur des Zeichengebrauchs überhaupt (z.B. über die
angebliche Nichtselbstrückbezüglichkeit a l l e r sinnvollen

Sätze) als Sätze einer philosophischen Metasprache im Verhältnis
zur Konstruktion formalisierter Sprach-Systeme und zur empirischen
Semiotik anzuerkennen. Kurz: die philosophische Semiotik müßte auf
apriorische Bedingungen der Möglichkeit und Gültigkeit der empirischen Semiotik und ihrer eigenen Sprachkonstruktion reflektieren
können.
Hiermit ist nun aber schon festgestellt, daß auch das Morrissche
Schema des triadischen Parallelismus von empirischer und formaler
Syntaktik, Semantik und Pragmatik der Peirceschen Konzeption der
Dreistelligkeit der Zeichenrelation, entgegen dem ersten Eindruck,
keineswegs Rechnung trägt. In Wahrheit kommt das von Peirce in
seiner normativen Logik der Forschung postulierte Erkenntnisobjekt -
die I n t e r p r e t a t i o n s g e m e i n s c h a f t der
Wissenschaftler, die über ihre Problemsituation sich verständigen
und über die Geltung ihrer Resultate (einschließlich der interpre-
tierten Sprachformalisierungen) zu einem argumentativen Konsens
kommen könnte - schon bei Morris so wenig vor wie bei Carnap. Der
Grund dafür liegt darin, daß Morris, im Geiste des Logischen
Empirismus und der b e h a v i o r i s t i s c h e n R e d u k-
t i o n des amerikanischen Pragmatismus eine (t r a n s z e n-
d e n t a l e) R e f l e x i o n des aktuellen kommunikativen
Sprachgebrauchs von vornherein für unmöglich erklärt, da er - wie
zu jener Zeit allgemein üblich - die Reflexion auf internalisierte
Regeln oder Handlungsnormen einerseits mit introspektiver Selbstbeobachtung gleichsetzt, andererseits das methodologische Verbot der
Selbstrückbezüglichkeit respektieren möchte.[23] Er muß daher die
pragmatische Subjekt-Dimension wissenschaftlicher Erkenntnis
einschließlich der eigenen philosophischen Argumente zum Thema einer
empirischen Beobachtung des zeichenvermittelten Verhaltens erklären.
Im Sinne einer behavioristischen Reduktion vollzieht er in seinem
Hauptwerk "Signs, Language and Behavior" von 1946 die von Dewey
geforderte pragmatische Integration der Semiotik, einschließlich der
"formativen" Regeln der Sprachkonstruktion, die er als planendes
Verhalten auffaßt. Es ist aber klar, daß eine solche Wissenschaft,
ganz abgesehen von den schwerwiegenden Einwänden gegen die Möglichkeit einer empirischen Sprachwissenschaft auf behavioristischer
Grundlage,[24] jedenfalls die von Peirce der pragmatischen Semiotik
zugedachte Aufgabe einer Transformation der Kantischen Vernunftkritik nicht erfüllen kann. So befestigt gerade Morris, der die
Pragmatik als dritte Dimension in die sprachanalytische Philosophie
einführte, durch seinen Reduktionismus zugleich die "anstractive

fallacy" der analytischen Wissenschaftslogik als einer Wissenschaftstheorie ohne erkennendes Subjekt.[25] (Vgl. hierzu den Versuch
einer schematischen Darstellung der durch Morris herbeigeführten
Problemsituation in Figur I: Die durchgezogenen Linien bezeichnen
die von Morris - und vom Logischen Empirismus - thematisierten
Dimensionen der Zeichen- bzw. Sprachfunktion; die gestrichelten
Linien dagegen die im Sinne einer "abstractive fallacy" nicht
reflektierten transzendentalpragmatischen Problem-Aspekte).

III. D i e   i l l e g i t i m e   A b s t r a k t i o n   v o n
d e n   t r a n s z e n d e n t a l p r a g m a t i s c h e n
V o r a u s s e t z u n g e n   d e r   z e i c h e n v e r m i t-
t e l t e n   E r k e n n t n i s   i n   d e r   a n a l y-
t i s c h e n   W i s s e n s c h a f t s l o g i k
Die illegitime Abstraktion der analytischen Wissenschaftslogik von
der, nur durch transzendentalpragmatische Reflexion zu thematisierenden, Subjekt-Dimension der zeichenvermittelten Erkenntnis läßt
sich m.E. an den folgenden aporetischen Konsequenzen verdeutlichen,
die hier nur kurz skizziert werden können.[26]
1. Die philosophische Argumentation der analytischen Wissenschaftslogik vollzieht sich, ihren eigenen Voraussetzungen zufolge, bis
heute immer noch in der eigentlich illegitimen, vorwissenschaft-
lichen "Para-Sprache", die bereits im "Tractatus logico-philosophicus" als "Erläuterungs"- bzw. "Leiter"-Sprache zugleich postuliert
und desavouiert wurde. Da eine methodisch legitime Sprache erst
durch die entscheidungsabhängige Konstruktion syntaktisch-semantischer Systeme begründet wird, so kann der in allen System-Konven-
tionen schon vorausgesetzte Sinn philosophischer und interdiszi-
plinärer Verständigung in seinem methodologischen Stellenwert nicht
bestimmt werden.
1.1. In krasser Form zeigt sich die daraus resultierende Aporie in
der - im Sinne des Logischen Empirismus konsequenten - Forderung
Carnaps, daß die Verständigung über die Applizierbarkeit einer
konstruierten Wissenschaftssprache durch behavioristische
Beobachtung der (selbst eine Beobachtungssprache anwendenden) empirischen Wissenschaftler zu erfolgen habe.Versucht man, sich die
praktischen Konsequenzen dieser Forderung einer empirischen Reduktion
der Sprachpragmatik vorzustellen, so ergibt sich m.E. folgende
Alternative: Entweder wird die Carnapsche Forderung streng befolgt:
dann muß die Beobachtung der empirischen Wissenschaftler wiederum
beobachtet werden und so fort ad infinitum. Zu einer Verständigung
zwischen den Sprach-Konstrukteuren und den empirischen Wissenschaft-

lern wird es dann überhaupt nicht kommen. Oder aber es wird zugegeben, daß der Wissenschaftstheoretiker immer schon über eine Sprache
verfügen muß, in der er sich mit sich selbst und seinen Kollegen
über die Ziele und Voraussetzungen der Sprachkonstruktion verständigen kann: dann wird sich herausstellen, daß auch die empirischen
Wissenschaftler durch Reflexion in dieser Sprache auf die sprachlichen Bedingungen der Möglichkeit und Gültigkeit ihrer Wissenschaft
an der metaszientifischen Kommunikation der Wissenschaftstheoretiker
teilnehmen müssen, wenn eine Verständigung über die Applizierbarkeit
einer Wissenschafts-Sprache zustandekommen soll. Kurz: Die Sprache
einer transzendentalen Sprachpragmatik erweist sich als soziales
Medium der Wissenschaftstheorie. (Im Falle der verstehenden Sozialwissenschaften werden sogar die Objekte der Wissenschaftssprache als
Subjekt-Objekte in einem gewissen Maße an der transzendentalpragmatischen Kommunikation müssen teilnehmen können, da ihr Verhalten nur
in solchen Begriffen verständlich gemacht werden kann, welche die
Akteure prinzipiell zu ihrem Selbstverständnis müßten verwenden
können.[27] Die Sprache der Transzendentalpragmatik erweist sich insofern als Sprache der Selbstreflexion der menschlichen Kommunikationsgemeinschaft als des Subjekt-Objektes der Wissenschaft.
2. Zu den inhaltlichen Konsequenzen der illegitimen Abstraktion von
der transzendentalpragmatischen Subjektproblematik der zeichenvermittelten Erkenntnis gehört eine entsprechende Verkürzung der
methodologischen Rekonstruktion der sg. "E r k e n n t n i s -
S y s t e m a t i s i e r u n g e n". So wird z.B. die K a u s a l-
E r k l ä r u n g anhand des z w e i s t e l l i g e n
S c h e m a s "x erklärt y" logisch-systematisch (d.h. mit Hilfe
eines formalisierten syntaktisch-semantischen Sprach-Systems) im
Sinne des Hempel-Oppenheim-Modells der d e d u k t i v -
n o m o l o g i s c h e n Erklärung rekonstruiert. Das im Sinne der
Dreistelligkeit jedes Erkenntnisaktes zu "x erklärt y" zugehörige
"für Person A" (A erkennt ja die Notwendigkeit des Eintretens von y
vermittels der das Explanans enthaltenden Hypothese x) wird in die
Psychologie verwiesen[28]- als ob nicht die Gemeinschaft der Wissenschaftler (auch im Falle der Psychologie selbst) zu einem normativ
verbindlichen Konsens darüber gelangen müßte, ob x (als im Sinne des
Wissensstandes theoretisch relevante Antwort auf eine Problemsituation) eine gültige Erklärung für das Phänomen y darstellt.
2.1. Da mit dem Erkenntnissubjekt zugleich die Problemsituation
(Fragestellung, Erkenntnisinteresse, Wissensstand, Vorverständnis
usw.) abgeblendet wird, so entsteht der Eindruck, synthetische

Erkenntnisleistungen, welche die intersubjektiv gültige Einheit der
Weltinterpretation herzustellen (bzw. im Falle der Störung wieder-
herzustellen) haben, könnten auf Deduktionen, die im Rahmen eines
syntaktischen Formalismus abbildbar sind, r e d u z i e r t
werden. So erscheint z.B. die Kausalerklärung als Deduktion des
E x p l a n a n d u m aus dem E x p l a n a n s , und nicht etwa
als Auffindung eines theoretisch relevanten Explanans, aus dem sich
das Explanandum deduzieren läßt. Die k a t e g o r i a l e
Problematik der zeitlich schematisierbaren Kausalnotwendigkeit
scheint so im Sinne des Neo-Humeanismus durch formallogische Notwendigkeit von Deduktion einerseits, empirischer Bestätigung von
Regelmäßigkeiten andererseits ersetzbar zu sein. Die Folge davon ist
die Ununterscheidbarkeit von kausalanalytisch relevanten ("theorie-
geladenen") Gesetzeshypothesen und Ad-hoc-Generalisierungen, welche
Prämissen für das deduktiv-nomologische Schema liefern, ohne die
Frage nach der Ursache der Phänomene zu beantworten. (Beispiel:
"Alles Eis wird von Wasser getragen" als Obersatz in der Erklärung
des Umstandes, daß ein bestimmtes Stück Eis vom Wasser getragen
wird. - Als ob nicht die prinzipiell experimentell wiederholbare
Feststellung, daß Eis vom Wasser getragen wird, allerst ein im Sinne
der Naturwissenschaft kausal erklärbares Phänomen konstituiert.)[29]
2.1.1. Die Reduktion der synthetischen Erkenntnisleistung auf den in
formalisierten Sprachen abbildbaren deduktiven Aspekt ihrer Systematisierung hat zur Folge, daß verschiedenartige Erkenntnisleistungen,
die auf verschiedenartige Problemsituationen antworten, als
"logisch-systematisch" aufeinander reduzierbar erscheinen. So
erscheint z.B. die logische Struktur von K a u s a l e r k l ä -
r u n g , P r o g n o s e und e m p i r i s c h e r Ü b e r -
p r ü f u n g im "Abstraktionsfenster" der syntaktisch-semantischen
Modellbildung als identisch. Die Unterschiede zwischen den drei
Prozeduren erscheinen als empirisch-psychologisch erklärbar, - als
ob nicht die E r k l ä r u n g als synthetische Erkenntnisleistung
(als innovative, abduktive Hypothese im Sinne von Peirce) den Er-
kenntnisstand der Wissenschaft verändert (unter Umständen neue
Theorien produzieren muß), während die P r o g n o s e die vorausgesetzte Erklärung nur anwendet und die e m p i r i s c h e
Ü b e r p r ü f u n g die Geltung der Erklärung mit Hilfe der durch
sie möglichen Prognosen erhärten oder erschüttern soll. Will man
diese Unterschiede als psychologische qualifizieren, so muß man
jedenfalls zugeben, daß sie nicht zu den Resultaten der
e m p i r i s c h g e n e r a l i s i e r e n d e n Psychologie

gehören, sondern zu deren Bedingungen der Möglichkeit und Gültigkeit
keit.

2.1.2. Deutlicher noch wird der nicht empirische, sondern
t r a n s z e n d e n t a l p r a g m a t i s c h e Charakter der
erörterten Unterschiede, wenn man bedenkt, daß auch die Unterschiede
zwischen K a u s a l - E r k l ä r u n g und o b j e k t i v -
t e l e o l o g i s c h e r F u n k t i o n a l a n a l y s e bzw.
zwischen K a u s a l - E r k l ä r u n g und s u b j e k t i v -
t e l e o l o g i s c h e m (z w e c k r a t i o n a l e m)
V e r s t e h e n menschlicher Handlungen - Unterschiede also, die
verschiedene Erkenntnis-Methoden zu begründen scheinen, die auf ganz
verschiedene Fragen antworten - von der analytischen Wissenschaftslogik als bloß psychologisch-heuristisch relevant betrachtet werden.
Es kann an dieser Stelle nicht das Problem des e i n h e i t s -
w i s s e n s c h a f t l i c h e n R e d u k t i o n i s m u s in
seiner ganzen Komplexität aufgeworfen und diskutiert werden. Ich
möchte jedoch die Vermutung äußern, daß die gesamte Strategie der
R e d u k t i o n aller wissenschaftlichen Erkenntnis-Systematisierungen auf das Hempel-Oppenheim-Modell der Erklärung ihre scheinbare
Berechtigung der illegitimen Abstraktion von den transzendentalpragmatischen Bedingungen der Möglichkeit der zeichenvermittelten
Erkenntnis verdankt.

Ein Indiz dafür, daß dem einheitswissenschaftlichen Reduktionismus
eine "abstractive fallacy" zugrundeliegt, liegt allein schon darin,
daß die (syntaktisch-semantische) Abstraktion vom leitenden
Erkenntnisinteresse als Bedingung der Möglichkeit eines wissenschaftlichen Sprachspiels offenbar nicht konsequent durchgehalten
werden kann, ohne die wissenschaftslogischen Rekonstruktionen als
trivial zu erweisen. So wird zwar im Falle des z w e c k r a t i o -
n a l e n V e r s t e h e n s u n d d e r F u n k t i o n a l -
a n a l y s e das primäre Interesse an normativ zu rechtfertigenden
guten Gründen des Handelns bzw. am objektiv teleologischen Bezug auf
einen Soll-Zustand als bloß p s y c h o l o g i s c h -
h e u r i s t i s c h erklärt, nicht aber in derselben Weise das
Interesse an der Erklärung aus Kausalgesetzen (die sich in techno-
logisches Verfügungswissen umsetzen läßt). Dieses letztere Erkenntnisinteresse wird vielmehr gerade dann als selbstverständlich implizit vorausgesetzt, wenn das Motiv-Verstehen als "bloß psychologisch-
heuristische Hilfsfunktion" im Dienste der Kausalerklärung menschlichen Verhaltens bezeichnet und das normativ rechtfertigende zweck-
rationale Verstehen auf eine wertneutrale Erklärung reduziert wird,

deren E x p l a n a n s aus Maximen qua Gesetzen und einem
v o l i t i o n a l - k o g n i t i v e n K o m p l e x qua
Ursachen oder Antecedenzbedingungen bestehen soll. Es zeigt sich
also, daß die sg. l o g i s c h - s y s t e m a t i s c h e
(s y n t a k t i s c h - s e m a n t i s c h e) Abstraktion von den
pragmatischen Voraussetzungen der Erkenntnis-Systematisierungen in
der analytischen Wissenschaftslogik de facto die Funktion hat, jene
transzendentalpragmatischen Voraussetzungen des kausalanalytisch
(bzw. statistisch) erklärenden Sprachspiels der Naturwissenschaft
zu verabsolutieren.
Vergleicht man diese Situation mit der älteren, naturalistischen
Reduktionsstrategie des Positivismus-Szientismus, so kann man die
scheinbar metaphysisch neutrale Reduktionsstrategie der analytischen
Wissenschaftslogik nur als "ideologisch" (im Sinne eines Erkenntnisinteressen verschleiernden falschen wissenschaftstheoretischen
Bewußtseins) bezeichnen.[30] Das ideologische Moment des Sprachspiels
der reduktionistischen Wissenschaftslogik läßt sich m.E. nur dadurch
aufheben, daß man die transzendentalpragmatischen Voraussetzungen
(Erkenntnisinteressen, Fragestellungen usw.) offenlegt, welche als
sinnkonstitutive Momente die verschiedenen Sprachspiele der metho-
dologisch verschiedenen Erkenntnis-Systematisierungen bestimmen. Es
würde sich dann zeigen, daß man einen scharfen Unterschied zu machen
hat zwischen solchen ("externen") Erkenntnismotivationen, welche nur
im p s y c h o l o g i s c h - g e n e t i s c h e n Sinn den
"context of discovery", nicht aber den wissenschaftstheoretischen
"context of justification" bestimmen, und andererseits jenen
("internen", transzendentalpragmatischen) Bedingungen der
Möglichkeit wissenschaftlicher Fragestellungen, welche den "context
of discovery" mit dem möglichen "context of justification" im Sinne
eines einheitlichen Sprachspiels zusammenschließen. So begründet
z.B. das Interesse am "Verstehen", das die Frage nach "Zielen" oder
"Gründen von menschlichen Handlungen" leitet, ein methodisch rele-
vantes Sprachspiel, in dem a priori die möglichen Antworten und die
Überprüfung der Richtigkeit dieser Antworten nicht - wie im Falle
der "Erklärung" - durch kommunikationsfreie "Beobachtung" zu
erhalten sind.[31]
Die im vorigen explizierte These einer t r a n s z e n d e n t a l-
p r a g m a t i s c h e n M e t a p r o b l e m a t i k der
s y n t a k t i s c h - s e m a n t i s c h e n Sprachkonstruktion
und Wissenschaftslogik besagt nicht etwa, daß die, hauptsächlich von
Carnap begründete, Methode der Formalisierung der Wissenschafts-

sprache rückgängig zu machen wäre. Sie besagt lediglich, daß diese
Methode als ein Weg "indirekter logischer Klärung" der in der
natürlichen Sprache gebrauchten, pragmatisch situierten Argumente
anzusehen ist. Ich beziehe mich hier auf eine These von
Y.Bar-Hillel[32] und versuche, sie im Sinne meines Ansatzes auszuwer-
ten. Es geht dann gewissermaßen um eine t r a n s z e n d e n -
t a l p r a g m a t i s c h e Begründung des Sinns der k o n -
s t r u k t i v e n S e m a n t i k.
Die Konstruktion semantischer "frameworks", wie sie Carnap in seinem
grundlegenden Aufsatz "Empirism, Semantics and Ontology"[33] charakterisiert hat, kann zunächst einmal selbst schon als s e m a n -
t i s c h e Transformation der "kopernikanischen Wendung" Kants
verstanden werden: denn die "semantical frameworks" schreiben ja
nach Carnap der Natur oder der Welt die ontologische Struktur
gewissermaßen vor (man hat in diesem Zusammenhang von "Onto-
Semantik" gesprochen).[34] Aber der Unterschied zwischen Carnaps und
Kants Version der "kopernikanischen Wende" liegt in Folgendem:
Während Kant im Sinne einer theoretischen Transzendentalphilosophie
qua Metaphysik der Erfahrung davon ausgeht, daß der Verstand der
Natur das (formale) Gesetz der Erscheinung vorschreibt, geht Carnap
gewissermaßen dazu über, die "kopernikanische Wendung" in die Praxis
umzusetzen - freilich in eine Praxis ohne transzendentale Reflexion
auf ihre Bedingungen der Möglichkeit und Gültigkeit. Er legt durch
die Konstruktion eines Systems von semantischen Regeln die Grund-
begriffe möglicher Weltbeschreibung fest, entzieht aber die kon-
ventionelle Festlegung dieser transzendentalen Bedingungen der
Erfahrung t h e o r e t i s c h e r Reflexion, indem er sie zu
einer Angelegenheit der P r a x i s erklärt, - der Praxis im Sinne
von "Entscheidung".
Nun läßt sich aber m.E. die syntaktisch-semantische Sprachkonstruktion nur dann im Sinne Bar-Hillels als "indirekte" Klärung der
Argumentation auffassen und in ihrem praktischen Effekt einschätzen,
wenn man auf die u m g a n g s s p r a c h l i c h e
V e r s t ä n d i g u n g als Bedingung der Möglichkeit und Gültigkeit der applikativen I n t e r p r e t a t i o n des semantischen
Systems und damit der Legitimation der in die Konstruktion der
"frameworks" eingehenden "Konventionen" reflektiert.[35] Solche
Reflexionen zu unterlassen oder gar aus der Philosophie auszuschließen, würde auf eine "abstractive fallacy" hinauslaufen; denn
nur in der natürlichen Sprache kann die virtuelle fragmentarische
Klärung möglicher Weltbeschreibung, die durch ein semantisches

System bloß projektiert wird, im Sinne einer Verbesserung der
A r g u m e n t a t i o n - d.h. hier: der   i n t e r p e r s o -
n a l e n   K o m m u n i k a t i o n   über die deiktisch fixierbare
Welterfahrung aktualisiert werden. In einem semantischen System
dagegen kann es nur "Sätze", nicht aber kommunikative "Sprechakte"
(speechacts) geben und demzufolge auch keine   D e i x i s   in dem
Sinne, daß durch sie der propositionale Sinn von Sätzen hier und
jetzt auf mögliche Erfahrung bezogen werden könnte, - oder in dem
Sinn, daß die Sätze durch   p e r s o n a l e   D e i x i s   der
zugehörigen Sprechakte in der interpersonalen Diskussion situiert
werden könnten - nicht zu reden davon, daß der hermeneutische
Zusammenhang der Argumentation mit einer geschichtlichen Problemsituation nur in der umgangssprachlichen Kommunikation hergestellt
werden kann.

(Die soeben angedeutete Notwendigkeit einer   t r a n s z e n d e n -
t a l p r a g m a t i s c h e n   R e f l e x i o n   auf die Bedingungen umgangssprachlicher Verständigung scheint mir aber auch durch
die von der Erlanger Schule vorgeschlagene Methode einer unmittelbar
im   D i a l o g   ansetzenden und somit   d i r e k t e n   Methode der
Sprach-Rekonstruktion bestätigt zu werden. Denn bereits die methodische Einführung der Junktoren und Quantoren im Dialogspiel der
P r o t o l o g i k, vollends aber die Einführung der Prädikatoren,
die zum Aufbau einer   O r t h o - S p r a c h e   der   P r o t o -
p h y s i k, der   P r o t o e t h i k   oder der   P r o t o j u r i -
d i k   erforderlich sind, setzt - als diskutierbare Rekonstruktion -
die ganze Umgangssprache einschließlich der Bildungssprache schon
voraus. Die transzendentale Voraussetzung der Umgangssprache auf
seiten des einführenden Lehrers zeigt sich m.E. darin, daß er mit
der Einführung der Prädikatoren bereits in die theoretische Auseinandersetzung mit der Tradition eintritt und deshalb eine wohlüberlegte Strategie der Einführung befolgen muß, um tatsächlich
P r o t o l o g i k,   P r o t o p h y s i k,   P r o t o e t h i k
usw. aufzubauen und nicht etwas anderes.[36] Auf seiten der Schüler,
die in die   O r t h o - S p r a c h e   eingeführt werden sollen,
wird die Sprachkompetenz im Sinne des Verstehens der Umgangssprache
ebenfalls prinzipiell vorausgesetzt, da sonst die methodische Einübung der Orthosprache für sie nicht auf   S p r a c h - R e k o n -
s t r u k t i o n, sondern auf   A b r i c h t u n g   hinauslaufen
würde. Auch für die   d i r e k t e   R e k o n ᴨ t r u k t i o n   der
Sprache bedeutet die transzendentale Voraussetzung der umgangssprachlichen Verständigung selbstverständlich nicht, daß die Umgangs-

sprache als unveränderliche Autorität vorausgesetzt würde; eher wird
sie als ein Schiff vorausgesetzt, das während der Fahrt umgebaut
werden muß. Der Umbau geschieht hier durch unmittelbar
r e f l e x i o n s a b h ä n g i g e R e k o n s t r u k t i o n,
während die "indirekte" Sprachklärung der "logischen Semantik"
primär durch e n t s c h e i d u n g s a b h ä n g i g e
S y s t e m - K o n s t r u k t i o n die Struktur der Umgangssprache erhellt. In beiden Fällen aber muß die Anwendung auf die
Lebenspraxis letztlich durch umgangssprachliche Verständigung zustandegebracht werden, da nur diese die Sprache situieren, d.h.
i n t e r p e r s o n a l und im H i e r u n d J e t z t der
Erfahrung festmachen kann.)
Die philosophische Tragweite der soeben angedeuteten transzendentalpragmatischen Sinngebung der logischen Sprachkonstruktion läßt sich
m.E. an zwei Konsequenzen verdeutlichen, von denen die eine einen
positiven, die andere einen negativ-kritischen Charakter hat:
1. Eine positive - auch wissenschaftstheoretisch relevante -
Konsequenz der Akzeptierung des transzendentalpragmatischen Sinnhorizonts der Sprach-(Re)-Konstruktion liegt darin, daß man den
methodologischen Ursprungsort der hermeneutischen Geisteswissenschaften - z.B. der Wissenschaftshistorie - nicht, wie in dem m.E.
sinnlosen Versuch des methodologischen Reduktionismus, auf der
Ebene der e m p i r i s c h - a n a l y t i s c h e n
S c i e n c e ansiedelt, sondern auf der Metaebene der
t r a n s z e n d e n t a l p r a g m a t i s c h e n V e r-
s t ä n d i g u n g über den Sinn der empirisch-analytischen
Wissenschaft.[37] Zwischen logischer Sprach-Konstruktion und
hermeneutischer Rekonstruktion der sprachlichen Überlieferung
bestünde dann ein t r a n s z e n d e n t a l p r a g m a t i-
s c h e r (und zugleich) t r a n s z e n d e n t a l -
h e r m e n e u t i s c h e r) Zusammenhang folgender Art: Die
logische Sprach-(Re)-Konstruktion einerseits ist im Hinblick auf die
Möglichkeit einer transzendentalpragmatischen Interpretation ihrer
Konstrukte - z.B. um die Adäquatheitsbedingungen von Begriffsexpli-
kationen sicherzustellen - auf die hermeneutische Rekonstruktion der
sprachlich-kulturellen Überlieferung und damit gewissermaßen des
eigenen Welt-Vorverständnisses angewiesen; die hermeneutische Rekonstruktion der Überlieferung - z.B. literarischer, philosophischer
und wissenschaftshistorischer Dokumente - andererseits ist im Hinblick auf die Möglichkeit einer sprachlich explizierenden und
reflexiv überholenden Interpretation[38] auf konstruktive Entwürfe der

Sinnexplikation und Präzisierung angewiesen, wie sie in der konstruktiven Sprachlogik abstraktiv thematisiert werden. Implizit sind
sowohl das konstruktive wie das hermeneutische Moment der Sinn-
klärung immer schon in den Geisteswissenschaften wie in der Sprachlogik enthalten gewesen - nur mit polar entgegengesetzter Akzen-
tuierung und mehr oder weniger unreflektiert.[39]

2. Eine negativ kritische Konsequenz der Akzeptierung des transzendentalpragmatischen Sinnhorizonts der syntaktisch-semantischen
Sprachkonstruktion liegt m.E. darin, daß man davon ablassen muß,
unmittelbar von den "frameworks" der modernen Wissenschaftslogik aus
die Beziehung zur philosophischen Tradition - insbesondere zur
aristotelisch-scholastischen O n t o l o g i e - herstellen zu
wollen. Dieser Ansatz einer "Onto-Semantik", der mit der transzendentalpragmatischen Reflexion zugleich das Erbe der neuzeitlichen
Erkenntniskritik ignoriert, muß unter den gegenwärtigen Bedingungen
möglicher "framework"-Konstruktion unweigerlich in einen philosophisch nicht mehr verständlichen Relativismus der "Weltbilder"
hineinführen.[40] M.a.W.: Man wird die von Descartes bis Husserl
bestehende Auszeichnung des Selbstbewußtseins der Erkenntnis, und
damit des Evidenz- oder Gewißheitsbegriffs der Wahrheit, nicht
einfach zugunsten eines ontosemantischen Korrespondenzbegriffs der
Wahrheit rückgängig machen können, sondern wird beide Aspekte des
Wahrheitsbegriffs in einer transzendentalpragmatischen Konsensus-
Theorie der Wahrheit "aufheben" müssen.[41] Der wesentliche Grund
dieser Forderung liegt m.E. in dem Umstand, daß die Problematik der
intersubjektiven Sinnverständigung sowohl in der Ontosemantik wie
andererseits in der Selbstverständigung über die Evidenz schon vorausgesetzt ist. Kurz: Die sprachanalytische Philosophie unseres
Jahrhunderts wird nur dann als E r s t e   P h i l o s o p h i e
(prima philosophia) auftreten können, wenn sie auf der Ebene einer
transzendentalen Sprachpragmatik sowohl die antik-scholastische
Ontologie wie die neuzeitliche Erkenntnistheorie "aufzuheben"
vermag.[42]

Die Gegenprobe zu der hier postulierten Konzeption einer
t r a n s z e n d e n t a l e n   S p r a c h p r a g m a t i k wird
m.E. durch die Konzeption einer   t r a n s z e n d e n t a l e n
O n t o s e m a n t i k   geliefert, wei sie der junge Wittgenstein
im "Tractatus logico-philosophicus" ausgearbeitet hat. Ihre Pointe
liegt darin, daß die Problematik des Erkenntnissubjekts (und damit
die Kantische Problematik der Transzendentalphilosophie) und die
Problematik der ontologischen Form der Welt als Problematik der

logischen Form der Sprache und der beschreibbaren Welt ineinsge-
setzt werden: Das transzendentale Erkenntnissubjekt ist ebenso wie
die logische Form der Sprache die "Grenze der Welt" (Wittgenstein).
Wird dies aber unterstellt, dann wäre es, wie Wittgenstein mit Recht
feststellt, weder notwendig noch möglich, sich über diese Form
philosophisch zu verständigen: "Solipsismus" und "Realismus" würden
zusammenfallen, weil jeder a priori mit derselben Welt konfrontiert
wäre und die interpersonale Kommunikation nicht den Charakter der
m e t a s p r a c h l i c h e n   S i n n v e r s t ä n d i g u n g ,
sondern allenfalls den Charakter einer reflexionsfreien Ü b e r -
t r a g u n g   v o n   I n f o r m a t i o n s - S i g n a l e n
haben könnte.[43] Mit anderen Worten: Eine t r a n s z e n d e n -
t a l e   O n t o - S e m a n t i k   kann, wie der "Tractatus" auf
paradoxe Weise **zeigt**, die für den Menschen charakteristische Form
der sprachlichen Kommunikation, die immer zugleich Verständigung
über die Sachen und metasprachliche Verständigung über die Sprache
einschließt, gerade nicht verständlich machen. Sie kann daher auch
nicht die von Kant postulierte Einheit des Gegenstandsbewußtseins
und des Selbstbewußtseins, die für menschliche Erkenntnis charakteristisch ist, in sprachphilosophischer Form zum Ausdruck bringen.

ANMERKUNGEN:

1.   Unsere Formulierung ist hier bewußt vage gehalten, da es darum
geht, eine allgemeine Denkhaltung zu charakterisieren, deren Begründung keineswegs geklärt ist, die aber gerade deswegen als ein prak-
tisches Denktabu fungiert. Ungeklärt sind z.B. Fragen wie diese:
M u ß die Selbstrückbezüglichkeit der natürlichen Sprache in
Widersprüche führen (ist insofern etwa die natürliche Sprache in-
konsistent), oder ist die Selbstrückbezüglichkeit der natürlichen
Sprache lediglich ein Hindernis für die Konstruktion einer - a
priori widerspruchsfreien - formalisierten Sprache? - Im ersten Fall
ist es unverständlich, wie die implizite Selbstrückbezüglichkeit der
philosophisch universalen Sätze der Typentheorie bzw. der logischen
Semantik, sofern sie die Notwendigkeit der Sprachspaltung begründet,
gerechtfertigt werden soll. Im letzten Fall liegt es nahe, die philosophische - und d.h. metaszientifische und metalogische - Sprache
vom Verbot der Selbstrückbezüglichkeit auszunehmen.
2.   Vgl. K.O. Apel, Sprache als Thema und Medium der Reflexion, in:
M a n   a n d   W o r l d, 3/4 (1970), pp. 323-337.
3.   Vgl. I. Kant, A n t h r o p o l o g i e   i n   p r a g m a t i-
s c h e r   H i n s i c h t, in: S ä m t l. W e r k e, Hrsg. v.
K. Vorländer, Bd.4, Leipzig 1920, p. 101.
4.   Vgl. meinen Aufsatz, Die Entfaltung der sprachanalytischen
Philosophie und das Problem der Geisteswissenschaften, in:
P h i l o s. J a h r b u c h, 72.Jg. (1965); englische Übersetzung:
Analytic Philosophy of Language and the Geisteswissenschaften, in:
F o u n d a t i o n s   o f   L a n g u a g e, suppl. series, vol.5,
Reidel, Dordrecht 1967.
5.   Vgl. K.O. Apel, Die Kommunikationsgemeinschaft als transzen-
dentale Voraussetzung der Sozialwissenschaften, in: N e u e
H e f t e   f ü r   P h i l o s o p h i e 2/3 (1972), S. 1-40. Auch
in K.O. Apel, T r a n s f o r m a t i o n   d e r   P h i l o s o-
p h i e, Bd II, Frankfurt 1973.
6.   Vgl. D. Wunderlich, Pragmatik, Sprachsituation, Deixis, in:
L i l i, Jg.1 (1971). Ferner: J. Habermas, Vorbereitende Bemerkungen
zu einer Theorie der kommunikativen Kompetenz, in: J. Habermas u.
N. Luhmann, T h e o r i e   d e r   G e s e l l s c h a f t   o d e r
S o z i a l t e c h n o l o g i e, Frankfurt 1971. Dazu K.O. Apel,
Noam Chomskys Sprachtheorie und die Philosophie der Gegenwart, in:
T r a n s f o r m a t i o n   d e r   P h i l o s o p h i e, a.a.O.
7.   s. Anm.6
8.   Vgl. dazu den Diskussionsband von C. Lyas (ed): P h i l o-
s o p h y   a n d   L i n g u i s t i c s, London 1971.
9.   Vgl. hierzu vorläufig meine Aufsätze zu Wittgenstein und
Chomsky in: T r a n s f o r m a t i o n   d e r   P h i l o s o-
p h i e, a.a.O.
10. Vgl. hierzu meine folgenden Arbeiten: Der philosophische
Hintergrund der Entstehung des Pragmatismus bei Ch.S. Peirce, in:
K.O. Apel (ed.), Ch.S. Peirce, S c h r i f t e n I, Frankfurt
1967, S. 13-154. Ferner: Peirces Denkweg vom Pragmatismus zum Prag-
matizismus, in: K.O. Apel (ed.), Ch.S. Peirce, S c h r i f t e n
II, Frankfurt 1970, S. 11-214. Ferner: K.O. Apel, From Kant to
Peirce: The Semiotic Transformation of Transcendental Philosophy,
in: L.W. Beck (ed.), P r o c e e d i n g s   o f   t h e   T h i r d
I n t e r n a t. K a n t - C o n g r e s s 1970, Dordrecht 1972,
p. 90-104. Ferner: K.O. Apel, Szientismus oder transzendentale
Hermeneutik? Zur Frage nach dem Subjekt der Zeicheninterpretation
in der Semiotik des Pragmatismus, in: H e r m e n e u t i k   u n d
D i a l e k t i k (hrsg. v. R. Bubner), Tübingen 1970, Bd.I,
S. 105-145.
11. Kant reduziert keineswegs die dreistellige Erkenntnisrelation

schlechtweg auf eine zweistellige, aber er denkt die Begriffsvermittlung der Erkenntnis ohne die zugehörige Zeichen- bzw. Sprach-
vermittlung.
12. Hierin steckt in der Tat die erste transzendental-semiotisch
begründete K o n s e n s - Theorie der Wahrheit. Sie soll allerdings - nach Peirce - die ontologische K o r r e s p o n d e n z-
theorie und die neuzeitlich-erkenntnistheoretische E v i d e n z-
theorie der Wahrheit nicht exclusiv ersetzen, sondern eher integrieren oder aufheben. Die Wahrheit der Korrespondenz- bzw. Evidenztheo-
rie wird von Peirce den "index"- und "ikon"-gestützten synthetischen
Schlußverfahren zugeordnet, ohne die alle Konsens-Bildung durch Sym-
bol-Interpretation leer bleiben müßte. - Soviel vorläufig zu der
Kontroverse zwischen J.Habermas (Vorbereitende Bemerkungen zu einer
Theorie der kommunikativen Kompetenz, in J. Habermas / N. Luhmann,
T h e o r i e d e r G e s e l l s c h a f t o d e r S o z i a l-
t e c h n o l o g i e, Frankfurt 1971) und A.Beckermann (Die reali-
stischen Voraussetzungen der Konsenstheorie von J.Habermas, in:
Z t s c h r. f. A l l g. W i s s e n s c h a f t s t h e o r i e,
III/1 1972). Vgl. jetzt auch J. Habermas, Wahrheitstheorien, in:
F e s t s c h r i f t f ü r W. S c h u l z (erscheint demnächst).
13. Vgl. G. Wartenberg, L o g i s c h e r S o z i a l i s m u s:
Die Transformation der Kantischen Transzendentalphilosophie durch
Charles S. Peirce, Frankfurt 1971.
14. Vgl. J. Royce, T h e P r o b l e m o f C h r i s t i a n i-
t y, Vol.II, New York 1913. Dazu John E. Smith, R o y c e ' s
S o c i a l I n f i n i t e, New York 1940, und K. Th. Humbach,
D a s V e r h ä l t n i s v o n E i n z e l p e r s o n u n d
G e m e i n s c h a f t n a c h J o s i a h R o y c e, Heidelberg
1962. Ferner K. O. Apel, Szientismus oder transtendentale Hermeneutik?, a.a.O., Teil III.
15. G. H. Mead, M i n d, S e l f a n d S o c i e t y, Chicago
1934, p. 327.
16. Für eine moderne Explikation dieser Idee vgl. die Arbeiten von
J.Haberma in: J. Habermas / N. Luhmann, a.a.O.: ferner meine Aufsätze in: T r a n s f o r m a t i o n d e r P h i l o s o p h i e
Frankfurt 1973, Bd.II, 2.Teil: ferner meine Aufsätze: The Apriori of
Communication and the Foundation of the Humanities, in: M a n
a n d W o r l d, 5/1 (1972) und: The Transcendental Conception of
Language-Communication and the Idea of a First Philosophy, in:
C o m m u n i c a t i o n Nr.2 (1973).
17. Ch. Morris, F o u n d a t i o n s o f t h e T h e o r y
o f S i g n s, Chicago 1938 (dtsch: G r u n d l a g e n d e r
Z e i c h e n t h e o r i e, München 1972).
18. Vgl. John Dewey, Peirce's Theory of Linguistic Signs, Thought
and Meaning, in: J o u r n a l o f P h i l o s o p h y, 43 (1946)
p. 85-95: Letter by Ch.Morris, ebda. p. 196: Reply by Dewey, ebda.
p. 280: Rejoinder by Morris, ebda. p. 363-364.
19. Vgl. R. Carnap, F o u n d a t i o n s o f L o g i c a n d
Ma t h e m a t i c s, Chicago 1939, p. 6: und: I n t r o d u c-
t i o n t o S e m a n t i c s, Cambridge/Mass. 1942, 84. - Dazu
Ch. Morris, S i g n s, L a n g u a g e a n d B e h a v i o r,
New York 1946, p. 279, note 8.
20. Vgl. R. Carnap, On Some Concepts of Pragmatics, in: P h i l-
o s. S t u d i e s VI (1955), pp. 85-91 (wiederabgedruckt in
M e a n i n g a n d N e c e s s i t y, 2.ed. Chicago 1956, App.E).
21. Diese Frage konzentriert sich zur Zeit auf die Arbeiten von R.
Montague, die wohl den neuesten Stand des Versuchs einer Formalisierung der "Pragmatik" repräsentieren. Vgl. z.B. den Artikel:
Pragmatics, in: R. Klibansky (ed.), C o n t e m p o r a r y
P h i l o s o p h y I, Firenze, Nuova Italia, 1968, pp. 102-122:
ferner: Universal Grammar, in: T h e o r i a XXXVI, 1970, pp. 373-

398 (deutsch mit Einleitung von H. Schnelle bei Vieweg/Braunschweig
1971); ferner: Pragmatics and Intensional Logic, in: S y n -
t h e s e XXII, 1970, pp. 69-94, und in D. Davidson / G. Harman
(eds.) S e m a n t i c s   o f   N a t u r a l   L a n g u a g e,
Reidel, Dordrecht 1972.
22. Vgl. zuletzt b.B. W.Stegmüllers Behandlung der pragmatischen
Dimension der "Erklärung" in seinem Buch P r o b l e m e   u n d
E r g e b n i s s e   d e r   W i s s e n s c h a f t s t h e o r i e
u n d   A n a l y t i s c h e n   P h i l o s o p h i e, Bd.I, Berlin-
Heidelberg-New York 1969.
23. Vgl. hierzu besonders Ch. Morris, G r u n d l a g e n   d e r
Z e i c h e n t h e o r i e, S. 50f und S. 57ff. Vgl. ferner:
S i g n s,   L a n g u a g e   a n d   B e h a v i o r, a.a.O. p. 279,
Note C. Die Paradoxie der Selbstanwendung des Postulats des nicht-
selbstrückbezüglichen Sprachgebrauchs, der schon Russell's Typentheorie selbst unterlag, zeigt sich bei Morris etwa in der folgenden
Passage (a.a.O. p. 220): "Does semiotic signify itself? An affirmative answer can be given to this question, without contradictions
arising, provided we recognize that no sign denotes its own signification....So while no statement denotes all significations, there
is no signification about which a statement cannot be made. In this
way a statement can be made without semiotics about any sign, inc
including the signs of this book, though no body of statements about
signs is the totality of statements which can be made about signs."
- Wenngleich die zuletzt gemachte Aussage trivialerweise wahr ist,
so trägt sie doch in keiner Weise ihrem eigenen Allgemeinheitsan-
spruch Rechnung, der sich auf die Bedeutung aller nur möglichen
Zeichen erstreckt. Und sollte dies nicht das Paradigma aller philosophischen Aussagen der Semiotik sein? - Die Antwort, die Morris
hierauf zu geben hat, dürfte in dem von uns ausgelassenen Satz enthalten sein. Er lautet: "This assertion (sc. "No signs denotes its
own signification"),itself part of Logic, is an analytic formative
ascriptor: since the signification of a sign is not itself a deno-
tatum of the sign."
Offenbar möchte Ch.Morris, ebenso wie die Vertreter des Logischen
Empirismus, die philosophischen Sätze als analytische Sätze der
Logik auffassen, um die vollständige Disjunktion von analytischen
und synthetischen Sätzen bzw. von Logik und empirischer Wissenschaft
aufrecht zu erhalten. Auch die These dieser vollständigen Disjunktion müßte demnach als analytisch aufgefaßt werden. Daß hierin eine
gefährliche Immunisierung philosophischer Behauptungen liegt, zeigt
jedoch gerade der obige Satz, mit dem Morris sich ausdrücklich auf
Russells Typentheorie beruft. Wir haben bereits erwähnt, daß er der
eigenen impliziten Selbstrückbezüglichkeit widerspricht. Darüber
hinaus widerspricht er jedoch der expliziten Selbstrückbezüglichkeit
der von Austin entdeckten "performativen" Ausdrücke. Der Ausdruck
"Ich verspreche hiermit,..." bezeichnet tatsächlich seine eigene
Bedeutung, nämlich die Bedingung, unter der er etwas bezeichnet, die
durch den Sprechakt des Versprechens hergestellt wird. Aber spricht
diese Widerlegung nicht lediglich dafür, daß philosophische **Aussagen**
empirisch sind, wenn sie nicht analytisch sind?
24. Vgl. insbesondere die Kritik Chomskys an Skinners
V e r b a l   B e h a v i o r   in: L a n g u a g e, 35, p. 26-58.
25. Interessanterweise hat Karl Popper diese Grundkonstellation der
analytischen Philosophie, derzufolge die Subjekt-Dimension der Erkenntnis einer empirischen Disziplin zufallen muß, in seiner Spät-
philosophie sogar im Sinne einer Metaphysik vorkantischen Stils, die
den Ursprung aller Normen in einer platonischen "Dritten Welt" ver-
ankert, bestätigt und zu begründen versucht. Vgl. insbesondere die
Aufsätze: Epistemology without a Knowing Subject, und: On the **Theory**
of the Objective Mind, in K. Popper, O b j e c t i v e

K n o w l e d g e, Oxford 1972. - Der "kritische Konventionalismus"
der Philosophie der offenen Gesellschaft hätte m.E. eine andere L
Lösung des Problems der normativen Grundlagen der Erkenntnis, eine
Lösung im Geiste des transzendentalen Pragmatismus von Peirce, nahe-
gelegt.
26. Eine ausführliche Studie über: "Die Idee einer transzendentalen
Pragmatik und die Grundlagen der Wissenschaftstheorie" ist in Vor-
bereitung.
27. Das von P. Winch (T h e   I d e a   o f   a   S o c i a l
S c i e n c e   a n d   i t s   R e l a t i o n   t o   P h i l o s o-
p h y, London 1958) vertretene Prinzip der prinzipiellen Gemeinsam-
keit der Sprache für Subjekt und Objekt der Sozialwissenschaften
wird von uns nur als ein kontrafaktisches Postulat akzeptiert, da
sonst - wie bei Winch selbst - die Möglichkeit ideologiekritischen
Hinterfragens soziokultureller Sprachspiele abgeschnitten würde.
Vgl. hierzu K. O. Apel, Die Kommunikationsgemeinschaft als transzendentale Voraussetzung der Sozialwissenschaften, in: N e u e
H e f t e   f ü r   P h i l o s o p h i e, Heft 2/3 (1972), wiederabgedruckt in: T r a n s f o r m a t i o n   d e r   P h i l o s o-
p h i e, Bd.II, Frankfurt 1973.
28. Vgl. hierzu z.B. W. Stegmüller, P r o b l e m e   u n d
R e s u l t a t e..., BdII, a.a.O.
29. Vgl. hierzu G. Radnitzky C o n t e m p o r a r y   S c h o
S c h o o l s   o f   M e t a s c i e n c e, sec. edition Göteborg
1970, Vol.I, pp. 146. Vgl. auch A. Wellmer, M e t h o d o l o g i e
a l s   E r k e n n t n i s t h e o r i e, Frankfurt 1967, Kap.IV:
Das Basisproblem. Ferner: ders., E r k l ä r u n g   u n d
K a u s a l i t ä t: Zur Kritik des Hempel-Oppenheim-Modells der
Erklärung, ungedruckte Habil.-Schrift.
30. Zur p e t i t i o   p r i n c i p i i   spitzt sich diese Ver-
schleierung transzendental-pragmatischer Voraussetzungen zu, wenn
dem "Verstehens-Theoretiker" (d.h. dem Vertreter einer nicht szientistisch reduzierbaren hermeneutischen Methodologie der Geisteswissenschaften) unterstellt wird, er verteidige eine - womöglich
irrationale - K o n k u r r e n z m e t h o d e   zur wissenschaftlichen "Erklärung" und man ihm dann zeigt, daß diese nur geringen
Erklärungswert hat.
31. Vgl. hierzu K. O. Apel, Communication and the Foundation of the
Humanities, in: A c t a   S o c i o l o g i c a, 15/1 (1972),
pp. 7-26. Erweiterte Fassung in: M a n   a n d   W o r l d, 5/1
(1972), pp. 3-37.
32. Vgl. Y. Bar-Hillel, Argumentation in Pragmatic Languages, in:
Y. Bar-Hillel, A s p e c t s   o f   L a n g u a g e, Jerusalem 1970,
pp. 206-221.
33. R. Carnap, Empirism, Semantics and Ontology, in: R e v u e
I n t e r n a t i o n a l e   d e   P h i l o s o p h i e, 11/1950,
wiederabgedruckt in: L. Linsky (ed.), S e m a n t i c s   a n d
t h e   P h i l o s o p h y   o f   L a n g u a g e, Urbana 1972.
34. Vgl. z.B. G. Janoska, D i e   s p r a c h l i c h e n   G r u n
G r u n d l a g e n   d e r   P h i l o s o p h i e, Graz 1962, und
E. K. Specht, S p r a c h e   u n d   S e i n, Berlin 1967.
35. Geschieht dies, so könnte sich zeigen, daß schon die Anschauungsformen und Kategorien, durch die nach Kant der Verstand der N
Natur das Gesetzt vorschreibt, als Bestandteil eines Sprachspiels
aufgefaßt werden müssen, das seine Legitimation darin hat, daß es
zusammen mit den zugehörigen experimentellen Tätigkeiten p r a k-
t i z i e r t   werden kann und auch heute noch im Sinne des methodischen Primats der "Protophysik" (P.Lorenzen) praktiziert werden
muß. "Protophysik" einerseits, syntaktisch-semantisch projektierte
Theorie-Sprachen andererseits würden sich als zwei - **eventuell**
transzendentalpragmatisch-erkenntnisanthropolo**gisch z**u vermittelnde

- Aspekte moderner Transformation der "kopernikanischen Wende" Kants
erweisen.
36. Ein Beispiel für solche wohlüberlegte - hermeneutisch ver-
mittelte! - Strategie der Einführung der Ortho-Sprache ist m.E. die
L o g i s c h e   P r o p ä d e u t i k von Kamlah-Lorenzen (Mann-
heim 1967).
37. Anhand unseres Diagramms (Figur I am Ende des Beitrags) läßt
sich zeigen, daß in der Tat jedes hermeneutische Verstehen der em-
pirsch-objektiv vorfindlichen Sprach-Handlungen bzw. ihrer Produkte
die empiristische Reduktion der transzendentalen Dimension der
Kommunikation (s. Reduktionspfeile!) der Tendenz nach rückgängig
macht, d.h. die historisch objektivierte Kommunikation in die
gegenwärtige intersubjektive (= noch nicht objektivierte!) Kommunikation (s. Bereich der gestrichelten Linien!) zu integrieren versucht. - Eine instruktive Illustration der unbestreitbaren Notwendigkeit dieser Rückgängigmachung des Reduktionismus liefert die
Debatte zwischen Th.Kuhn und der Popper-Schule in I.Lakatos /
A.Musgrave (eds.), C r i t i c i s m   a n d   t h e   G r o w t h
o f   K n o w l e d g e, Cambridge 1970. Da Kuhn seine wissenschafts-
historischen Einsichten anfangs im Namen einer empirischen Psychologie bzw. Soziologie zu vertreten scheint (vgl. bs. p. 21f.) und die
Popperianer sich als normative Wissenschaftlogiker verstehen, die an
der "Dritten Welt" des "objektiven Geistes" orientiert sind, so
scheint zunächst gar kein Dialog zwischen beiden Seiten möglich zu
sein. In der Tat könnte eine empirisch-analytische Sozialwissenschaft im Sinne des Szientismus immer nur Objekt, nicht aber meta-
szientifischer Gesprächspartner der normativen Wissenschaftstheorie
sein. Zuletzt zeigt sich jedoch, daß die Kuhnsche Wissenschaftshistorie zu v e r s t e h e n beansprucht, warum die Wissenschaftler a u s   g u t e n   G r ü n d e n oft anderst gehandelt haben
bzw. anderst handeln müssen, als es der "naive Falsifikationismus"
vorschreibt (vgl. bes. Kuhns Replik, pp. 231 ff.). Hier zeigt sich,
daß Wissenschaftshistorie keine wertfreie "behavioral science" ist,
die etwa das Durchschnittsverhalten von Wissenschaftlern aus Gesetzen erklären müßte, sondern ihre h e r m e n e u t i s c h e
Pointe aus dem Versuch entfaltet, gewissermaßen als Vermittler eine
Methoden-Diskussion zwischen den modernen Wissenschaftstheoretikern
und den verstorbenen Praktikern möglich zu machen.
38. Es geht hier um den guten Sinn des alten hermeneutischen Topos,
daß man einen Autor nur insofern versteht, als man ihn besser versteht, als er sich selbst verstehen konnte.
39. Es sollte auch nicht vergessen werden, daß "Logik" (bzw.
"Dialektik"), "Grammatik", "Rhetorik" und "Hermeneutik" als
"Technai Logikai" ("artes sermonicales") gleich alt und gleich ursprünglich sind. Alle aufgeführten Titel lassen sich schon bei
Plato belegen; und wenn nicht alles täuscht, so ist gegenwärtig ein
Prozess der philosophisch-wissenschaftlichen Rekonstruktion des
Systems der "artes sermonicales" im Gang.
40. Wissenschaftstheoretisch reflektiert sich diese Problematik
m.E. im "Theorienpluralismus" oder genauer: in der Kuhn-Feyerabend-
These der "Inkommensurabilität" wissenschaftlicher Theorien oder
Sprachspiel-Paradigmata. In der Ebene des Vergleichs semantischer
Systeme dürfte diese Theorie - ebenso wie die Sapir-Whorff-These
der sg. "Metalinguistik" - stichhaltig sein. In der transzendentalpragmatischen Ebene der Verständigung dürfte dagegen der Anspruch
des wissenschaflichen Erkenntnisfortschritts - bzw. des interlingu-
alen Verständigungsfortschritts - zu recht bestehen. Wenn z.B. zwei
inkommensurable Theorien im Sinne Feyerabends zur wechselseitigen
Falsifikation ihrer beobachtbaren Konsequenzen benutzt werden
sollen, dann muß es zumindest möglich sein, mittels der nicht vollständig semantisch relativierbaren D e i x i s das für beide

Theorien gemeinsame Reale zu identifizieren. Weitere transzendental-
pragmatische Voraussetzungen aller physikalischen Theorien im Sinne
einer methodisch-apriorischen Protophysik dürften durch das mit dem
Apriori des technisch präzisierbaren Leibeingriffs in die Natur ver-
knüpfte Erkenntnisinteresse am objektiven Verfügungswissen bedingt
sein. Insofern spricht der unbestreitbare Fortschritt in der tech-
nologischen Herrschaft über die Natur für die Möglichkeit eines
theoretischen Fortschritts, und das heißt letztlich: gegen die
Inkommensurabilitätsthese.

41. Vgl. Anmerkung 12.

42. Vgl. hierzu meinen Aufsatz: The Transcendental Conception of
Language-Communication and the Idea of a First Philosophy, a.a.O.

43. Denkt man sich die menschliche Sprachkompetenz als auf einem
angeborenen Regelsystem beruhende Satzgenerationskompetenz im Sinne
Chomsky's, ohne diesen Aspekt durch die (transzendentalpragmatische)
Konzeption einer "kommunikativen Kompetenz" (Habermas) zu ergänzen,
so reproduziert sich m.E. die Apori des "Tractatus": die kommunikative "Performanz" ist dann nichts weiter als rein monologische
Aktualisierung eines fertigen Sprach-Systems + Nachrichtenüber-
tragung. Das Sprachsystem kann nicht - zumindest auch - als immer
wieder erneuerte Institutionalisierung der Kommunikation begriffen
werden. Vgl. hierzu: K. O. Apel, Noam Chomskys Sprachtheorie und die
Philosophie der Gegenwart, a.a.O.

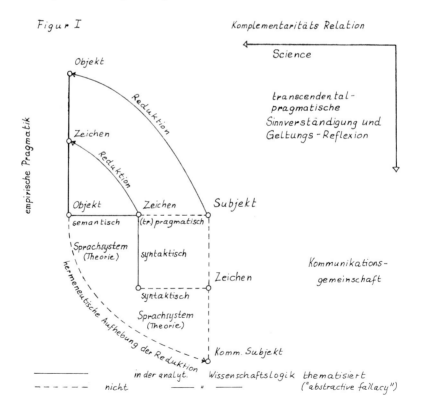

Figur I   Komplementaritäts Relation

ESSLER:

Die Ausführungen von Herrn Apel zeigen, daß im sogenannten "Positi-
vismus-Streit" sich Gegensätze aufgeschaukelt haben, die sachlich
nicht gerechtfertigt sind, daß da Standpunkte eingenommen worden
sind, die man bei einer ruhigen Debatte bestimmt nicht akzeptiert
hätte, und die Kontrahenten von damals und ihre Schüler stimmen
weitgehend in Thesen überein, über die man sich damals die Köpfe
heiß geredet hat. Natürlich ist es nicht so, daß es überhaupt keine
Gegensätze mehr gibt, und es wäre für Sie langweilig, wenn ich nicht
auf solche hinweisen würde. Aber wichtig ist es, daß wir beginnen,
uns nun zu verstehen.

Der Begriff "Verstehen" markiert einen der Punkte, in dem sich die
hermeneutische Schule, der Herr Apel zumindest teilweise zuzurechnen
ist, von der analytischen Schule der Philosophie unterscheidet. Für
Herrn Apel ist "Verstehen" eine Grundkategorie, die vor allem in den
Geisteswissenschaften methodisch zu verwerten ist. In der Analytischen Philosophie wird immer wieder auf die enge Beziehung zwischen
V e r s t e h e n und E r k l ä r e n hingewiesen. Für mich ist
V e r s t e h e n eine spezielle Art des h y p o t h e t i c a l
r e a s o n i n g , des D e n k e n s a l s o b, das sich sprachlich häufig in i r r e a l e n K o n d i t i o n a l s ä t z e n
äußert. Diesen mehr speziellen Unterschied werde ich jedoch im
Folgenden nicht ausführen. Ich möchte vielmehr versuchen, ein für
die Frage der Kommunikation grundsätzliches Problem anzuschneiden,
nämlich die Frage, worin sich die Kommunikation vollzieht; in
Zusammenhang damit kann man dann prüfen, was mit dem Ausdruck
"unbegrenzte Kommunikationsgemeinschaft" sinnvollerweise zu
v e r s t e h e n ist, d.h. hier: wie man ihn zweckmäßigerweise
g e b r a u c h t .

Mein Standpunkt ist der der Formalsprachenphilosophen, nicht der der
ordinary-language-Philosophen, nicht oder jedenfalls nur zum Teil
der der Hermeneutiker. Die Alltagssprachen-Philosophen versuchen,
die lebenden Sprachen durch unzählige Einzelanalysen zu erhellen,
während die Hermeneutiker danach trachten, sie durch eine Gesamt-
schau zu erfassen. Goethe hat hinsichtlich der Naturwissenschaften
wahlweise den einen oder den anderen dieser beiden Standpunkte eingenommen und sich von dem der experimentierenden Naturwissenschaftler, die die Wirklichkeit nicht so lassen, wie sie ist, die sie
vielmehr bewußt verändern, bewußt distanziert.[1] Mein sprachphilosophischer Standpunkt ist nun gerade der der Methode der experimentellen Betrachtung der Sprache, die versucht, an Modellen Sachen zu

zeigen, an Modellen, die so in der uns vorgegebenen Sprachrealität
nicht verwirklicht sind, aber die versucht, mit Verfeinerung und
Präzisierung dieser Modelle diese vorgegebene Wirklichkeit zu
approximieren. Denn Modelle gehören zur Wirklichkeit; sie sind nicht
die g a n z e Wirklichkeit, aber sie erlauben uns, diese gedank-
lich zu erschließen, indem vielschichtige Dinge durch einfache
konstituiert werden und wir dadurch in die Lage versetzt werden,
diese Vielschichtigkeit zu v e r s t e h e n.
Was Kunstsprachen oder formale Sprachen sind, ist bekannt. Sie
bestehen aus 1. einem Wörterverzeichnis, 2. einer Grammatik, die ein
Regelsystem enthält, das erklärt, wie man aus Ausdrücken Sätze,
komplexe Ausdrücke bilden kann, 3. die ein Regelsystem zum Gebrauch
der Ausdrücke in Kontexten enthält, wobei die Ausdrücke durch dieses
Regelsystem zu Begriffen werden (wobei den Ausdrücken durch dieses
System Intensionen zugeschrieben werden, wie man auch manchmal
sagt), und 4. auch aus einer partiellen oder totalen semantischen
Interpretation; im angelsächsischen Sprachgebrauch sagt man statt
"semantische Interpretation" in diesem Sinn auch "mengentheoretische Interpretation" oder "modelltheoretische Interpretation". Auf
Grund dieser Interpretation werden die Ausdrücke, die sprachliche
Entitäten sind, Zeichen für etwas, so daß diese Zeichen für Kommunikationszwecke verwendet werden können. Ohne diese vorausgesetzte
semantische Interpretation wären die Sätze bloße sprachliche Gebilde
ohne Mitteilungswert, so wie uns auch die Schachfiguren nichts über
unsere Welt mitteilen können, und ein S p r a c h s p i e l hätte
dann kommunikativ den gleichen Wert wie ein S c h a c h s p i e l.
Zu untersuchen bleibt noch, in welchem Verhältnis die so charakteri-
sierten S p r a c h e n zu den n a t ü r l i c h e n S p r a -
c h e n (oder A l l t a g s s p r a c h e n), zu den K u n s t-
s p r a c h e n (oder f o r m a l e n S p r a c h e n), zu den
l e b e n d e n S p r a c h e n und zu den t o t e n S p r a -
c h e n stehen. Tote Sprachen sind eindeutig (wenn auch nicht in
jedem Falle explizit) fixiert, sie werden nicht mehr verändert.
Lebende Sprachen hingegen werden verändert, wobei sich diese Änderungen im Normalfall durch ihren Gebrauch und durch die Bedürfnisse
der Sprachbenützer ergeben; nur ganz selten werden solche Änderungen
durch willkürliche Eingriffe einer relativ kleinen Gruppe von Personen erzwungen, etwa, wenn durch irgendeine sich kompetent fühlen-
de Kommission bestimmt wird, daß alle Wörter klein zu schreiben
sind, oder aber, wenn sich eine solche eines Tages einmal aufraffen
würde, die geschriebene Sprache der gesprochenen anzugleichen.

Natürliche Sprachen haben sich aus den Sprachen der Gebärden und der
Schreie der Primaten durch Änderungen der genetischen Voraussetzungen wie auch der Bedürfnisse der einzelnen Personen hinsichtlich der
Kommunikation entwickelt; unüberschaubar viele Mitglieder der jewei-
ligen Kommunikationsgemeinschaft haben zu dieser Entwicklung und
damit zu den jetzigen Formen der menschlichen Sprachen beigetragen.
Kunstsprachen **hingegen sind von überschaubar vielen Personen** (und
oft nur von einer einzigen) in relativ kurzer Zeit so gut wie vollständig entwickelt worden, und zwar im Normalfall mit dem Blick auf
bewußt vorgegebene Zwecke: hinsichtlich der Sprache der "Principia
Mathematica" von Russell und Whitehead war der Zweck die Präzisierung des Logikbegriffs, und hinsichtlich Esperanto von Zamenhof war
dies der Wunsch nach Völkerversöhnung und Abbau nationaler Gegensätze, die sich meist an Sprachgegensätzen entzünden.
Es bedarf wohl keiner weiteren Begründung, daß die Begriffe "natürliche Sprache" und "lebende Sprache" intensionsverschieden sind und
daß gleiches von "Kunstsprache" und "tote Sprache" gilt. Nicht
weiter begründet zu werden braucht auch, daß nicht nur natürliche
Sprachen und lebende Sprachen, sondern auch tote Sprachen und Kunstsprachen für Kommunikationszwecke geeignet sind.
Ich möchte nun einige p e r s u a s i v e a r g u m e n t s für
die These vortragen, daß n a t ü r l i c h e S p r a c h e n
keine S p r a c h e n im vorhin angegebenen Sinn sind, d.h. keine
Sprachen, die durch Vokabular, Grammatik, Regelsystem und Interpretation eindeutig bestimmt sind.
Auf den ersten Blick erscheint diese These, die man auch schlagwort-
artig durch "Natürliche Sprachen gibt es nicht" wiedergeben kann,
widersinnig zu sein: Das Hochdeutsche, so wird man behaupten, ist
eine natürliche Sprache und existiert, da man mit dem Duden das
Vokabular hat, da ihre Grammatik exakt beschrieben werden kann (und
auch teilweise schon ist), da mit dem Grimmschen Wörterbuch und
anderen anerkannten Wortfeldanalysen für die wichtigsten Ausdrücke
der Sprache Regeln zu ihrem Gebrauch gegeben sind[2] und da man auf
diese Weise im Prinzip in der Lage ist, die semantische Interpretation zu ermitteln.
Diese Behauptung ist jedoch irreführend, wie man sich durch folgende
Überlegungen vergegenwärtigen kann: Wenn zwei Personen miteinander
in Kommunikation treten, dann ist es wahrscheinlich, daß sie
n i c h t d i e g l e i c h e S p r a c h e verwenden, und zwar
ist dies umso wahrscheinlicher, je komplexer die vorgegebene
n o r m i e r t e S p r a c h e ist, an **die** sich beide halten

wollen; wenn diese etwa das Hochdeutsche ist, so ist der Wortschatz
der beiden mit an Sicherheit grenzender Wahrscheinlichkeit verschieden, beide verwenden vermutlich nicht genau die gleiche Grammatik
zur Bildung von Sätzen, ihre Regelsysteme zum Gebrauch der Ausdrücke
sind aller Wahrscheinlichkeit nach verschieden, weshalb sie diese
Ausdrücke vermutlich auch nicht gleich interpretieren. Sie sprechen
also nicht die gleiche Sprache, wenn man den Ausdruck "Sprache" so
verwendet, wie dies vorhin angedeutet worden ist.

Es ist naheliegend, dem folgendes entgegenzuhalten: "Selbstverständlich gibt es immer Abweichungen von Normen, nicht nur hinsichtlich
der richtigen Verwendung des Hochdeutschen, sondern auch etwa hinsichtlich der richtigen Durchführung einer Versuchsvorschrift;
Ergebnis solcher Abweichungen sind dann im Normalfall Fehler, und
zwar in einem Fall fehlerhafte Abweichungen vom Hochdeutschen, im
anderen hingegen Meßfehler. Dem widerspricht nicht, daß die Abweichungen gelegentlich durch Gesetze bzw. durch Zusatznormen erfaßt
werden können, sei es durch Beschreibung eines Dialekts, sei es
durch Identifizierung von Störfaktoren." Diese Analogie zwischen
Physik und Linguistik ist wichtig und meines Wissens bisher von
niemanden ausgearbeitet worden. Sie trifft jedoch das vorhin an-
geschnittene Problem nicht vollständig. Man kann sich nämlich ohne
Mühe zwei Gesprächspartner vorstellen, die annähernd das gleiche
Vokabular und annähernd die gleiche Grammatik benützen, die jedoch
Ausdrücke wie "Kritk", "Emanzipation", "Dogmatismus", "Ideologie",
"Freiheit" usw. so unterschiedlich verwenden, daß sie keine Kommunikationsbasis mehr haben, daß sie sich also nicht mehr v e r -
s t e h e n können, jedenfalls nicht mehr in jenen Sachen, zu
deren Formulierung sie derartige Begriffe benötigen.
Selbstverständlich werden sie sich in e i n i g e n Bereichen
verstehen, etwa wenn sie Sätze formulieren, in denen nur Ausdrücke
der Art "Baum", "Wein", "Anti-Baby-Pille" usw. vorkommen: hinsichtlich dieser stimmen ihre Regelsysteme nämlich (praktisch) überein,
hier geht es ihnen also besser als in einem Gespräch mit einem Gast,
der nur Suaheli spricht und dessen Sprache sie nicht kennen;
zwischen ihnen gibt es also nach wie vor eine b e g r e n z t e
K o m m u n i k a t i o n s g e m e i n s c h a f t .
Die Grenzen der Kommunikation werden zwischen verschiedenen Mit-
gliedern einer Sprachgemeinschaft verschieden liegen, doch ist nicht
anzunehmen, daß die Gesamtheit der Benützer einer normierten Sprache
kein Gemeinsames Kommunikationsgebiet mehr haben, so daß zwischen
den individuellen Variationen nur noch die Relation der

F a m i l i e n ä h n l i c h k e i t besteht: jene Ausdrücke, mit
denen wir Mitteilungen machen, die zu unseren unmittelbaren Lebens-
bedürfnissen gehören, wie "Mensch", "Brot" usw., sind fest mit bestimmten Regeln (mit bestimmten Intensionen) verbunden, andere, wie
etwa "Kunstwerk", "Freundschaft" usw., weniger, und noch andere, wie
"Interpretation", "Logik", "Dialektik" usw., offenbar überhaupt
nicht. Hinsichtlich dessen, was die Menschen als entscheidend für
ihre Lebensbedürfnisse a n s e h e n , scheinen sie also nicht
bereit zu sein, die Kommunikationsbasis mutwillig zu zerbrechen.
Zu beantworten bleibt die Frage, was mit dem Postulat einer
u n b e g r e n t z t e n K o m m u n i k a t i o n s g e m e i n -
s c h a f t ausgesagt sein kann, wie man diese zu v e r s t e -
h e n hat. Dazu ist folgendes zu sagen: 1. Die gängigen Kommunika-
tionssprachen als n o r m i e r t e S p r a c h e n (wie etwa das
Hochdeutsche) sind K u n s t s p r a c h e n und haben von ihren
Schöpfern die Tendenz erhalten, t o t e S p r a c h e n zu sein.
2. Die einzelnen Mitglieder eines Sprachraums haben die F ä h i g-
k e i t (die D i s p o s i t i o n), sich solche normierten
Sprachen vollständig anzueignen. 3. Folglich haben zwei beliebige
Gesprächspartner dieses Sprachraums die Fähigkeit, ihre individuellen Sprachen (die partielle und Abweichungen enthaltende Realisie-
rungen jener Dispositionen sind) so abzuändern, daß sie schließlich
eine g e m e i n s a m e S p r a c h e benützen. 4. Darüberhinaus
gibt es mindestens eine normierte Sprache von der Art, daß alle
Menschen die Fähigkeit haben, sie sich vollständig anzueignen.
5. Da sich die einzelnen normierten Sprachen der Menschen in dieser
Hinsicht nicht prinzipiell voneinander unterscheiden, haben somit
alle Menschen die Fähigkeit, sich jede Sprache vollständig anzueignen. 6. Folglich haben beliebige Gesprächspartner die Fähigkeit,
ihre individuellen Sprachen so abzuändern, daß sie, als Folge davon,
eine g e m e i n s a m e S p r a c h e benützen.
Das, was wir "natürliche Sprache" nennen, ist somit eine Disposition
und keine Realität (d.h. keine vorgegebene Sprache, so wie Kunstsprachen vorgegeben sind); sie ist nur in vergleichsweise wenigen
Fällen und nur unter außergewöhnlichen Bedingungen vollständig realisiert, etwa wenn Sprachforscher sie in allen Details untersuchen.
Die Realisierung einer solchen Disposition, einer solchen natürlichen Sprache, führt somit zu einer Kunstsprache, die wegen des sub-
jektiv verständlichen Bedürfnisses solches Forschers, ihre Ergebnisse zu verewigen, außerdem die Tendenz hat, eine tote Sprache zu
werden.

Daß die sogenannten "natürlichen Sprachen" so gut wie nie realisiert
sein sollen und daß sie in diesem Sinn praktisch nicht existieren,
wird manchen verblüffen. Er wird, wenn er dieses Ergebnis nicht akzeptieren will, versuchen müssen, den Unterschied zwischen natürlichen Sprachen und Kunstsprachen anders zu charakterisieren. Naheliegend sind folgende Versuche:
1. "Natürliche Sprachen unterscheiden sich von Kunstsprachen wesentlich dadurch, daß sie Indikatoren enthalten, also von der Art "ich",
"du", "dies", "dort", usw., sowie Regeln zu deren Gebrauch in Co-
texten und Kontexten." Diese Behauptung ist jedoch falsch. Richtig
ist lediglich, daß es von kleineren oder größeren Sprachgruppen
benutzte Sprachen gibt, die solche Indikatoren enthalten, wie etwa
das normierte Deutsch und das normierte Englisch, und daß es einzelne Kunstsprachen gibt, die diese nicht enthalten, wie etwa die
Sprache der "Principia Mathematica". Falsch ist, daß es keine Kunstsprachen gibt, die sie enthalten, und es ist denkbar, daß es auch
einzelne gewachsene Sprachen von Stämmen in wenig erforschten Zeiten
oder Gebieten gibt oder gegeben hat, die sie ebenfalls nicht enthalten. - Daß man Indikatoren in jedem Fall Kunstsprachen wie auch
Alltagssprachen zur Abkürzung und Vereinfachung der Ausdrucksweise
hinzufügen kann, ist nicht zu bestreiten, ist aber ebenfalls als
Unterscheidungskriterium ungeeignet. Wer sich aber entschlossen hat,
eine normierte Alltagssprache und ihre Logik zum Gegenstand seiner
Untersuchungen zu machen, der tut damit im Prinzip nicht anderes
als einer, der eine Kunstsprache und deren Logik reflektiert. Beide
sind nur in beschränktem Maße im Alltag realisiert, die eine vielleicht mehr, die andere hingegen weniger. Aber es ist nur ein gra-
dueller und kein prinzipieller Unterschied.
2. Folgender Unterschied kann allerdings nicht geleugnet werden: die
gewachsenen Sprachen unseres Alltags drücken zumindest teilweise
unsere Lebensgewohnheiten, unsere Lebensbedürfnisse und unsere Welt-
anschauung aus, während Kunstsprachen wegen ihres experimentellen
Charakters darauf häufig keine Rücksicht nehmen. Ich sehe diesen
Unterschied jedoch gerade als zureichenden Grund dafür an, sich mit
Kunstsprachen zu befassen; denn Sprachen des Alltags haben im allgemeinen eine geringe Variabilität und eine große Konservativität, und
drücken dann weniger u n s e r e Lebensbedürfnisse und Weltan-
schauungen, sondern vielmehr die v e r g a n g e n e r Z e i t e n
aus. U n s e r e Bedürfnisse können sich ja inzwischen geändert
haben, und es könnte sich für eine solche neue Situation eine
a n d e r e Weltsicht als adäquate erweisen. Wer neue Sprachen

konzipiert, schafft damit zumindest gelegentlich neue Arten des
Denkens und verhilft auf jeden Fall sich und anderen dazu, sich von
den Fesseln der hergebrachten und unreflektierten Sprachen zu befreien und deren Vorzüge wie auch Nachteile mit denen der neuen zu
vergleichen.

3. Man wird geneigt sein, folgenden Unterschied zwischen Kunstsprachen und Sprachen des Alltags zu sehen: "Kunstsprachen sind i.a. der
Gegenstand des Reflektierens, während diese Reflexionen gerade in
der Alltagssprache oder in Alltagssprachen vorgenommen und vollzogen
werden." Richtig ist hieran soviel, daß dies h ä u f i g so ist.
Falsch ist, daß man Alltagssprachen n i c h t zum Gegenstand der
Untersuchungen m a c h e n kann, und daß man Reflexionen über
andere Sprachen nicht in Kunstsprachen formulieren oder vollziehen
kann.

4. Naheliegend ist dann der Einwand, daß die Alltagssprachen immer
letzte Metasprachen sein müssen. Alle Kunstsprachen erhalten demnach
ihren Sinn erst dadurch, daß ihren Ausdrücken vermittels der Alltagssprachen Bedeutungen zugeordnet werden. Ohne diese Zuordnungen
bleiben sie uninterpretierte und unverständliche Kalküle. Dies gilt
ohne Zweifel für die erstmalige Vermittlung einer Kunstsprache wie
sie auch für den gilt, dessen Muttersprache z.B. eine Variation des
Deutschen ist und der eine Spielart des Englischen erlernen möchte.
Ohne sein ihm verständliches Deutsch als Muttersprache bleibt ihm
der Kalkül E n g l i s c h unverständlich. Aber das ändert sich
mit den Jahren, wenn er mit dem Englischen hinreichend vertraut
geworden ist. Und seinen Kindern, die vielleicht nur Englisch
können, wird es lächerlich vorkommen, wenn ihnen ein Philosoph erklären würde, daß Deutsch ihre letzte Metasprache wäre, und sie ihre
Sprache nur verstünden, weil sie durch die deutsche Alltagssprache
interpretiert sei. Ähnlich kann man bei Esperanto argumentieren und
in gleicher Weise bei jeder anderen Kunstsprache. Der Einwand ist
also unhaltbar.

5. Er könnte jedoch in folgender Weise modifiziert werden: "Eine
Alltagssprache besteht aus einer Folge von Sprachstufen, wobei diese
Folge nicht ein für allemal determiniert ist. Je nachdem, über
welche Teile der Alltagssprache man reflektieren möchte, ob über
einen, der nur Aussagen über die Dinge der Außenwelt enthält, oder
über einen, der zusätzlich Reflexionen über diese Aussagen enthält,
oder über einen, der außerdem noch Reflexionen über diese Reflexionen enthält, usw., wird diese Folge zweigliedrig, dreigliedrig,
viergliedrig, und so fort. Kunstsprachen sind hingegen stets

e i n e Sprache." Diese Behauptung beruht auf einem falschen Ver-
ständnis von Kunstsprachen. In diesen sind, wenn sie von ihren
Schöpfern nicht so ausdrucksarm gestaltet worden sind, durchaus
Reflexionen über andere Sprachen möglich, und da diese anderen
Sprachen in der vorgegebenen Kunstsprache als Kalkül entworfen und
beschrieben werden, lassen sich in ihr auch die entsprechenden
Sprachstufungen wiedergeben. Da man Kunstsprachen genauso ändern
kann wie natürliche Sprachen - man denke nur an die verschiedenen
Änderungen der Sprache der "Principia Mathematica" - lassen sich auf
diese Weise auch Arten von Reflexionssprachen in ihr darstellen.
6. Dann aber ist es naheliegend, jenen Einwand folgendermaßen abzu-
wandeln: "Sprachen des Alltags sind reflexiv, Kunstsprachen sind es
nicht; d.h., in einer Sprache des Alltags kann über eben diese
Sprache als Ganzes reflektiert werden, in Kunstsprachen jedoch nur
über andere Sprachen." Doch auch dies ist unzutreffend: denn einmal
kann man, wie wir seit Gödel wissen, bestimmte Aussagen ü b e r
eine Sprache auch i n dieser Sprache formulieren, und wem das
Verfahren der Gödelisierung suspekt ist, den darf ich auf Quines
Protosyntax verweisen, die bekanntlich selbstanwendbar ist. Zum
anderen wird man sich fragen müssen, wo die Grenzen dieser
Reflexionsmöglichkeiten liegen...Diesen Punkt möchte ich etwas ausführlicher behandeln, nicht weil ich hier etwas Neues zu sagen
hätte - wer sich um diese Fragen ernsthaft bemüht hat, weiß schon
längst, wo diese Grenzen liegen - sondern weil die sogenannten
"kritischen Theorien" in diesem Punkt eine beispiellose Kritiklosig-
keit an den Tag gelegt haben.
Gegeben sei eine Sprache - es muß nicht unbedingt eine Kunstsprache
sein - d.h., gegeben sei ein Wörterverzeichnis, eine Grammatik, die
besagt, wie aus den Wörtern Sätze und komplexe Ausdrücke gebildet
werden können, für die Konstante der Sprache ein System von Regeln,
womit jeder Konstante eine Intension zugeordnet wird und eine semantische (modelltheoretische, mengentheoretische) Interpretation
dieser Sprache. Durch diese Interpretation werden bestimmte Wörter
der Sprache im Sinne von Frege (nicht im Sinne der ordinary language
philosophy) Bedeutungsträger, d.h. Zeichen für etwas und somit für
Mitteilungszwecke brauchbar. Bezugnehmend auf diese Interpretation
kann der Wahrheitsbegriff für die Sätze der Sprache rekursiv
definiert werden. Für das Folgende ist allerdings d i e s e Einführung des Wahrheitsbegriffs nicht wesentlich, d.h. er könnte auch
ande rs eingeführt werden, vorausgesetzt, daß hierbei die im wesentlichen auch schon auf Aristoteles und Platon zurückgehende

T a r s k i - K o n v e n t i o n   erfüllt ist. Es wird zusätzlich
vorausgesetzt, daß für diese Sprache eine Logik definiert ist, sei
es über den Wahrheitsbegriff, sei es anders, daß das Gesamtsystem
S p r a c h e   p l u s   L o g i k   widerspruchsfrei ist und daß es
genügend ausdrucksreich ist: letzteres soll einschließen, daß in ihr
die für sie definierten syntaktischen Begriffe wie "Wort", "Satz",
usw. ausdrückbar sind. Dann kann bewiesen werden (und ist erstmals
von Tarski bewiesen worden), daß weder der für diese Sprache definierte Interpretationsbegriff noch der für sie definierte Wahrheitsbegriff in ihr ausdrückbar ist, daß es also keine Ausdrücke dieser
Sprache und den ihnen zugeordneten Regelsystemen für ihren Gebrauch
gibt, die im Sinne der vorgegebenen Interpretation und der durch sie
gegebenen Übersetzungsmöglichkeit   den Interpretationsbegriff und
den Wahrheitsbegriff in dieser Sprache ausdrücken. Es kann dann also
in dieser Sprache wohl über syntaktische Merkmale dieser Sprache
gesprochen werden, nicht aber - wegen der vorausgesetzten Widerspruchsfreiheit des Gesamtsystems - über die Interpretation ihrer
Ausdrücke und über die Wahrheit ihrer Aussagen.
Dieses Ergebnis verdient festgehalten zu werden: Reflexionen in
einer Sprache und über diese Sprache - und, wenn ich das richtig
sehe, verstehen sich hermeneutische Reflexionen immer als derartige
Reflexionen - erfassen nicht den genuin semantischen Bereich, der
für Kommunikationszwecke relevant ist. Das Überhören solcher Ergebnisse der Metalogik ist, glaube ich, heute nur ganz schwer zu entschuldigen.
Es ist nun naheliegend, zu versuchen, diese Grenzen der Reflexion
und des Reflektierens folgerdermaßen zu hintergehen: Es wird die
Syntax nicht durch eine Semantik, sondern durch eine Pragmatik ergänzt, wobei hier gleichgültig ist, ob es sich um eine empirische
oder um eine transzendentale handelt. Es liegt auf der Hand, wohin
dieser Ausweg führt. Wenn diese Pragmatik weder explizit noch implizit ein sematisches Vokabular enthält, wird sie durchaus in der
vorgegebenen Sprache formulierbar sein, so daß   nach wie vor   i n
der Sprache   ü b e r   diese Sprache und ihre Methodologie reflektiert werden kann. Nur ist bei dieser Methodologie der semantische
Aspekt und damit der für die Kommunikation relevante Teil der
Sprache   a u s g e k l a m m e r t   (um mit den Schwaben zu sprechen). Wenn die Pragmatik jedoch zumindest implizit eine Semantik
in diesem Sinne enthält, dann sind deren Begriffe sowie jene pragmatischen, mittels derer sie definierbar sind, nicht in der Sprache
ausdrückbar und gehören damit nicht zum Bereich der in dieser

Sprache möglichen Reflexionen. Unter der Voraussetzung der Widerspruchsfreiheit des Gesamtsystems S p r a c h e p l u s L o g i k
gibt es also in ihr Grenzen des Reflektierens, die man nicht über-
sehen sollte.

ANMERKUNGEN

1.   Vgl. R. Carnap, P h i l o s o p h i c a l F o u n d a-
t i o n s o f P h y s i c s, Abschnitt 4, sowie W. K. Essler,
W i s s e n s c h a f t s t h e o r i e III, Kap.V.
2.   Auch viele Gesetze können als solche Regeln zum Gebrauch von
Ausdrücken verstanden werden, etwa das Weingesetz, das den Gebrauch
des Ausdrucks "Wein" bestimmt (und überdies noch Verkäufern von
Flüssigkeiten, die sich nicht an diesen Gebrauch halten, mit
Sanktionen droht).

BAR-HILLEL:

I have decided to simply skip my prepared talk, since it would make
little sense to burden you with so many topics at one time. Let us,
therefore, concentrate upon the problems discussed by Apel and
Essler; this should do for this morning and probably for a few more
days.

I shall, then, restrict myself to a number of independent comments
and hope that somehow a more general view will emerge.

Let me start with a paraphrase of Heine: "Denn es will mich schier
bedünken, daß die beiden Vorträge, die wir eben gehört haben,
keineswegs stinken." I see no serious difficulties in an attempt to
synthesize the views of Apel and Essler - and of a few others, for
good measure -, similar to the attempt I made in Amsterdam in 1967
at a Sympósium on F o r m a l L o g i c a n d S e m a n t i c s
held during the Third International Congress for Logic, Methodology
and Philosophy of Science (a summary of which was published by
J.F. Staal in F o u n d a t i o n s o f L a n g u a g e, 5 (1969)
pp. 256-284) to establish an e n t e n t e c o r d i a l e
between Oxford, M.I.T. and U.C.L.A., an e n t e n t e which I
regarded then and regard now as not only possible but even as
necessary if we want to arrive at a reasonable conception of
language and philosophy of language.

(1) It has always been a strange phenomenon for me, for which I have
no serious explanation to this very day, that Kant, who lectured
and published about everything on earth, not only on theoretical and
practical philosophy, but also on astronomy, geography, anthropology
and almost any other subject on which lectures were given at the
time in German universities, did not envolve any philosophy of
language worth this name, that language was never a problem for him
and was hardly discussed by him beyond commonplaces. For me, then,
Apel's interpretation is close to self-evident. What Kant should
have discussed under the heading of philosophy of language he,
unfortunately, treated as transcendental philosophy, so that Apel's
proposed transformation is for me the most natural thing.

(2) I am not sure whether the opposition between behaviouristic
pragmatics and transcendental pragmatics, mentioned by Apel, is a
substantial one and whether it would not be worth while, and perhaps
even necessary, at least for those who would like to avoid the
associations which are traditionally connected with the word
"transcendental", to employ a different formulation. I think that
"transcendental", to paraphrase Carnap, is only a not too clear

fusion of three rather different concepts. The first element is
"mental". In the last years it has turned out that behaviouristic
pragmatics is indeed not enough. Since Chomsky only few authors are
afraid of the word "mental". The second element could be termed
"hyper-hypothesis" ("Oberhypothese"), following Stegmüller, i.e.
something that is presupposed in the discussion of hypotheses proper
and not questioned during this discussion, though every hyper-
hypothesis can, of course, itself be questioned when the opportunity
arises. The third element is "methodology". If I remember correctly,
this word did not occur in either Apel's or Essler's talks. If we
understand "transcendental" as a combination of "mental", "hyper-
hypothesis" and "methodology", we can eliminate the metaphysical
associations connected with it in standard philosophical usage, and
then, to paraphrase Quine's well-known remark about "ontology", we
can use it freely, as I myself (and Chomsky before me) started to do
recently, after a boycott of three decades or so.
(3) The sentence I am now dead is by no means ill-formed or
ungrammatical. In my logic lectures I often tell the story about
that eccentric English lord, from whose coffin, when all his family
had sorrowfully assembled for his burial, there emerged, loud and
clear, a (tape-recorded) speech beginning with Now that I am dead...
- I shall spare you the end of the story. Let me only insist that
the stunning impact of this speech was due in part precisely to the
fact that the sentence I am dead, forming part of it, was not
ungrammatical. The situation can, of course, be much better
described by stating that the u t t e r a n c e of this sentence,
under the circumstances, was odd, bizarre, strange, etc. I regard it
as very annoying to construct the s y n t a x of English in such a
way as to deny this string its sentential character. The price one
would have to pay for such a conception seems to me so high that I,
for one, am not willing to pay it.
(4) The arguments presented by Essler for the necessity, or at least
the importance, of using constructed languages and for the
H i n t e r g e h b a r k e i t (avoidability) of the natural
languages, even as ultimate metalanguages, did not fully convince
me. I would like to call your attention to what I still regard as
the best discussion by far of the problem of constructed languages
versus natural languages, in particular with regard to the treatment
of philosophical problems, between Strawson and Carnap in T h e
P h i l o s o p h y   o f   R u d o l f   C a r n a p (1963).
Some of Essler's formulations - whose major intention was probably

épater le bourgeois - might irritate some people so
much that they will no longer see the truth behind them. For
instance, I would not recommend using such formulations as "There
are no natural languages". There exist already other, less
misleading, formulations for what Essler intended to say thereby.
I cannot see why we should not use them for clarifying the
situation. Most of us know that, i n a d d i t i o n to
languages, there exist dialects, idiolects, language stages,
language varieties, language registers and the like. If a Bavarian
does not understand a Prussian - whatever this may mean - , then
this fact can easily be described in customary formulation. Whether
it is useful to interpolate between natural languages and
constructed languages a "third", such as "normal" (or "regimented",
or "cannonical") natural languages, should be carefully studied.
I, for one, tend to believe that such an interpolation will turn out
to be of use, perhaps even of decisive importance.
(5) I have often expressed my belief that there could not be any
natural languages which will not contain deictic or anaphoric
expressions. Their occurrence in these languages, to use a
fashionable term, is a s u b s t a n t i v e u n i v e r s a l.
My claim is not based on an inductive generalization from the five
or six languages with which I am familiar. I would rather want to
insist that a language which contains no deictic or anaphoric
expressions is just not "natural". To see my point, let me ask you,
once more, to perform the following thought experiment: In 1984, the
world government prohibits the use of such expressions in verbal
communications. What would happen?

DISKUSSION:

Ungeheuer: Danke schön, Herr Bar-Hillel. Bevor ich Herrn Apel zu
sprechen bitte, möchte ich gerne Herrn Essler Gelegenheit geben,
ganz kurz zu den Äußerungen von Herrn Bar-Hillel Stellung zu nehmen.
Essler: Selbstverständlich habe ich nicht behaupten wollen, ich
spräche keine natürliche Sprache. Jetzt zum Beispiel tue ich es! Ich
kenne die Diskussion zwischen Carnap und Strawson und halte sie
nicht für ganz so gut wie Herr Bar-Hillel, sonst hätte ich darüber
referiert. Vielleicht sollte man, bis man hier klar sieht, über
n a t ü r l i c h e S p r a c h e n oder o r d i n a r y
l a n g u a g e s überhaupt nicht reden, sondern stattdessen über
b e n u t z t e S p r a c h e n sowie über n o r m i e r t e
S p r a c h e n; das würde, glaube ich, manche Verwirrung vermeiden.
Benutzte Sprachen können nämlich Kunstsprachen wie auch natürliche
sein.
Bar-Hillel: Nur eine schnelle Bemerkung! Das ist verwirrend!
Natürliche Sprache ist keineswegs dasselbe wie ordinary language.
Ich möchte Sie davor warnen. Herr von Savigny, der ja nicht hier
ist, hat große Schwierigkeiten gehabt, als er die Worte "ordinary
language" ins Deutsche hat übersetzen müssen. Was ist dabei heraus-
gekommen?
Essler: "Normalsprache".
Bar-Hillel: "Normalsprache" - was wahrscheinlich kein normaler
Deutscher überhaupt verstehen kann.
Ungeheuer: Sind Sie so sicher, daß "ordinary language" im Englischen
so eindeutig ist?
Bar-Hillel: Nein, das bestimmt nicht. Aber, daß keine Korrespondenz
zwischen "ordinary language" und "natürlicher Sprache" besteht,
dessen bin ich mir sicher!
Ungeheuer: Jetzt würde ich gern Herrn Apel Gelegenheit zur Beantwortung der Frage von Herrn Bar-Hillel geben. Herr Apel, wenn Sie
einverstanden sind, konzentrieren wir uns vielleicht auf den ersten
Punkt, den Herr Bar-Hillel erwähnt hat; die möglichen Vorstellungen
Carnaps über das, was "transzendental" heißt. Unsere Problematik ist
genau, inwieweit eine transzendentale Pragmatik, ob universal oder
nicht, die Bedingungen der Möglichkeit für zwischenmenschliche
Kommunikation enthält. Wie d a s zu verstehen ist, könnte sich
vielleicht auch aus den Bemerkungen von Herrn Apel ergeben. Vorweg
würde ich aber gerne gern Herrn Bar-Hillel bitten, noch einmal die
Komponenten anzugeben, die in seinem Verständnis und in Anlehnung an

Carnap eine Vermischung darstellen und das repräsentieren, was bei
Herrn Apel als das Transzendentale aufgebaut wird.
Bar-Hillel: Carnap hat im Jahre 1934 von Erkenntnistheorie als einer
unklaren Vermischung von **drei bestimmten** Elementen gesprochen. Ich
wollte damit keineswegs behaupten, daß meine analoge Behauptung über
"transzendent" Carnap zuzuschieben sei. Was ich sagen wollte, war,
daß es in der Tat drei Elemente gibt, die von der behavioristischen
Pragmatik nicht oder jedenfalls nicht genügend behandelt werden.
Die Reduktion der mentalistischen Ausdrücke auf behavioristische ist
bisher mißglückt. Aus dem Mißlingen dieses Versuches sollte man
natürlich nicht folgern, daß mentalistische Terme nicht benutzt
werden dürfen. Das zweite Element ist dann: Methodologie. Ich
glaube, daß das, was Herr Apel bei Kant die Bedingungen der Möglichkeit nennt, in der Methodologie von Wissenschaften heutzutage behandelt wird. Drittens: das Element der Oberhypothese. Wenn ich Hypothesen oder Theorien vergleichen will, einschätzen will, zwischen
ihnen wählen will, so ist es beinahe selbstverständlich, daß man
häufig von einer in diesem Zusammenhang nicht mehr hinterfra**gten**
oder thematisierten Oberhypothese ausgeht. Nicht nur ist das keineswegs eine irgendwie zu beanstandende, sondern eine absolut notwendi-
ge Arbeitsweise, wobei, wie gesagt, diese Oberhypothese selbstverständlich bei passender Gelegenheit wieder thematisiert und hinter-
fragt werden kann. Eine Untersuchung kann dann in diesem Sinne
transzendental sein, daß sie auf Oberhypothesen beruht, die bei
dieser Gelegenheit nicht in Frage gestellt werden. Wenn jemand in
diesem Zusammenhang auch das Wort "metaphysisch" wieder einführen
will, habe ich persönlich auch nichts dagegen. Oberhypothesen bilden
dann den gesunden Kern der sogenannten "metaphysischen Anfangsgründe
der Wissenschaft." Wenn diese Formulierung jemanden helfen wird,
seinen metaphysischen Komplex loszuwerden, dann würde ich mich
freuen.
Ungeheuer: Wenn **Sie damit** einverstanden sind, hören wir zuerst die
Antwort von Herrn Apel. Ich bitte aber, im Auge zu behalten, daß die
von Herrn Bar-Hillel gezeigte Toleranz doch nicht die sachliche
Differenz beeinträchtigt.
Apel: **Ja,** wir wollen uns verständigen, das ist klar. Aber es darf
natürlich nicht die Fraternisierung auf Kosten des möglichen Consens
gehen. Ich darf vielleicht dies vorausschicken: ich habe immer dies
grandiose Unternehmen des Logischen Empirismus gerade deshalb bewun-
dert, weil es ein klar geschnittenes Modell war, das unter Umständen
eben auch klar scheitern konnte und von dem jemand dann etwas lernen

kann. Deswegen halte ich es - ich darf das vielleicht einmal sagen -
nicht für fruchtbar, wenn die eine Seite so tolerant argumentiert,
als wolle sie sagen: "Wir Logische Empiristen sind gar nicht so
schlimme Menschen, wie das immer hingestellt wird." Dabei werden nur
zu oft Dinge, die vorher in einer harten Form wirklich einmal behauptet worden sind, so langsam aus dem Verkehr gezogen, ohne daß
öffentlich auch darüber reflektiert worden ist, was nun eigentlich
dabei herausgekommen ist, was sich bewährt hat und was gescheitert
ist. Entschuldigen Sie bitte, wenn das so hart klingt.
Ich möchte gerne zwei Statements machen: Eines zum Titel "Transzendentalpragmatik" und eines zum Thema "Verhältnis von Kunstsprache
und - wie man das Ding auch nennen soll - "Umgangssprache" oder
"natürliche Sprache" (das ist ein besonderes Problem!)". Zunächst zu
dem Thema "Transzendentalpragmatik", und ob das, was ich im Sinne
hatte, getroffen wird durch das , was Herr Bar-Hillel jetzt aus-
geführt hat. Ich möchte der Reihe nach vorgehen: Zuerst zum Punkt
"Mentalismus" versus "Behaviorismus". Dazu würde ich sagen: in der
Form, wie es Herr Bar-Hillel jetzt gesagt hat, ist es nicht genau
das, was mich eigentlich interessiert. Ich bin eigentlich davon
überzeugt, daß dieser Gegensatz ("Mentalismus" - "Behaviorismus")
nicht der entscheidende und interessante ist. Ich glaube, man
könnte mit einer gewissen Übertreibung sagen: der ist interessant
in Zusammenhang der Kontroverse zwischen Behaviorismus und Introspektionismus, sehr wohl, aber nicht bei dem, was ich jetzt meine.
Man könnte sagen: beides - Behaviorismus und Mentalismus qua Introspektionismus - enthält einen Begriff von Beobachtung! Die einen
denken an externe Beobachtungen und die anderen an Selbstbeobachtung. Aber worum es z.B. in der Hermeneutik geht oder in dem, was
ich transzendentale hermeneutische Reflexion nenne - da geht es
nicht um Selbstbeobachtung oder Introspektion. Vielmehr geht es in
einem anderen Sinn um "Mentalismus"! Ich würde beinahe folgendes
einander entgegenstellen: I n t r o s p e k t i v e B e o b -
a c h t u n g e n u n d e x t e r n e B e o b a c h t u n g e n
im Sinne des Behaviorismus gehören auf die e i n e Seite und auf
die a n d e r e Seite gehört S e l b s t v e r s t ä n d n i s
i n d e r S i t u a t i o n, i m p l i z i t o d e r e x p l i -
z i t r e f l e x i v e s S e l b s t v e r s t ä n d n i s, das
ohne Schwierigkeiten umgesetzt werden kann in das Verständnis der
Anderen im Rahmen eines Sprachspiels, in dem beide Seiten beteiligt
sind - oder einer symbolisch vermittelten Interaktion im Sinne von
Georg Herbert Mead. Und das war die von mir intendierte Pointe,

wenn ich sagte: wenn man durch hermeneutisches Verstehen in ein
Sprachspiel hineinkommt, dann holt man es gewissermaßen zurück in
die transzendentale Dimension, dann sind wir plötzlich in der
intersubjektiven oder interpersonalen Beziehung der transzendentalen
Kommunikationsgemeinschaft (s. Schema I). Hier besteht also noch ein
Problem jenseits von Behaviorismus und Mentalismus (im Sinne von
Introspektionismus).
Dann zweitens "Methodologie"! Methodologie ist ja besonders das
Stichwort der "Popperschen" Richtung der modernen Wissenschaftstheorie und analytischen Philosophie. Dazu würde ich sagen: Ich habe
in der Tat die Ambition, daß in die transzendental-pragmatische
Wissenschaftstheorie, die von den Bedingungen der Möglichkeit und
Gültigkeit von Erkenntnis, von Wissenschaft handeln soll, das methodologische Problem hineingehört und "aufzuheben" ist. Und deshalb
habe ich die normativen Prinzipien im Sinne der geforderten Consens-
bildung in der unbegrenzten Kommunikationsgemeinschaft eingeführt;
denn das ist ein Punkt - das möchte ich betonen -, der mich mit
Popper verbindet und auch mit Erlangen, mit Lorenzen selbstverständlich. Normative Prinzipien sind unbedingt erforderlich; sie ersetzen sogar in gewisser Weise das, was bei Kant immer schon garantiert war durch eine metaphysische Setzung eines "Bewußtseins überhaupt", das objektiv gültige Erkenntnis ihrer Form nach a priori
garantiert. Dieser Rest von dogmatischer Metaphysik soll in einer
transzendentalen Pragmatik abgeschafft werden. Was dann übrigbleibt,
ist dies: wir sind auf Gedeih und Verderb auf V e r s t ä n d i -
g u n g angewiesen. Deswegen brauchen wir im Sinne Kants regulative
Prinzipien und Postulate, normative Postulate; das bleibt vom Kantianismus übrig. Das bedeutet nicht,daß ich nun mit Popper in jeder
Hinsicht übereinstimme; denn jetzt muß gleich noch dazu gesagt werden, daß der transzendental-philosophische Anspruch mehr ist als nur
der methodologische Anspruch. Vielleicht kann man das aber besser
erläutern, wenn man zum dritten Punkt übergeht: Oberhypothesen!
Hier scheint mir jetzt ein Mißverständnis im Spiel zu sein, wenn ich
recht sehe. Mir scheint, daß heute zwei Tendenzen da sind, von der
analytischen Wissenschaftslogik zu einer transformierten Transzendentalphilosophie überzugehen. Die eine Tendenz hält sich m.E. immer
noch in der semantischen Ebene der Abstraktion vom **Erkenntnissubjekt**
Was ich jetzt meine, hat man neuerdings "Ontosemantik" genannt. (Der
Terminus ist von Herrn G.Janoska eingeführt worden und ist dann von
Herrn Specht, der ja hier wohl anwesend ist, aufgenommen worden.)
In dieser Diskussion liegen m.E. die Bestrebungen, daß man allerlei

"frameworks", sei es Theorien, sei es Sprachspiel-Rahmen, daß man
sie als Regelsysteme interpretiert (ich glaube, auch in dem neuesten
Buch von Herrn Essler ist das so) und zeigt, was ja richtig ist:
Hier ist - in Gestalt syntaktisch-semantischer Regeln oder impliziter
ter Definitionen, die mit der Theoriebildung eingeführt werden - ein
Moment des Synthetisch-Apriorischen vorausgesetzt. Die "frameworks"
haben gewissermaßen eine quasi transzendentale Funktion. Ich würde
nun sagen: in dieser Ebene des Denkens kann man dann auch von Oberhypothesen reden. Dabei bleibt man immer noch in der Dimension
möglicher semantischer Regel-Systeme, möglicher theoretischer
Rahmen. Was mir da fehlt,ist: hinter allen möglichen theoretischen
Rahmen steckt dies: daß wir uns über sie verständigen. Wollen Sie
sich bitte mal einen theoretischen Hyper-Rahmen im Sinne von Oberhypothesen vorstellen! Welcher Rahmen könnte die von mir gemeinte
transzendentale Funktion ausüben? Da besteht immer noch ein Problem
der K o n v e n t i o n, das er sozusagen im Rücken hat. Bei dieser
Gelegenheit sollte man doch beachten, daß alle Entwicklungen der
modernen Wissenschaftstheorie auf ein letztes Restproblem hinausge-
laufen sind: bei Popper, bei Carnap und auch bei Wittgenstein ergibt
sich das Problem , daß da irgendwo K o n v e n t i o n e n (Über-
einkünfte) eingeführt werden müssen. Hinter den Konventionen nun
steckt mein Problem: die Frage: W a s   s i n d   d i e   B e d i n-
g u n g e n   d e r   M ö g l i c h k e i t   u n d   G ü l t i g k e i t
v o n   K o n v e n t i o n e n? Denn die Konventionen werden auch
noch in der Kommunikationsgemeinschaft der Wissenschaftler, im Vor-
blick auf mögliche Zweckmäßigkeit und im Anschluß an wissenschafts-
geschichtliche Kontexte zustandegebracht. Warum soll man nun nicht
fragen dürfen nach den Bedingungen der Möglichkeit und Gültigkeit
zweckmäßiger Konventionen? Damit ist m.E. das Problem der Reflexion
auf die Bedingungen der Möglichkeit einer Verständigung in der
Interpretationsgemeinschaft der Wissenschaftler gestellt; und das
ist erst meine Dimension einer transzendentalen Pragmatik. Soviel
vielleicht zu Herrn Bar-Hillel.
Und dann käme als zweites noch eine Bemerkung zu Herrn Essler.
Zunächst einmal kann ich Herrn Essler sehr weit entgegenkommen. Denn
ich bin von Hause aus, als hermeneutisch-geschichtlich denkender
Mensch, wie Sie das ja in meinem Buch von 1963 noch verfolgen können,
daran gewöhnt, diese Dinge gar nicht in solch abstrakten Dichotomien
zu denken wie: Kunstsprache versus "ordinary language" (oder was das
Gegenstück sein soll), sondern ich hätte zunächst eher so gedacht:
Schon seit dem wir Definitionen haben, und damit Begriffe, Logik

und Grammatik und dergleichen, seit den Griechen also, zeigt sich,
daß die Sprache nicht ein Naturgebilde ist. Das wußte ja Humboldt
schon, daß Sprache wie alles Kulturelle, zugleich künstlich u n d
natürlich ist. Deswegen ja auch der Streit "Thesei" versus "Physei"
schon im Altertum. Deswegen auch Sprachformierung in der
Renaissance; "lingua regulata" als das große Thema! Die Sprache ist
als naturwüchsige immer unfertig; sie fordert uns geradezu auf, an
ihr zu arbeiten, und mit der Einführung der Definitionen in der
griechischen Philosophie wurde ja ein ganz enormer Schritt in diese
Richtung getan, denn seitdem haben wir Begriffsbildung; und es ist
ein interessantes Phänomen, daß in der Ebene der philosophisch-
wissenschaftlichen Begriffsbildung, die immer noch in den "natürlichen" Sprachen vor sich geht, bereits eine enorme semantische Ver-
einheitlichung der Bildungssprache stattgefunden hat - oberhalb der
Ebene der sogenannten Muttersprachen mit ihren "inhaltlichen Fel-
dern" usw. Die Ebene der durch Definition vermittelten philosophisch
-wissenschaftlichen Bildungssprache ist schon der Anfang, wenn Sie
so wollen, von Kunstsprache; und die Leibnizsche Idee einer künstlichen Universalsprache der Wissenschaft ist gewissermaßen nur die
historische Aufgipfelung dieses Prinzips. Und ich könnte mich dazu
verstehen, im gewissen Sinne mit Wittgenstein die Kunstsprachen -
übrigens meine ich nicht Esperanto in diesem Zusammenhang, sondern
nur die formalisierten Sprachen der Wissenschaftslogik - ebenso wie
die älteren Fachsprachen, an denen schon Leibniz so enorm interessiert war, als "Vorstädte" der immer schon gebrauchteñ Sprache zu
bezeichnen. Aber dann entsteht doch die ernste Frage: inwiefern kann
man denn eigentlich sagen, man kann eine Kunstsprache gebrauchen?
Was heißt das denn, wenn man eine Kunstsprache gebraucht? Was geschieht denn da? Geschieht da nicht dies, daß man dann das formal-
sprachliche System wieder zurückintegriert in den immer schon bestehenden Sprachgebrauch, wo dann die Deixis hinzukommt und die
interpersonale Kommunikation, - daß man es also wieder zurückintegriert in die gebrauchte Sprache, und das ist ja eben die natürlich-
künstliche Umgangssprache. Diese natürlich-künstliche Gebrauchssprache würde ich der Kunstsprache entgegenstellen. Aber diese Ent-
gegenstellung, meine ich, sollte man nicht in Frage stellen, und
zwar aus folgendem Grund: Es hatte ja eine geniale Pointe, als man
sagte, wir wollen einmal von der gebrauchten Sprache im ganzen ab-
strahieren, als man mit G.Boole sagte: wir wollen erst einen syntaktischen Kalkül entwerfen und diesen dann semantisch interpretieren. Es hatte insofern eine geniale Pointe, als man da von vielem

abstrahierte, was die Gebrauchssprachen universal verwendbar und
logisch problematisch macht. Wenn Herr Essler jetzt so vorgehen
möchte, daß er auch die pragmatischen Vorzüge der (natürlich-
künstlichen) Gebrauchssprache für die Kunstsprachen reklamiert,
dann sieht das für mich so aus: - Ich darf das mal an einem
nis verdeutlichen - : Ich hatte mal eine Diskussion mit dem Kyber-
netiker Karl Steinbuch über die Frage, ob wir jemals imstande sein
würden, Computer zu konstruieren, die den Menschen total simulieren!
Diese Frage war natürlich im Sinne einer metaphysischen Diskussion
überhaupt nicht zwischen uns zu behandeln! Aber schließlich kam ich
auf folgenden Einfall: Ich sagte Herrn Steinbuch, der die totale
Simulation verteidigte: Sie scheinen mir zwei unvereinbare Ziele zu
verfolgen, - und ich habe den Verdacht, daß das jetzt auch hier in
Herrn Esslers Argumentationsstrategie so ist. - Man kann doch nicht
folgendes beides wollen: 1. den gewaltigen Vorteil der reinen Abstraktion, der Klarheit und Präzision eines semantischen Systems,
das z.B. a priori gegen Widersprüche gesichert ist und deshalb
Selbst-Reflexion nicht zuläßt, eines Modells, in dem man die "indirekte Klärung" der pragmatischen Argumentation im Sinne Bar-
Hillels erreichen kann, und 2. zur gleichen Zeit dann auch noch die
Vorteile der Umgangssprache haben, die eben in diesem Sinne nicht
klar und logisch konsistent ist, die aber an die Situation an-
knüpfen kann mit Deixis usw. und ihre eigene Metasprache ist. In der
angeführten Computerproblematik ist es m.E. dasselbe: So wie ich
verstehe, will Herr Steinbuch dies beides: Er will mit der totalen
Simulation des Menschen durch Computer einerseits den Gipfel der
Technologie erreichen, d.h. aber, der technischen Kontrolle des
Menschen über die Natur, und er will dadurch notwendigerweise
gleichzeitig den Computer so geheimnisvoll machen wie den Menschen.
Dann aber ist der Computer selbst ebenso unkontrollierbar wie der
Mensch, und daraus habe ich die Konsequenz gezogen: Dann werden wir
mit den Computern im Sinne der Hermeneutik kommunizieren müssen und
auch Computer-Ideologiekritik treiben müssen. Ich verstehe dieses
Paradoxon als ein Argument für eine Transzendentalpragmatik oder
Hermeneutik der selbstreflexiven menschlichen Umgangssprache, die
zwar nicht den Ansprüchen Tarskis an ein logisch-semantisches System
entspricht, in der wir aber - z.B. hier - ü b e r Computer und
ü b e r formale Präzisionssprachen diskutieren können.
Ungeheuer: Herr Essler, wäre es Ihnen möglich, daß sie die Problematik "Natürliche Sprachen - Kunstsprachen" in ihrer Bemerkung nicht
ausklammern, sie aber nur insoweit berühren, als es zu dem ersten

Komplex gehört. Die Verbindung ist ja von Herrn Apel zuletzt auch
deutlich gemacht worden.

Essler: Ich wollte das eine sogar ganz weglassen, aber wenn Sie
wollen, sage ich noch ein Wort dazu. Ich habe nie vorgehabt, zu
leugnen, daß es einen Unterschied zwischen "use" und "mention"
gibt; daß es benutzte Sprachen gibt, ist im Gegenteil sogar eine
Voraussetzung meiner Argumentation. - Ich habe an anderer Stelle,und
damit komme ich zu dem zurück, was ich sagen wollte, geschrieben,
daß man nicht einfach nur bei Konventionen stehenbleiben kann, daß
es vielmehr Möglichkeiten gibt, sich über Konventionen auseinander-
zusetzen. Ich möchte nun versuchen, eine wichtige These von Herrn
Apel zu rekonstruieren und hoffe, daß ich ihn hierbei verstanden
habe. Sie sagen, wenn man zwei Sprachspiele untersucht und zeigen
will, daß das eine für einen bestimmten Zweck vorteilhafter ist als
das andere, dann müsse man das von einem archimedischen Punkt aus
machen. Man brauche dazu bereits eine Sprache, die aber nicht
gleichzeitig wieder Gegenstand der Untersuchung sein könne, über den
Vorteil bzw. Nachteil ich mich ebenfalls vergewissern müsse,
sondern ich bräuchte einen archimedischen Punkt. Die Sprache müsse
in irgendeinem Sinne vorgegeben sein - das haben sie "transzendental" genannt.

Apel: Die letzte Metasprache meinte ich!

Essler: Ja, auf das komme ich auch noch zurück. Hinsichtlich der
Frage, welche Sprache für Reflexionen die geeignetste ist, kann man,
je nachdem, welche man für diese Reflexionen b e n ü t z t, zu
einer der beiden folgenden Situationen gelangen:
a) Die b e n ü t z t e S p r a c h e (und insbesondere das System
von Regeln, das den Gebrauch der Ausdrücke der Sprache bestimmt) ist
von der Art, daß durch sie unter denjenigen Sprachen, über die
reflektiert wird, eine einzige als die geeignetste ausgezeichnet
wird, nämlich jene, die mit ihr formal gleich ist (bzw., falls dies
mehrere sind, alle von diesen); solche Sprachen gibt es offenbar:
ihre Benützer sind, erkenntnistheoretisch gesehen, an einem toten
Punkt angelangt (wobei sie selber umgekehrt meinen, sie seien im
definitiven Besitz der Wahrheit). Die Argumentation ist für sie
stets kreisförmig: Alles, was sie sagen, kehrt wie ein Bumerang zu
ihren Grundsätzen zurück.
b) Die b e n ü t z t e S p r a c h e ist von der Art, daß sie
einer Selbstkorrektur fähig ist, daß also nicht schon durch ihr
Begriffssystem (bzw. durch die Art, in der es gehandhabt wird) aus-
geschlossen wird, daß man bei Untersuchungen von Sprachspielen stets

zu dem Ergebnis gelangen muß, daß man eine optimale Sprache verwendet. Voraussetzung dafür, daß dieser Fall eintreten kann, ist,
daß man die eigene Sprache nicht dogmatisch (d.h. unwiderruflich)
akzeptiert hat und daß das darin enthaltene Begriffssystem somit
offen für Korrekturen ist; dann ist man nicht mehr in einem solchen
Kreis gefangen.

Mit "letzte Metasprache" können zwei Aspekte gemeint sein. Ich bin
vorhin nur auf den einen eingegangen, als ich versucht habe, zu
zeigen, daß eine letzte M e t a s p r a c h e genausowenig
existiert wie die g r ö ß t e O r d i n a l z a h l, daß sie
nicht das ist, was übrig bleibt, wenn man alle Sprachen abzieht,
über die in ihr reflektiert werden kann. Der andere Aspekt ist von
Herrn Bar-Hillel angeschnitten worden, daß man nämlich, um eine
Sprache erlernen zu können, bereits eine Sprache braucht, und daß
für jeden einzelnen die erstmalig erlernte Sprache somit die letzte
Metasprache ist. Das haben Sie doch vorhin behauptet, oder täusche
ich mich da?

Bar-Hillel: Nein, keineswegs, sondern: Es muß irgendeine Sprache
geben, deren Erwerb nicht mit Hilfe einer anderen Sprache geschieht.

Essler: Das heißt also, daß das die erste Sprache ist, die die
Kinder erlernen?

Bar-Hillel: Zum Beispiel! Was auch sehr natürlich ist!

Essler: Das ist eben die Frage, ob es wirklich so natürlich ist, daß
die Kinder als t a b u l a r a s a geboren werden, ohne ein
zumindest rudimentäres Hintergrundwissen (formaler Art, d.h. ein
begriffliches Wissen), ohne zumindest partiell vorprogrammiert zu
sein. Sie können natürlich der Ansicht sein, daß Chomskys Thesen von
den angeborenen Ideen üble Metaphysik sind und daß man, wie schon
früher immer wieder behauptet worden ist, Begriffe durch Hinweise
lernt. Das ist der Kern dessen, was Herr Lorenz schreibt, das
steht auch im Kamlah-Lorenzen drin, und das ist Gemeingut aller
Erlanger. Dieses Lernen von Begriffen ist eine Art von Induktion
(wie schon Aristoteles gesehen hat). Daß mit der Behauptung, man
lerne Begriffe durch Hinweise, mehr Probleme aufgeworfen als gelöst
werden, da man induktive Methoden nicht ohne Voraussetzungen
formaler Natur (d.h. nicht ohne ein Wissen über die Begriffe) adäquat verwenden kann, dürfte doch ein Ergebnis sein, das durch die
Goodmanschen Paradoxien hinreichend klargelegt worden ist. (Ausführlicher bin ich auf diese Fragen in meinen Büchern "Wissenschaftstheorie II" (Kap.I) und "Analytische Philosophie I" (Kap. IV)
eingegangen.) Ich sehe nicht, wie man dieses Problem umgehen kann,

wenn man in der Methodologie des Wort "Hinweisdefinition" durch
"Exemplifizierung" ersetzt.

Bar-Hillel: Das neue Wort ist "exemplifiziert".

Essler: Es ist gleichgültig, welche W o r t e man dann noch hat.
Daß die Hinweisdefinitionen eine Art von induktivem Erlernen der
Sprache sind, war früher klar, daß es da im Prinzip unendlich viele
Mehrdeutungen, Fehldeutungen gibt, war auch klar, und genauso, daß
man sich das Nicht-zustande-Kommen solcher Fehldeutungen nur so
erklären kann, daß uns irgendwelche Alternativen (Regel-Systeme oder
Theorien zum Gebrauch der betreffenden Ausdrücke der Sprache) vorgegeben sind. Ich glaube, das war das, was auch Sie gestern gesagt
haben, das scheint eigentlich fast notwendig zu sein. Ich habe in
dem Buch von Lorenz nichts, wirklich nichts, über diese Problematik
gefunden.

Ungeheuer: Darf ich die Mitglieder des Panel darum bitten,
vielleicht nicht immer von "den Erlangern" zu sprechen, um Herrn
Lorenz nicht in ständige Schwierigkeiten zu bringen. Jedesmal, wenn
das Wort fällt, zuckt er zusammen. - Ich meine, wir müssen doch zu
einer Klärung des Fundierungsverhältnisses zwischen Sprachen kommen.
Dies aber als bloßes Bedingungsverhältnis gedacht bei Hierarchien
von Metasprachen oder bei Rückführung von Sprachen auf etwas, was
zu diesen Sprachen hinführt, aber selbst keine Sprache ist, wie es
möglicherweise von Kant als transzendental hätte verstanden werden
können - wenn er es gedacht hätte. Auf der anderen Seite ist bei dem
ständigen Hinweis auf Ontogenese oder Phylogenese nicht klar, ob er
sich auf eine Person bezieht, wie im Fall der Kindersprache. Das
Kind hat ja zunächst keine Sprache, aber möglicherweise wird zur
Spracherlernung doch eine Sprache benutzt, nur nicht gerade
s e i n e Sprache. Das würde ich doch bitten, klarzustellen. Denn
meinen Sie es nun wirklich auf eine Person bezogen, wie vielleicht
Herr Bar-Hillel, oder meinen Sie es auf mehrere Personen bezogen?
Wenn es auf eine Gemeinschaft, eine Gruppe bezogen ist, dann ist
immer eine Sprache vorhanden.

Apel: Also zum Problem Metasprachenhierarchie, letzte Metasprache
und Reflexion. Ich würde sagen, auch hier muß man eine gewisse
Pointe dieser ganzen logischen Semantik unbedingt festhalten und
retten. Die bestand ja gerade darin: das Selbstreflexionsverhältnis,
das man in der natürlichen Umgangssprache hat, wenn sie gebraucht
wird, dieses eben zu suspendieren, um gewisse Schwierigkeiten gar
nicht erst aufkommen zu lassen. Das fängt schon in der Typentheorie
an. Nach meinem Verständnis wird das, was früher in der Transzenden-

talphilosophie "Reflexion" genannt wurde, seitdem ersetzt durch das
Verhältnis von Objektsprache, Metasprache, Metametasprache usw., und
in dieser modernen Art des Denkens im Sinne der logischen Semantik
kann es keine letzte Metasprache geben; denn es geht ja immer
weiter! Und ich will jetzt etwas sehr Radikales sagen: Für mich
liegt der Hauptwert und die Hauptkonsequenz des "Tractatus" von
Wittgenstein darin, daß Wittgenstein gezeigt hat, daß dann keine
Philosophie mehr möglich ist, wenn Selbst-Reflexion im transzendentalphilosophischen Sinn nicht möglich ist. Er hat die ganze Meta-
sprachen-Problematik in gewisser Weise antizipiert und ausdrücklich
gesagt, daß die Form, die transzendentale Bedingung des Sprechens
ist, so niemals eingeholt wird, sie ist deshalb für ihn überhaupt
nicht aussagbar, sie "zeigt sich" nur. Das ist die wunderbar
doxe Pointe des "Tractatus". Nimmt man sie wörtlich, dann gibt es
eben keine Philosophie mehr, und in der Tat: Carnap hat diese Folge-
rung zu ziehen versucht: Philosophen sind dann eben nur noch Kon-
strukteure von Sprachen, und das, was sie da tun, nämlich die
Sprache zu konstruieren, das ist reine "Praxis". Diese schafft dann
erst die Bedingungen einer theoretischen Sprache. Dann entsteht
freilich in aller Schärfe das Problem: Darf bzw. muß man nicht auf
die Bedingungen der Möglichkeit und Gültigkeit von Konventionen reflektieren, die der Konzeption von "semantical frameworks" zugrunde-
liegen? Kommt hier nicht die alte transzendentalphilosophische
Reflexions-Problematik als transzendentalpragmatische wieder, als
Problematik der natürlichen Reflexion in der Sprache auf die
Sprache? Das ist es, was ich in einem metaphorischen Sinne in dem
Buch von 1963 die aktualiter, im Gebrauch, letzte Metasprache genannt habe. Und in dem Zusammenhang habe ich auch den Terminus der
Umgangssprache "Nichthintergehbarkeit" verwendet; und in einem recht
verstandenen Sinne halte ich daran fest, an der Nichthintergehbar-
keitsthese. (Ich muß leider sagen, daß die Auseinandersetzung, die
daraufhin in den Kantstudien geführt worden ist und alles, was
daraufhin bis jetzt gesagt worden ist, nicht die Pointe trifft, die
ich im Auge gehabt habe mit "Nichthintergehbarkeit". Ich habe dabei
nicht im Auge gehabt, daß man die Umgangssprache etwa nicht sollte
rekonstruieren können. Bar-Hillels Konzeption der sogenannten "indi-
rekten Klärung" oder umgangssprachlichen Argumentation durch die logische Semantik der Formalsprachen kommt mir sogar außerordentlich
entgegen. "Indirekte Klärung" setzt ja gerade voraus, daß man das
kunstsprachliche System nicht in den Gebrauch hereinzieht, sondern
es als ein Vermittlungsmoment betrachtet, durch das indirekt geklärt

werden soll, was in der pragmatischen Dimension seinen Ursprung hat.
Ich fasse die letzten beiden papers von Herrn Bar-Hillel gerade in
dieser Richtung auf.
Bar-Hillel: Darf ich dazu ganz kurz was sagen! Ich hoffe, daß Herr
Lorenz bei meinen Bemerkungen nicht aufgezuckt ist. Ich hoffe, daß
ich ihn korrekt interpretiert habe, um hinzuzufügen, daß ich mit
seinen Auffassungen übereinstimme. Daß Kinder, um mit Spracherwerb
beginnen zu können, dazu in der Tat eingeborene Fähigkeiten haben
müssen, daß ist für mich so selbstverständlich, daß ich es nicht
einmal erwähnt habe. Die Drohung, die Herr Apel aus Wittgenstein
herauslesen wollte, daß, wenn seine Konzeption nicht stimmt, dann
keine Philosophie möglich ist, erschüttert mich nicht. Aber die
Drohung, die ich daraus gezogen habe, daß nämlich dann kein Verständnis von dem, was Sprache ist, möglich ist, erschüttert mich!
Irgendwann, bevor ich siebzig und zu alt dafür bin, will ich mal
verstehen, wie Sprache funktioniert. Ich weiß natürlich, daß
Wittgenstein dazu nicht weniger, vielleicht sogar mehr als viele
andere, vielleicht als jeder andere geleistet hat. Das ist alles,
was ich dazu noch sagen wollte. Ach ja, Carnap und Hempel haben
übrigens öffentlich über ihre Meinungsänderungen reflektiert.
Carnap hat darüber sehr ausführlich in seiner Autobiographie und den
"Replies" in dem Buche "Rudolf Carnap" referiert, und die letzten
Änderungen der Auffassung Hempels über den logischen Empirizismus
sind von ihm in aller Öffentlichkeit, z.B. im letzten Kongress der
Philosophie der Wissenschaften in Bukarest, dargestellt worden.
Eine kurze Bemerkung noch, aber die sollen Sie ruhig gleich wieder
vergessen, weil sie uns vom Hauptthema abführt. Ich selber habe mich
mit dem Problem beschäftigt, in welcher Art von Sprache wir uns mit
Computern unterhalten wollen, wenn wir mit ihnen alles Mögliche an-
stellen wollen, was ungefähr dem entspricht, was wir mit Menschen
machen können. In der Tat habe ich dann behauptet, daß diese Kon-
versationssprachen mit Computern pragmatische Sprachen werden
müssen. Ob Herr Steinbuch diese Formulierungen akzeptieren würde,
weiß ich nicht. Aber daß das so ist, ist mir klar, und es ist mir
auch klar, daß das haargenau das ist, was im Augenblick geschieht.
Ungeheuer: Ich möchte jetzt Wortmeldungen aus dem Auditorium zu-
lassen. Darf ich aber darauf hinweisen, daß wir zwei Problemstellungen hatten. Ich würde gerne weiterhin bei der ersten bleiben,
sie scheint mir noch lange nicht klar zu sein. Im Panel existiert
jetzt ein scheinbares Einverständnis, vor allen Dingen in dem, was
"transzendental" heißen kann. Aber es k a n n eigentlich zwischen

den Beteiligten bis jetzt keine Übereinstimmung geben, soweit ich
die Sache sehe. Würden Sie also den zweiten Komplex bitte nur insoweit tangieren, als er mit dem ersten zusammenhängt.

Essler: Darf ich das ganz kurz noch einmal an einem Beispiel sagen.
Herr Apel sagt mit "transzendental": Es gibt eine Sprache, von der
aus man alle Sprachspiele beurteilen kann, die also transzendental
vorgegeben ist.

Ungeheuer: Er kann nicht sagen, "es gibt"!

Essler: Er hat eine solche Wendung vorhin gebraucht: "Zu jeder...hat
man...", das ist der Unterschied der Quantoren.

Apel: In gewissem Sinne kann ich sagen, die Umgangssprache muß dazu
benutzt werden, wobei jetzt Umgangssprache bitte nicht im Gegensatz
zu Bildungssprache zu verstehen ist, sondern das treffen soll, was
nicht ein konstruiertes System ist, sondern festgemacht werden kann
an die interpersonale Kommunikation und hier und jetzt an der Erfahrung. Das, was auch Selbstreflexion erlauben muß.

Ungeheuer: Wir können später nochmal darauf zurückkommen. Es liegen
zwei schriftliche Anmeldungen von Herrn Staal und Herrn Lorenz vor.

Staal: I would like to make three points about the main issue. The
first point: I am not convinced that there is such a thing as
"transcendental pragmatics". If there is no such thing I am not
convinced that such a thing should be created. I am not taking the
lines which Bar-Hillel has taken.
The second point is a point of detail that seems to me significant
because you said it was interesting that the word "Wissen" in German
functions in the same way as the English "know".

Apel: Not in all respects!

Staal: In some respects! For instance in the respect that we were
talking about, namely, that if you say "I know that p", then the
speaker presupposes the truth of "p". Now I say that it is not
interesting. I say that if it were not so we would not translate
"know" by "Wissen" and "Wissen" by "know".
The third point is a little longer. I would not dare to say anything
about these "Bedingungen der Möglichkeit". I would like to say
something about one of the philosophical backgrounds which you have
used.Let us look at the concept of "Sprachspiele" which you took
from Wittgenstein. Now you also mentioned, rightly, I think that in
Wittgenstein you find this concept of "Tiefengrammatik". This
concept has something to do with the concept of logical form which
is related to Frege and Russell but which has definitely something
to do with what is done in the M.I.T. "transcendental linguistics".

Now I would say that in Wittgenstein there is an absolute contradiction between what he says about "Tiefengrammatik" which he touches
rather briefly and what he says in general when he says philosophy
leaves everything as it is, we should not do analysis and so on.
A "Tiefengrammatik" is a concept that you can only arrive at when you
you are willing to do some analysis and when you are not willing to
leave everything as it is. If you leave everything as it is,then you
arrive at such concepts as "Sprachspiele" because "Sprachspiele" are
as it were isolated domains in which words, sentences are used in a
certain way. Now if you want to relate those "Sprachspiele" to each
other you have to do "Tiefengrammatik", you have to do analysis
which Wittgenstein has done a little bit against his prescript but
which in general, I think, in accordance to what he says to himself,
he does not do. I think it really makes variable sense to make use
of such a concept of "Sprachspiele", or, for instance, to try to
clarify it as you do by saying they should be pragmatically and
semantically consistent or they should have something to do with
truth. You want to avoid such cases as Peter Winch's one who arrives
at this kind of relativism by,as it were,putting these conditions on
"Sprachspiele". But that is what "Sprachspiele" are, they are rather
vague and they are only acceptable if one does not want to analyse.
If a "Sprachspiel" had ever to be consistent, then our scientific
"Sprachspiele" would not be "Sprachspiele". In most cases when we do
linguistics or any sciences we just hope that we will be able one
day to show that these are consistent. We are a long way from
that.
Apel: Um zwischen uns eine Verständigung herbeizuführen, Herr Staal,
dazu bedürfte es natürlich längerer Zeit. Hier würde ich beinahe nur
noch am transzendentalen Ideal festhalten, am regulativen Prinzip,
und die faktische Möglichkeit tatsächlich sehr stark bezweifeln. Es
ist natürlich sowieso klar, daß heute viele Leute - aber das war
eigentlich immer so - Transzendental-Philosophie nicht unbedingt für
notwendig halten.Daß wir z.B. nicht sagen können, einer weiß etwas,
wenn das, was er weiß, unserer Meinung nach nicht der Fall ist, das
ist zwar nicht so eindrucksvoll wie die Beispiele des späten
Wittgensteins für das, was man nicht sagen kann, aber wenn man auch
schon dieses Beispiel nicht für interessant hält, dann muß ich
sagen, in der Tat verstehe ich oft, daß man transzendentale Sprach-
pragmatik nicht für unbedingt notwendig hält. Und daß man sich dann
auch nicht dazu verstehen kann, daß es das geben sollte. Die Rede-
weise, daß es das gibt, würde ich übrigens niemals anwenden, sondern

es ist für mich ein Postulat, daß es eine tranzendental-pragmatische
Philosophie geben sollte, um die Probleme zu bewältigen, die sich
philosophisch in der gegenwärtigen Situation stellen. Unter anderem
z.B. das folgende Problem: Was sollen wir tun angesichts der zahl-
losen "frameworks" der Wissenschaftssprache, die heute vorgeschlagen werden, mit jeweiliger Formalisierung, mit jeweiliger Notation.
Ich weiß nicht, ob sich jeder schon einmal Gedanken darüber gemacht
hat, wie das heute in unseren Universitäten schon aussieht, daß der
eine Mathematiker sagt: Das, was mein Kollege tut, das ist eine andere Mathematik, das versteh' ich nicht mehr. Ich sehe voraus, daß es
Verständigungswissenschaftler geben wird, die sich nur noch damit
beschäftigen werden, die Verständigung zwischen den Naturwissenschaften herzustellen. Das werden keine "empirischen Naturwissenschaftler" sein, auch keine Philosophen, dazwischen wird sich noch
etwas etablieren: eine neue Art von hermeneutischen Wissenschaften.
Es ist sehr interessant, daß einerseits die heutigen Wissenschaften
immer stärker zur wissenschaftstheoretischen Selbstreflexion tendie-
ren, diese selbst aber immer mehr zur Wissenschaftshistorie übergeht. Hier haben sich prächtige Beispiele einer nicht empirischen,
aber auch nicht logischen Wissenschaft inzwischen ergeben. Das Beispiel einer normativ-hermeneutischen Wissenschaft hat z.B. der
Popperianer Imre Lakatos angegeben: "Interne Rekonstruktion" der
Wissenschaftsgeschichte.

Lenz: Ich war doch ein bißchen verwundert über diese leichtfertige
Denunziation des Behaviorismus in der Diskussion hier. Das ging mir
ein bißchen sehr eilig. Ich hatte auch den Eindruck, als ob die Prä-
dikatisierung als antimentalistisch sich mehr auf einen Behaviorismus zwischen 1913 und 1920 bezieht. Es gibt aber doch danach, immerhin vor 1930 George H. Mead, es gibt danach die Behavioristen, die
sich mit Vermittlungsprozesstheorien gerade in Bezug auf Sprache beschäftigt haben, aufgrund deren ich wissen möchte, ob man einfach in
dieser Weise von Herrn Apel die Wissenschaftslogik außer acht lassen
darf. Ich möchte das an einem historischen Beispiel von Spracherwerb
verdeutlichen. Setzen wir folgenden Fall, den ich einmal normal-
sprachlich und einmal behavioristisch beschreiben kann. Ein Baby hat
eine Empfindung, die Eltern sehen dies und sagen: "Es tut ihm weh".
Das Baby lernt darauf, in Zukunft zu sagen, "es tut mir weh".
Behavioristisch handelt es sich um Stimuli, intraceptive Stimuli,
auf die Reflexe von seiten des Babys erfolgen. Diese Reflexe sind
Stimuli für die Eltern als Erziehungspersonen. Sie antworten darauf
mit einem verbal behavior: "es tut ihm weh", und nach mehrfachem

Vorfallen dieser Ereignisse kommt das Baby immer beim Auftreten
dieser Stimuli zu einer konditionierten Reaktion, daß es ihm weh
tut. Weiterhin, da beim erstmaligen Auftreten dieser Behavior-
Korrelate die Eltern gesagt haben: "es tut ihm weh", wird nunmehr an
dem Reiz auch die Schmerzreaktion als solche wieder konditioniert,
so daß, wenn die Eltern "es tut ihm weh" sagen, ein residualer
Schmerzakt als Inhalt, als Bewußtseinsinhalt, und nunmehr als Vorstellung existent ist. Tatsächlich hatte G.H.Mead dem Behaviorismus
vorgeworfen, er erkenne keine Empfindungen an, obwohl doch jedermann
weiß, daß es welche gibt. Und der Behaviorismus hat daraufhin mit
dieser Vermittlungsprozesstheorie geantwortet, wonach Bewußtseins-
akte verständlich gemacht oder umgedeutet werden konnten als
Behavior. Nun frage ich: handelt es sich hierbei um eine transzendentale Pragmatik, und muß man, wenn man von solchen Miniaturbau
steinen ausgeht, wirklich auf Ihre Seite überwechseln?
Bar-Hillel: Als ich von "behavioristisch" sprach (doch zuvor will
ich zugeben, daß der Terminus eventuell vielleicht überhaupt nicht
benutzt werden sollte), hatte ich keineswegs 1920 im Sinne, sondern
die 1960-Theorien von Skinner und Osgood. A priori, aus irgendwelchen metaphysischen Ansätzen, zu glauben, daß man mentalistische
Ausdrücke nicht benutzen darf, weil sie tabu sind, scheint mir heute
nicht nehr akzeptabel zu sein.
Ungeheuer: Aber Herr Bar-Hillel, darf ich vielleicht in Ihrem Sinne,
vielleicht aber auch aus eigenem Antrieb heraus nachfragen. Ich
meine, daß ihre Darstellung zu dramatisch ist. Ihre Frage müßte
doch eigentlich lauten: gibt es eine ernsthafte Theoriebildung, in
der beispielsweise theoretische und empirische Begriffe unterschieden werden können und die auch in Bezug auf die Gesetze der empirischen Basis ausreicht? Das ist doch die entscheidende Frage.
Bar-Hillel: Die Antwort ist nein! Weder Skinner noch Osgood ist
imstande, die Psychologie in irgendeinem adäquaten Ausmaße zu beschreiben. Und solange das nicht geschieht, sehe ich keinen anderen
Weg, als mich mentalistisch auszudrücken, obwohl ich nichts dagegen
habe, wenn jemand irgendwann mal das auf irgendeine Weise auf behavioristische oder physiologische Redeweisen wird reduzieren können.
Es ist doch wohl auch von e i n e r Wissenschaft zuviel verlangt,
daß sie allein imstande sein sollte, alles zu erklären. Wir sind
wahrscheinlich auf mentalistische Begriffe angewiesen, um uns zu
verständigen.
Ungeheuer: Ich meine, die einzige Konsequenz daraus ist doch nur,
daß dieses Argument nicht verwendet werden kann, um behavioristische

oder mentalistische Theoriebildungen nur deswegen abzuweisen, weil
sie nicht vollständig sind.
Bar-Hillel: Nein! Der Vollständigkeitsanspruch der behavioristischen
Pragmatik muß abgewiesen werden.
Ungeheuer: Ja, aber auch von allen anderen!
Bar-Hillel: Von jedem, das muß von jedem abgewiesen werden! Heute,
1972!
Apel: Ich möchte auch versuchen, etwas zum Behaviorismusproblem zu
sagen. Zunächst, würde ich sagen, muß man zwischen zwei ganz verschiedenen Fragen unterscheiden, nämlich erstens der Frage: ist es
möglich, daß die empirischen Wissenschaften vom menschlichen Handeln einschließlich der Sprachhandlungen auf der Grundlage, sagen
wir eines fortgeschrittenen Behaviorismus behandelt werden können.
Das ist die erste Frage. Die zweite Frage ist dann die: Kann selbst
unter der Voraussetzung einer positiven Beantwortung der ersten
Frage die Funktion, die einer Transzendentalpragmatik zugedacht
werden muß im Haushalt der Wissenschaft (nämlich auf die Bedingungen
der Möglichkeit und Gültigkeit der Wissenschaft zu reflektieren),
kann die jemals auf behavioristischer Grundlage als lösbar gedacht
werden? Dann würde ich zunächst sagen: die zweite Frage, und das ist
ja eigentlich mein Problem, kann aus ganz anderem Grunde als die
erste Frage nicht positiv beantwortet werden. Es läßt sich gar
nicht denken, daß überhaupt eine empirisch beschreibende oder er-
klärende Wissenschaft diese Funktion einer transzendentalen Gel-
tungsreflexion sollte übernehmen können; denn sie würde selber
diese Probleme aufwerfen, oder auf jeden Fall derartige Probleme im
Rücken haben: solche der Methodologie, normativer Methodologie, und
der Frage des "In-Geltung-Setzens", also das Problem, das eventuell
durch "Konvention" gelöst werden muß. D i e s Problem kann nicht
behavioristisch gelöst werden. Sie können nicht die Konvention, die
hinter der Geltung der behavioristischen Sätze steht, noch mal mit
behavioristischer Beschreibung und Erklärung lösen wollen. Das ist
keine empirische Frage. Für mich ist das philosophisch a priori unmöglich. Das ist der wichtigste Teil meiner Erklärung. Jetzt aber
zur zweiten Frage, genauer: zur ersten Frage: ob die Sozialwissenschaften in einem anspruchsvollen Sinne auf die Basis des Behaviorismus gestellt werden könnten? Dies würde ich, aus anderen Gründen
allerdings, auch für aussichtslos halten. Da würden Sie vielleicht
einwenden - und das ist natürlich ein Standardargument des Positivismus seit Comte - was wir n o c h nicht können, werden wir
später können; wir fangen ja erst an; der Fortschritt ist unbegrenzt.

Aber ich möchte meinen: es gibt da gewisse "crucial experiments",
oder: es gibt da gewisse Phänomene, angesichts derer die Dinge sich
entscheiden lassen. Für mich war in meiner Erfahrung da etwa folgendes wichtig: erstens einmal Peirces Begriff von der dreistelligen
Zeichenrelation, vom durch Zeichen sich vermittelnden Intendieren
von etwas als etwas. Den Anspruch, daß Ch.Morris dies Phänomen hätte
umsetzen können in die behavioristische Theorie, habe ich geprüft
und ich glaube, sagen zu können, daß dies nicht gelang. Dann habe
ich mehrere für mich wichtige Bestätigungen erhalten, etwa durch den
Aufsatz von Chomsky über Skinners "Verbal Behavior". Hier geht es
ja nicht nur um intentionale Handlungen, sondern um noch viel mehr:
um grammatische Regeln, die den Sprecher in den Stand setzen, auch
bisher nie gehörte Sätze zu bilden. Das ist alles impliziert im
Kompetenzbegriff. Dieses Phänomen der Kompetenz, das erst Chomsky
überhaupt entdeckt hat, dieses Phänomen kann man m.E. überhaupt
nicht entdecken auf der Basis des Behaviorismus. Und dann gibt es
noch einige andere "crucial experiments" in diesem Sinn. Es gibt
freilich Leute, die sprechen von "Behavioral Science", wenn sie
etwas meinen, was wissenschaftstheoretisch ganz harmlos ist. Wenn
z.B. gestern in der Diskussion über Psychoanalyse Herr Watzlawick
von empirischer Beobachtung und Deskription von Verhalten sprach,
dann stellte sich nachher für mich heraus, daß er etwas meint, was
wir alle auch meinen, wenn wir von verstehbarem Handeln reden. Es
handelte sich um "Verhaltensbeobachtung" aufgrund hermeneutischer
Erfahrungen; Verstehen von Intentionen, stillschweigendem Mitspielen
des Spiels, Verstehen der zugrundeliegenden Konventionen und der
möglichen Handlungsstrategien von Gewinn und Verlust usw. Wenn das
dann auch "Behavior" sein soll, dann ist das einfach nur eine Ver-
harmlosung des Problems. Da freu ich mich dann immer über so etwas
wie Carnaps Radikalismus. Der hat 1954 noch einmal ganz hart das
Problem diskutiert, ob man das Intensionalitätsproblem der "belief-
sentences" behavioristisch auflösen kann. Und da hat sich gezeigt,
daß das nicht möglich ist. Der Norweger Hans Stjervheim, Schüler
von Arne Naess , hat in seiner Dissertation "Objectivism and the
study of man" (Oslo, 1959) mit sprachanalytischen Methoden gezeigt,
daß man unter behavioristischen Voraussetzungen für "affirmativ
reagieren" auf den Satz "The world is round" H u s t e n ein-
setzen kann. Das ist für mich auch ein "crucial experiment" gewesen.
Lieb: Ich bin eigentlich philosophisch ein schlichtes Gemüt. Es
scheint mir, daß bei dem Versuch, hier eine transzendentale Pragmatik zu kreieren, wesentliche Dinge vermischt wurden, von denen ich

immer geglaubt habe, man sollte sie auseinanderhalten. Auf der
einen Seite haben wir Pragmatik, traditionell als einen Zweig einer
empirischen Wissenschaft. Ob das nun behavioristisch oder mentalistisch ist, ist in diesem Zusammenhang völlig belanglos. Auf der
anderen Seite haben wir etwa Kants transzendentale Ästhetik, was
heute in den Bereich eines Zweiges der Philosophie fällt, den man
Erkenntnistheorie nennen könnte. Daneben kommt hier über die Hermeneutik etwas herein: das Stehen in einer kommunikativen Situation
und Ähnliches, worauf dann hier der Ausdruck Pragmatik angewandt
wurde. Wir hätten also Pragmatik, Zweig einer empirischen Wissenschaft, dann den Versuch, so wie ich es sehe, die Problematik
dessen, was traditionellerweise in der Erkenntnistheorie behandelt
wurde, gleichzeitig zu behandeln mit dem Unterschied zwischen dem
Stehen und Handeln in einer Situation und dem Betrachten dieser Situation. Und dieses, scheint mir, sollte zusammengefaßt werden unter
"transzendentaler Pragmatik". Ich sehe den Versuch einer solchen
Zusammenfassung als verhängnisvoll für die Klärung der vorhandenen
Sachverhalte an.

Ungeheuer: Warum verhängnisvoll? Das müssen Sie noch kurz erläutern!

Lieb: Verhängnisvoll deshalb, weil ich kaum einen Zusammenhang sehe
zwischen erkenntnistheoretischen Problemen und dem Problem, in einer
Kommunikationssituation zu stehen, d.h. also, dem Stehen in einer
Kommunikationssituation, die Tatsache, daß Kommunizieren etwas anderes ist als Reflektieren über Kommunizieren, hat m.E. mit den Problemen, die in der Erkenntnistheorie behandelt werden, nahezu nichts
zu tun. Es erschwert eine Erklärung, weil Disparates zusammenge-
bracht wird, und ich sehe nicht ein, warum die legitime Berechtigung
transzendentaler Fragestellung im traditionellen Sinn und die legitime Berechtigung der Untersuchungen, die in der Hermeneutik vorliegen, irgendwas, wieso die Berechtigung nicht schon klar ist,
warum man dann noch den Namen einer empirischen Wissenschaft hier
hinzunehmen muß, die Frage hatte ich.

Ungeheuer: Herr Apel, würden Sie etwas dazu sagen!

Apel: Zunächst muß ich das zurückweisen, daß es eine Selbstverständlichkeit ist, daß Pragmatik Zweig einer empirischen Wissenschaft
ist! Wer die Geschichte kennt, der weiß, daß es ganz anders war.
Der Terminus "Pragmatik" ist eingeführt worden von Morris in einer
bestimmten Situation der Entwicklung des logischen Empirismus als
Ergänzung von Syntax und Semantik, und Syntax und Semantik, wie sie
damals gebraucht wurden in der Wissenschaftslogik, waren bestimmt
nicht empirisch gemeint. Als Morris die Pragmatik einführte, hat

sich erst das Problem ergeben, was das wohl sein würde; in meinem
Referat habe ich das ausführlicher und genauer dargelegt. Da haben
sich zwei Vorschläge herausgestellt, einmal der, das Problem der
Pragmatik behavioristisch-empirisch zu behandeln, und das war
Morris' eigener Vorschlag, dem auch Carnap gefolgt ist; allerdings
hat Morris von vornherein hinzugesetzt: man muß das Problem auch in
Form einer reinen Pragmatik behandeln können, d.h. konstruktiv! Das
hat Carnap dann schließlich auch aufgenommen, und es ist dann ja auch
Programmpunkt in den Werken von "Martin" und anderen. Für mich noch
viel wichtiger ist jedoch, daß hinter dem Pragmatik-Vorschlag von
Morris Peirce stand, den ich erst später studierte. Dabei sah ich,
daß Peirce eine grandiose Konzeption von Pragmatik hat, die von
Morris absolut nicht verstanden worden ist, die man von Kant aus
verstehen muß. Allerdings wird dann vieles verändert. Und jetzt
komme ich zu dem zweiten Thema: daß es verwirrend sein soll, daß man
die traditionelle Problematik der Erkenntnistheorie, also einer
Bewußtseinstheorie mit Bewußtseinsvermögen und transzendentaler
Synthese der Apperzeption, daß man die transformiert im Sinne der
Semiotik, im Sinne der Pragmatik.
Ungeheuer: Darf ich Sie unterbrechen? Nicht "verwirren" ist gesagt
worden. Es wurde zuerst gesagt, es sei "verhängnisvoll"! Dann haben
wir es dahingehend aufgeklärt, daß dieser Konstruktionsversuch etwas
über die Bedingungen der Möglichkeit von Kommunikation aussagen soll
und dies aus vielen Gründen nicht zutreffen kann.
Apel: Ich muß zunächst einmal folgendes klarmachen: Das wir heute
erkenntnistheoretische Problematik transformieren, indem wir nicht
mehr mit den Kategorien Bewußtsein, Bewußtseinsvermögen, Synthesis
der Apperzeption, Vorstellung, Einheit des Bewußtseins usw. reden,
sondern das umzusetzen suchen in semiotische Termini, ist erstens
historisch schon vorgemacht worden von Peirce - er hat mehrere Arbeiten darüber geschrieben -, zweitens halte ich das aus vielen anderen Gründen für äußerst plausibel. Ich gehöre zu denjenigen, die
Erkenntnis heute folgendermaßen auffassen: ich erkenne etwas, d.h.,
ich verständige mich mit mir selber über etwas. Das Problem der
I n t e r p r e t a t i o n mit Hilfe von Zeichen und Sprachen
ist immer mit drin. Ernst Cassirer hat den ersten Schritt in diese
Richtung gemacht, indem er das Symbol als Vermittlungsinstrument in
die Kantische Erkenntnisproblematik hineinbrachte. Peirce hat Kant
viel radikaler und großartiger transformiert - in diesem Punkte.
Auch die Überwindung des m e t h o d i s c h e n S o l i p s i s-
m u s der klassischen Erkenntnistheorie gehört in diesen Zusammen-

hang. Wie Plato schon sagte, ist das Denken "Gespräch mit sich
selbst". Erkennen ist dementsprechend immer schon eine Internali-
sierung der Verständigung in der Kommunikationsgemeinschaft. Das
gilt für jeden Akt g ü l t i g e r Erkenntnis. Denn es ist z.B.
wissenschaftstheoretisch uninteressant, wenn ich eine private Erleb-
nisgewißheit habe, die ich nicht in bestätigbare oder bestreitbare
Behauptungen umsetzen kann. Wenn die Erkenntnis Interpretations-
charakter hat, dann ist sie immer schon integriert in den Zusammenhang der Verständigung, und es geht insofern in der Erkenntnistheorie um die Verständigung und die Verständigungsgemeinschaft, und
deshalb nenne ich das auch in anderen Arbeiten "transzendental-
hermeneutisch". "Transzendental-hermeneutisch" und "transzendental-
pragmatisch" bezeichnen zwei Aspekte desselben Grundkonzepts. Es ist
natürlich klar, daß ich jetzt darüber nicht hinreichend ausführlich
sprechen kann. Ich möchte nur auf eins hinweisen: Ich bin nicht der
Einzige, der in dieser Richtung vorgeht, weder heute noch historisch
gesehen. Ich habe versucht, immer wieder auf Peirce hinzuweisen und
ihn unter diesem Gesichtspunkt neu zu studieren. Außerdem sind heute
aber viele unterwegs in dieser Richtung, z.B. J.Habermas.
Und nun zu einem letzten Problem: Das Problem der transzendentalpragmatischen Bedingungen der Möglichkeit, des In-Geltung-Setzens
wissenschaftlicher Erkenntnis, stellt sich natürlich auch als das
Problem der Bedingungen der Möglichkeit kommunikationswissenschaft-
licher Erkenntnis. Das ist freilich ein Spezialproblem, bei dem ganz
klar wird, daß Sinn- und Geltungsverständigung eine transzendentale
Funktion ist und nicht etwas, was etwa empirische Kommunikations-
wissenschaften behandeln könnten: die bedürfen ja, wie ich eben
sagte, selbst der wissenschaftstheoretisch philosophischen Reflexionen auf ihre Bedingungen der Möglichkeit und Gültigkeit.
Ungeheuer: Herr Apel, ein Unterschied ist hier doch zu machen:
ob es die Bedingungen der Möglichkeit oder der Gültigkeit für
kommunikationswissenschaftliche Erkenntnis oder für Kommunikations-
Akte selbst sind. Sie haben eben das erste angesprochen. Sie haben
aber in Ihrem Vortrag, und auch darauf wurde gerade hingewiesen, das
zweite auch genannt, und das ist die Problematik! Nicht so sehr das
erste, weil Sie mit Ihrem Postulat konstruktiv nachweisen können,
daß es nur auf diese Weise geht. Aber das zweite: Die Kommunika-
tionsakte sind erst in diesem Erklärungsversuch möglich dadurch,
daß sie transzendental sind.
Apel: Ich muß hier vielleicht folgendes einschieben: Bei Kant sieht
es noch so aus, als ob das Transzendentale im Gegensatz zu dem

Empirischen etwas Besonderes, also gewissermaßen eine metaphysische
Sphäre bezeichnet. Bei Wittgenstein ist es im "Tractatus" die Grenze
der Welt und verschwindet da übrigens für die Diskussion dieses
Jahrhunderts. Wenn ich nun hier eine Transformation der Kantischen
Bewußtseinsphilosophie in eine Philosophie der transzendentalen
Verständigung propagiere, dann ist diese Verständigung in keiner
Weise ein besonderes metaphysisches Gebilde. Es ist die Kommunikation z.B., die wir hier durchführen.
Menschliche Kommunikation kann man unter verschiedenen Gesichtspunkten in einem verschiedenen Stellenwert betrachten. Man kann sie
empirisch erforschen, wobei man m.E. Methoden anwenden muß, die
schon zeigen, daß es sich da nicht um empirische N a t u r w i s-
s e n s c h a f t e n handelt. Aber diese unsere Kommunikation, die
nichts Mysteriöses hat, die kann auch betrachtet werden unter dem
Gesichtspunkt, daß es sich dabei um die Bedingung der Möglichkeit
unserer Verständigung überhaupt handelt (und also auch von der
empirischen Kommunikationswissenschaft). Es ändert sich dann der
Stellenwert der thematisierten Kommunikation und die Art der **Thema-
tisierung**; und es muß z.B. dann, wenn ich sie in den transzendentalen Stellenwert einrücke, das Methodologische hereinkommen, dann
müssen normative Prinzipien und Postulate eingeführt werden. Da ist
z.B. das höchste Postulat, daß in unserer kommunikativen Verständigung hier die transzendentale Einheit der Interpretation angestrebt
werden soll. Ich glaube, daß gerade **das**, was wir hier tun, ein ganz
ausgezeichnetes Beispiel für den transzendentalen Stellenwert, für
die transzendentale Funktion der Kommunikation ist; denn wir behalten uns hier immer die letzte Metaposition vor. Wir lassen uns jetzt
als Kommunikationspartner nicht empirisch thematisieren, sondern,
wenn wir hier etwas empirisch thematisieren, dann behalten wir uns
die transzendentale Funktion vor. Bitte **versuchen** Sie es nur einmal
versuchsweise für fünf Minuten zu überdenken, daß selbst wenn wir
hier einen der Kommunikationsteilnehmer in seinen **Aktionen thematisieren** wollen, daß wir in demselben Moment komplementär dazu sofort
die transzendentale Funktion davon trennen würden und uns als der
Gemeinschaft hier vorbehalten würden, die zur Verständigung darüber
kommen will. Es geht um diese letzte Dimension, deswegen letzte
Metasprache, letzte!
<u>Lorenzer</u>: Ich möchte eine kleine Vorbemerkung machen. Ich glaube,
es ist gestern nicht ganz deutlich geworden, was für eine Funktion
hier ein psychoanalytischer Beitrag haben kann. Das möchte ich doch
noch etwas deutlicher machen. Ich meine, in diesem Kreis kann er nur

die Funktion haben, einige Fragen aufzuwerfen, z.B.: Soll nicht
Wesentliches an den Grundannahmen der Psychoanalyse preisgegeben
werden? Nun können Sie diese Frage für relativ belanglos halten.
Immerhin können bestimmte Fragen nur von einer bestimmten Position
her gelöst werden. Zu dieser Diskussion hier möchte ich Folgendes
sagen: Die m.E. essentielle Grundannahme psychoanalytischer Praxis,
nämlich die der lebensgeschichtlichen Aufarbeitung, läßt sich
zweifellos nur einlösen, wenn man die von Herrn Apel kontrovers zu
Herrn Essler aufgestellte Position der transzendentalen Reflexion
festhält. Ich möchte das jetzt nur als eine Behauptung formulieren
und zu einem zweiten, wichtigeren und auch einleuchtenderen Punkt
übergehen: zu den Unterscheidungen von Kunstsprachen und natürlichen
Sprachen. Aus der wesentlichen Grundposition der Psychoanalyse,
nämlich der Triebtheorie, ergibt sich Folgendes: Wenn wir überhaupt
versuchen wollen, psychoanalytische Annahmen mit Sprachtheorie zu
verbinden oder sprachtheoretisch zu formulieren, so kann doch eine
wesentliche Annahme dieser triebtheoretischen Fundierung nur heißen,
daß Triebe, d.h. also Triebmomente des Kindes in seiner isolierten
Subjektivität bei dem Prozess der Einübung in Interaktionen, bei
dem, was von Herrn Lorenz unter dem Titel der Einführungssituation
gekennzeichnet wurde, in Inhalte der Sprache eingebracht werden. Das
bedeutet aber doch, daß damit die Naturdialektik in der Auseinandersetzung mit der inneren Natur in einer Weise hereingebracht wird,
die sich nicht mit der Forderung nach einer Widerspruchsfreiheit
vertragen kann. Ich würde also sagen, daß mindestens eine Sprache,
die eingeübt wird, das Merkmal der Widersprüchlichkeit und der Un-
klarheit enthalten muß.
Ungeheuer: Danke schön!

MODAL-LOGICAL INVESTIGATION OF COMMUNICATIVE ACTIONS

Panel: E.M.Barth, Rijksuniversiteit of Utrecht
       R. Hilpinen, University of Turku
       T.C.Potts, The University of Leeds

Chairman: G. Hasenjaeger, University of Bonn

February, 18th, morning session.

BARTH:

UNTIMELY REMARKS ON THE LOGIC OF "THE MODALITIES" IN NATURAL
LANGUAGE

The topic I have been asked to take up is the relevance of modal
logic to the activities of persons working either in linguistics or
in communication studies. This topic is too large and has to be
limited in some way or other. My remarks will be addressed to those
who are interested in modal or other logic from tne point of view of
the search for a "natural logic", a logic inherent to the mental
capacities of human beings and somehow reflected in (the rules of)
the natural languages. The idea that such a natural logic exists and
finds its expression in grammatical phenomena and rules has recently
been re-introduced in an influential article by G.Lakoff.[1] I shall
try to convey why I have no confidence in this idea. In order to do
so I shall, largely by way of examples, raise the problem of the
likely meanings of overt and explicit occurences of certain alethic
modal expressions which are very frequently found in the ordinary
usage of European languages. No attempt will be made to estimate the
general value of the basic notions in the semantics of modern modal
logic for the grammatical study of other kinds of intensional
expressions. What is more, when speaking of modal logic I have in
mind logic in the sense of a theory of inference, and not only in
the sense of rules for well-formedness and rules that allow us to
distinguish non-synonymous paraphrases of ambiguous sentences.
As a working hypothesis for grammarians, I would expect the
following assumption to be more fertile than the assumption of a
natural modal logic: t h e   (o n e   a n d   o n l y) n a t u r a l
m o d a l   l o g i c   e i t h e r   d o e s   n o t   e x i s t   o r
e l s e   i s   a   r e g r e t t a b l e   p h e n o m e n o n. There
are three possible inter-relationships between modal logic and the
European languages, which are the only ones I know anything about.
Either these languages have been influenced by more than one modal
logic, or some modal logics have been influenced by some of these
languages, or else there has been a mutual interaction. In the two
millennia since the earliest modal logic, the latter is by far the
most likely. Unless Natural Language and its logic somehow preceded
man, we should expect natural languages to reflect all these modal
"logics", at least the older ones and those which have not been so
well worked out.
In order to show that this is the most fertile working hypothesis

I start with a number of historical remarks.

E a r l y   m o d e r n   l o g i c. Modern logic is roughly a hundred
years old, if we take Frege's "Begriffsschrift" as the real turning
point, rather than the work of Boole. During the first half of those
hundred years hardly a word was said about modalities. The founders
of modern logic, Boole, Frege, Russell, and their contemporaries had
no use for modal operators in solving their problems. Russell wanted
to deal with everything, and did so. He wrote on a huge number of
real philosophical problems and also discussed earlier attempts to
solve them without feeling any need for a calculus - in the sense of
a formalized logical syntax - containing expressions like
'necessarily' and 'possibly'. These expressions did not belong among
his analytical tools.

T h e   f i r s t   e x t e n s i o n s   o f   m o d e r n   s y n t a x
a n d   s e m a n t i c s. When Fregean syntax and theory of
inference had been around for almost forty years, the American
philosopher C.I.Lewis tried to do something constuctive in order to
meet the frequent complaints about the truth-functional reading of
the conditional 'if...then...' taken for granted by most logicians
(L.E.J.Brouwer did not see himself as a logician). This attempt led
Lewis into axiomatic investigations of a number of uses of the
expressions 'it is possibly the case that...' and 'it is necessarily
the case that...', all of which had a certain "intuitive support",
as one often says when unable to offer any better justification.
At about the same time, and as a result of reading Aristotle's "De
Interpretatione", the Polish logician Jan Łukasiewicz became
interested in the relationship between the problem of determinism
and that of the truth-value of statements about non-necessary, yet
not impossible future events, like the statement: There will be a
sea-battle tomorrow. In order to solve the problem of their
evaluation with respect to truth and falsity he invoked an
additional third irreducible truth-value, call it   t e r t i u m, to
be ascribed to statements about   f u t u r e   c o n t i n g e n t s,
i.e. future events which may or may not take place. By adding this
new truth-value to the set of semantic primitives Lukasiewicz so
widened the framework of theoretical logic that it became possible
to accomodate the expressions 'necessarily', 'possibly', and
'contingently' from an inferential point of view within truth-
functional logic. That is to say, it became possible to give a
clear meaning to these expressions by defining them as unary (one-

argument) truth-functional operators upon sentences, just like the
expression 'not', or 'it is not the case that'.

The fit with n a t u r a l (read:traditionally conventional) uses
of these modal expressions was not too good. However, the fit
between the (two-valued) truth-functional inclusive 'or' and natural
uses of that word is not perfect either; jet that is no good reason
for rejecting the truth-functional definition, which is at least as
valuable as the other uses of 'or'.

T h e s e c o n d w a v e. After another period of forty years,
that is to say about 1960, Kripke, Hintikka, and Kanger introduced
a completely different type of semantics for languages whose syntax
contains modal operators, while retaining the principle of two-
valuedness. The best-known version of this type of semantics is
Kripke's Leibniz-inspired p o s s i b l e w o r l d s -ontologies.
This approach is more attractive from every point of view than the
a d h o c introduction of additional truth-values in the style of
Lukasiewicz. Since then, modal logic has been at the centre of
interest in logic itself and is attracting an increasing number of
very able persons, both philosophers and mathematicians. No doubt
there is some ground to hope that this may ultimately lead to a real
philosophical break-through for mankind. On the other hand it cannot
be denied that many, if not all, logicians are more proficient
in producing variants on other systems than in expect them to be
good for. In any case, the proposals for modal axiom systems,
ontologies and other models are multiplying like rabbits. The new
approach gave logicians a new scientific paradigm, and the field
of modal logic has definitely become accepted as what Thomas Kuhn
has called a "normal science". Today you can be a modal logician in
the same culturally relaxed manner as you can be a dentist. Yet
nobody is anywhere near to making a choice between the uncountably
many new definitions of 'necessarily' and 'possibly' which are every
year loaded upon us.

T h e s c e p t i c s. It should be noted that not everyone has
climbed upon the modal band-wagon. Thus the logical positivist
Gustav Bergmann, always sceptical of fancy words and notions, has
expressed the simple opinion that modal logic is good for absolutely
nothing at all.[2] He said that in 1960, however, which is so long ago
as to make his verdict irrelevant with respect to the second wave.
More significantly, another American logician, Richard Martin, has
quite recently written very ironically about "modal logic and its

train",[3] clearly seeing it as a fashionable but superfluous
playground - too fashionable. Other sceptics are W.V.O.Quine (see
below), P.T.Geach, and D.Davidson, who for various reasons warns us
against an uncritical reliance upon modal logic and its semantic
apparatus. The number of total sceptics among logicians is, however,
relatively small and seems to be decreasing. This, however, is due
to the fact that the focus of interest within modal logic as a
discipline has shifted from the modalities in the narrower sense to
the study of all kinds of intensional operators and verbs. That
leaves us with an unsolved problem with respect to the meanings of
alethic modalities in natural languages.

" A c c e p t   t h e   c h a i n s   o f   n e c e s s i t y ! " At the
other **end** of the philosophical spectrum there is, e.g., the English
Hegelian philosopher J.N.Findlay, who in 1963 expressed the
following opinion, and reprinted it in 1970: "Philosophy may well,
therefore, have the task of putting the philosopher back into the
chains of necessity--chains willingly and happily accepted--after he
has enjoyed the intoxication of a liberating logic--such as that of
Russell in the "Principia Mathematica"--which has given him too
many wings."[4]

Findlay is more honest than some, but has not personally contributed
to the clarification of the concepts of necessity and possibility
which he and many other traditional philosophers have in mind.

Q u i n e   v e r s u s   e s s e n t i a l i s m. Those concepts,
however vague, are in fact very common in our culture and can be
traced back to Aristotle. It is more than doubtful whether these
(unsuccessful) conceptual structures and the use(s) of 'necessarily'
and 'possibly' which go with them are studied by modern modal
logicians. Nevertheless, anyone who looks into articles and books
discussing the merits of contemporary modal logic cannot fail to
observe that some modern logicians, headed by W.V.O.Quine, are very
sceptical especially about so-called quantified modal logic. This
scepticism derives from a fear that by developing modal logic we may
re-establish the linguistic and conceptual structures which Quine
sums up under the name of "Aristotelian essentialism". The quotation
from Findlay may serve as an indication that there is a general and
very real cultural basis for this fear. Quine and others are
especially sceptical about the justification of languages which
allow, as all natural languages do, a free syntactic interplay of
modal expressi ns with the usual quantifier-expressions '(for)

every' and '(for) some' or 'there is at least one'. These languages
are said to be philosophically questionable if their syntax allows
a modal operator, within whose scope only a predicate (a propositional function) falls, itself to occur within the scope of a quantifier, so that an expression s o m e t h i n g   i s   (p o s s i-
b l y   F) will count as grammatical. Such a sentence, saying that
there are things in the domain of discourse with the property of
being possibly F, does indeed smack of essentialism. If you can have
the property of being possibly F, then it is also at least meaningful to say that you can have the property of being necessarily F.
Quine, no less than Jean-Paul Sartre, seems repelled by this idea. No
qualms are felt if modal operators may only appear in front, as in
p o s s i b l y   s o m e t h i n g   i s   F . A sentence of this form
consists of a well-formed (closed) sentence preceded by a
propositional operator 'possibly', the use of which, therefore, does
not go beyond what is permitted by the syntactical rules of
propositional modal logic. The objections to quantified modal logic,
or modal quantified logic (modal predicate logic), are often
presented as a criticism of the formula known as the Barcan-formula,
which some logicians have regarded as a tautology and, hence,
a   f o r t i o r i   as well-formed:

$$\Diamond(Ex)Fx \rightarrow (Ex)\Diamond Fx,$$

read: i f   i t   i s   p o s s i b l e   t h a t   s o m e t h i n g
i s   F ,   t h e n   t h e r e   i s   s o m e t h i n g   w h i c h
i s   p o s s i b l y   F (or: w h i c h   p o s s i b l y   i s   F).
According to those logicians, therefore, from the truth of a
sentence of the form p o s s i b l y   s o m e t h i n g   i s   F
one may infer not only the well-formedness of the corresponding
sentence s o m e t h i n g   i s   (p o s s i b l y   F), but even
its truth.[5]

" A   s i m p l e   f a l l a c y " :   q u a n t i f i e r s   o r
m o d a l i t i e s ?   Among the many acute observations made by
G.E.Moore on the logic and illogic which are embedded in ordinary
language, one is especially relevant for what I want to bring out
here: that a study of the grammar of modalities and of many other
expressions in natural languages should be based upon a firm
understanding of the old as well as of the modern theories of the
logic of the words 'all', 'any', 'some', 'there is', 'none', and the
like, and of the different ways in which these theories interlock
with other pieces of logical theory (theories), such as the theories
of certain connectives ('or', 'not'), of predication, of relations,

of substitution, of description, etc. so as to form entirely
different conceptual structures. Moore's observation is, I think,
of a far deeper significance with respect to natural language than
he himself seems to have realized. Moore says that there are at
least two senses of the word 'possibly', or 'may be', and that if
you confound them, you may turn up with some weird results.[6] He
cites the sentence It is possible for a human being to be of the
female sex, which can be paraphrased   s a l v a   v e r i t a t e
in a number of ways, all containing some modal locution:

(1a) I t   i s   p o s s i b l e   f o r   a human being t o   b e   o f
      the female sex

(1b) Human being s   m a y   b e   of the female sex

Many German authors prefer the following vernacular:

(1c) D e r   Mensch   k a n n   weiblich sein,

thus combining a modal expression 'kann sein' with a definite
article. The importance of this will become clearer later on.

Moore first compares sentences like (1) to universal statements
without modal expressions, such as

(2a) All human beings are mortal,

·or, as one often says,

(2b) Human beings are mortal.

Again I add a German variant:

(2c) D e r   Mensch   i s t   sterblich.

He now introduces the assumption that the sentences (1), like the
sentences (2), have universal import, and subsequently carries this
assumption a d   a b s u r d u m. If one of the variants of (1), in
that sense which makes it a true sentence, is to have universal
import, then it must be a sentence in which the modal expression
comes a f t e r the universal quantifier: Every human being may be
of the female sex, since the opposite order would make (1) a false
sentence. The most natural symbolization of this in modern logic is:

(3)   (x) $\left[Hx \to \Diamond Fx \right]$,

with 'x is of the female sex' as the argument of the modal operator
This way of paraphrasing (1) yields, together with

(4)   I, G.E.Moore, am a human being,

the remarkable result

(5)   I, G.E.Moore, may be of the female sex.

Since Moore knew that he was no woman this is obviously false when
'may be' is understood in the epistemic sense of 'it is unknown
whether'.

From this Moore draws the conclusion that the sentences (1) cannot
be taken to express universal statements at all, and that 'possible'
in (1a) has a meaning which cannot even be approached by assuming it
to be an operator modifying the predicate Fx . The truth is, Moore
says, that (1) is nothing but a misleading manner of expressing
what may be expressed just as well by the simple particular
proposition
(6)   Some human being are of the female sex,
or, more briefly,
(6')   Some H are F.
And from (6) and (4), (5) does not follow. The lesson to be drawn
from this is: do not read a modality where a mere particularity is
"meant".

Moore refers to the argument form which takes us from (1) and (4)
to (5) as "this simple fallacy". His point is that as soon as we
take (1) to be of the form (3), this fallacy is forced upon us.

T h i s   f a l l a c y   i s   a   f e a t u r e   o f   t h e   o l d
N P + V P - l o g i c   (s u b j e c t - p r e d i c a t e
l o g i c.) Now it happens to be the case that this simple fallacy
is a fundamental systematic feature of perhaps the greater part of
traditional logic, the logic that was in residence, so to speak, in
the universities before Frege's new logic of the quantifiers was
generally accepted. In the first place, practically all earlier
logicians assumed the logically correct grouping of words in a
particular sentence like (6) to be
(7)   (Some human beings) (are of the female sex),
or, more briefly,
(7')   (Some H) (is F),
with 'Some H' as a noun phrase or subject term. Second, a great many
of them proceeded from (7) to one of the variants of (1), usually
to (1c) when the language in question was German. The first is a
purely syntactic principle, the second an inferential one. Together
these two principles constitute the basis of t r a d i t i o n a l
logical essentialism, and the "chains of necessity" which Findlay
so dearly misses in the Frege-Russell logic are welded from
precisely these principles.

It should be noted at this point that due to the lack of individual
variables in the pre-Fregean variants of logical syntax, all
logicians before Frege understood (7) in such a way that if we want
to describe it in modern technical terms, then we shall have to say

that (7) was taken to contain a second-order quantifier, not a first-order one. The truth of (7) was assumed to imply or to "presuppose" the existence of a general entity. Most older forms of logical thinking rest upon this assumption.[7]

Modal operators in combination with Fregean quantificational syntax. On the principles of Fregean syntax, the right analysis of (6) is, by approximation,

(8)   Some (is H and F)

i.e.,

(8')   There is something which (is H and F).

This sentence contains no noun-phrase whatsoever and therefore does not suggest (1c) or one of the other variants of (1) as a paraphrase. Nobody would think of deriving or inferring (1c) **from** (6) when the brackets are put as in (8) and (8').

The reader may now want to draw the conclusion that if one starts out from Frege's syntax and logic of the quantifiers, one does not run the risk of landing oneself in essentialism of any kind and that modal logic, even "quantified" (a highly misleading expression!) logic of the expressions 'necessarily' and 'possibly' will be all right. That may be so; I think we do not really know that yet. The fact that one road to essentialism has been blocked does not exclude the possibility that other roads are still open or may be created while going along.

Moore's argument rests upon the assumption that (5), the sentence I, G.E.Moore, may be of the female sex, is false, and this again rests upon the assumption that 'may be' is given a meaning which I have here called e p i s t e m i c p o s s i b i l i t y : it is unknown whether.... Moore himself does not call it by that name. He speaks of "a confusion of two different uses of the word 'possible' or 'may'". He seems to take into account only their epistemic use and, in addition, the use of these terms to paraphrase sentences beginning with 'some'.

P u r t i l l o n l o g i c a l p o s s i b i l i t y. Moore's argument was recently taken up by Purtill,[8] who points out that 'possibly' and 'may' can be given a meaning which differs from either of those considered by Moore. Purtill holds that although (1) may be misleading if 'possibly' is used in one **sense** (in the above sense of e p i s t e m i c p o s s i b i l i t y), it is not misleading but simply true if you use it in a weaker or at least

different sense, even if we cast (1) into the form of (3), as Moore
was apparently not willing to do. This other sense he calls "logical
possibility", to which belongs a notion of "logical necessity".
"Surely the sex of any individual is always a matter of contingent
fact and never a matter of logical necessity," he writes, thereby
trying to make us accept (3) as true, and a f o r t i o r i as
well-formed. But he glosses over both that very many people,
especially theologians, have thought otherwise, and also that there
is more than one way of denying the statement: "A person's sex is a
matter of logical necessity". Let us take G.E.Moore as an example,
as he did himself. On the Leibniz-inspired semantics of modern modal
logic, the latter statement would mean:

(a) there is an individual essence, G.E.Moore "as such", which (or
who) exists in all possible worlds (of some as yet unspecified kind)
and which (who) is a male in all those possible worlds, maleness
being an essential characteristic.

This outlook is denied by someone who holds:

(b) there is an individual essence, G.E.Moore "as such", which
exists in all possible worlds and which is a male in the present
world and a female in some other conceivable world.

That is clearly Purtill's own outlook, and presumably that of most
modern logicians. But (a) can also be denied in the following
manner:

(c) "individuals have no essences"
as John Stuart Mill put it, and which is also Quine's outlook. This
means that the question whether a logically g o o d syntax ought
to generate sentences of the form m i s p o s s i b l y F is
still open. It would be premature to defend a definitive standpoint
here, but I object to the idea that there is in our culture a more
or less clear and semantically non-redundant - semantically "deep",
if you like - notion called 'logical necessity' which (i) is studied
by modern logicians and which (ii) already has something to do with
the construction and inner system of our natural languages. If it
cannot be established that a certain meaning of the expressions
'logical necessity' or 'logical possibility' is a reasonably clear
pre-scientific concept, then we cannot go on to look into the
natural languages for embodiments of that meaning. In my opinion,
no pre-scientific, unambiguous and intellectually non-redundant
meaning related to the meaning which Purtill, for instance, ascribes

to the expressions 'logically possible' and 'logically necessary'
exists, at least not in common usage.

My first argument for this is that in pre-Fregean logic, and notably
in the rationalist and idealist logic of 'all' and 'some', sentences
like (1) above expressed a kind of possibility which w a s
considered to be a logical one, though it was often regarded as
ontological, epistemological, metaphysical, etc. at the same time;
at any rate, it was part and parcel of rationalist and idealist
logical theory. This logical theory or, **perhaps one should say, this**
logical conception, produced a great amount of verbal utterances
which cannot in any **reasonable** and unprejudiced way be isolated
from 'natural' uses of language. Modern natural languages have
features which quite clearly point to the impact of that old
unsuccessful notion - as Moore unwittingly demonstrated.That notion
can therefore, **alas,** be said to be present in natural language and
hence to be a part of Natural Logic.

The second argument has to do with the meanings allotted to these
frequently used expressions, 'is possible', or 'may be', and 'is
necessarily', or 'must be', by the semantic systems of modern modal
logic, and with the likelihood that these meanings have, more than
incidentally, counterparts in the natural languages. Those modern
notions, I shall argue, are (as yet) absent from Natural Logic.

Purtill, who takes (3) to be well-formed and true, has also to
accept (5) as true, since, as he points out, the argument

$$(x) \left[Hx \longrightarrow \Diamond Fx \right]$$

(9)   Hm

$$\therefore \Diamond Fm$$

is logically valid, at least as long as one accepts the rules of
m o d u s   p o n e n s   and the   d i c t u m   d e   o m n i, or
universal instantiation (the latter rule is in fact rejected in
some modal systems, but Purtill does not go into that). By ending
his discussion right here, Purtill, like so many others, probably
succeeds in making many readers believe that there already exists
in human communication a clear and simple notion of logical
necessity, and connected with a clear and simple and not unimportant
notion of logical possibility, which simply lies here awaiting the
right logician to come along and provide the correct description of
what every competent user of "natural" language means and always has

meant. Now suppose that 'm' does not abbreviate 'G.E.Moore', but
rather the name of Moore's father and let us try to adopt a historical perspective, which admittedly is not easy, asking the following
question: on what grounds can one maintain that "the idealized
speaker", the average competent user of a natural language who lived,
for instance, two hundred years ago, really recognized, consciously
or subconsciously, different meanings behind 'm may be a female',
'the father of Moore may be a female', 'the father, who belongs to
Moore, may be a female', 'the father, a man by definition of Fatherness, who belongs to Moore, may be a female', '(that) father, who is
necessarily a male, and who belongs to Moore, may be a female'? What
about the idealized average competent user of English four hundred
years ago? Or of Latin, eight hundred years ago? Or was that not a
natural language, and if not, where does the limit go?

One need not go as far as saying that no difference between sentences such as the four above was recognized before our time, but I
do think there is little reason for holding that the differences (if
any) which were recognized by Leibniz or by Kant were t h e
s a m e as those recognized by modern logicians. And why, if competence is not relative to a certain time in history, which in the
eyes of a great number of linguists it clearly is not, should
intelligent men like Leibniz and Kant be expelled from the class of
competent users of language?

The problems concerning the modalities have a parallel in the
theory of negation: the sentence The King of France i s n o t a
monarch is, given Russell's theory of descriptions, true in one
sense and contradictory in another. The same holds of The father of
Moore i s p o s s i b l y a female. Kant, too, distinguished between two kinds of negation, since then often called "privative" and
"limitative" or "infinite" negation. But just as it would be a mistake to assume that Kant's notions of negation were the same as the
two senses (if I may call them that) of the spaced n o t in this
example, so it would be a mistake to think that the notions of possibility distinguished by "the" competent user of language are those
of modern logicians. Kant's two negations were in fact assumed to be
significant in connection with general and not in connection with
individual subject terms; "Fatherness", entailing "Maleness", would
be such a term. Kant o u g h t to have said that the necessity of
a distinction arises in connection with definite descriptions, and
the reason why he did not should, I think, be sought in his inabili-

ty to distinguish definite from generic descriptions. Much the same
may be expected to hold for older distinctions between notions of
possibility.

Let us face it: the notion or notions of logical necessity studied
by modern logicians are not pre-fabricated, they are being made up,
constructed, in our century. This is certainly the case where modal
expressions 'necessary' and 'possibly', or 'must' and 'may' or
'can', are used in connection with quantifiers or articles (descriptions), which in natural languages happens all the time. The very
fact that there are almost as many modal systems as there are modal
logicians is a strong argument in favour of my thesis. As one modal
logician puts it: "The modalities can be m a d e formally respect-
able, free from logical difficulties"[9] (space mine). They are not
so by themselves, i.e. on the strength of the rules of any natural
language and its logic. Contemporary modal logic is a study that
assumes the new logic of 'some', which comprises the rule of existential instantiation, furthermore polyadic (relational) predication
and iterated and internal quantification, inclusive disjunctions, a
theory of descriptions, and the distinction between first and higher
order quantification. Older modal notions, however, belonged to a
conceptual network built up from the analysis of 'some' exemplified
in (7) above, monadic (substantival) predication, single external
quantifiers, exclusive disjunctions, no theory of descriptions, and
articles in the place of second-order quantifiers. Each of these
older principles suffices to produce, or induce, vague and intrac-
table modalities, as attempts at the solution of logical (inferential) problems of language. A student of the grammar of natural
languages is likely to meet occurrences of "the modalities" deriving
from these sources far more often than he will meet references to
notions of logical necessity and possibility resembling the notions
which are being isolated and even created by modern modal logicians.
He will meet a number of occurrences of modal expressions which are
either nonsense or else intellectually eliminable in a more or less
obvious manner in favour of other logical constants (such as the inclusive 'or'), which the notions discussed by modern modal logicians
are not intended to be. It seems to me that he will have to be prepared for this encounter, and I doubt that a study of modern modal
logic in isolation from earlier, less successful but intellectually
influential logical theories will so prepare him.

L a k o f f 's e x a m p l e. For those who consider the features
of language illustrated in Moore's fallacy as too superficial and as
too obviously misleading to be worthy of scholarly attention, I have
a neat surprise. On the first page of the very article in which he
expresses his belief in a natural logic as that (one) logic which is
somehow embedded in (any) natural language, Lakoff offers the
following example of what he regards as a valid argument:

(1)   The members of the royal family are visiting dignitaries.

(2)   Visiting dignitaries can be boring.

(3)   a. Therefore, the members of the royal family can be boring.
"Thus if 'visiting' is assumed to be a modifier of the head noun
'dignitaries'", Lakoff says, "then (3a) follows as a logical
consequence."

In a logic for which that holds, the following argument is another
piece of valid inference:

(1')   The members of the presidential (Heinemann) family are
        German visiting dignitaries.

(2')   German visiting dignitaries can be ferocious.

(3')   Therefore, the members of the presidential family can be
        ferocious.

As P.T.Geach in the title of his latest book says: logic matters.
The second argument is a clear counter-example to the logical
validity of the English form of Lakoff's argument. These are better
examples of Moore's simple fallacy than Moore's own example: Lakoff
says "can be", not 'may be', even in the conclusion, and cannot
therefore be rescued by Purtill. Besides, if (2') has the form
$(x) [Gx \rightarrow \Diamond Fx]$, then it would have no more informative value than
$(x) [\text{Wombat } x \rightarrow \Diamond \text{Ferocious } x]$, which is also true but which only
says that any completely non-ferocious animal like a wombat is (say)
a tiger in some other conceivable world in an unspecified set of
such "worlds".[10] So that would be a very unreasonable interpretation
of (2') when uttered as a statement of natural language. Lakoff's
example therefore expresses no modal argument in the sense of modern
modal logic and thus a f o r t i o r i not a valid one. It may
be used to express, but then only incompletely, an inductive
argument of some kind, with hidden time references and variables and
with a suppressed premiss or condition to the effect that nothing
is known about the members of the royal/presidential family that can
be used to refute the conclusion. The logical status of the latter
assumption has often been an object of discussion. We need not go

into that discussion here, for since he says that the conclusion
"follows as a logical consequence", Lakoff has in all likelihood
not had this kind of inductive argument in mind either. I think
we should rather say that, as it stands, Lakoff's example is simply
invalid. Since man is a prejudiced **animal** his example may well
belong to a natural logic, but hardly to a normative one. Has the
time not come to take a more critical attitude towards natural
languages, and to ask from which natural un-logic this kind of
locution derives?

NOTES

1.   George Lakoff, Linguistics and natural logic, S y n t h e s e
22 (1970), pp. 151-271.

2.   Gustav Bergmann, The philosophical significance of modal logic,
M i n d, n.s. 69 (1960), pp. 466-485.

3.   Richard Martin, L o g i c, L a n g u a g e a n d
M e t a p h y s i c s, New York and London 1971, p. 17.

4.   J.N. Findlay, A s c e n t t o t h e A b s o l u t e,
London and New York 1970, p. 120.

5   For a discussion of various sorts of essentialism defined in
terms of modal logic, see Terence Parsons, Essentialism and
quantified modal logic, T h e P h i l o s o p h i c a l
R e v i e w, LXXVIII (1969), pp. 35-52; also published in: Leonard
Linsky (ed.), R e f e r e n c e a n d M o d a l i t y, Oxford
. 1971.

6.   G.E. Moore, P h i l o s o p h i c a l P a p e r s, London
1956, pp.

7.   This is discussed in E.M. Barth, D e l o g i c a v a n d e
l i d w o o r d e n i n d e t r a d i t i o n e l e
f i l o s o f i e, Leiden 1971, ch. X. English translation
forthcoming under the title: T h e l o g i c o f t h e
A r t i c l e s i n T r a d i t i o n a l P h i l o s o p h y.
A S t u d y i n C o n c e p t u a l S t r u c t u r e s (Reidel,
Dordrecht, spring 1974).

8.   Richard L. Purtill, L o g i c f o r P h i l o s o p h e r s,
New York etc. 1971, pp. 119-122, 265-267.

9.   Dagfinn Føllesdal, Quine on Modality, S y n t h e s e 19
(1968-69), p. 156. Føllesdal italicizes "formally", not "made".

10. Purtill would seem to agree with this: "Thus the alternative
analysis of the crucial premise does not produce a version of the
parallel argument which is a good argument and at the same time
leads to the conclusion that, in any interesting sense, Moore may be
of the female sex" (o.c., p. 267).

HILPINEN:
ON THE SEMANTICS OF PERSONAL DIRECTIVES[*]

I. D i r e c t i v e s   a n d   F i a t s

In this paper I shall illustrate the modal-logical investigation of
communicative acts by means of an example. I shall consider some
aspects of the logic of c o m m a n d s   or   d i r e c t i v e s.
The latter expression is derived from Albert Hofstadter and J.C.C.
McKinsey's classic paper "On the Logic of Imperatives".[1] Hofstadter
and McKinsey distinguish two types of imperatives,
d i r e c t i v e s   and   f i a t s. Directives contain reference
to an "addressee" or a "recipient" to whom the command is directed,
whereas fiats are impersonal; they do not indicate who is to carry
out the command. Thus John, open the door is a directive, and Let
there be light is a fiat.[2] A similar distinction can be drawn
between 'personal' and 'impersonal' ought-propositions or deontic
statements. Hector-Neri Castañeda has presented this distinction as
a contrast between the O u g h t - t o - d o and the O u g h t -
t o - b e. According to Castañeda,

> "Deontic statements divide neatly into (i) those that involve
> agents and support imperatives, and (ii) those that involve
> states of affairs and are agentless and have by themselves
> nothing to do with imperatives. The former belong to what used
> to be called the O u g h t - t o - d o and the latter to the
> O u g h t - t o - b e."[3]

This distinction is perhaps not quite as clear-cut as Castañeda
seems to believe. For instance, the imperative John, be quiet!
(or John ought to be quiet) involves an agent a n d a state of
affairs (that John be quiet). However, if it is formulated only in
terms of agency, it is clearly analogous to Hofstadter and
McKinsey's distinction between directives and fiats: agential
deontic propositions are similar to directives, and agentless
propositions similar to fiats.[4]

Deontic logicians have often observed that oughts and obligations
are normally relative to persons: they are some person's oughts and
obligations. Nevertheless, most systems of deontic logic seem to
deal with impersonal oughts (or fiats) alone, they contain no
reference to agents. If agents are mentioned at all, it is assumed
that the normative concepts under discussion are relative to a
single person, and explicit reference to this person is unnecessary.[5]
In such systems the problems related to agency cannot be discussed

in a systematic manner.

This paper will concentrate on questions related to agency; other
logical and philosophical problems concerning commands and
imperatives (for instance, the problem of temporal reference in the
case of imperatives) will not be discussed here.[6]
Commands can be expressed in several different ways; for instance,
the command that Mary kiss Peter (where Mary is the addressee) can
be expressed by an imperative sentence
(1)   Mary, kiss Peter!
or by a deontic sentence
(2)   Mary shall kiss Peter,
which involves a personal s h a l l (personal obligation).
(2) will be termed the d e o n t i c c o u n t e r p a r t of (1).
The command (1) can also be expressed in a more explicit form
(3)   I command you (Mary) to kiss Peter.
We may call (1) the i m p e r a t i v e f o r m u l a t i o n,
(2) the d e o n t i c f o r m u l a t i o n, and (3) the p e r-
f o r m a t i v e f o r m u l a t i o n of the command that Mary
kiss Peter. All these formulations can be used to express the same
'basic meaning' (the same command or request),[7] and we can assume
that a given logical relationship holds between two imperatives if
and only if this relationship holds between their deontic counterparts (and between the corresponding performatives). Thus I shall
assume that the logic of imperatives (or the logic of commands) is
identical with the logic of personal deontic propositions, and imperatives can be regarded as expressing personal 'imperative
obligations.'[8]

II. T h e L o g i c a l F o r m o f D i r e c t i v e s
What is the 'logical form' or the 'deep structure' of the directive
expressed by (1) - (3)? From the semantical viewpoint, the formulation (3) seems more explicit than (1) or (2), and the following formulation is perhaps even more explicit:
(4)   I command you (Mary) that you kiss Peter.
(4) shows the main semantical components of a command: (i) the
s o u r c e or the speaker (expressed by "I"),)ii) the a d-
d r e s s e e ("you"), (iii) the c o n t e n t of the command
("that you kiss Peter"), and (iv) the c o m m a n d f u n c-
t i o n - expressed by the verb "command". According to this analysis, the command function is a **ternary** function which takes (i)-
(iii) as arguments and yiels a command. (1) and (2) contain no ref-

erence to the source of the command, otherwise their semantical
structure is similar to that of (3) and (4).
In this paper I shall analyse directives in the form expressed by
personal deontic sentences, and treat the command function and its
first argument (the source) as an unanalysed whole. This is tanta-
mount to the assumption that the source of the command is always
constant. Thus simple directives can be expressed by sentences of
the form

(5) $O(a,F)$,

where 'a' is a name of an agent, 'F' is a sentence, and 'O' is
a functor which takes a name and a sentence as arguments and makes a
directive sentence. (5) can be read 'a has an imperative obligation
that F' or simply 'F is obligatory for a'. Normally 'F' is an
action sentence or a description of some individual event (which may
or may not involve the individual a), but we shall not formally restrict the second argument of 'O' to such sentences. However, it
will be assumed that no deontic operator (for instance, the O -oper-
ator) occurs in 'F': in this paper I shall not consider the it-
e r a t i o n of the O -operator.[9] The concept of imperative permissibility can be defined in terms of 'O' in the customary way:

(6) $P(a,F) \equiv \sim O(a, \sim F)$.

'$P(a,F)$' means simply that a has no imperative obligation that $\sim F$.

III. C o n d i t i o n s   o f   C o n s i s t e n c y   f o r
    I m p e r a t i v e   O b l i g a t i o n s

When is a set of directives consistent? Let us consider first the
imperative obligations of a single person a_1. It seems natural to
require that at least the following minimal condition is satisfied:

(A1)   If a set of sentences A is consistent and
         $\{O(a_1,F_1), O(a_1,F_2), \ldots, O(a_1,F_n), P(a_1,G)\} \subseteq A$,
         then $\{F_1, F_2, \ldots F_n, G\}$ is consistent.

(A1) says that the imperative obligations of a person are jointly
consistent only if they can be simultaneously fulfilled, and G is
imperatively permissible for a_1 only if it can be realized in conjunction with a_1's obligations. According to the standard semantics
for deontic logic, a condition similar to (A1) holds for absolute
obligations or f i a t s.[10] (A1) is in accord with the view that
the standard deontic logic is interpretable as the logic of directives for a single agent. Consider now a set of directives involving
imperative obligations of several agents a_1. It seems plausible to
generalize (A1) to such systems as well: a system of directives

for a_1, a_2,...,is consistent only if it is possible for every agent a_i to fulfill his obligations without preventing others from carrying out their duties, and G is permissible for a_i if and only if it is compatible with his obligations. Thus we obtain the condition

(A2)   If a set of sentences M is consistent and
$$\{O(a_1, F_1^1), O(a_1, F_2^1),..., O(a_1, F_{n_1}^1),..., O(a_1, F_1^1),...,$$
$$O(a_1, F_{n_1}^1),..., P(a_i, G)\} \subseteq \mathit{M}, \text{ then } \{F_1^1, F_2^1,..., F_{n_1}^1,$$
$$..., F_1^1,..., F_{n_1}^1,...\} \text{ and } \{F_1^1,..., F_{n_1}^1, G\} \text{ are}$$
consistent.

According to (A1) and (A2), the standard semantics of deontic logic is applicable to the obligations of each agent a_i. Thus the truth-conditions of '$O(a_i,F)$' and '$P(a_i,G)$' can be defined in terms of models similar to those used in deontic logic. A m o d e l of the propositional logic of directives is a structure $\langle W, \mathcal{R}, V \rangle$, where $W = \{v, v', w, w',...\}$ is a set of possible worlds or points of reference, $\mathcal{R} = \{R_1, R_2,..., R_i,...\}$ is a set of binary relations defined on W such that a relation R_i is assigned to each agent a_i (i = 1,2,...) (R_i is termed the relation of directive a_i - alternativeness), and V is the valuation function of the model: V assigns a truth-value (0 or 1) to each sentence-letter at every point $v \in W$; the values of complex sentences are defined inductively in the usual way. The truth-conditions of '$O(a_i,F)$' and '$P(a_i,F)$' are defined as follows:

(C.O) $V(O(a_i,F),v) = 1$ if and only if $V(F,v') = 1$
         for every $v' \in W$ such that $R_i(v,v')$.

(C.P) $V(P(a_i,F),v) = 1$ if and only if $V(F,v') = 1$
         for some $v' \in W$ such that $R_i(v,v')$.

(A1) is satisfied if every $v \in W$ has an alternative v' such that everything that is obligatory for a_i at v is true at v'; thus we shall assume that all models satisfy the condition

(B1)   For every $v \in W$, there is a point v' such that
         $R_i(v,v')$.

Condition (A2) requires that every $v \in W$ has an alternative in which e v e r y agent has fulfilled his obligations, that is,

(B2)   For every $v \in W$, there is a point $v' \in W$
         such that $\bigcap_{i \in I} R_i(v,v')$,

where I is the set of all individual indices i. From the intuitive standpoint, v' is a world in which everything that is obligatory (at v) for s o m e agent is true. The main burden of (A2) was

to ensure that this is possible, and all **agents can fulfill their**
duties simultaneously.[11]

IV The Definability of Directives in
    terms of Fiats

To simplify the following discussion, I introduce the **following**
abbreviations:

(7) $R^* = \bigcap_{i \in I} R_i$,

           $W_v^* =$ the set of points $v' \in W$ such that $R^*(v,v')$, and

           $W_v^i =$ the set of points $v'' \in W$ such that $R_i(v,v'')$.

According to **(B2)**, every W_v^* is a nonempty set, and $W_v^* \subset W_v^i$ **for**
every $i \in I$. Let O^* be a new modal operator such that $O^* F$ is true
at $v \in W$ if and only if F is true at every point $v' \in W_v^*$, that is

(C.O*) $V(O^* F, v) = 1$ if and only if $V(F, v') = 1$

           for every $v' \in W$ such that $R^*(v,v')$.

The O^* -operator is termed the f i a t - o p e r a t o r
r e l a t e d t o O $(-,-)$. (B2) implies that every $v \in W$ has at
least one alternative v' such that $R^*(v,v')$; hence O^* is
similar to the standard **obligation** operator (or ought-operator) of
deontic logic. R^* is termed the f i a t a l t e r n a t i v e -
n e s s r e l a t i o n on W.

Let $\mathcal{P} = \left\{ S_1, S_2, \dots \right\}$ be a family of relations on W such that
every $S_i \in \mathcal{P}$ satisfies the **condition**

(C1) $R_i(v,v'')$ if and only if $S_i(v,v'')$ for

           some $v' \in W_v^*$.

According to (7), $R^* \subset R_i$ for every $i \in I$. This follows from
condition (C1) as well if we assume that the relations $S_i \in \mathcal{P}$ are
reflexive in W. Let $D(-,-)$ be a new modal operator defined by
the following semantical rule:

(C.D) $V(D(a_i,F),v) = 1$ if and only if $V(F,v') = 1$

           for every $v' \in W$ such that $S_i(v,v')$.

According to (C.O*), (C1) and (C.D), '$O(a_i,F)$' is true at v
if and only if '$D(a_i,F)$' is true at every point v' such that
$R^*(v,v')$. Thus

(8) $O(a_i,F) \equiv O^* D(a_i,F)$

is a logical truth.

In his paper "Some Main Problems of Deontic Logic" Jaakko Hintikka
has raised the question of "whether, and if so how, 'personal'
obligations and permissions can be defined in terms of impersonal
ones."[12] We can regard (8) as a definition of this kind. Instead of
taking the relations $R_i \in \mathcal{R}$ as semantic primitives, we can define
the models of personal directives as structures $\langle W, R^*, \mathcal{J}, v \rangle$,
where R^* is a fiat alternativeness relation on W, and $\mathcal{J}$ is a
set of reflexive relations on W such that a relation $S_i \in \mathcal{J}$ is
assigned to each agent a_i $(i = 1,2,...)$. The directive
alternativeness relations R_i can now be defined in terms of R^*
and S_i by (C1): each R_i is the relative product of R^* and
S_i.[13] (The relation R^* is now regarded as a primitive notion, not
defined in terms of $\mathcal{R}$.) The philosophical significance of this
analysis of $O(-,-)$ depends on the interpretation of the D-operator.
A personal obligation 'F is obligatory for a_i' can be expressed
in terms of an impersonal concept of obligation e.g. by using the
locution 'It is obligatory that a_i sees to it that F'; thus it
seems natural to read '$D(a_i,F)$' as 'a_i sees to it that F' or
'a_i brings it about that F' or simply 'a_i is the a g e n t of
F'. Thus '$D(-,-)$' can be termed an a g e n c y - o p e r a t o r.
This interpretation of 'D' will be dicussed in greater detail in
Section V.

The operators O^* and D enable us to make distinctions which
cannot be made in terms of the directive operator O alone.
Let P^* be the (absolute) m a y - operator related to O^*, that
is

(9) $P^* F \equiv \sim O^* \sim F$,

and let $C(a_i,F) \equiv \sim D(a_i, \sim F)$; thus

(C.C) $V(C(a_i,F),v) = 1$ if and only if $V(F,v) = 1$
           for some $v' \in W$ such that $S_i(v,v')$.

According to (8), the imperative permissibility of F for a_i
can be expressed by

(10) $P(a_i,F) \equiv \sim O^* D(a_i, \sim F)$
                     $\equiv P^* C(a_i,F)$.

However, in terms of O^* and D it is possible to define also
another notion of imperative permission, viz.

(11) $P^* D(a_i,F) \equiv \sim O \sim D(a_i,F)$.

$D(a_i,F)$ implies $C(a_i,F)$: consequently (11) implies (10), but
not conversely. Thus it seems appropriate to call (10) a w e a k
permission and (11) a s t r o n g permission: if $'P^{\times}C(a_i,F)'$
is true, F is weakly permissible for a_i, whereas $'P^{\times}D(a_i,F)'$
means that F is strongly permissible for a_i. The concept of
strong permission cannot be defined in terms of $'O(a_i,F)'$.
If 'D' is interpreted as an agency-operator, the weak
permissibility of F for a_i means that a_i may let F happen,
and the strong permissibility of F means that a_i may bring it
about that F (a_i may "do" F).

V. The Interpretation of D

Many philosophers have suggested that the concept of personal
s h a l l can be defined in terms of the absolute s h a l l
and some notion indicating agency.
For instance, Hofstadter and McKinsey say that if
"proper symbolic devices were introduced for the formalization
of imperatives, [the distinction between directives and fiats]
could be made in a syntactical manner. Thus we could
distinguish between imperatives which possess a certain
operator - the directive operator formed by putting a name

within sqare brackets - as $[$ Henry $]$ (Let it be the case that
Henry does not forget to stop at the grocery)!, and imperatives
which do not possess this operator, e.g. Let it be the case
that Henry does not forget to stop at the grocery!"[14]

In his paper "On the Semantics of the Ought-to-do" Hector-Neri
Castañeda has analysed directives in terms of an ought-operator
and a p r e s c r i p t i v e c o m p o n e n t.
Prescriptives contain at least one individual considered as an
a g e n t: Castañeda expresses agency by underlining the individual
term in question. (A special function symbol, such as   'D', would
of course do the same job.)[15]

Stig Kanger[16] has defined personal directives by schemata similar
to (11). He regards the schema

   Ought(X sees to it that $F(X,Y)$)

as an explication of the expression

   X has a right in relation to Y to the effect that $F(X,Y)$.

Kanger and Kanger[17] have proposed similar explications of different
types of (personal) rights. In his book "The Logical Form of
Imperatives" Brian F. Chellas has studied the definability of
directives in terms of a fiat-operator and a personal D -operator
in detail. Chellas has pointed out that the directive alternativeness relations R_i can be defined by (D3). He has termed the
relations S_i "investigative alternativeness relations".[18]
The logic of the D -operator has been studied by Ingmar Pörn and
by Lennart Åqvist. They translate 'D(a,F)' as 'a brings it
about that F'.[19]

The logic of the D - operator is similar to that of the modal
necessity operator. Certain principles of this logic are not in
agreement with the translations 'a does F', 'a is the agent
of F', 'a sees to it that F', and 'a brings it about that F'.
For instance, if F is a logical truth, D(a,F) is also logically
true, but it is clearly false or nonsensical to say that some person
is the agent of a logical truth. Let Z_v^i be the set of points
$v' \in W$ such that $S_i(v,v')$. The points $v' \in Z_v^i$ represent worlds

compatible with everything done by a_i. If F is an event which is
necessary for a_i in the sense that a_i has no control over F,
'F' is true in all worlds $v' \epsilon Z_v^i$, and hence 'D(a_i,F)' is true at v.
However, lack of control over some event or state of affairs seems
to be the very opposite of agency, and in this case the translation
of 'D(a_i,F)' in terms of agency seems seriously misleading.

This difficulty can be solved by distinguishing two complementary
aspects of action and agency. When we say that a is the agent of
F, we normally mean that the actions of a are, in the
circumstances in question, sufficient to make F true. This can be
termed the s u f f i c i e n t   c o n d i t i o n   a s p e c t   of
agency. This aspect does not exhaust the concept of agency, however:
if a is the agent of F, we also assume that the actions of a
are, in some **sense**, necessary for the occurence of F, and F is
not u n a v o i d a b l e for a. This may be termed the
n e c e s s a r y   c o n d i t i o n   a s p e c t of agency.[20] The
D -operator expresses only the former aspect of agency: thus
'D(a,F)' may be true even if a 's actions are not necessary for
the occurecce of F. Let 'E_v^i' be a sentence which is true at v'
if and only if $v' \epsilon Z_v^i$ ('E_v^i' can be thought of as a description of
what a_i does at v). According to (C.D), 'D(a_i,F)' is true at
v if and only if '$E_v^i \supset F$' holds at every point $v \epsilon W$, i.e., if E_v^i
is a sufficient condition of F. If F itself is causally or
logically necessary, anything is (causally or logically) sufficient
for F, and consequently 'D(a_i,F)' is always true. Thus we may
translate 'D(a_i,F)' as 'the **actions of** a_i are (logically or
causally) sufficient for F' (or 'the actions of a_i are a
sufficient condition of F'). A more complete analysis of agency
should include both aspects; a very simple analysis of this type is
(14) D(a,F) & M(a,$\sim$F),
where 'M(a,$\sim$F)' means that $\sim$ F is possible for a.[21]

In the context of directives the sufficient condition aspect of
agency is more important than the necessary condition aspect. If
a has an imperative obligation that F, the actions of a must be
sufficient to ensure that F is the case, but this obligation does
not necessarily require any specific acts on the part of a.
A directive is a command g i v e n t o a to **see** to it that F
is the case, not a norm to the effect that a ought to be the
agent of F (in the full sense of agency).
In a recent paper on agency Donald Davidson has argued that "a man

is the agent of an act if what he does can be described under an
aspect that makes is intentional",[22] and all actions can be
described as bodily movements of the agent. If 'bodily movement' is
understood in a sufficiently wide sense, we can say that people can
do things only through bodily movements, and doing c o n s i s t s
of certain movements.[23]
Actions described as bodily movements are termed by Davidson
p r i m i t i v e   a c t i o n s: thus, according to Davidson, "if
an event is an action, then under some description(s) it is
primitive, and under some description(s) it is intentional."[24]
Primitive actions can also be termed 'voluntary movements'.
According to Davidson's analysis of agency, $'D(a_i,F)'$ can be
interpreted as 'the voluntary movements of a_i are sufficient for
F'.

VI. O n   C o l l e c t i v e   A g e n c y

In some cases the "addressee" of a directive is not a single person,
but a group. For instance, a father may tell his sons:
(15) Boys, this table must be carried upstairs!
This command is given to a group of boys, and it requires that the
group do something. (15) can be expressed in terms of O^* and D
as follows:
(16) O^*D(Boys, the table is carried upstairs)
In (16) the first argument of 'D' is not an individual, but a set
of persons. Agents of this kind may be termed collective agents or
a g e n t - s e t s. If the D - operator is used for the expression
of collective agency, the **syntactical** and semantical rules
concerning D und C must be changed in such a way that the first
argument of D and C refers to a set, and the S -relations $s \in \int$
are **assigned** to sets, not to individuals. Let U be a set of
individual agents. We shall assume that all nonempty subsets of U
are agent-sets; agent-sets will be denoted by the letters A, B,
C... Individual agents can be represented by unit sets. Let S_A be
the instigative alternativeness relation for A. The truth of
$'D(A,F)'$ at the point $v \in W$ is defined by
$(C.D_c)$ $V(D(A,F),v) = 1$ if and only if $V(F,v') = 1$
              for every $v' \in W$ such that $S_A(v,v')$.
The truth of $'C(A,F)'$ is defined analogously. Again we shall
assume that
$(C.S_{refl})$ Every relation $S_A \in \int$ is reflexive.
The directive alternativeness relations R_A can be defined in

analogy with (D3).

According to the interpretation of 'D' given in the end of
section VI, 'D($\{a\}$,F)' means that the primitive actions or
voluntary movements of a are sufficient for F. If the same
interpretation is applied to collective agents, 'D(A,F)' means
that the primitive actions (or voluntary movements) of the group A
are sufficient for F. It is not entirely clear what can be meant
by the 'voluntary movements' of a group. However, it is clear that
a group can do something only if the members of the group do
something, and it is plausible to assume that the primitive actions
of a group are constituted, in some way or other, by the primitive
actions of the members of the group. We shall make this relationship
more definite and identify the voluntary movements of a group with
the voluntary movements of its members, and understand group action
in such a way that it includes individual action. If 'primitive
action' is understood 'physicalistically' (and this is how
Davidson interprets it), this identification is in fact fairly
obvious and unproblematic.

Thus the primitive actions of a group include the primitive actions
of its subsets and of its members. If 'E_v^A' is a description of the
primitive actions of A and 'E_v^B' is a description of the
primitive actions of B , $A \subset B$ implies that 'E_v^B' implies 'E_v^A' ,
and consequently the primitive actions of B are sufficient for F
if the primitive actions of A are sufficient for F. Thus

(17) $D(A,F) \supset D(B,F)$

is valid if $A \subset B$. (17) is valid if the relations $S_A \in \int$ satisfy the
following condition:

(C.S$\subset$)   If $A \subset B$, $S_B(v,v')$ implies $S_A(v,v')$.

If z_v^A and z_v^B are defined as the sets of those points for which
$S_A(v,v')$ and $S_B(v,v')$ holds, respectively, $z_v^B \subset z_v^A$ whenever
$A \subset B$.[25]

(C.S$\subset$) simplifies the models of collective directives considerably,
and   is in agreement with our interpretation of 'D'. The set z_v^A
is the set of those worlds compatible with everything done by A.
It is clear that the primitive actions (or movements) of a large
group restrict the range of possibilities more than the acts of a
small group (other things being equal): any group of agents
necessarily accomplishes at least as much as any of its subgroups.
The command (15) does not require that every boy in the group
addressed to should take part in the act of carrying the table
upstairs. If some subset of the group (in the case of a normal-

sized table two or three boys should suffice) carries the table upstairs, the imperative obligation expressed by (16) has been fulfilled, and the sentence 'D(Boys, The table is carried upstairs)' is true at every $v' \in W_v^*$. This presupposes the principle (C.S$\subset$). A directive '$O^*D(A,F)$' says that F must be brought about by A in some way or other, but it does not say h o w it must be brought about.[26]

(C.S$\subset$) may seem paradoxical as a general principle concerning agency. If a does F, it is normally incorrect to say, for instance, that a and b do F. Some apparent counter-examples of this kind can be explained away by pointing out that the second argument of 'D' must be a complete (closed) sentence, not an open sentence. The D -operator is applied to (descriptions of) individual acts, not to generic acts or act-predicates. The conditional (17) holds only if both the antecedent and the consequent refer to the same individual event or state. (C.S$\subset$) does not require that, e.g., Peter attacked Tom should imply Peter and John attacked Tom. Moreover, the assumption that any nonempty subset of U is an agent-set is perhaps unrealistic. Normally only certain "natural groups" are considered as agent-sets. An analysis of the concept of natural groups cannot be attempted here, however. (The logic of action cannot determine what counts as a natural group.)

Another partial explanation of the seemingly paradoxical character of (C.S$\subset$) and (17) depends on the fact that the D -operator expresses only the sufficient condition aspect of agency. If A and B are disjoint sets and A is the agent of F, the primitive actions of B are irrelevant or superfluous as far as F is concerned, and it is thus misleading to say that $A \cup B$ is the agent of F. Nevertheless, the primitive actions of $A \cup B$ are s u f f i c i e n t for F. A situation in which both A and B are "essential" agent-components can be described in terms of the D -operator as follows:

(18) $D(A \cup B,F)$ & $\sim D(A,F)$ & $\sim D(B,F)$.

We can regard (18) as a definition of genuine group action or c o o p e r a t i v e a c t i o n.

The "paradox" involved in (C.S$\subset$) bears resemblance to the well-known R o s s ' s p a r a d o x of deontic logic. In the standard system of deontic logic,

(19) $O^*F \supset O^*(F \lor G)$

is a valid principle. For instance, an obligation to mail a letter

implies an obligation to mail or burn it. Many philosophers have
felt that this is paradoxical: the alleged paradox is termed 'Ross's
paradox'.[27] The D -operator satisfies a similar principle,

(20) $D(A,F) \supset D(A, F \lor G)$.

According to (D.S$\subset$), an analogous principle holds also for the
first argument of 'D':

(21) $D(A,F) \supset D(A \cup B,F)$;

if the primitive actions of A are sufficient for F, then the
primitive actions of $A \cup B$ are sufficient for F. (21) implies

(22) $O^*D(A,F) \supset O^*D(A \cup B,F)$.

Let $A = \{a\}$ and $B = \{b\}$. The following alternatives are
consistent with $D(A \cup B,F)$:

(23)   (i) $D(\{a\},F)$ & $D(\{b\},F)$,

            (ii) $D(\{a\},F)$ & $\sim D(\{b\},F)$,

            (iii) $\sim D(\{a\},F)$ & $D(\{b\},F)$, and

            (iv) $\sim D(\{a\},F)$ & $\sim D(\{b\},F)$ & $D(\{a,b\},F)$.

(23) lists all the possible ways in which F can be brought about
by $\{a,b\}$. '$D(\{a,b\},F)$' implies the disjunction of (23.i - iv) and
is implied by each of the disjuncts. (23.i) is a case in which the
action of both a and b (each) are sufficient for F,[28] in cases
(ii) and (iii) F is brought about by the actions of a and by the
actions of b, respectively, and (iv) is a case of cooperative group
action. According to (23), the consequent of (22) can be formulated
as a disjunctive obligation, and (22) is an instance of (19). The
statement that F is brought about by A is stronger than the
statement that F is brought about by $A \cup B$, and '$O^*D(A,F)$' is
more informative than '$O^*D(A \cup B,F)$'. In general, speakers make as
informative statements as they are in a position to make.[29] If a
person is known to have an obligation that F, it is usually
misleading or uninformative to say that he has an obligation that
F $\lor$ G, and if F is brought about by A, it is misleading to say
that F is brought about by $A \cup B$.

Panel 4   175

NOTES

* This paper is an expanded version of the talk given at the 3rd
IKP-Colloquium. An earlier version of this paper appeared in
A j a t u s 35 (1973). The analysis of directives presented in
sections III and V is similar to that presented by Brian F. Chellas
in T h e L o g i c a l F o r m o f I m p e r a t i v e s
(Perry Lane Press, Stanford 1969) (cf. Notes 11 and 13).

1. P h i l o s o p h y o f S c i e n c e 6 (1939), pp 446-457.

2. The distinction between directives and fiats is not always
clear. For instance, in his dissertation T h e L o g i c a l
F o r m o f I m p e r a t i v e s Brian F. Chellas says that
Close the door is a fiat (Perry Lane Press, Standord 1969, p. 26).
However, according to grammarians, the sentence Close the door is
obtained by an "imperative transformation" from You close the door.
The former sentence is merely an abbreviation of the latter, and
apparently both should be classified as directives (at least from
the semantical viewpoint). See Roderick A. Jacobs and Peter S.
Rosenbaum, E n g l i s h T r a n s f o r m a t i o n a l
G r a m m a r, Blaisdell Publ. Co., Waltham, Mass. 1968, pp. 32-33.

3. Hector-Neri Castañeda, On the Semantics of the Ought-to-do,
S y n t h e s e 21 (1970), pp. 449-468, cf. p 452.

4. Nicholas Rescher (T h e L o g i c o f C o m m a n d s,
Dover Publications, New York 1966, p. 18) has distinguished between
"action-performance commands" and "state-realization commands";
this distinction is different from that between agential and
agentless ought-statements. Here we are mainly interested in the
latter distinction.

5. See Jaakko Hintikka, S o m e M a i n P r o b l e m s o f
D e o n t i c L o g i c, in D e o n t i c L o g i c:
I n t r o d u c t o r y a n d S y s t e m a t i c R e a d i n g s
(ed. by R. Hilpinen), D. Reidel, Dordrecht 1971, p. 60.

6. The problems of temporal reference in the case of imperatives
have been discussed e.g. in Brian F. Chellas, T h e L o g i c a l
F o r m o f I m p e r a t i v e s, Chapter IV, and Imperatives,
T h e o r i a 37 (1971), pp. 114-129. This aspect of commands has
also been emphasized by Nicholas Rescher; see T h e L o g i c o f
C o m m a n d s (especially p. 123).

7. In the terminology of John Searle's theory of speech acts we
can say that the 'basic meaning' of an utterance is determined

(mainly) by its i l l o c u t i o n a r y   f o r c e   and its
p r o p o s i t i o n a l   c o n t e n t. Cf. John Searle,
S p e e c h   A c t s, Cambridge Univ. Press, Cambridge 1969, pp. 22-
33.

8.   Cf. Brian F. Chellas, T h e   L o g i c a l   F o r m   o f
I m p e r a t i v e s, Chapter I. Yehoshua Bar-Hillel has emphasized
that "there exists no logic that covers all English imperative
sentences", but there exists "a logic of commands (and of
instructions, and of encouragements, etc.) issued by uttering
English imperative sentences" (Imperative Inference, A n a l y s i s
26 (1966), pp. 79-82: reprinted in A s p e c t s   o f
L a n g u a g e (by Y. Bar-Hillel), North-Holland, Amsterdam 1970,
pp. 146-149). This view is accepted here, even though the somewhat
misleading expression 'logic of imperatives' is occasionally used.

9.   In his paper "Imperatives" Brian F. Chellas discusses the
iteration of imperative operators, but comes to the conclusion that
"iteration of the imperative operators is completely vacuous"
(p. 124). Chellas considers only fiats, but the same seems to be
true of directives as well.

10. Cf. Dagfinn Føllesdal and Risto Hilpinen, Deontic Logic: An
Introduction, in D e o n t i c   L o g i c : I n t r o d u c t o r y
and S y s t e m a t i c   R e a d i n g s (ed. by R. Hilpinen),
p. 16.

11. This analysis of directives is similar to that presented by
Brian F. Chellas: see T h e   L o g i c a l   F o r m   o f
I m p e r a t i v e s, p. 56.

12. Jaakko Hintikka, Some Main Problems of Deontic Logic, in
D e o n t i c   L o g i c : I n t r o d u c t o r y   a n d
S y s t e m a t i c   R e a d i n g s, p.60.

13. The results of this section are not new. The analysis of
directives presented here is due to Brian F. Chellas: see T h e
L o g i c a l   F o r m   o f   I m p e r a t i v e s, Chapter III,
section 4 (especially pp. 62-64).

14. On the logic of Imperatives, p. 446

15. On the Semantics of the Ought-to-do, pp. 461-464

16. Stig Kanger, New Foundations for Ethical Theory, in
D e o n t i c   L o g i c : I n t r o d u c t o r y   a n d
S y s t e m a t i c   R e a d i n g s, pp 36-58; see p. 42.

17. Stig Kanger and Helle Kanger, Rights and Parliamentarism, in C o n t e m p o r a r y   P h i l o s o p h y   i n S c a n d i n a v i a (ed. by R.E. Olson and A. Paul), John Hopkins Press, Baltimore 1972, pp. 213-236; cf. pp. 214-216. (An earlier version of this paper appeared in T h e o r i a   32   (1966), pp. 85-115.)

18. T h e   L o g i c a l   F o r m   o f   I m p e r a t i v e s, p. 64.

19. See Ingmar Pörn, T h e   L o g i c   o f   P o w e r , Basil Blackwell, Oxford 1970, pp. 2-16, E l e m e n t s   o f   S o c i a l A n a l y s i s, Philosophical Studies published by the Philosophical Society and the Department of Philosophy, University of Uppsala, No. 10, Uppsala 1971, pp. 1-9, and Lennart Åqvist, P e r f o r m a t i v e s   a n d   V e r i f i a b i l i t y   b y t h e   U s e   o f   L a n g u a g e, Philosophical Studies published by the Philosophical Society and the Department of Philosophy, University of Uppsala, No. 14, Uppsala 1972, pp. 10-12. Pörn and Åqvist call 'D' and 'C' "praxiological operators".

20. The necessary condition aspect of agency has been emphasized by by G.H. von Wright in An Essay on Deontic Logic and the General Theory of Action, A c t a   P h i l o s o p h i c a   F e n n i c a 21, North-Holland, Amsterdam 1968: "Every description of an action contains, in a concealed form, an counterfactual conditional statement. When we say, e.g., that an agent opened a window, we imply that, had it not been for the agent's interference, the window would, on that occasion, have remained closed" (p 43). This counterfactual element is related to the necessary condition aspect of action.

21. This notion of 'personal possibility' has been studied in Risto Hilpinen, An Analysis of Relativised Modalities, in P h i l o s o p h i c a l   L o g i c (ed. by J.W. Davis et al.), D. Reidel, Dordrecht 1969, pp. 181-193. 'D' and 'M' are not logically independent, but their relationship cannot be studied here.

22. Donald Davidson, Agency, in A g e n t, A c t i o n, a n d R e a s o n (ed. by R. Binkley, R. Bronaugh and A. Marras), University of Toronto Press, Toronto 1971, pp. 3-25: cf. p. 7.

23. Agency, pp. 11-13 and 23.

24. Agency, p. 25.

25. This entails the validity of $'O^*D(A,F) \supset O^*D(A \cup B,F)'$. The
converse of (17) does not hold: it is possible that the actions of
$A \cup B$ are sufficient for F, but those of A are not.
$'O^*D(A \cup B,F)'$ does not imply $'O^*D(A,F)'$: for instance, no proper
subset of the agent-set mentioned in (15) has an imperative
obligation to carry to the table upstairs. If $'O^*D(C,F)'$ is true,
but $'O^*D(A,F)'$ holds for no proper subset A of C, we can say
that F is obligatory for the w h o l e group C. In this case
$'O^*D(C,F)'$ expresses a g e n u i n e or nontrivial collective
obligation of the group C.

26. In T h e L o g i c o f C o m m a n d s Nicholas Rescher
discusses commands directed to groups. According to Rescher, a
command is addressed to a group collectively if it is addressed to
an "indifferent subgroup of the members of the group possibly
including the entire lot" (p. 12). This conception of a collective
command fits with our interpretation of the D-operator, except that
it is misleading to say that a command is directed to an
"indifferent subgroup of a group" (there is no such addressee): the
command is addressed to the entire group, but it can be carried out
by a subgroup. According to Rescher, a command can be addressed to
a group of recipients also d i s t r i b u t i v e l y : in this
case it is addressed to each individual member of the group (for
instance: "Every one of you chaps raise your right hand!" (p. 12).
According to the present analysis, distributive commands express
sets of individual directives; they do not require any 'group
action'.

27. This paradox was first pointed out by Alf Ross in Imperatives
and Logic, T h e o r i a 7 (1941), pp. 53-71.

28. In his book N o r m a n d A c t i o n (Routledge and Kegan
Paul, London 1963, pp. 44-45) G.H. von Wright considers a case in
which "two persons at the same time shoot a third" so that "each
shot individually would have killed him". This is an example of
(25.i). It is easy to see why this is a perplexing case of agency:
from the sufficient condition aspect of agency, both persons are
agents of the killing (and hence (25.i) is true), but from the
necessary condition aspect neither (alone) is an agent. Several
"paradoxical" cases of this type are mentioned and discussed in
H.L.A. Hart and A.M.Honore, C a u s a t i o n i n t h e L a w,
Oxford University Press, Oxford 1959.

29. This 'requirement of efficient communication' has been
formulated by H.P. Grice as follows: "One should not make a weaker
statement rather than a stronger one unless there are good reasons
for so doing" (The Causal Theory of Perception, in
P e r c e i v i n g ,   S e n s i n g, a n d   K n o w i n g (ed.
by R. Swartz), Anchor Books, Doubleday & Co., Garden City 1965,
pp. 438-472; p. 450).

POTTS:

MODAL LOGIC AND AUXILIARY VERBS

1 A l e t h i c M o d a l L o g i c

This paper is primarily about the categorization of certain
auxiliary verbs within the framework of Fregean grammer (cp. Potts,
1974a): its theme, in logical terminology, is that they are more
like quantifiers than like propositional operators. The account
given by Hilpinen (1973) of one of these auxiliaries also provides
an opportunity to detail some of the shortcomings of model theory as
a method for linguistics, thus illustrating the position which has
been argued generally by Jardine and Jardine (1974) and also by
myself (1974b,c). The paper contains, in addition, a positive
methodological thesis, that syntax is a part of a theory of meaning,
which ought not to be opposed to semantics, and that it is always
the first part: so that if our syntax is wrong, the theory of
meaning which is built upon it will inevitably be wrong too.

Logicians use the terms 'syntax' and 'semantics' in different senses
from linguists. Now that diplomatic relations between linguists and
logicians have been restored, this is giving rise to much confusion.
Traditionally, sytax is a theory of the possible combinations of
expressions in a language, where the method is to group the
expressions into categories and then to specify permissible
combinations in terms of the categories. If the boundary between
permissible and impermissible expressions is intended to coincide
with that between expressions having a meaning in the language and
nonsensical ones, then syntax is already a weak theory of meaning,
to the extent that it tells us what expressions have a meaning and
what expressions do not.

In the past, grammarians have not already been clear as to the aim
of a syntactic theory: until we know what is meant by 'grammatical',
it is no explanation to say that syntax fixes the borderline between
grammatical and ungrammatical expressions. For two notions of
grammaticality must be distinguished: according to the first, an
expression is ungrammatical if and only if it is nonsense, according
to the second, if and only if it is not a form of expression to be
found in the particular language under consideration (cp. Wittgenstein, 1922, 4.002 - 4.0031).   We must therefore also distinguish
between two types of syntax, both of which are necessary to
theoretical linguistics: the syntax which is concerned with
grammaticality in the first sense, I shall call l o g i c a l

syntax, that which is concerned with grammaticality in the second,
l i n g u i s t i c syntax. These terms are to be mere labels of
convenience, carrying no implication that logical syntax is
independent of language in general.

We understand a complex expression from our knowledge of the
meanings of its components and the manner in which they are
combined; a theory of meaning must, accordingly, presuppose an
account of the structures of complex expressions - their logical,
not their lingusitic structures. Where consideration of complex
expressions is restricted to propositions (those expressions which
we account as being true or untrue), two methods have been developed
by logicians for explaining their meanings in terms of the meanings
of their components. The first is to charakterize valid inferences
by recourse to the logical structures of their premisses and
conclusions, the second to specify the truth-conditions of any
proposition by reference to its logical structure. Logicians call
the first method syntactic and the second semantic, so 'syntax' in
this sense is a theory of consequences, while 'semantics' is a
theory of truth; both methods presuppose an account of which I have
called logical syntax ana are, hence, quite distinct from it.

The relevance of logical consequence to meaning can be explained as
follows. Let us say that two propositions have the same s e n s e
just in case all and only the conclusions which may be validly be
drawn from one of them, in combination with any set of further
premisses, may validly be drawn from the other, in combination with
the same set; and let us say that the sense of any expression other
than a proposition is the contribution which it makes to the senses
of propositions in which it occurs. 'Sense' will be used throughout
this paper with this technical meaning. It is then part of
understanding a proposition that we know its sense, at least
implicitly, though sense is not the only ingredient in the meaning
of a proposition or of expressions in general. But if we can specify
the sense of an expression, we shall have given an account of one
important aspect of its meaning and, if we can do the same for a
range of expressions, we shall be well on the way to giving an
account to the sense of every proposition.
The technique involves distinguishing between two kinds of component
in the structures of propositions, those in virtue of which a given
inference is valid, commonly called c o n s t a n t s, and those,
which are irrelevant to its validity to the extent that whatever

other expressions, of the same categories, were substituted for
them, we should still have a valid inference; the latter are
commonly termed v a r i a b l e s. The division between constants
and variables may have to be drawn differently, even for a single
proposition, in different inferences, for the validity of one
inference may turn upon a component which is irrelevant to the
validity of another inference. In representing the pattern or
structure of which a given valid inference is an example, the
appropriate distinction between constants and variables must be
marked: thus the variables are replaced by s c h e m a t i c
s y m b o l s which tell us only the categories of the variables
and the manner in which they are combined with each other and with
the constants. By substituting any expressions of the specified
categories for the schematic symbols, we shall always obtain a
proposition having a logical structure in common with the original
proposition respresented. The use of schematic symbols is essential
to logic, enabling us to exhibit a logical structure or
p r o p o s i t i o n - s c h e m a for any proposition and an
argument-schema for any argument. The constants may also be, and in
modern logic are, represented by symbols; this is often convenient,
but not essential.

The two methods employed by logicians both presuppose a fixed
division between constants and variables and a logical syntax
specified in terms of the constants and schematic symbols. In its
most elegant form, the first method then takes each constant in turn
and considers the simplest proposition-schema in which it may occur,
stating one rule for introducing the schema in an argument and one
rule for eliminating it. Complex proposition-schemas can then be
broken down or built up by successive applications of these rules,
with whose aid new argument-schemas can then be derived. Providing
that the resulting system is consistent, the pairs of rules taken
together then define the senses of the constants.

The second method again starts with the simplest proposition-schema
for each constant, but now specifies its truth-conditions. Since the
proposition-schema contains schematic symbols it is not itself
either true or untrue, so the procedure is to state, for each
possible substitution for the schematic symbols, whether the
resulting proposition is true or untrue. This method is only
practicable when some principle can be found for classifying the
possible subsitutions into denumerable groups. It is, however, more

fundamental than the first, because logical consequence can be
defined in terms of truth: since a valid consequence never leads
from true premisses to a false conclusion, an argument-schema will
be valid just in case every substitution for its schematic symbols
which yields true premisses also yields a true conlusion. Thus this
second method provides a criterion by which the inference-rules
resulting from the first method can be judged, while the
definitions for the simple proposition-schemas again define the
senses of the constants and together determine the truth-conditions
of complex proposition-schemas.

Each of these methods aims to give us an account of the sense of a
proposition in terms of its logical structure, since each
concentrates, constant by constant, upon the simplest proposition-
schema in which it can occur, the senses of complex propositions
then being determined by those of their components and the way in
which the latter are combined. Neither method, however, can give us
a c o m p l e t e account of the sense of any proposition, but
only of its sense so far as it is determined by the constants which
it contains; for the range of constants was fixed beforehand,
whereas a proposition which is an example of one schema may also
have logical consequences whose validity could only be shown by a
d i f f e r e n t division between its constant and variable
components. It is this limitation which has motivated alethic modal
logic.

During the nineteenth century and under the influence of Hume and
Kant, the notion of l o g i c a l   t r u t h came to occupy a
central position in logical theory. A proposition-schema is
logically true if it is true for e v e r y substitution for its
schematic symbols and any proposition which is an example of such a
schema is a t a u t o l o g y . A tautology is thus true quite
independently of how things stand in the world, just as a self-
contradictory proposition, which is the negation of a tautology, is
false in all circumstances; both are limiting and degenerate cases
of propositions. Their truth or falsity, indeed, is wholly
determined by the senses of their constant components and their
structures. Given truth-definitions for the constants, therefore, we
shall always be able to determine what schemas containing them are
logically true or logically false.

The range of constants available in present-day logic is, however,
pitifully small: negation, conjunction, disjunction, implication,

universal and existential quantification and identity - a mere
seven. Thus only those tautologies which are logically true in
virtue of the senses of t h e s e constants can be shown to be
such. The moral which logicians o u g h t to have drawn was to
enlarge their vocabulary of constants, but, as a matter of history,
their reaction was to construct, instead, a logical system in which
it could be a s s e r t e d, but not shown, that a schema was
tautological or self-contradictory. This is alethic modal logic, in
which two constants, meaning respectively 'It is logically true
that...' and 'It is consistent (to suppose) that...', are added to
the vocabulary of propositional or predicate logic.

This enterprise could claim some continuity with traditional modal
logic, which was concerned in the first instance with the adverbs
'necessarily' and 'possibly'. The keystone of traditional modal
logic was the validity of the inferences from 'necessarily p' to
'p' and from 'p' to 'possibly p' and, although traditional
logicians were not unaware that 'necessary' and 'possible' have more
than one meaning in natural language (cp. Aristotle, Metaphysics
δ 12), they did not develop these distinctions in the context of
modal logic. Provided that 'necessarily' and 'possibly' are used
with correlative meanings, however, traditional modal logic is
applicable; unfortunately, the history of philosopy contains many
examples of fallacies which can be exposed with this simple
apparatus. One meaning of 'necessarily' (though a very untraditional
one: cp. Hintikka, 1957) is 'It is necessarily t r u e that...',
with the correlative 'It is possibly true that...'. It is then but a
short step to identify necessary with logical truth and possible
truth with consistency, so that alethic modal logic appears as the
development of one interpretation of traditional modal logic.

More accurately, it could be described from the logician's
'syntactic' point of view as a theory of consequences of
consequences, or, from his 'semantic' point of view as a theory of
the truth of logical truth. Thus, to take the 'syntactic' account
first, the schema: 'Necessarily, if p, then q' will s a y that
'q' is a logical consequence of 'p'; but it will not be possible,
of course, to d e r i v e 'q' from 'p' in a system of alethic
modal logic. We could, however, derive 'Necessarily, if not q, then
not p' from 'Necessarily, if p, then q', thereby showing that
'"not p" is a logical consequence of "not q"' is a logical
consequence of ' "q" is a logical consequence of "p"'; and this

example will be typical of the types of consequence which we can prove.

From the 'semantic' point of view, the task is to specify the truth-conditions of 'necessarily p', i.e. of 'It is a logical truth that p'. But this cannot be done in terms of the structure of 'p', because a n y proposition may be substituted for 'p'. Instead, we are told that 'p' is necessary just in case it is true in every consistent world, where a 'world' is given by its description in a set of propositions. Thus this amounts to saying that 'p' is logically true just in case it is a member of every consistent set of propositions. Whether a given substitution for 'p' satisfies this condition could not be determined, but the truth-definition nevertheless allows us to fix the logical relationships of propositions which are necessary, simply true and possible. For example, if 'p' is logically true, then it must be consistent, for what is true in e v e r y consistent set of propositions is true in s o m e consistent set, i.e. possible, i.e. consistent.

Alethic modal logic might have justified the energy which has been expended upon it if it had led us to a clearer understanding of the concepts of logical consequence and logical truth. Its effect, however, has been just the opposite, to increase the confusion in their regard. The modal operators have been assigned by logicians to the same category as negation, i.e. the category of expressions which turn a proposition into a proposition: 1PP, if we use 'P' for the basic category of propositions. Since the valour of any such expression is of the same category as its argumentor, namely P, it can always be iterated; but it is far from clear what it could mean to say, e.g. 'it is logically true that it is logically true that p'. Logicians, consequently, proposed various simplifications, for example that the expression above should be regarded as equivalent to the plain 'It is logically true that p'. The meanings of iterated alethic modalities being unclear from the start, however, there is no general agreement as to which simplifications, if any, best represent the notion of logical truth and, since there are many different simplifications each of which is consistent, the result has been a proliferation of alethic modal systems.

The inter-relationship between these systems have been greatly clarified by the device of making worlds possible, not absolutely, but relative to other worlds and, simultaneously, restricting the definition of necessity to truth in every world which is possible

relative to this world. By specifying the relation in different
ways, each of the various systems may then be obtained and their
properties may also be more easily investigated. But these technical
advances have shed no light upon the concepts of logical consequence
and logical truth, nor could they be expected to do so: for by
allowing us to s a y that a proposition is logically true without
showing the structure in virtue of which it is so, alethic modal
logic forces us to treat an i n t e r n a l property of propositions as if it were an e x t e r n a l one (cp. Wittgenstein
1922, 4.1211-4.1252, for an explanation of this distinction and its
application here). It trades the original explanation of logical
truth, which could at least be applied to proposition-schemas
containing constants of predicate logic, for a definition which can
only be applied to schemas containing the operators 'It is logically
true that...' or 'It is consistent (to suppose) that...'. By so
doing, it rules out from the start any possibility of explaining why
certain propositions are true or false independently of how things
stand in the world, although they are not examples of tautologies of
predicate logic or their negations.

Alethic modal logic is thus totally misconceived from the very
beginning. If modal logic were to progress, it was certainly
requisite that it should distinguish between the different meanings
of 'necessary' and 'possible' and not rest content with one logic
for the lot; indeed, the connexions between those meanings are
themselves suitable matter for logical investigation. The most
urgent task for logic today is to extend its range of constants,
instead of playing ever more sophisticated games with the few
already available, for this is the only means by which it can codify
valid consequences and clarify concepts which at present elude its
powers of representation and expression. Now the semantic field
which, after that covered by predicate logic, pervades language most
extensively is the one concerned with change and causality. Very few
topics are immune from its influence, though its dissociation from
number theory and the recent close association between logic and the
foundations of arithmetic may well explain, historically, why it has
been for so long neglected.

The first step in extending logic to this field must be to formulate
a logical syntax for the new constants. This in itself is a
difficult undertaking, upon which I can only hope to make a small
and tentative beginning here. It has frequently been noted that

'necessarily' and 'possibly' are often used to indicate
c a u s a l necessity and possibility, so this is one direction in
which traditional modal logic might be developed. These meanings of
the two adverbs are also closely related to one use of the
auxiliary verbs 'must' and 'can' ('be able to'): the latter, indeed,
is typically used to express what Aristotle called
p o t e n t i a l i t i e s and distinguished into passive
potentialities, what a thing can b e c o m e, and active
potentialities, what a thing can d o, including what it can
c a u s e. 'Can' is, therefore, at the heart of the semantic field
of change and causality and deserves closer syntactic investigation.

The simplest propositions containing 'can' are those in which it is
preceded by a proper name and followed by a verb. Where the proper
name is that of an animal, 'can' may often be paraphrased by 'knows
how to', as in:
(1)   John can drive.
But this paraphrase is not always possible, e.g.
(2)   Mary can sleep for twelve hours at a stretch.
It depends not only upon the subject to which the potentialitiy is
attributed being an animal, but also upon the meaning of the verb,
which must describe a skill. In what follws, I shall ignore this
difference.

Potentialities, according to an Aristotelian dictum, are known to us
from their actualizations; translating this into logical terms, the
sense of
(3)   John is driving
must be related to that of (1) and the sense of
(4)   Mary has slept for twelve hours at a stretch
to that of (2). One might hesitate to say that (3) entails (1) or
that (4) entails (2), on the ground that repeated performances of
the types described by (3) and (4) would be requisite to justify the
ascription of the corresponding potentialities, but even so, it is
clear that the same proper name and the same verb must occur in (3)
as in (1) and in (4) as in (2).

If we now introduce N as the basic category of proper names, in
addition to P as the basic category of propositions, then by
removing the proper names from (3) and (4), we shall be left with
two expressions of category 1PN, ' ξ is driving' and ' ξ has slept for
twelve hours at a stretch '. Similarly, by removing the proper names
from (1) and (2), we obtain the result that ' ξ can drive' and

' ɩ can sleep for twelve hours at a stretch' are also expressions of
the same category, 1PN. The two pairs differ in that the aspect of
the verb in each of the first pair (continuous in (1), perfective in
(2)) has been replaced by 'can' in each of the second pair.
Restricted to P and N as basic categories of our grammar, there is
no means of categorizing aspects; the requisite extension of the
grammar is beyond the scope of this paper, so I shall have to ignore
them and suppose that the expressions of category 1PN obtained from
(3) and (4) actually occur in (1) and (2) respectively. In that
case, the most straightforward hypothesis about the category of
'can' and the one which accords most closely with its linguistic
syntax is that it serves to turn an expression of category 1PN into
another of the same category. Its own category would then be 2PN1PN,
so that we can also describe it as turning a proper name and a one-
place predicate into a proposition.

Linguistic syntax, as Russell rightly maintained, is the guide, but
cannot be the master of logical syntax. So far as English linguistic syntax is concerned, the sign of negation 'not', also turns a
predicate into a predicate; yet there are excellent logical reasons
for assigning it to category 1PP rather than to category 2PN1PN.
Might not the same go for 'can'? Perhaps we should, for logical
purposes, paraphrase (1) by, e.g.

(5)   It is (causally) possible that John is driving,
regarding (1) as containing (3) i n   t o t o, as a subordinate
proposition. We have, in any case, assumed that the predicate of (3)
actually occurs in (1), so there could be no objection upon that
score. An Aristotelian might object that, whereas potentialities are
ascribed to substances, this analysis would reduce them to
properties of events, no means now being available for picking out
the possessor of the potentiality; but this objection would only
carry weight if an analysis like (5) could be shown to lead to
l o g i c a l difficulties.

There is, indeed, such a proof, which we owe to Anselm (De veritate,
8 a d   f i n e m). Informally, we could say of a proposition like
(6)   Fischer can beat Spassky at chess
that it ascribes a potentiality to Fischer, but a corresponding
relative   l a c k of ability to Spassky, and that a lack of
ability is not itself a species of ability or of potentiality.
If, however, (6) may be paraphrased by
(7)   It is (causally) possible that Fischer beats Spassky at

chess,

then, since 'Spassky was beaten by Fischer at chess' has the same
sense and, therefore, the same logical structure as 'Fischer beats
Spassky at chess', (7) will be equivalent to

(8)   It is (causally) possible that Spassky is beaten by
           Fischer at chess,

which, in turn, should paraphrase

(9)   Spassky can be beaten by Fischer at chess.

E x h y p o t h e s i, 'can' must have the same sense in (9) as in
(7), so if (7) means that Fischer is able to beat Spassky, then (9)
must mean that Spassky is able to be beaten by Fischer: it is not
open to us to give 'can' a weaker meaning in (9) than in (7). But
there is no such ability as the ability to be beaten by Fischer, so
(9) is not merely not equivalent to (7); under the hypothesis, no
meaning can be attached to it at all.

This is conclusive evidence against assigning 'can' to category 1PP,
but the difficulty could be avoided by giving it, instead, the
category 2PNP, using for paraphrasing a schema like

(10)   It is (causally) possible for a that p,

e.g. 'It is (causally) possible for Fischer that Fischer beats
Spassky'. The argument of the last paragraph will then only take us
as far as: 'It is (causally) possible for Fischer that Spassky is
beaten by Fischer', but will not allow us to substitute 'Spassky'
for the first occurrence of 'Fischer'. This proposal, however, lands
us, instead, in even worse trouble, for in adopting the category
2PNP for 'can', we must allow a n y proposition to be substituted
for 'p' in schema (10); we cannot require, for instance, that 'a'
should occur in 'p'. So we cannot reject as ill-formed, for example

(11)   It is (causally) possible for John that Mary sleeps for
           twelve hours at a stretch.

There is no way of construing this in terms of some ability of John:
we cannot speak of one object having an ability for a n o t h e r
object to do or undergo something.

The first analysis is therefore confirmed and we can represent the
logical structure of (1) and (6) by:

(S1) N^1 $2PN^1 1P^2N_3$ $1P^2N_3$
           John   can   drive
           Fischer   can   beat Spassky at chess

A corresponding logical notation would be   '$M_x aFx$', but we should
note that although this analysis serves to differentiate (6) from
(9), it does not exclude the latter as ill-formed: the difference is

simply that between '$M_x aFxb$' and '$M_x bFax$'. The Anselmian argument, however, shows that 'can', in the sense with which we are concerned, may not be combined with a predicate in the passive voice.
This is certainly a point of logical syntax and it shows that the
categorization 2PN1PN is still not correct; but it cannot be re-
solved within a P-N grammar, in which 2PN1PN is the nearest approximation.

As the logical notation brings out, expressions of category 2PN1PN
are like quantifiers (category 1P1PN), except for having a second
argumentor-place,for a proper name. This difference, however, makes
them iterable, since the structure
(S2) $2PN1P^1N_2$ $2P^1N_21PN$
is, as a whole, itself of category 2PN1PN. But 'can' is not iterable, and this is again a point of logical syntax. The reason why it
is not iterable and the reason that it cannot be combined with passive predicates could well be the same, that the sense of every
predicate which it can qualify contains some component which it
"neutralizes" and which is somehow associated with only one of the
argumentor-places in a polyadic predicate. Correct identification of
this component would then be of great importance for giving an account, whether "syntactic" or "semantic", of the sense of 'can'.
Meanwhile, however, it is worth pointing out that analogues to consequences which are valid for the alethic modal operators can easily be formulated for '$M_x \xi \phi x$'. We could even introduce a corresponding "strong" operator '$L_x \xi \phi x$', defined by:
(D1) $L_x aFx \Vdash \neg M_x a \neg Fx$
so that '$L_x aFx$' would mean 'a cannot not F' or 'a is not able
not to F'. The question is whether, at this stage, anything would
be gained thereby; the familiar paths of alethic modal logic may
turn out to be cul-de-sacs in the logic of potentiality.

2 D e o n t i c   L o g i c   a n d   P e r s o n a l
   O b l i g a t i o n
Considerable efforts have been made by logicians during the last two
decades to enlarge logic's vocabulary of constants, first by the
'syntactic' and, more recently, by the 'semantic' method. Yet they
have taken alethic modal logic as their paradigm, making practically
no innovations in logical syntax: new constants have regularly been
assigned to one of the three categories 1PP, 2PPP and 2PNP, almost
as though the second level were sacred to the quantifiers. Deontic
logic is an example germane to the present topic: propositions ex-

pressing obligation and permission have been analyzed by paraphrases embodying the expressions 'it is obligatory that...' and 'it
is permissible that...', assigned to category 1PP.

At one moment, there was a chance for an alternative analysis to
gain a foothold: von Wright (1951), basing his work on the analogy
between the meaning of 'necessary', 'impossible' and 'possible', on
the one hand, and 'obligatory', 'forbidden', and 'permissible', on
the other, formulated a system of deontic logic in which the constants 'it is obligatory to...' and 'it is permissible to...' were
completed into propositions by verbs of action, e.g.

(12)   It is forbidden to smoke.

If action-verbs are expressions of first level - an assumption which
again ignores complications arising from tense, aspect and mood -
then 'it is obligatory to...' and 'it is permissible to...' must be
expressions of second level; more precisely, if they are completed
into propositions by one-place predicates (category 1PN), their own
category will be 1P1PN, the same as that of the quantifiers. An appropriate logical notation would then be 'O_xFx' and 'P_xFx'.

Verbs of action, of course, have varying polyadicities; thus, from a
proposition like:

(13)   It is forbidden to smoke cigarettes

one might conclude that "smoke" belongs to category 2PNN. But one
need not, on that account, say that the category of 'it is forbidden
to...' is 1P2PNN in (12), but 1P1PN in (13). In the absence of any
qualification of the kind provided by (13), (12) means that it is
forbidden to smoke a n y t h i n g, the second argumentor-place of
"smoke" thus being filled by an implicit quantifier to yield a one-
place predicate; in this example, the quantifier is universal, while
in others it is existential. A similar account will apply to verbs
of category 3PNNN, where two implicit quantifiers are to be posited.

Unfortunately, von Wright did not adopt a notation which showed that
his deontic constants were expressions of second level; he simply
used 'Op' and 'Pp', which left it open to subsequent authors to
re-interpret his system so that propositions were to be substituted
for 'p'. Under the influence of Mally (1926) and Prior (1955), this
is the direction which deontic logic has subsequently taken; even
von Wright has now fallen into line (1968).

The second level notation proposed above suffers from the limitation
that it cannot be used to represent propositions expressing
p e r s o n a l obligations, such as:

(14)   John ought to marry Mary

But this disadvantage is easily overcome: 'ought to' ('is obliged to'), like 'can', is an auxiliary verb, which suggests that it, too, might be assigned to category 2PN1PN. The logical structure of (14) will then also be represented by (S1), ignoring the complexity of the predicate ' ξ marries Mary'. The relationship between 'ought to' and 'it is obligatory to' is then quite straightforward: propositions like (12) and (13) are general prohibitions, embracing everyone, so, using '$O_x \xi \phi x$' to represent 'ought to', we can define:

(D2) $O_x Fx \vdash \bigwedge_y O_x yFx$,

the domain of the universal quantifier being restricted to persons. The sense of (12) would then be given by:

(15)   Everyone ought/is obliged not to smoke

and this is, indeed, what would normally be intended by (12); the "No smoking" sign in a railway compartment merely restricts the prohibition to those who choose to occupy that compartment.

Hilpinen (1973) has proposed a different logical syntax for personal obligation, using a constant of category 2PNP, whose sense he explains both directly, using the "semantic" method, and also by a componential analysis into the 1PP obligation constant of "standard" deontic logic and a constant of personal agency of category 2PNP; the senses of each of these constants are also specified by the "semantic" method and it is shown that their combined sense is that of the personal obligation constant. I am here concerned primarily with the issues in logical syntax which are raised by this account, but it will also be necessary to consider Hilpinen's specification of the senses of his constants, since he proceeds in the opposite order to what which was been followed here, asking about the linguistic interpretations only a f t e r he has specified their senses.

Hilpinen's starting-point is the "standard" deontic logic in which the two constants are 'it is obligatory that...' and 'it is permissible that...', both of category 1PP. These can, of course, be used to express p a r t i c u l a r obligations, as in:

(16)   It is obligatory that John marries Mary,

but they do so i m p e r s o n a l l y: thus (16) does not tell us whether the obligation devolves upon John, upon Mary, or upon both. We should not confuse 'it is obligatory that...' with 'it is obligatory to...'; the latter expresses u n i v e r s a l, not impersonal obligation.

Noticing this limitation of the "standard" notation, Hilpinen
proposes a new constant of category 2PNP, whose intended meaning is
conveyed by the schema:
(17)   Oap : it is obligatory for a that p
Thus (14) would be paraphrased, on this analysis, by
(18)   It is obligatory for John that John marries Mary.
Now Anselm makes a parallel point about 'ought' to this point about
'can' (De veritate, 8): thus, if
(19)   Fischer has an obligation to beat Spassky,
it does not follow that
(20)   Spassky has an obligation to be beaten by Fischer.
The parallel extends still further, for if 'ought to' means the
same as 'has an obligation to', then it, too, may not be combined
with a passive predicate; in order to construe (20), we should have
to regard it as short for Spassky has an obligation t o a l l o w
h i m s e l f to be beaten by Fischer. The 'Oap' notation is able
to differentiate (20) from (19), but not to show that (20) is ill-
formed; as with potentiality, however, that is beyond the powers of
a P-N grammar.

By assigning 'ought' to category 2PNP, a parallel difficulty is
produced to that wich arose from assigning 'can' to that category:
we cannot reject as ill-formed an expression like:
(21)   It is obligatory for Mary that John does not smoke.
But how can Mary have an obligation with regard to what John does?
In order to give a meaning to (21), we must suppose that it has the
same sense as:
(22)   It is obligatory that Mary p r e v e n t s John from
            smoking.
This brings out the motivation for the componential analysis
proposed by Hilpinen: the sense of schema (17) is to be given, quite
generally, by:
(23)   ODap : It is obligatory that a brings it about that p,
in which 'O' is now the i m p e r s o n a l "standard" deontic
constant and 'D' a constant expressing personal agency (Hilpinen
has some reservations about rendering 'Dap' by 'a brings it about
that p', which I shall consider in section 3).

This account of personal obligation is forced upon him by the 2PNP
categorization, since schema (17) must yield a well-formed
proposition w h a t e v e r proposition we substitute for 'p'.
Now we may readily admit that people sometimes have obligations to

effect a particular result, or to bring about or prevent a specified
state of affairs. Thus a physician's obligation is to bring it about
that his patients are healthy, the choice of means being a matter
for his own discretion. But this is a special case of personal
obligation, which, in general, is an obligation to a c t, or
refrain from acting, in some way, rather than to effect a specific
result. Language affords us the facility of describing an action in
terms of its result, by incorporating a causal expression into the
description; thus the special case can be subsumed under the general
one and we can say, e.g., that a physician's obligation is to
c u r e his patients.

Even in the special case, the componential analysis does not succeed
in its aim. Schema (17) makes it clear that it is a who has the
obligation that p should be the case; schema (23), by contrast,
merely says that a 's bringing it about that p is obligatory.
It would be quite compatible with the latter that some second party,
b, should have the obligation, which he fulfils by bringing it
about that a, in turn, brings it about that p. There is a tacit
assumption in Hilpinen's analysis that if a brings it about that p,
then a will also be the agent m o r a l l y responsible for p
being the case; but this assumption is not embodied in his truth-
definition of 'Dap', as will be shown in section 3. Nor is it, in
general, built into the senses of verbs of action; in the absence of
any counter-indication we normally assume that the agent is also
morally responsible, but it is not contradictory to say that someone
accidentally or unintentionally did so-and-so.

The source of the mistake lies in the "standard" deontic logic,
which should never have been taken as the starting-point for an
account of 'ought'. The notion of a state of affairs (what is
described by a proposition) as being obligatory or permitted is a
peculiar one, for which the logical syntax of natural language
offers no support. We have to consider, in this connexion, what
gives our concept of obligation its p o i n t in human life. It is
clear, at the very least, that the concept would lose its point, not
just in a Parmenidean world which was not subject to change,but even
in a changing world which w e, nevertheless, could not influence.
One may say that it presupposes persons as causes of change; to that
extent, Hilpinen is right in thinking that it is somehow tied up
with the semantic field of change and causality , though this is not
alone enough to explain it. But it does explain why it is

meaningless to suppose that states of affairs, in general, are the
subjects of obligation; if w e are not involved in those states,
either as actors or as bringing them about, then the only background
against which obligation can make an appearance is lacking.
Logicians, if they hope to elucidate some of the ways in which
language r e a l l y works, should not allow familiar and
convenient notations to blind them to such considerations; otherwise
logic will merely become a straight-jacket for language, telling us,
not how it d o e s work, but how logicians think it o u g h t to
work.

These tendencies become still more apparent in the 'standard
semantics' for deontic logic, of which an account is to be found in
Føllesdal and Hilpinen (1971, 15-21). This method is an extension of
that used in alethic modal logic, beginning with a definition of a
relation between consistent 'worlds':

(D3) $R(M_i,M_j) \Vdash$ p in M_i if it is obligatory that p in M_j
                                        (cp. p. 17)

We are then told that a state of affairs will be obligatory in a
given consistent world just in case it actually holds in every
consistent world which stands in this relation to the given world,
that is:

(D4)   Op in M $\Vdash$ p in every M_i such that $R(M_i,M)$
                                        (cp. (F5), p. 18)

These can be combined into the following composite definition:

(D5)   Op in M $\Vdash$ p in every M_i such that
        (q in M_i if it is obligatory that p in M)

But since 'Op' represents 'it is obligatory that p', this amounts,
in ordinary language, to saying that a state of affairs is
obligatory in this world just in case it actually holds in every
consistent world in which a state of affairs holds if and only if it
is obligatory in this world.

One could hardly ask for a nicer example of a circular definition;
in order to understand it, we must first understand the sense of
'obligatory', which occurs in the defining clause, but is also the
very notion which is ostensibly being defined. If we do already
understand it, we can just say that 'Op' is to have the same sense
as 'it is obligatory that p', omitting all reference to consistent
worlds. The "definition" may succeed, in conjunction with the truth-
definitions of the other constants of the calculus, in determining
the validity of certain sequents and the (logical) truth of certain

formulas, but whether these sequents and formulas represent valid argument-schemas and logical truths must remain an open question. If the truth-definition, though circular, is not actually false to our notion of obligation, we can expect the argument-schemas to be valid and the proposition-schemas logically true, but incomplete with respect to the linguistic constant: they will capture a part of its sense, but not its whole sense.

That (D5) is, in fact, f a l s e to our notion of obligation is readily apparent. Since a logically true proposition-schema is true in every consistent world without exception, it will hold in the deontic logic that

$$\text{if} \models \alpha \quad , \text{then} \models \text{O} \, \alpha$$

But in these circumstances, we cannot even speak of a state of affairs being obligatory, for a tautology is true in every state of affairs and so represents none. We could, indeed, s a y, for example, 'It is obligatory that not both p and not p': but unless by 'obligatory' we meant 'a logical truth', or something of the sort, this form of words would be totally meaningless. Obligation serves to regulate conduct, but conduct is quite irrelevant to the truth of tautologies. It must, therefore, be the first care of any account of an obligation constant to show that the result of combining it with a tautology will be an ill-formed expression. If it is assigned to category 1PP, this will, of course, be impossible. Modal logicians may be inclined to retort that although their usage in this respect departs somewhat from natural language, no great harm comes of it. On the contrary, it blinds them to one of the most important features of the concept of obligation.

The intuitive idea which (D5) is intended to capture is that a set of obligations is consistent only if every obligation in it can be fulfilled simultaneously (cp. Føllesdal and Hilpinen, p. 16). Hilpinen adapts this requirement to his constant of personal obligation, extending it so that a set of personal obligations of several agents is to be consistent only if all the obligations can be fulfilled simultaneously: that is, everyone must be able to fulfil his own obligations without thereby preventing anyone else from carrying out h i s duties (pp. 6-7, (A2)). A requirement of this type is plausible for universal obligations: when it is applied to personal obligations, it runs counter to all experience. Personal obligations, unlike universal ones, can be i n c u r r e d, for instance by making a promise or signing a

contract. There is nothing to prevent a single person from painting
himself into a corner in which it is logically impossible for him to
fulfil all of his obligations. Some people do this quite
deliberately: we call one version of it "double-crossing" (cp.
Hitler's diplomacy). Text-books of moral theology discuss cases of
conflicting obligations, but they do not, with the exception of
undertakings contrary to a universal obligation, take the easy way
out of saying that at least one of the conflicting obligations is
not binding. We can, indeed, say that a person o u g h t not to
incur conflicting obligations deliberately, but that is one of the
differences between 'ought' and 'can'; Hilpinen's requirement, by
contrast, would be a passport to immorality, the more so when
applied to the totality of moral agents.

This condition upon personal obligations is not a subsidiary part of
Hilpinen's account, which might easily be modified; it is virtually
a l l that he has to say about the notion. Yet it should, surely,be
rather obvious that we are not going to be able to say anything very
interesting about obligation if we only concept to which we can
appeal is that of consistency, much less be able to characterize its
sense. In order to specify the circumstances in which propositions
like (14) or (12) are true, we should have to consider a wide range
of human institutions. The question must also be raised whether
sentences containing deontic expressions are propositions at all,
but not, rather, disguised commands. Hilpinen, indeed, calls
sentences ascribing personal obligations 'personal
d i r e c t i v e s' and begins his discussion with an explanation
of directives which assimilates them to commands; but, although it
cannot be asked whether a command is true or untrue, Hilpinen
assumes that the 'semantic' method can be applied to directives,
thus treating them as propositions.

The semantic field of natural language which includes deontic
expressions is evidently highly complex and presupposes other
semantic fields of which, at present, we have a very imperfect
understanding. Until this groundwork has been accomplished,
logicians will not be able to reveal anything about this concepts
which is likely to be of serious interest to moral philosophers. To
approach this task with inadequate tools is to run the risk of
bungling it so badly that moral philosophers will conclude that, as
far as they are concerned, logic can be written off as a bad job.
Indeed, I fear that this is already happening, which is a great

pity: for there is plenty of room for logical acumen in moral
philosophy, even though the time is not yet ripe for any systematic
application there of formal methods. My own suggestion with regard
to the category of 'ought' must therefore be regarded as only a
first step; it does not yet answer all the difficulties which I have
raised in reference to Hilpinen's proposal. Perhaps the most that
can be said at present is that obligation, like potentiality, is a
concept of second level, which the "standard" deontic logic has mis-
represented as a concept of first level.

3 C a u s a l i t y   a n d   C h a n g e
Although, for the reasons given in the previous section, a
componential analysis of the sense of 'ought' into impersonal
obligation and personal agency is to be rejected, 'ought' being,
rather, itself a component in the notion of u n i v e r s a l
obligation, Hilpinen's constant 'D' is, nevertheless, of
considerable independent interest. Hilpinen's own preferred
"translation" of the constant is:
(24)   Dap: the actions of a are (logically or causally)
          sufficient that p.
The constant is thus clearly intended as a means of representing one
type of causal proposition, even though it will also represent some
propositions which are not causal at all. The latter, however,
constitute Hilpinen's principle ground for rejecting the
"translation":
(25)   Dap: a brings it about that p.

These non-causal propositions are introduced by the truth-definition
of 'Dap', which follows the general pattern of that for 'Oap'.
Hilpinen first defines a relation S_a between consistent "worlds",
whose intuitive sense is given by:
(D6) $S_a(M_i,M_j) \Vdash$ M_i is a world compatible with everything
          done by a in M_j,
the truth-definition of 'Dap' then being:
(D7)   Dap in M $\Vdash$ p in every M_i such that $S_a(M_i,M_j)$
                                              (cp. (C.D), p.12)
From these we can again obtain a composite definition:
(D8)   Dap in M $\Vdash$ p in every M_i compatible with everything
          done by a in M.
As before with 'Op' and 'Oap', this definition has the result
that 'Dap' will be true whenever a logical truth is substituted for
'p'. This explains the "logically" in (24) and Hilpinen's rejection

of (25). Further, it shows that 'Dap' does not imply the
m o r a l responsibility of a for its being the case that p; but
there is, in any case, no suggestion of moral responsibility in (24).

The words 'compatible' and 'done' in the truth-definition call for
some comment. One might be incline to distinguish between logical
and causal compatibility: for instance, it would not be causally
compatible with putting a kettle of water on a gas burner that the
water should become progressively colder and freeze, but this might
be acceptable in a science-fiction story. In (D8), however, 'compatible' means 'logically compatible'; that is, M_i will be compatible
with M_j just in case $M_i \cup M_j$ is a consistent set of propositions.

What is done by a can presumably be described by a proposition of
the form 'Fa'. Now if 'Fa' be substituted for 'p' in (D8), we
shall then, e x h y p o t h e s i, have Fa in every M_i compatible with everything (which includes F) done by a in M. Hence:
(26)   Fa $\models$ DaFa
This is covered by the 'logically' in (24): if 'Fa' describes one
of the actions of a, then the actions of a are indeed logically
sufficient that Fa. Consequently, in cases where the "causality" of
(24) rather than the "logically" is operative, 'p' cannot itself
describe one of the actions or things done by a.

The relationship between 'p' and what is done by a in these
cases can be clarified by considering schema (25). If a brought it
about that p, we can always ask h o w a brought it about; in the
most straight-forward examples, the answer will take the form 'by F-
ing', where 'F' is a verb of action. With this information, we can
construct a proposition which will exemplify the schema:
(27)   a brought it about that p by F -ing
which, in turn, is "convertible" into
(28)   p because Fa,
though propositions of the form (28) are not universally convertible
into form (27). Now (D8) tells us that, in these circumstances, the
supposition that Fa will be inconsistent with the supposition that
not- p; and that is to say that (28), when obtained from (27), is to
mean that 'p' is a l o g i c a l consequence of 'Fa'. But what
(27) means is that p is the r e s u l t of a's F -ing; the
causal, not the logical result. If a brought it about that p by
F -ing, then it must be consistent to suppose that Fa, but,
nevertheless, not- p. Otherwise causality is reduced to logical
consequence. This is precisely the effect of Hilpinen's truth—

definition. Anselm noticed this fallacy and argued against it. (D e
c a s u   d i a b o l i, 2-3).

Once again, it should be obvious that we are not going to be able to
explain the notion of causality in terms of logical consequence and/
or consistency. Further, any truth-definition of schema (25) which
makes 'Dap' true if a logical truth is substituted for 'p' will
be on the wrong foot from the start. Hilpinen admits that it is
false or nonsential to say that someone is the agent of a logical
truth and that lack of control over a state of affairs seems to be
the very opposite of agency (pp. 15-16). He proposes to remedy the
difficulty by representing schema (25) by

(29)   Dap ∧ Ma¬p,

where the "translation" of 'Map' is

(30)   Map: it is (logically) possible for a that p   (p. 17).
No truth-definition is given for this new constant, but the idea
seems to be that a brought it about that p just in case his
actions were sufficient that p, but, nevertheless, it is possible
to suppose that they were not, i.e. possible to suppose that he
acted otherwise, not that the same actions had a different outcome,
which would contradict (D8). If the truth-definition of 'Dap'
already e x c l u d e s causality, however, this device cannot
introduce it. Of course, what we are up against here is a
philosophical theory of causality which has been allowed to
prejudice logic.

Schema (25) presents us with a constant which is to some extent
artificial, in that causal propositions are not normally expressed
with the aid of 'bring it about that'. As a result, one cannot
object to the assignment of this constant to category 2PNP. But it
then becomes important to consider how 'bring it about that' is
related to 'cause to'; do they have the same sense or not? The story
of Procrustes yields an argument which appears to show that they do
not. Procrustes was in the habit to amputating or elongating his
guests in order to make them fit his guest-bed exactly. The end
result, upon each occasion was that his guest was the same length
as his guest-bed, which is the same as saying that his guest-bed was
the same length as his guest. Now if a proposition contains a
subordinate proposition, we ought not to be able to change the sense
of the former by substituting for the latter another proposition
which has the same sense as it. Well, it makes no difference whether
we say

(31)   Procrustes brought it about that his guest was the same
            length as his guest-bed
or
(32)   Procrustes brought it about that his guest-bed was the
            same length as his guest
By contrast,
(33)   Procrustes caused his guest to be the same length as his
            guest bed
could be taken to imply that it was the guest who underwent the
change and
(34)   Procrustes caused his guest-bed to be the same length as
            his guest
that he altered the length of his guest-bed, instead. In that case,
(34) would have a different sense from (33).

If we leave the argument here, the conclusion to be drawn, by
parallel analyses to those for 'can' in section 1 and 'ought' in
section 2, is that 'come to' should be assigned to category 3PNN1PN,
its second argumentor-place then being filled by the name of the
patient. But whereas we could dismiss **first level expressions** of
potentiality and obligation as mistaken, a place would still have
to be found for a first level expression of causality, for there are
many causal propositions which do not identify a patient. Thus if
someone caused two sticks to be the same length, did he alter the
lengths of both of them or only of one and, if the latter, which
one? Yet it is clearly also of great importance to us to have a
linguistic means of identifying the patient if we need to do so: the
difference between (33) and (34) is a difference between criminal
assault, on the one hand, and hospitable preparations, on the other.

Closer inspection of (33) and (34) suggests a better solution. As
they stand, it would be quite possible, if somewhat less natural, to
construe (33) as having exactly the same **sense** as **(31) and (34) as**
having exactly the same **sense** as (32); (33) and (34) would then also
have the same sense. However, if 'be' in (33) and (34) **were replaced**
by 'become', this construction would no longer be possible; **but then**
(35)   Procrustes's guest became the same length as his guest-bed
does not have the same sense as
(36)   Procrustes's guest-bed became the same length as his
            guest,
for 'became' now serves to identify the thing that changed.

This pair of examples will recall the l o c u s   c l a s s i c u s
in Plato (Theaetetus, 155) where the relationship between
(37)   Theaetetus became taller than Socrates
and
(38)   Socrates became shorter than Theaetetus
is considered. Now 'became' is short for 'come to be' and 'come to'
is yet another auxiliary verb, which can combine with other verbs
as well as 'be', e.g. 'come to have', 'come to understand'. If
'come to' is to identify what changes and thereby differentiate the
logical structures of (35) and (37) from those of (36) and (38), it
must be assigned to category 2PN1PN and not to category 1PP. There
is, however, a closely related expression of category 1PP, the
Biblical 'it came to pass that...' or, in a more contemporary form,
'it came about that...'. Hence, however, there is a manifest
phonological difference; it is not that we have two different senses
of 'come', but, rather, two different   e x p r e s s i o n s,
'come (to)' and 'come   a b o u t   (that)'.

An objection may still be raised to this account. Comparative
constructions (including the 'as... as...'form) contain t w o
verbs, one of which can often be suppressed; but in some
propositions, both must appear, e.g.
(39)   Theaetetus   i s   now older than Socrates   w a s   when he
            was executed.
Accordingly, there are also two verbs in
(40)   Theaetetus was taller than Socrates (was),
either of which can be qualified by 'come to'. If the first, we get
(37), but if the second,
(41)   Theaetetus was taller than Socrates came to be,
which will have the same sense as (38). Consequently, we could
exhibit the difference of logical structure between (37) and (38)
with 'come about that', which would simply have a different scope in
each proposition. Thus (41) could be re-cast as:
(42)   Theaetetus was taller than it came about that Socrates
            was.
An expression of category 2PN1PN would then be unnecessary.

A definitive answer to this objection would call for a logical
analysis of comparative and similar constructions, which is not
available. One could, of course, give the   a p r i o r i   reply
that if 'come to' can always be eliminated in favour of 'come about
that', we should never be able to pick out, linguistically, an

object as having changed. But enough is already clear for us to do
better than this. Intuitively, (41) does n o t appear to have the
same sense as (38), but, rather, to mean 'Socrates never became as
tall as Theaetetus was'. This would be explained if, as several
linguists have suggested, the 'than' of the comparative construction
contains an element of negation. Suppose that we exhibit this by
paraphrasing (40) as:
(43)   Theaetetus was s o tall: and not: Socrates was
           t h a t tall.
Then the corresponding paraphrase of (42), in which the 'than'
precedes the 'came about that', will be:
(44)   Theaetetus was s o tall: and not: it came about that
           Socrates was t h a t tall.
In order to obtain a structure with the same sense as (38), we
should need:
(45)   Theaetetus was s o tall: and: it came about that
           Socrates was not t h a t tall.
But this cannot be achieved within a comparative construction, in
which the 'than' combines the 'and' and the 'not' so that they
cannot be separated.

Given an expression of category 2PN1PN, however, we can combine it
with e i t h e r of the predicates ' ξ was taller than Socrates
was' or 'Theaetetus was taller than ζ was', the latter having the
same sense as ' ζ was shorter than Theaetetus was'. In the first
case we obtain the predicate ' ξ became taller than Socrates was',
in the second ' ζ became shorter than Socrates was', the 'than'
('and not') in both cases coming w i t h i n the scope of 'come
to'. Using ' $C_x \xi \phi x$ ' to represent 'come to', the two structures can
be exhibited as follows:
(37S) C_x Theaetetus (x was s o tall: and not: Socrates was
           t h a t tall)
(38S) C_x Socrates (Theaetetus was s o tall: and not: x was
           t h a t tall)
It is then no longer necessary to worry about the internal
structures of comparative and similar constructions; we can simply
consider them as two-place predicates completed by two proper names.
Then, using 'F ξ ζ ' to represent ' ξ was the same length as   ',
the difference between (35) and (36) is that between ' $C_x aFxb$ '   and
' $C_x bFax$ '. So we shall now be able to represent (33) by ' $DaC_x bFxc$ '
and (34) by ' $DaC_x cFbx$ ', the suppressed 'come to' element picking

out the respective patients and, at the same time, blocking any
proof of logical equivalence between the two propositions.

The conclusion to be drawn from this discussion is that 'cause to'
and 'bring it about that' are expressions of the same category 2PNP,
the latter expression being merely a convenient paraphrase for the
former which exhibits more clearly the logical structure of causal
propositions. This view has been implicitly challenged by Harman
(1972, p.39), who cites the propositions

(46)   A short circuit caused a house that Jack built to burn
          down

and

(47)   A short circuit caused Jack to build a house that burned
          down,

whose senses differ, in spite of the equivalence between A house
that Jack built burned down and Jack built a house that burned down.
This, however, is to confuse linguistic with logical syntax. It
cannot be assumed that each of the two equivalent propositions
occurs, respectively, as a subordinate proposition in (46) and (47).
Once this assumption is dropped, it is easy to account for the
difference in sense by a difference of scope in 'cause to' as
between the two propositions. There is even an outward sign of this
in the linguistic syntax: only one verb occurs in the infinitive in
each example and it is a different verb in each case.

The logical form of what Harman takes to be the subordinate
proposition would be represented in standard logical practice as
'$\bigvee_x(Fax \wedge Gx)$', the range of the existential quantifier being
restricted to houses. There is an obvious difficulty about
quantifying over short circuits, but this feature of the example
is accidental, so let us suppose that 'A short circuit' is replaced
by 'Peter' in both examples; it makes no difference to Harman's
point. Then the representation which we need for (46) is:

(46S) $\bigvee_x(Fax \wedge DbGx)$: for some house, Jack built it and Peter

while that required for (47) is:

(47S) $\bigvee_x(DbFax \wedge Gx)$: for some house, Peter caused Jack to
           build it and it burned down

There is no objection to a prenex existential quantifier
representing something which e x   h y p o t h e s i   no longer
exists; it is enough to justify its use that Jack   d i d   build the
house and that it   d i d, therefore, at some time exist (cp. the use

of proper names of deceased persons).

The sense of certain verbs is repugnant to qualification by 'come
to', among them verbs describing actions which take time; thus 'come
to walk' is ill-formed (though not: How did you come to walk from
John O'Groats to Land's End? in which 'How did you come to...?' has
the sense of 'How did it come about that you...?'). The reason for
this is that such verbs already describe changes: to walk from John
O'Groats to Land's End is one way of coming to be at Land's End,
having been at John O'Groats. 'Come to', like 'can' and 'ought',
cannot be iterated, so it, too, can only be provisionally assigned
to category 2PN1PN. We cannot generalize from this example and say
that 'come to' is a component in the sense of all such verbs,
however; it takes time to polish a table, for instance, but it would
be empty to say that the table comes to be polished. Nevertheless,
these verbs do identify what changes and that is enough to ensure
that when they fall within the scope of 'cause to', ambiguity on
that score is excluded.

In some cases, there is a double change. Thus, if Pilate caused some
Roman soldiers to crucify a thief, then the soldiers were patients
with respect to Pilate, but agents with respect to the thief. We can
say here that the soldiers were Pilate's i n s t r u m e n t s in
crucifying the thief; this suggests that we might also use the
constant 'cause to' in an analysis of the senses of propositions
employing the instrumental case, expressed in English by the
preposition 'with'. For example, if we can have
(48)   A key opened the door,
then we might specify the sense of
(49)   John opened the door with a key
by
(50)   John caused a key to open the door.
Of course, propositions of type (50) will not always "convert" into
propositions of type (49): we cannot say that Pilate crucified a
thief w i t h some soldiers in this sense of 'with': the
instrument(s) must be inanimate.

Some verbs of action also contain 'cause to' as a component in their
senses. This is quite explicit in the Semitic languages, in which,
for many verbs 'F', it is possible with a single prefix to form a
verb meaning 'cause to F': in German, the prefix 'be-' often has
the same function. In English, however, the same change of sense is
frequently effected by using a verb transitively instead of

intransitively; thus (48) itself could be paraphrased by:

(51)   A key caused the door to open.

These few examples, which could easily be multiplied, show how useful a constant representing 'cause to' or 'bring it about that' would be in analyzing the logical structure of a wide range of propositions, but, although they support the assignment of these expressions to category 2PNP, they do not advance the task of giving a truth-definition for schema (25). Yet it would be premature to cast around for a truth-definition, assuming that the necessary logical syntax is already available. I drew attention earlier to Hilpinen's admission that it is false or nonsensical to say that someone is the agent of a logical truth; the difference between these two alternatives must now be pressed home. If 'bring it about that' belongs to category 2PNP, then it can be, at worst, false; if, on the other hand, it is nonsensical, then the category of 'bring it about that' cannot be 2PNP.

As with obligation, so with causality, we must consider the point of the concept: again, it would have no point in a Parmenidean world. In contrast to obligation, however, there would still be room for causality in a world which w e could not influence, provided that it could change and that some changes could be seen as proceeding from the behaviour of certain objects. The minimal requirements here are that propositions substituted for 'p' in schema (25) should be significantly tensed and that the 'How?' question should be admissible. Another way of putting this is that propositions substituted for 'p' must describe contingent states of the world, for this is what both makes their tense logically significant and provides an application for the 'How?' question. In that case it will be nonsense, and not merely false, to substitute a tautology or its negation for 'p' in the schema. Nor will tautologies and contradictions be the only inadmissible substitutions: scientific laws, for example, like Water boils at 100°C, will be equally inappropriate.

It seems, then, that there must be some as yet unidentified component in propositions which can be substituted for 'p' in schema (25) and that 'bring it about that' and 'cause to' latch onto this component, but without neutralizing it, for both can be iterated. It is also clear that this component is bound up with the concepts of time and change; for this reason, it must remain inaccessible to a P-N grammar. It does not follow, however, that it

is beyond the reach of logical syntax: no guarantees are to be found
that P and N are the only basic categories which logical syntax
requires. Nor does it follow that because 'bring it about that' and
'cause to' belong to a first level category with respect to a P-N
grammar that they belong to a first level category without
qualification. The senses of these expressions, as of any
expressions, determine their possibilities of combination, so by
specifying the latter we shall bring to light the logical features
which must be taken into account in specifying the former. The
essential clue to predicate logic, or the logic of generality, lay
in distinguishing sharply between proper names and functors of
second level; it is my conjecture that the essential clue to the
logic of change and causality lies in the identification of a
further basic category.

REFERENCES

Føllesdal,D., and Hilpinen,R. (1971), Deontic Logic: An
    Introduction, in R. Hilpinen (editor), D e o n t i c
    L o g i c : I n t r o d u c t o r y   a n d   S y s t e m a t i c
    R e a d i n g s; Dordrecht: Reidel, 1-35.

Hilpinen,R. (1973), On the Semantics of Personal Directives,
    A j a t u s 35; re-printed in this volume (page references to
    the latter).

Hintikka,J.K.K. (1957), Necessity, Universality and Time in
    Aristotle, A j a t u s 20. 65-90.

Jardine,N., and Jardine,C.J. (1974), The Status of Model-Theoretic
    Semantics, in E.L. Keenan (editor), P r o c e e d i n g s   o f
    t h e   C o l l o q u i u m   o n   S e m a n t i c s   o f
    N a t u r a l   L a n g u a g e s, Cambridge, April, 1973;
    Cambridge: Cambridge University Press.

Mally,E. (1926), G r u n d g e s e t z e   d e s   S o l l e n s :
    E l e m e n t e   d e r   L o g i   d e s   W i l l e n s; Graz;
    reprinted in L o g i s c h e   S c h r i f t e n; Dordrecht:
    Reidel, 1971.

Potts,T.C. (1974a), Fregean Grammar: A Formal Outline, in R. Posner
    (editor), a   c o l l e c t i o n   o f   p a p e r s   o n
    c a t e g o r i a l   g r a m m a r s; New York: The Seminar
    Press.

Potts, T.C. (1974b), Model Theory and Linguistics, in E.L. Keenan
    (editor), P r o c e e d i n g s   o f   t h e
    C o l l o q u i u m   o n   S e m a n t i c s   o f
    N a t u r a l   L a n g u a g e s, Cambridge, April, 1973;
    Cambridge: Cambridge University Press.

Potts,T.C. (1974c), Montague's Semiotic: A Syllabus of Errors, in
    M. Bell (editor), P r o c e e d i n g s   o f   t h e
    L o g i c   C o n f e r e n c e, York, March. 1973; Oxford: at
    the Clarendon Press.

Prior,A.N. (1955), F o r m a l   L o g i c; Oxford: at the Clarendon
    Press.

Wittgenstein,L. (1922), T r a c t a t u s   L o g i c o -
    P h i l o s o p h i c u s; London: Routlegde and Kegan Paul.

von Wright,G.H. (1951), Deontic Logic, M i n d 60, 1-15; re-

printed in L o g i c a l S t u d i e s; London: Routledge and
    Kegan Paul.
von Wright,G.H. (1968), An Essay in Deontic Logic and the General
    Theory of Action, A c t a P h i l o s o p h i c a
    F e n n i c a 21; Amsterdam: North-Holland.

ACKNOWLEDGEMENTS
The author is indebted to his colleagues in the Department of
Philosophy of the University of Leeds, to whom an earlier version
of this paper was read at a senior seminar, for criticism and
suggestions.

DISCUSSION

Hasenjaeger: Even though only a smaller part was related to the
first talk, Mrs. Barth should first give her comments to Mr. Potts'
contribution.
Barth: I think Mr. Potts' remark was most interesting, and I am
quite willing to believe that medieval logicians would not make this
fallacy, which Moore had discussed, and which I discussed today
when they would be starting out from (1). But my point is actually a
different one that you can generate sentences of the form of (1) by
that analysis of particular sentences which was the only one known
before Frege and also known in the Middle Ages and that the sentence which resulted from that analysis was by a large number of
authors even then, and in fact in all centuries, as far as I have
been able to see, assumed to presuppose the truth of something like
(1c). I am much more interested in how you generate them, but of
course I should not like to imply that medieval logic was as bad as
idealistic logic, for instance.
Potts: Yes: one of the main points indeed remains. If you construe
such a proposition as being essentially a subject-predicate proposition, then you have to regard the "possible" as attaching to the
predicate, because even in my representation, it comes within the
scope of the quantifier. Hence, if you are limited to an analysis of
sentences which breaks them down in the first instance into a noun-
phrase and a verb-phrase, or into a subject and a predicate, you are
unable to bring out these logical distinctions.
Hilpinen: I wish to comment first on Mrs. Barth's paper. I have two
comments; one is a comment on a detail, another is a general comment. First I should like to comment on the example in which Mrs.
Barth derives from certain plausible-looking premisses the conclusion that "It is possible that Moore's father is a female". According to Mrs. Barth, this inference is unacceptable since the conclusion is clearly self-contradictory. I don't agree with this view. In
this case the description 'Moore's father' is used referentially; it
is similar to a name which picks out a certain individual (the individual who is in fact Moore's father), and the sentence "It is possible that Moore's father is a female" means that this individual
might have been a female. (The formulation used above is a bit misleading; "Moore's father might have been a female" would perhaps be
a more natural formulation of the conclusion.) This is not at all
contradictory (even though some people would say that it does not
make sense to speak about such possibilities). We know that people

can change sex, etc; sex does not seem to be an "essential" property of individuals. We can also say that "Moore's father might have
been a female" is consistent if it is interpreted as a modal proposition d e r e, but inconsistent if interpreted as a proposition
d e d i c t o. (The d e d i c t o interpretation implies that
some individual might have been both Moore's father and a female at
the same time.) Distinctions of this kind can be elucidated with the
help of modal logic.

My second comment on Mrs. Barth's paper is a general one, and is
related to what Mr. Potts already said. Mrs. Barth only gives examples about the use of the modal expression 'necessary' and 'possible' in natural language. This gives a restricted and unrepresenta-
tive view of the application of modal logic to the analysis of natural language. It would be more natural and more interesting to take
as examples various intensional verbs, for instance "know", "hope",
"believe", "look for", etc. If modal logic is applied to the analysis of intensional verbs, the philosophical problems and perplexi-
ties concerning essences and essentialism (which are prominent in
the case of possibility and necessity) do not arise. Problems concerning necessity and possibility are not typical or even good examples of the application of intensional or modal logic to the semantical analysis of natural language.

Then I should like to comment briefly on some points raised by Mr.
Potts. At the beginning of his talk Mr. Potts suggested that the
rule of necessitation of modal logic may be unacceptable in the
logic of directives. This rule is problematic in most applications
of modal logic; in this respect the D-operator is not an exceptional
case. The acceptability of the rule of necessitation depends on the
interpretation of 'D'. In my paper I attempted to sketch an interpretation consistent with this rule.

Mr. Potts' proposal that the D-operator should be applied to open
sentences or predicates instead of closed sentences is very interesting and seems very plausible in cases in which we say that a
person does something t o s o m e i n d i v i d u a l. However, I
am not convinced that Mr. Potts' proposal works equally well in
other cases (or is an improvement over my D-operator). I cannot make
detailed comments on this proposal before I have worked out the
semantics of Mr. Potts' D-operator; on the basis of syntactical considerations alone I am not able to evaluate it. Nevertheless Mr.
Potts' example shows clearly that if the D-operator is applied to
closed sentences, the second argument of 'D' cannot always be a

s t a t e (which results from the agent's action); in some cases it
must be a description of an e v e n t.

Barth: May I for the sake of completeness make a couple of remarks
in answer to what Mr. Hilpinen said. In the first place, you
suggested that the expression My father may be understood as a name.
I fail to see what you can mean by this in such a way as to make it
relevant for a formalized theory of modalities. 'My father' is a
term and 'father' is a function and you obtain that term 'Moore's
father' by applying this functional relation to a certain argument.
It is not a name in the strong sense of the word, at least.
Secondly, I like to point out that, of course, I have made no
attempt to express my view on the study of all kinds of modalities
as a whole. I explicitly said that I was going to speak only of
alethic modalities, but I may not have said it distinctly enough.
These alethic modalities are found in natural languages. I wanted to
show one way in which they have commonly been produced, one reason
why they are still with us. About epistemic and deontic logics I
have no quarrels at all, and in fact, not about the alethic
modalities either, as long as we are aware of the fact that we are
constructing them rather than finding them: at least, we are not,
when formulating logical theory, simply describing them: for the
meaning of the alethic modal operators will be a function of, among
other things, underlying non-modal logic. And so the "meaning" of
modal operators cannot be discussed in absence of a logical theory.
So what one can possibly be looking for as "meaning" of the modal
operators, will in fact depend on the theory one has already
adopted with respect to the logic of other logical particles. What
one can possibly be looking for in fact varies very strongly with
the choice of your previous logical steps. This is what I have tried
to bring out, and that has much less relevance to the study of the
deontic modalities, for instance, than to the alethic ones.

Hilpinen: I should like to return to the example about Moore's
father. If the description 'moore's father' is used purely
referentially (as a 'rigid designator'), it is not inconsistent to
say that Moore's father might have been a woman - or that Moore's
father might not have been Moore's father. This can be shown more
clearly if the modal expression 'possible' (or 'might') is replaced
by some intensional verbs, for instance, the verb "believe". It is
conceivable that some person might have said to the son of George
Eliot: I used to believe that your mother was a man. This is not
inconsistent - and everyone understands what it means. (This

illustrates my earlier remark that various intensional verbs provide
better and more natural examples of the application of modal logic
to natural language than modal expressions proper.)

Bertrand Russell has given (in "On Denoting") a similar example of
the referential use of descriptions. Russell's example is about a
yacht owner whom someone told I thought your yacht was longer than
it is.

Suppes: I like to make a comment, following up what Hilpinen said, I
take up Mr. Potts' closing remark. It seemes to me that a very good
case has been made in the literature, but the difficulty with modal
logic, and the many papers that have been written, is, that people
have not given a semantics. They have relied upon unstructured
intuition. The mistake has indeed been to try to do a syntactical
theory without a proper semantics. The second remark is: it doesn't
seem to me that from the standpoint of linguistics there is any
serious sense in which you are doing syntax. For example, a notation
as $D_x(a,b,Fxc)$ is certainly not the syntax of natural language.
Already some case must be made, presumably semanticly based, as to
how that expression is to be related to any expression in ordinary
language.

Potts: Well, I certainly want to reply to that! First, I think
that the traditional dichotomy between syntax and semantics is
totally misconceived. We have been offered what some people call
"semantics", which from the philosophical point of view is totally
unenlightening. I does not seem to me to beginn to give an account
of the meanings of 'necessary' or 'possible'. Certainly it provides
a means of proving certain formal properties of modal systems, and
it is quite in order as a mathematical technique, but the essential
idea that we define necessity as truth in all possible worlds, does
not help me at all until I know what a possible world is. But when I
know what a possible world is, I know what it means to say that it
is possible that p and, hence, if 'it is necessary that p' means
'it is not possible that not p', I already know what 'necessary'
means. When I use the term 'semantics', I mean, on the contrary,
an account of the meaning of the sentence which could be given as an
explanation to somebody who did not understand it. I do not mean a
sophisticated mathematical device for proving meta-theorems about a
formal system. In this sense, it seems to me that one must begin
semantics by giving a clear account of the structure of sentences.
It is urged against me that the type of analysis which I have
proposed gives no account of the structure of natural language. But

one can speak of the structure of natural language in two senses.
One is the structure that we need in order to explain the
s e n s e   of the sentence, and I assume that the latter, which is
logically complex, must be explained as made up in some way out of
the senses of its constituents. One can also talk about the
structure of a sentence to refer to the forms of expression used in
a particular natural language. This corresponds roughly to one
distinction that transformational grammarians have drawn between
deep structure and surface structure. Now my claim is that the
structure relevant to the   m e a n i n g s   of causal propositions
and to propositions ascribing personal obligation cannot be as
Hilpinen described it, since, if it were, fallacious inferences
would thereby be licensed. If a structural description allows
fallacious inferences, we do not need any sophisticated mathematics
in order to see that it is incorrect.

Bar-Hillel: I still have to come back to the argument of Professor
Suppes and to generalize it. I think what he said applies almost
equally well to what Hilpinen said and to what Mrs. Barth said.
There is no obvious relationship at all between all the things we
have heard today and what is happening in natural languages. There
is a very interesting not obvious relationship, but this has been
left probably in the background. Let me go into details. The logic
of imperatives which you are dealing with is a logic of commands. It
is a logic of speech-acts. The relationship between an imperative
sentence and a command in English or any language is a very peculiar
one. Not by any utterance of an imperative sentence does one give a
command, and vice versa. So what you gave us is one particular logic
of commands, pointing out personal interest, etc. The application
will be a very indirect one, and that application is a very wrong
way to go. So what you did, to put it in slogan terms, was a
conceptual analysis and was not a linguistic analysis. This, for
instance, shows up in Potts' counterexample. The only thing is that
if you say 'I cause a to be b' the English expression is slightly
assymetrical. So that if Procrustes caused the bed to fit the
length of the man, then we would probably interpret it that he did
something to the bed, whereas if he caused the man to fit the length
of the bed, we would probably interpret it that he did something to
the man. And this is not much more difficult than to say that 'a is
bigger than b' is not at all always the same as 'b is smaller
than   a'. To the last issue of syntax and sematics, I think, we
cannot let it go by that. This issue has to

be continued. Suppes surely had in mind a more legitimate sense of
the word "semantic". What Mr. Potts was telling us right now has
surely nothing to do with syntax at all, I would replace it exactly
by the term 'conceptual'. What Mr. Potts and Hilpinen gave us was a
conceptual analysis of certain operators. But this has nothing to do
at all with language in any sense whatsoever. The relationship
between this conceptual analysis and the analysis of what is going
on in natural language has directly not even been touched. I think
that linguists will now require of philosophical logicians that they
should develop systems which should be much clearer and more
directly applicable to natural languages than it has been so far.
Suppes: I think, Bar-Hillel and I are in agreement on somebody's
issues. I was addressing a question to your (Potts) remark about
semantics in a general sense. And in fact I would take it to be on
the side of semantics and not syntax. I would consider an account of
the sense and the way in which the sense of the sentence is
constructed from the sense of its parts a problem of semantics and
not a problem of syntax. And I think that would be customary usage
to take it that way. What I find strange in your remarks in response
to mine is: you object to a model-theoretic semantics like Kripke-
semantics or something of that kind because there isn't an explicit
definition of "possible worlds". But you immediately refer yourself
to other kinds of operators that seem to me of no better kind. I
mean that have in fact more weaknesses of knowing exactly what is
being talked about, a very good example being 'deep structure'. I
mean the Kripke-semantics as a concept is a more sharply defined
concept than , to use that favorable word of linguistics, the
abstract concept of 'deep structure'. The same has to be said of the
concept of sense. So, what I find is a kind of prejudice, I would
say, regarding which particular abstract concepts you think are
relevant. I think the issue really is in the case of semantics
whether a model-theoretic semantics is relevant to the analysis of
natural language. I think your view is that it is not, and my view
is that it is.
Potts: I used terms such as 'deep structure' simply because I
thought they would be familiar to most people here and thus the
easiest and quickest means of conveying my point. But I did also
explain first the notions which I intended, before introducing the
terminology, so I do not regard myself as committed to the latter.
Before coming to Suppes's point about model-theoretic semantics,
when I expect to raise a hornet's nest, I should like to return

to Bar-Hillel's remarks on converse relations like 'a is bigger than
b' and 'b is smaller than a'. There may indeed be certain
differences of meaning here, but, if so, they do not affect logical
consequence. To give another example, 'a bought b from c' has
the same logical force as 'c sold b to a', even though, as a
shop-keeper once told me, dissatisfied customers always say You
s o l d me this and never I b o u g h t this from you. That
difference is a difference of meaning and an important one; its
explanation lies, no doubt, in the context of utterance. Yet it does
not affect that aspect of meaning which Frege called the 'conceptual
content' of a proposition, or, as I should prefer to say, its
l o g i c a l f o r c e.
Now I regard logical force as the fundamental aspect of meaning and
syntax, in the sense of structural description, as essential to its
elucidation. Nothing that either Suppes or Bar-Hillel has said
persuades me that the analysis which I presented is irrelevant to
explaining the logical force of sentences of ordinary language. To
be sure, Bar-Hillel is correct in saying that I have given no
account of how to obtain sentences from formulas in the symbolism
which I proposed, but one cannot do everything in twenty minutes!
I am prepared to render such an account, and do not consider it such
a difficult task.
To turn now to model-theoretic semantics, philosophers since the
time of Aristotle, and in our day linguists and logicians, have been
obsessed by a mistaken prejudice about the concept of meaning, to
the effect that if an expression means something, then there must be
something, some entity, for which it stands. This idea is built into
model-theoretic semantics (excepting, perhaps, the recent paper by
Hiz) and is quite clearly stated in Tarski's paper on truth. It is
supposed that incomplete expressions stand for progressively more
complex set-theoretical entities, which are their meanings.
To my mind, this theory of meaning was decisively refuted by
Wittgenstein, who rightly claimed that standing for something is a
s p e c i a l feature of proper names, which differentiates them
from every other kind of expression and, in particular, from the
logical constants ("and", "or", "if... then...", etc.), whose
meaning does not consist in standing for anything. The same applies
to predicates in general. Anyone who wants to sell model-theoretic
semantics to us has an obligation to consider Wittgenstein's
arguments on this point; perhaps he was wrong, but at least we are
entitled to know why.

Bar-Hillel: When you say that Taski's model-theory is not good
enough for natural languages, I have to remind you that we have
the so-called intensional model-theory for a number of years. Why
should this be disregarded? Whether these intensional model-theories
can in some sense be reduced to extensional model-theories has been
discussed since Carnap's paper of 1947 by dozens of people. I leave
this totally open. Reduceable or not, we have a perfectly workable
intensional model-theory and this is still the by far most
impressive means that logicians have put at our hands. We should by
no means be ready to give this up. Finally again, it is not just a
terminological question of command and imperative. Let me repeat
this old example to show that the utterance of a disjunctive
imperative on no account means   giving a disjunctive command: Hans
is interfered with the teacher and the teacher says: Hans, either
shut up or leave the room! Whereupon Hans gets up and leaves the
room. Now the teacher carries him immediately to the headmaster and
accuses him of misbehaving.
So, switching from imperative logic to logic of commands is not
quite a terminological affair but it is something rather essential.
Hilpinen: I wish to reply to what Professor Bar-Hillel said about
the logic of commands and the logic of imperatives. I regard this as
a purely terminological difference. I have thought that the
expression 'imperative' can be used to refer to a meaning category,
but if this is not the case, I am ready to change my terminology and
speak only about the 'logic of commands'. Secondly, I believe that
the possible world-semantics of modal logic (or some refined version
of it) is applicable to the semantic analysis of n a t u r a l
language, and in some areas it seems to be the best and most
fruitful semantical theory available.
Keenan: I want to comment on two points. First, with respect to Mr.
Potts' remarks about actives and passives in similar propositional
content. It came up about seven or eight years ago within the
framework of transformational syntax, a problem, as far as I can see
see, in most important respects analogous to the one he brought up
only where the difference in question was one of active and passive
sentences. The argument was that actives and passives had different
content in some sense because the result of embedding them did not
preserve meaning. Thus John persuaded Fred to be examined by a
doctor did not mean the same thing as John persuaded the doctor to
examine Fred , though apparently the only difference is that the
embedded sentence is passive quite analogous to your His bed was as

long as his guest - case. And the solution that was proposed was
rather analogous to this syntactically, that is, "persuade" was to
be considered as a three-place predicate taking roughly two names
and a sentence as an argument, where the second argument nonetheless
had to be the same as the subject of the embedded sentence. I am not
clear from your notation, how you will show that John caused Fred to
break the window implies that Fred broke the window. That is that in
some sense "Fred", the second argument here in the first sentence,
is understood as in some sense the subject of "break", the reason
being that there is not any identity indicated in your notation
between arguments of the sentence and any of the mayor arguments of
the functor. Secondly just a remark about the utility of model-
theoretic semantics. It seems to me that the only serious notion of
consequence that has been proposed has been Tarski's, and the only
serious clear and systematic implementation of that has been
basically the model-theory he proposed. The justification of it
surely is that if we represent sentences in an extensional way,
think of predicates as referring to sets as names as referring to
entities etc., we can show that sentences, pricipally those of very
elementary mathematical languages, with respect to the semantics
that has been proposed, imply the right sentences. Every student
either works hard or has rich parents does not entail Either every
student works hard or every student has rich parents. It is the
fact that under that semantics those two sentences come out
independently that justifies using it. I think that the principal
justification then is on it gives the right results as regards our
judgements of (relatedness) sentences, not as regards fundamental
intuitions about whether predicates denote, or names denote in that
sense.

Kummer:I have a question to Mr. Hilpinen. If you have John eats an
apple you would have to split this into John caused something and a
part for which I can ask What did he cause?. I cannot think of some
state or event which would not be ad hoc. I don't see that this
could be a way of changing action sentences into simpler components.

Hilpinen: In that case the sentence radical would be That John ate
an apple. The function of the D-operator is merely to indicate the
individual considered as an agent, and bring out the element of
intentionality related to agency. In the case of John ate an apple
the role of the D-operator seems rather trivial, but it is not as
trivial e.g. in cases in which the sentence radical does not contain
the name of the agent.

Keenan: If you take John ate an apple as the sentence embedded under
your modal operator and define as you suggested John may eat the
apple as being, if I remember, It's not the case than John ought not
to eat the apple, it seems to me that this is an unenlightening
treatment of negation embedded in such contexts, because surely the
simple sentence John ought not to eat the apple entails It is not
the case that John ought to eat the apple in which case It's not the
case that John ought not to eat the apple is equivalent to John
ought to eat the apple which gives you by definition John may eat
the apple entails John ought to eat the apple.

Hilpinen: Now we should need a pen and paper, but I believe the
negations come out right.

Potts: May I intervene here? There is a difficulty about negation
and 'ought'-sentences in English. One cannot distinguish between
negations within the scope of "ought" and "ought" within the scope
of negation, because You not ought to do it is ungrammatical.
Normally 'a ought not to F' is construed as an internal negation.
But if, instead, we say 'a is obliged not to F', then we can
distinguish this from 'a is not obliged to F'. Once this
distinction is clearly made, I do not think that the entailment
which has been suggested is plausible any longer. But perhaps the
steps in the argument could be repeated, using the 'a is obliged to
F' form?

Keenan: Okay, John is obliged not to eat the apple surely entails
that It is not the case that John is obliged to eat the apple. But
John is permitted to eat the apple was by definition It is not the
case that John is obliged not to eat the apple. Was it not? Now
the simple sentence from above John is obliged not to eat the apple
entails It is not the case that John is obliged to eat the apple.
Then surely the negation of that whole thing entails the negation of
the other.

Potts: No, you can't get from John is not obliged not to eat the
apple to John is obliged to eat the apple. You can't cancel out the
two negations on either side of 'obliged to'.

Schnelle: My remark is an addition to what Bar-Hillel said. There is
usually an assumption by theoretical linguists and all logicians,
which is tacitly made, namely that what one is describing is not the
full system of all linguistic features which may occur on the actual
process of communication but rather a standardized or normalized
system behind it. And on this assumption the real discussion to
be made is whether such an abstraction is a useful or necessary one.

If the result would be that it is indeed useful then the reproaches made by Bar-Hillel would not really hit. So it's this methodological problem which should be attacked.

Potts: I think that the English proverb that we must learn to walk before we can learn to run is very relevant to linguistics just at the moment, but that it is little heeded. One must not expect to be able to deal with sentences like John is even taller than Peter until we can deal with those like John is taller than Peter. The analysis of comparartive constructions is not at all easy; I talked in my paper of second-level functors and regretted that they have as yet been so little explored: well, I believe that the analysis of comparative constructions calls for third-level functors, i.e., those which take a second-level functor as one of their arguments. So I would only claim that the syntactic methods of which I gave you an example this afternoon will eventually yield a store of standard forms in one or other of which everything which can be expressed in a language can be said, in a correct grammatical form. But I do not suppose that we shall necessarily be able to generate every variant and, when we come to idioms, I do not think that it is even reasonable for formal linguistics to aim to exhibit every idiom as rule-governed. May I remind you of Wittgenstein's comparison between language and an ancient city, parts of which were planned at one time, other parts at another, and which has grown up between-times quite haphazardly, without any planning at all (Philosophical Investigations, I.18). To try to bring every idiom under a rule is as vain an enterprise as trying to find a master-plan for the whole of such a city. Geach has given an excellent example of such an idiom in English: there is no rule about which names of diseases are preceded by the definite article and which are not. We say 't h e measles', 't h e heeby-jeebies', but plain 'meningitis', and so on, without rhyme or reason (Should Traditional Grammar Be Ended or Mended?, E d u c a t i o n a l R e v i e w 22 (1969, 1, 18-25).

Keenan: A small remark about Mr. Potts' last remark. I would be in complete agreement that a certain number of distributional proper-ties of lexical items are utterly arbitrary in a language and there is little order and little point in trying to describe them. But as an attitude of a working linguist, I don't think that attitude is tenable because we don't know which ones these are until we try.

Potts: In reply to Keenan, I would say that a linguist needs a good "logical nose" in order to sniff out important and regular features of language - if a metaphor drawn from the behaviour of dogs may be

allowed. I think that Fowler gives evidence of a good logical nose
in "Modern English Usage" and that a linguist can, in consequence,
learn much from it. In general, the distinctions which are likely to
be important are those which carry over into other languages: not
necessarily to every language, but at least to those in the same
family. The history of philosopy also contains lessons for
linguists: I mean the concepts which philosophers over the ages have
thought worthy of discussion. Perhaps they have not always made a
good selection, but for the most part the concepts to which they
have paid attention will, I think, turn out to be of importance for
linguists as well. In our present position, when so little of the
ground has been covered, it is surely wiser to concentrate on those
areas of language in which there is a high probability of important
results coming to light, rather than dissipating our energies upon
anything and everything.
Bar-Hillel: Mr. Potts has a certain tendency to embed age-old
fallacies: I think "One should not begin to run before one can walk"
is a deep-seated fallacy. I call it a one-step-at-a-time-fallacy.
This is as if there is a beginning and then there comes a second
step and then a third step. Should one really first finish with
syntax and then go over to semantics, then to pragmatics, or should
we follow the line which was pointed out yesterday, that is: go the
other way round? I would say, the proper approach is to start
anywhere you like, go back if it's necessary, go forward if it's
necessary, or turn in circles.
Staal: I used an expression yesterday which, in the context of this
discussion, could easily be interpreted as meaning something
different. Let me say something about the step-for-step-process and
about what is in the background of the mind of some of us, namely
this model-theoretic approach. Yesterday I said something that looks
as if I will believe in the step theory. That is by no means the
case at all. It was not meant in any sense chronologically, neither
applying to individuals nor applying to the progress of this science.
I would also like to give an example of what actually has happened
or is in the process of happening. The example which Bar-Hillel gave
about the synonymy or non-synonymy of actives and passives is clear.
One of the difficulties in the meeting between logic and natural
language is this: the quantifiers in most natural languages are
immediately attached to the noun phrases while quantifiers in logic,
as we all know, tend to heap together at the beginning of sentences.
Barth: Not necessarily.

<u>Staal</u>: No, not necessarily. In the surface form of sentences of
natural language they seem to attach to noun phrases or terms while
in logic they attach to sentences.

<u>Bar-Hillel</u>: In one-sorted logic they tend not! But in many sorted
logic they tend.

<u>Staal</u>: Now if you look at several of Montague's researches which are
so heavily model-theoretical you find that he constructed at least
one method of going from quantifiers in front of expressions to
quantifiers immediately attached to terms. Now linguists would have
to do it all over again   if they want to make that part of a
linguistic theory. But I think there is a lot that they could learn
from this kind of construction and they have not so far been able to
do so.

<u>Potts</u>: I owe Keenan a comment upon Tarski's definition of logical
consequence. He has claimed that it is the best definition of
logical consequence that we have and that it is spelled out by model
theory. Well, perhaps it is the best we have, but we should not be
complacent about it, for all that. It has been criticized by the
Kneales in "The Development of Logic" (pp. 640-644) for giving no
place to the element of necessity which we feel intuitively to be a
part of our notion of logical consequence. Tarski's definition
involves u n i v e r s a l i t y, but not necessity: 'α' is a
logical consequence of a set of formulas 'Γ' if and only if
e v e r y interpretation which satisfies 'Γ' also satisfies 'α'.
But even granting Tarski's definition, what strictly follows from it
is only that we shall be able to determine the truth-value of any
formula v i a the description which it gives of its parts. The
analogous thesis about the meaning of a sentence is that the latter
shall also be determined by the meanings of its parts and their
manner of combination; and with this I am in full agreement. Model-
theoretic semantics, however, goes as far beyond this, construing
every sentence as a functional expression and explaining a function
as a mapping, with truth or falsity as the objects onto which
various objects named by parts of the sentence are eventually
mapped. It is here that I disagree, not only with the friends of
model-theoretic semantics, but even with Frege, to whom the
function-argument analysis is orginally due. Frege's achievement in
applying the syntax of mathematical propositions to sentences of
natural language was a remarkable one, which made a decisive advance
upon the previous efforts of logicians and grammarians, but by
taking over at the same time the explanation of a function as a

mapping, he opened the way to positing a progression of ever
incomprehensible entities. With an intensional model-theoretic
semantics will come even more objectionable intentional entities.
In sum, there are, it seems to me, very serious objections to model-
theoretic semantics which its proponents must consider and answer.
Suppes: I think, Mr. Potts is quite right that one can raise
objections to predicates denoting sets and Tarski would agree with
that as an example of his own viewpoint. As he would state it, he is
a nominalist in his basic philosophy. But it seems to me that the
delicate issue is the following: I would like to draw a seventheenth
century comparison of a rather different sort. The objection of
seventeenth century Cartesians to Newtonian physics was that there
could not possibly be action on a distance corresponding to the idea
that a predicate cannot denote an **abstract object.** Now the force of
that objection was so great that a case must be made that Newton
himself was unprepared to accept action on a distance as a physical
idea. I think the difficulty is: when you say, we should read
Wittgenstein , we should believe in Frege, that is really not what
we are after. If you can propose, to take up Keenan's point, a
constructive and particular and definite **alternative** that has the
level of precision of **Tarski's** definition but that meets the
difficulties that you raise then you would have said something
interesting. If all you do, as in the case of Cartesian criticism on
Newton, is, say how can a predicate denote an abstract entity,
you were not able to propose a systematic theory that is an
alternative you have not really advanced in a **serious way** our
understanding of these problems. The point is that it is very clear
that the Tarski-approach goes a long way to giving an account of
much usage both in mathematical language and in systematic language
that is adjacent to. I can agree with you that we need something
more, but we need it in a systematic way.
Potts: What Suppes says is fair enough. I was once told that **no**
economist has ever abandoned an economic theory because it did not
fit the facts, but only because somebody prdoduced a more elegant
theory. One can understand this as a matter of psychology and so,
too, your demand for a better theory before abandoning model-
theoretic semantics. But when you also demand that it should have
the level of precision of Tarski's definitions of truth and of
logical consequence, I wonder whether you are not asking for
something which is inappropriate to the subject-matter. For the
logical particles, it may be a reasonable demand; e.g. their

meanings might be explained in terms of introduction and elimination
rules. However, it is not that we need to replace model-theoretic
semantics by o n e account of what it is for a word to have a
meaning. Rather, there are many different k i n d s of expression
in languages, and the way in which their meanings are to be explained
may be expected to differ from one kind to another. This, of course,
is one of Wittgenstein's theses. Thus the way in which one would
explain the meaning of a psychological verb may be quite different
from the method of explaining the meaning of a first-level functor.
Schnelle: But each of the accounts must have precision. It could not
possibly mean that it is inadequate.
Potts: Yes, indeed it must have rigour, but it must also have an
application. One of the worst features of model-theoretic semantics
is that it lacks an application. Consider, for example, the account
which it gives of the meaning of a monadic predicate. This is
supposed to map objects of the kind that can be named by proper
names onto truth-values. So if you ask me to explain to you the
meaning of "yawned" in Plato yawned, I tell you what all the
possible arguments of the expression ' ξ yawned' are and then which
of these it maps onto truth and which onto falsity. This would be an
i d i o t i c way of trying to explain the meaning of such a
predicate to anybody. But that is what a practical application of
model-theoretic semantics would come to.
Bar-Hillel: By no means! You don't do it with the prime number.
Whoever did this with the prime number?
Potts: No, not in this case, because here we have a r u l e for
computing the value of the function. But who has yet formulated a
rule for computing the values of ' ξ yawned', or any other first-
level functor of a natural language? Until this has been done,
model-theoretic semantics has not got off the ground.
Hilpinen: I agree with Mr. Potts' last remark. Mr. Potts' point is
illustrated by the problems which arise, for instance, when we
attempt to formulate criteria of intensional identity in epistemic
logic. No account of intensional identity which depends on logical
equivalence (or on the mappings from possible worlds to truth-
values) is fully satisfactory. We seem to need some sort of
algorithmic or rule-concept of intensional identity.
Potts: It has been suggested during the discussion, especially by
Bar-Hillel, that the methodological remarks which I have made commit
me to a step-by-step programme in linguistics: syntax first,
semantics later. But that presupposes a dichotomy between syntax and

semantics, which I explicitly rejected. In the first instance, I
wanted to justify giving a paper on what would traditionally be
called "syntax" in a conference on semantics and my point was that a
structural description which is intended to clarify the logical
force of a sentence is the first step towards explaining its
meaning. 'Συντάσσω' is "organize" and 'σημαίνω' is "signify", and my
view is simply that what a sentence signifies is partly determined
by the way in which its parts are organized: so, naturally, I think
that syntax is a part of semantics. I agree with Bar-Hillel to the
extent that we may start out with a hypothesis about the correct
structural description of a sentence, try to build upon that
description a fuller account of its meaning, and then find that we
run into difficulties which lead us to modify or reject the initial
hypothesis, so that both steps in the process interact. I suggest
that a formal grammar has two aims: first, to devise a notation for
describing the structure of a sentence which is relevant to its
meaning in which it is impossible to write down nonsense
(U n s i n n); second, to explain the meanings of sentences in
terms of the meanings of their constituents and the manner in which
the latter are combined. I have no objection to saying that syntax
has the first aim and semantics the second, so long as no one
insists that syntax has nothing to do with meaning.

Keenan: I would like to say that I would agree certainly that part
of the program of logical semantics is to represent in what way
meanings of complex things are functions of meanings of parts and
that principally what is done in the standard logic is to represent
how the truth of the model conditions of complex sentences are a
function of the truth of the model conditions of simpler sentences.
In fact, how truth conditions are assigned to the atomic sentences
is rather arbitrary and varies much more in different formulations
than do the truth conditions for quantified sentences. What is done
semantically in standard logic is contained in the definition of
truth in the model for quantified sentences and conjunctions and
disjunctions, and not in how they represent the truth conditions of
a simple predicate noun phrase sentence which is much more
arbitrary. Its justification basically is that we can show that the
right quantified sentences have the right consequences and are
independent of the right sentences rather than its kind of basic
intuitive appeal. The minimal intuitive appeal it has is simply none
or less that the truth we assign to the simple sentences is a
function of what we assign to the predicates and the names.

Hasenjaeger: I should like to add a certain remark about semantics, and perhaps you shout me down then since you might be most opposed. There was an idea about possible worlds and it was called just not understandable. Think about a world which is simple enough to be described by a stack of punched cards. Then the possible world to be described by this are just the possible situations of being holes or not being holes at appropriate places. Now reference to possible worlds just means this. And the semantics of modal logic, in the sense only of necessity and possibility, was interpreted by quantification about these possible worlds and "possible" for some possible worlds. So "necessary" is just for all possible worlds and "possible" for some possible worlds. And, of course, in this case there is no way to explain differences of iterated prefixes of modal operators.

Hilpinen: That idea was first presented in Carnap's "Meaning and Necessity".

Hasenjaeger: I think the essential contribution of Kripke to this was just to take this quantification not referring to all possible worlds in his restricted modal-sense, but to take just all worlds which are r e l a t e d in some sense to the proposed world. And so we know that some of the systems give just certain properties of this relation. And so Kripke really introduces a new tool for the investigation of what the meaning of this hidden relation is.

Potts: I agree: I think that Kripke made a great advance in modal logic which gave us a much clearer picture of the inter-relationships between the different modal systems. This is the r i g h t application of model theory and I am all for it!

Hasenjaeger: But at least we need an explanation of this hidden relation. And this should give a new working point for the intuitive parts of semantics.

Potts: Well, I don't think it has any application to natural languages, after the reasons that I have given. But I think that it is very interesting as a technical piece of work in logic.

Hasenjaeger: It could have an application. If you relate it with tense-logic then in the future there is something like open possibilities which will be closed by advancing of time. You can think about the possible holes as of the future possibilities of our model. If they become p r e s e n t, then the holes are there or not there and there are no other possibilities. And so referring to the open possibilities of the holes in the punched cards in the future is a kind of way to think about tense-logic.

CURRENT TENDENCIES IN LINGUISTIC SEMANTICS

Panel: E.L.Keenan, King's College Research Centre, Cambridge
       P.Suppes, Stanford University
       A.K.Joshi, University of Pennsylvania, Philadelphia
Chairman: T.C.Potts, The University of Leeds

February, 19th, morning session.

KEENAN:
LOGICAL PRESUPPOSITION IN NATURAL LANGUAGES

Summary
PART I
We present informally a logic, PL, which is expressively richer
than SL, standard first order predicate logic, but which contains
SL (with equality but without individual constants) as a proper
sublogic. The motivation of PL is to represent certain logical
properties of natural language not naturally representable in SL.

PART II
The syntax and (completely extensional) semantics of PL is
presented and some basic metatheorems are stated.

PART III
Direct evidence from universal grammar and indirect evidence from
transformational grammar is presented to show that the underlying
syntactic structure of natural language sentences(and noun phrases)
have the formal properties of our logical sentences (and noun
phrases).

The increased expressive power of PL over SL is due primarily to
the properties of PL discussed in A. and B. below.
A. PL f o r m a l l y d i s t i n g u i s h e s t w o w a y s
    a s e n t e n c e c a n b e u n t r u e
The intuition behind the distinction is this: A sentence is assigned
value zero if one of its presuppositions fails. It is assigned value
false, on the other hand, if its presuppositions hold but something
it asserts fails. In such cases its natural denial is true.
Thus (1) would be assigned value false in an interpretation in which
its natural denial (2) is true.

(1) The fact that Fred left early really surprised John
(2) No, it didn't (= No, the fact that Fred left early didn't
    surprise John)
Notice that both (1) and its denial (2) imply (3). If (3) isn't
true, then neither (1) nor (2) are true, and (1) is understood to be
resoundingly vacuous. The

(3) Fred left early

question whether the 'fact' expressed by (3) surprised John or not
simply doesn't arise since (3) doesn't express a fact.
We distinguish easily then the way in which (1) is untrue if (2) is
true from the way (1) is untrue if (3) fails. And in the latter case
we assign (1) value zero.
Given the false/zero distinction we can define:
DEF: S l o g i c a l l y p r e s u p p o s e s T just in case S
     is neither true nor false in each interpretation in which T is
     untrue.
Note that if S logically presupposes T, then it also logically
implies T (i.e. if S is true then T is, since T must be true when-
ever S is either true or false).
Thus we can define:
DEF: S l o g i c a l l y a s s e r t s T just in case S
     logically implies T and S does not logically presuppose T.
In other words, the assertions of a sentence S are what it claims
about the world beyond what it takes for granted (presupposes).
Thus (1) above presupposes (3). It merely asserts (4) below since it
is quite possible for both (4) and (1) to be false together, and
thus the untruth of (4) does not guarantee the logical vacuousness
of (1).

(4) Something surprised John

Notice that the consequences of a sentence S are exactly partitioned
by its assertions and presuppositions. That is, if S implies T (we
here and henceforth drop the use of 'logical'), then either S
asserts T or S presupposes T, but not both.
The facts of presupposition we have presented are directly
represented in PL since PL has predicates of the grammatical
category 'surprise' and it has a way of making noun phrases like
'the fact that S' from any given sentence S. Further such noun
phrases are interpreted formally in such a way that sentences which
have the same truth and falsehood conditions may nonetheless
determine different 'facts'. Thus we can show correctly that
although (5a) and (5b) always have the same truth value, (6a) and
(6b) are logically independent -- either can be true without the
other being true.

(5) a. John sold a coat to Mary
    b. Mary bought a coat from John
(6) a. It surprised Fred that John sold a coat to Mary
    b. It surprised Fred that Mary bought a coat from John

Similarly (7a) and (7b) never differ in truth value, but (8a) and
(8b) are logically independent.

(7) a. Some Republicans are atheists
    b. Some atheists are Republicans

(8) a. John will be surprised to learn that some Republicans are
       atheists
    b. John will be surprised to learn that some atheists are
       Republicans

B. PL t r e a t s f u l l n o u n p h r a s e s a s
   s e n t e n c e o p e r a t o r s (l i k e
   q u a n t i f i e r p h r a s e s i n SL). T h i s
   e n a b l e s u s t o d i s t i n g u i s h b a s i c
   o p a q u e a n d t r a n s p a r e n t r e a d i n g s
   o f s e n t e n c e s.
Thus in PL the gross logical structure of (9a) is (9b).

(9) a. Every doctor was drunk
    b. (every doctor,x) (x was drunk)

The noun phrase in (9b) consists of a common noun preceded by a
determiner every (some and the are treated analogously) and followed
by a pronoun (variable) which must occur free in the sentence

quantified into. (9a) can be converted into a complex noun phrase
(10a) simply by assigning it a pronominal index as in (10b).
And it is this index which is referenced when the complex NP is
used to quantify into further sentences as in (11).

(10) a. Every doctor who was drunk
     b.((every doctor,x) (x was drunk),y)
(11) a. Every doctor who was drunk left early
     b.((every doctor,x) (x was drunk),y) (y left early)

The basic difference in the transparent and opaque readings of (12)
then is indicated by (13a) and (13b) respectively.

(12)   John was surprised that the man who won was drunk
(13) a. (the man who won,x)(John was surprised that (x was drunk))
     b. John was surprised that ((the man who won,x)(x was drunk))

In the opaque reading, (13b), the information contained in the
phrase the man who won is part of the sentence which determines the
fact surprising to John. In the transparent reading it isn't. Our
definition of truth in an interpretation for such sentences as (13a)
and (13b) is such that they are logically independent.
In addition to distinguishing assertions from presuppositions and
opaque and transparent readings, certain specific sentence types
whose treatment is awkward in SL receive a natural analysis in PL.
We give two examples here.

1. There exist in PL sentences which
   assert nothing, not even themselves
   (theorem 6a, part II, section C).

This seems rather unintuitive. We can prove (theorem-9) that if a
sentence asserts anything,then it asserts itself. But there is a
degenerate class of sentences which assert nothing at all. Noticing
that every sentence does imply itself, it follows that a sentence
which does not assert itself does presuppose itself.
The sentences of (14) are such examples.

(14) a. The man who won won
     b. Every student who left early left early
     c. John is as tall as he is
     d. John's wife is John's wife
     e. John exists
     f. It bothers John that everything bothers him
     g. Mary kissed the man who John realized she kissed

(compare: Mary kissed the man who John thought she kissed)

The sentences of (14) are all rather odd. Their natural denials can never be true. For example the man who won didn't win is obviously contradictory on a literal reading. Such a sentence then would appear to be unfalsifiable. Yet none of them is logically true -- they all have some consequence which obviously may be false. For example (14a) implies that Some man won, which obviously need not be true.

PL resolves this paradox by showing that all the information in these sentences is presupposed. That part of the sentence which appears to assert something merely repeats information which has already been taken for granted. These sentences are odd then in that if they're meaningful (either true or false) then they must be true. Thus in PL such sentences are never false and the natural negations never true. But the sentences may be untrue if one of their presuppositions fails, in which case the sentence is assigned value zero.

2. There exist sentences in PL which are similar in meaning in that they have the same logical consequences (and so cannot be distinguished in SL), but which are logically distinct in that they have different presuppositions and assertions.

In other words, there are sentences which are true in the same interpretations but not false in the same ones , for one may assert something that the other presupposes. A rather clever example is the following: (15a) and (18a) have the same consequences since each implies the other. And each implies both (16) and (17), but (15a) presupposes (16) and only asserts (17). (18a) on the other hand presupposes (17) and merely asserts (16).

(15) a. Mary is the girl John loves
     b. Mary isn't the girl John loves
(16)   John loves just one girl
(17)   John loves Mary
(18) a. Mary is the only girl John loves
     b. Mary isn't the only girl John loves

(19) and (20) below illustrate a more usual example. Clearly they have the same truth conditions, yet (19) presupposes the first

conjunct of (20), whereas (20) itself merely asserts that conjunct.

(19) The king of France is bald

(20) There is exactly one king of France and anyone who is king of
     France is bald

A strong point of PL then is that we can show that (19) and (20)
have the same truth conditions but that (20) is false in a greater
number of cases than (19), which presupposes some material merely
asserted in (20).

In fact we can go farther than this. Intuitively (20) makes the
meaning of (19) more e x p l i c i t. We can explain this in PL on
the grounds that, of a sentence's consequences, the assertions are
more explicit than the presuppositions. It's the assertions that can
naturally be denied, and for that matter, naturally questioned.
Notice that Is the king of France bald? questions only baldness, not
the existence of the king. And Did it surprise John that Fred left?
does not question whether Fred left but only whether that fact was
surprising to John.

Thus we can define in PL:

DEF: T   m a k e s   S   m o r e   e x p l i c i t   just in case T and
     S   are true in the same interpretations, and the assertions of
     S are a proper subset of the assertions of T. (In other words,
     T asserts everything that S does and in addition it asserts
     something that S presupposes).

So we can show in PL that (20) makes (19) more explicit.

It happens often in linguistics and philosophy that one attempts to
"paraphrase" a complex sentence, or even "explain" its meaning, by
offering another sentence which is a conjunction of sentences, each
one of which states one of the ideas expressed in the original sentence.
We can to some extent justify this procedure by showing(in PL) that
of the various ways of forming complex sentences, conjunction is
assertion preserving. Therefore a paraphrase which introduces
conjunctions is likely to raise presupposed material up to the level
of assertion and thus be a more explicit rendering of the original.
We note then theorem-5 about PL: "if S and T each assert themselves
and they are completely independent (see DEF-4b,PartII) then (S & T)
asserts S and asserts T".

It is natural to wonder whether every sentence can be made fully
explicit in the above sense. That is, is it the case that for every
sentence S there is another sentence T whose assertions are exactly
the non-trivial consequences of S. (A sentence is called non-trivial

just in case it is untrue in some interpretation). Theorem-14 says
that the answer to this question is no (as regards the sentences of
PL). For example, sentences using proper names, such as <u>John left
early</u> presuppose <u>John exists</u>. But there is no sentence which merely
asserts that John exists for any such sentence would have to use the
name 'John' and thus would presuppose <u>John exists</u>. Notice that the
sentence <u>John exists</u> is one of those that presuppose themselves.
It can be untrue, but not false.
Even sentences whose presuppositions are due solely to factive
predicates, such as (21), which presupposes exactly the consequences
of (22), cannot be made fully explicit.

(21) Someone was surprised by the fact that someone flunked
(22) Someone flunked

Our language PL simply gives us no way of saying that the fact
expressed by (22) is in the surprise relation to someone without
putting (22) in a subordinate position in which it is logically
presupposed.
On the other hand the presuppositions due solely to definite
descriptions can be made fully explicit. That is, if the sentences
some definite descriptions are formed from can be made fully
explicit, and S, with a free occurrence of x, can be made fully
explicit, then so can (d,x)S.

PL, a P r e s u p p o s i t i o n a l   L o g i c   f o r
N a t u r a l   L a n g u a g e

A. T h e   S y n t a x   o f   t h e   P r e s u p p o s i t i o n a l
   L a n g u a g e   L

Determiners (Quantifiers): E, the, A
Structure Markers:), (, ,, fact
Predicates:
   Sentential: -, &, v
   Elementary: W, =, P',P'',...(each predicate symbol has a fixed
                               number of arguments--subject,object,
                               etc.--called the degree of that
                               symbol. The degree of W is 1,
                               the degree of = is 2.)

   Factive: R', R'',...
Noun Phrases (NP)
   Pronouns (NP$_{pro}$): x', x'',. . . y', y'',. . .

   Proper Nouns (NP$_{prop}$): p', p'',. . .

   Factive Nominalizations (NP$_{fact}$): defined as follows:

      If S is an L-sentence, then fact(S) is a NP$_{fact}$

   Quantified Noun Phrases (NP$_q$): the least set satisfying 1.-3.

      1. If p is a proper noun and
         x is a pronoun

         Then (p,x) is a(proper) quantified noun phrase

      2. If P is an elementary predicate symbol of degree one and
         d is a determiner and
         x is a pronoun

         Then (d P,x) is a quantified noun phrase

      3. If (NP$_q$S) is a quantified L-sentence and
         NP$_q$ is a quantified noun phrase which is not proper and
         x is a pronoun

         Then ((NP$_q$S),x) is a quantified noun phrase

L-sentence: the least set satisfying 1.-4. below:
   1. Atomic
      If P is an elementary predicate symbol of degree m and

$x_1, x_2, \ldots x_m$ **are** pronouns

Then $(Px_1x_2 \ldots x_m)$ is an atomic L-sentence

2. Combinations

    (a) If S is an L-sentence, then (-S) is an L-sentence

    (b) If $S_1, S_2, \ldots S_m$ are L-sentences, for m greater

    than 1,

        Then $(\& \ S_1, S_2, \ldots S_m)$ is an L-sentence and

        $(v \ S_1, S_2, \ldots S_m)$ is an L-sentence

3. Embeddings

    If R is a factive predicate symbol and

    fact(S) is a factive nominalization and

    x is a pronoun

    Then (R fact (S),x) is an embedding L-sentence

4. Quantified

    If (Q,x) is a quantified noun phrase and

    S is an L-sentence and

    x is a pronoun occuring in S and there is no occurence of a

    quantified noun phrase (Q',x) in S,

    Then ((Q,x)S) is a quantified L-sentence

This completes the statement of the syntax of L. For convenience in
the semantics we define:

    If (Q,x)S is a quantified sentence, then every occurrence of
the pronoun x which is to the right of the comma is said to
bound by Q. And an occurrence of a pronoun in an arbitrary
sentence S is a bound occurrence just in case it is bound
by some quantified noun phrase occurring in S.
Otherwise it is a free occurrence.

B. S e m a n t i c s   f o r   L

We define an interpretation of the language L to be a six-tuple
$(w_i, N_i, L_i, NP_{prop_i}, \{t, f, z\}, f_i)$ where:

1. w_i is an arbitrary non-empty set (called the world, or universe
of discourse of the
interpretation i

2. N_i is a set of symbols called discourse names such that:

    (a) no symbol in N_i is also in L

    (b) the cardinality of N_i equals that of w_i

3. L_i is the language obtained by adding N_i as a subcategory of
   Noun Phrase to the grammar of L and allowing discourse names to
   occur in sentences in exactly the positions in which free
   pronouns occur in L-sentences.

   Notice that for each interpretation i, the set of L-sentences is
   a proper subset of the set of L_i-sentences.

4. NP_{prop_i} is a subset of NP_{prop}

5. (t,f,z) is a set of three truth values, read _true_, _false_, _zero_.

6. f_i is any function which meets the following conditions:

       (6.1) for each elementary predicate symbol P of degree m,
   f_iP is a subset of w_i^m where w_i^m is the set of m-tuples
   of objects in w_i.

       (6.2) f_i = is the $\{(\underline{a},\underline{a}): \underline{a}$ is a member of $w_i\}$ and $f_i(W) = w_i$

       (6.3) for each pronoun x, f_ix is a member of w_i

       (6.4) for each discourse name n in N_i, f_in is a member of w_i
   such that:

           (a) for all n,m in N_i, $f_in = f_im$ iff n and m are the
   the same name and

           (b) for each $\underline{a}$ in w_i there is an n in N_i such that
   $f_in = \underline{a}$

   (In other words, f_i restricted to N_i is a 1-1 onto function
   $N_i \to w_i$)

       (6.5) for each atomic sentence $(Pc_1c_2 \ldots c_m)$,
   $$f_i(Pc_1c_2 \ldots c_m) = t \text{ iff } (f_ic_1, f_ic_2, \ldots f_ic_m)$$
   $$\text{is in } f_iP$$
   $$= f \text{ iff otherwise}$$

       Note that each c_j may be either a pronoun or a
   discourse name

       (6.6) $f_i(facts(S))$ = the set of alphabetic variants of S^+,
   the sentence obtained by replacing each
   free occurrence of a pronoun x in S by
   the discourse name n where $f_ix = f_in$

       (6.7) for each factive predicate symbol R, f_iR is a subset
   of the set of all pairs $(f_i(fact(S)),\underline{a})$, where $\underline{a}$
   is in w_i

       (6.8) for each embedding sentence $(R\ fact(S),c)$,
   $$f_i(R\ fact(S),c) = t \text{ iff } f_iS = t \text{ and } (f_i(fact(S)),f_ic)$$
   $$\text{is in } f_iR$$

$$= f \text{ iff } f_i S = t \text{ and } (f_i(\text{fact}(S)), f_i c)$$
$$\text{is not in } f_i R$$
$$= z \text{ iff otherwise}$$

(6.9) for Combinations,

(6.9a) $f_i{-}S = t$ iff $f_i S = f$
$\quad\quad f_i{-}S = f$ iff $f_i S = t$
$\quad\quad f_i{-}S = z$ iff $f_i S = z$

(6.9b) $f_i(\& \ S_1, S_2 m, \ldots S_m) = t$ iff for each conjunct S_j,
$$f_i S_j = t$$
$$= f \text{ iff } f_i S_j = f \text{ for some } S_j, \text{and}$$
$$f_i S_j \neq z \text{ for any } S_j$$
$$= z \text{ iff otherwise}$$

(6.9c) $f_i(v \ S_1, S_2, \ldots S_m) = t$ iff $f_i S_j = t$ for some
$$\text{disjunct } S_j$$
$$= f \text{ iff } f_i S_j = f \text{ for some}$$
$$\text{disjunct } S_j \text{ and}$$
$$f_i S_j \neq t \text{ for any disjunct } S_j$$
$$= z \text{ iff otherwise}$$

(6.10) for each proper noun p, $f_i p$ is in w_i iff p is in
NP_{prop_i}
Thus for each interpretation i, NP_{prop_i} is the set
of proper nouns which denote

(6.11) for each proper noun quantified sentence $(p,x)S$,
$\quad\quad f_i(p,s)S = t$ iff for some discourse name n,
$$f_i p = f_i n \text{ and } f_i S_n^x = t$$
$\quad\quad$ " $\quad\quad = f$ iff for some discourse name n,
$$f_i p = f_j n \text{ and } f_i S_n^x = f$$
$\quad\quad$ " $\quad\quad = z$ iff otherwise
(here and elsewhere we use S_n^x to mean the result of replacing each
free occurrence of the pronoun x in S by an occurrence of the
discourse name n)

(6.12) for each quantified noun phrase with definite article
$NP_{the} = ((\ldots ((\text{the } P, x_1)S_1, x_2)S_2, \ldots x_m)S_m, x)$
$f_i NP_{the}$ is in $\{f_i n: f_i(\& \ Pn, S_1{}^x_1, \ldots S_m{}^x_m) = t\}$
if that set has exactly one member. Otherwise
$f_i NP_{the}$ is not a member of w_i

(6.13) for each quantified sentence $(NP_{the}, x)S$

$f_i(NP_{the}, x)S = t$ iff for some discourse name n,
$$f_i NP_{the} = f_i n \text{ and } f_i S_n^x = t$$

" $= f$ iff for some discourse name n,
$$f_i NP_{the} = f_i n \text{ and } f_i S_n^x = f$$

" $= z$ iff otherwise

(6.14) for each $NP_A = ((\ldots((A\ P, x_1)S_1, x_2)S_2, \ldots x_m)S_m, x)$ and

for each $NP_E = ((\ldots((E\ P, x_1)S_1, x_2)S_2, \ldots x_m)S_m, x)$ we

have that $f_i NP_A = f_i NP_E$
$$= (f_i n:\quad f_i(\&Pn, S_1{}^x{}_1, \ldots S_m{}^x{}_m) = t)$$

(6.15) for each universally quantified sentence $(NP_A, x)S$,

$f_i(NP_A, x)S = t$ iff $f_i NP_A \neq$ the null set and for each

discourse name n such that $f_i n$ is in

$f_i NP_A$ we have that

$f_i S_n^x = t$

" $= f$ iff $f_i NP_A \neq$ the null set and $f_i S_n^x = f$

for some n such that $f_i n$ is in $f_i NP_A$

" $= z$ iff otherwise

(6.16) for each existentially quantified sentence $(NP_E, x)S$,

$f_i(NP_E, x)S = t$ iff $f_i(NP_E) \neq$ the null set and for some

discourse name n such that $f_i n$ is in

$f_i NP_E$, $f_i S_n^x = t$

" $= f$ iff both (a) and (b) hold:

(a) if $f_i NP_E \neq$ the null set then for some n such that
$f_i n$ is in $f_i NP_E$, $f_i S_n^x = f$ and for no such n does
$f_i S_n^x = t$

(b) if $f_i NP_e =$ the null set then there is a discourse
name n such that $f_i S_n^x \neq z$ (S is the sentence
quantified into by NP_E) and for each S_j that NP_E
is formed from (Remember that $NP_E =$
$(\ldots((E\ P, x_1)S_1, x_2)S_2, \ldots x_m)S_m)$ there is an n

such that $f_i S_j {}^x_h j \neq z$

$f_i(NP_E, x)S = z$ iff otherwise.

This completes the definition of interpretation for L.
We may now define:

DEF 1: A set of L-sentences S <u>logically implies</u> an L-sentence T iff
      for each interpretation i, if $f_i S' = t$ for each S' in S then
      $f_i T = t$

DEF 2: An L-sentence S <u>logically presupposes</u> an L-sentence T iff
      for each interpretation i, if $f_i T \neq t$ then $f_i S = z$

DEF 3: An L-sentence S <u>logically asserts</u> an L-sentence T iff S
      logically implies T and S does not logically presuppose T

DEF 4: (a) P(S), the set of possible truth values of the L-sentence
      S, is the set of all x $\in$ {t, f, z} such that for some
      interpretation i of the language L, $f_i S = x$
      (b) L-sentences S and T are <u>completely independent</u> iff for
      all x $\in$ P(S) and all y $\in$ P(T) there is an interpretation
      i such that $f_i S = x$ and $f_i T = y$

DEF 5: T <u>makes more explicit</u> S iff
      (1) the set of interpretations i such that $f_i T = t$ is the
      same as the set of interpretations j such that $f_j S = t$
      and
      (2) the assertions of S are a proper subset of the
      assertions of T

This completes the semantics of L. The function M below translates
SL into PL: (i) m(S) = S, for S atomic (having no individual
                      constants)
        (ii) m(-S) = -(m(S))
              m((S v T)) = (v m(S),m(T))
        (iii) m((Ex)S) = (EW,x)m(S)

NB: We have not put function symbols into the language of PL as
      they do not seem very useful in representing natural language.
      But we could add them easily,giving them the same semantics as
      in SL.

    C. S o m e B a s i c M e t a - T h e o r e m s a b o u t L
All the existence theorems are directly about L and are not
necessarily true of an arbitrary presupposition logic. The other
theorems follow directly from the definition of the logical
relations defined in B and do not depend on any particular

242   Keenan

properties of L. S and T are arbitrary L-sentences. We use <u>implies</u>,
<u>presupposes</u>, etc. for <u>logically implies</u>, <u>logically presupposes</u>, etc.

Thm-1:   a. S presupposes T iff -S presupposes T. That is,
             PR(S) = PR(-S)
          b. S presupposes T iff S implies T and -S implies T
          c. S presupposes T iff (v S, -S) implies T

Thm-2:   If S presupposes T then S presupposes every consequence of
          T (The consequences of T are the L-sentences it logically
          implies).

Thm-3:   a. S implies T iff either S asserts T or S presupposes T
          b. If S implies T then it is not the case that S both
             asserts T and also presupposes T.
             That is: a. CN(S) = AS(S) U PR(S)
                      b. AS(S) ∩ PR(S) = the empty set

Thm-4:   There exist S and T such that CN(S) = CN(T) but AS(S)≠AS(T)
          and PR(S) ≠ PR(T).

Thm-5:   There exist sentences which presuppose themselves.

Thm-6:   a. There exist sentences which assert nothing, not **even**
             themselves.
          b. There exist sentences which assert nothing and which are
             not logically true (i.e. true under all interpretations
             of the language L).

Thm-7:   A sentence asserts nothing iff it presupposes itself.

Thm-8:   A sentence asserts nothing iff it is false in no
          interpretation.

Thm-9:   A sentence asserts something iff it asserts itself.

Thm-10:   If T is logically true,then T asserts nothing and is
          asserted by nothing.

Thm-11:   There exist S, T, and T' such that S asserts T, T asserts T'
          and S does <u>not</u> assert T'. Thus assertion is not transitive.

Thm-12:   a. For all S there is a T such that CN(S) = PR(T)
          b. For all S there is a T such that PR(S) = CN(T)

Thm-13:   Presupposition is an undecidable relation in L
          Specifically the set of pairs (S,T) such that S presupposes
          T is a recursively enumerable set but is not recursive.

Thm-14:   It is not the case that the presuppositions of every
          sentence can be made fully explicit in L. That is, there
          exist S such that for every T, the assertions of T are <u>not</u>
          the same as the non-trivial presuppositions of S.
          (A non-trivial presupposition is one that is not logically
           true).

Thm-15: Conjunction in L has the assertion-conservation property.
That is, if S and T each assert themselves and they are
completely independent, then (&S,T) asserts S and (&S,T)
asserts T.

A. We shall argue that many natural languages present in surface
some or all of the many pronouns (variables) we have used in the
logical representations of sentences.
Recall that even apparently simple sentences in PL consist of a
full NP with a pronominal index followed by a sentence which
repeats this pronoun, (hereafter called the <u>interior</u> pronoun).
Thus the representation of (1a) below in PL is (1b), and (2a) is
represented by (2b).

(1) a. Every doctor left
    b.(every doctor,x)(x,left)

(2) a. John kissed Mary
    b.(John,x)(Mary,y)(x kissed y)

Many languages present interior pronouns in surface. The
Romanian(3) and Luganda(4) are typical.

(3) Am intîlnit-o pe sorî   sa
    (I) met   her   sister his(I met his sister)
(4) Mary ye- basse
    Mary she is sleeping

The important point to note here is that what appear to be verbs
with weak pronominal forms on them e.g. <u>yebasse</u> in (4), functions in
isolation as sentences. Thus if we had already identified Mary above
and wanted to say simply "she is sleeping", we would say simply
"yebasse". That ye- functions as a proform and not simply a person
marker is seen in that it agrees in noun class and number with the
full NP. In Luganda there are 16 distinct weak subject pronouns of
which <u>ye</u>- is merely one. The surface structure of (4) then is:

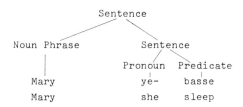

```
                    Sentence
              _____/  _____
     Noun Phrase              Sentence
         |                _____/  _____
                        Pronoun    Predicate
       Mary               ye-        basse
       Mary               she        sleep
```

This sentence differs from our logical structure then only in that
the coreference between the proform and the full NP is not indicated
by matching the proform with the index of the NP,but rather by its
agreement with the noun class and number of the NP. Consequently the
full NP 'Mary' carries no pronominal index.
The interest of the examples we have given lies in the fact that
they translate apparently simplex sentences in English.
The "redundant" proforms do not reflect any sort of topicalization
or dislocation. Other languages which exhibit similar occurences of
interior pronouns are: Swahili (and the Bantu languages generally),
Hadza (a non-Bantu African language), Chinookan, Iai (a Melanesian
language), Fijian and Spanish.
It happens less frequently across languages that what appears
indexical pronouns is retained in surface. Nonetheless in spoken
Czech (5) and Norwegian dialects (6),such pronouns do occur and form
a constituent with their coreferential NP, not with the verb phrase
or following sentence. Again no effect of topicalization is felt
here.

(5) Ona Věra má přijít domů na večeři
    She Vera is supposed to come home to dinner (Vanek, PIL)

(6) Han Per   er glad
    He Peter is happy

In fact, in certain rather restricted cases (7), in Romanian both the
indexical pronoun and the interior pronoun appear present in surface.
The same claim holds for Hadza (8) although there the occurrence of
the indexical pronouns is not obligatory and does serve a slight
emphasis function (but does not bring in any new logical
information).

(7) Lui   Gheorghe nu- i   plac   glumele
    To him George   not to him pleasing jokes
    (Jokes are not pleasing to George)

(8) Boko seseme   //o- ta- kwa boko nak'oma
    She lion   kill her she she buffalo
                      + past
    (The lioness killed the she-buffalo

Notice that, ignoring sense, the surface structure of (8) is almost
exactly the logical structure we would assign it:

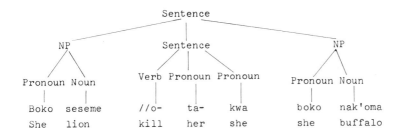

In complex sentences it is quite common across languages for the
interior pronouns to be present in surface. To consider only the
case of relative clause formation we note that it is the norm in
many languages to retain a personal pronoun in positions relativized
into. Note the Hebrew (9) and the Welsh (10).

(9) ha- iš še- ha- iša   hikta oto
    the man   that the woman hit   him (the man that the woman hit)

(10) dyma' r llyfr y   darllenais y   stori ynddo
     Here-is the book that I-read   the story in-it

The logical form we assign to these relative clauses provides the
basis for an interesting prediction concerning the relative
effectiveness of different relativization strategies across
languages. Note that the pronoun retaining languages present in
surface more of their logical structure than do the pronoun deleting
ones. In logical structure the complex noun phrase consists of a
head noun phrase followed by a sentence containing a proform which
refers back to the head noun. This sentence is present as a sentence
in the pronoun retaining languages precisely because the interior
pronoun is present in surface. Thus the subordinate"clause" in
Hebrew ha-iša hikta oto is a surface structure sentence and would be
used to say "the woman hit him", in a case where some male had
already been identified. But the subordinate clause in, say, English
"the woman hit" is not a sentence because it has no direct object,

the pronoun which represents this position in Hebrew not being
present.

We might expect then that pronoun retaining languages would admit
relativization into more difficult positions than pronoun deleting
ones, precisely because they make the logical structure more
explicit. This is in fact the case. Thus we can frequently
relativize into single members of coordinate NP, as in the Hebrew
(11), and also into relative clauses themselves, as in the
Welsh (12).

(11) Ani roa et ha- iš še- Mary makira oto ve- et išto
     I   see   the man that Mary knows him and   his wife

(12) Dyma'r   het y   gwn   y   dyn a'p i gadewodd ar y ford
     Here-is the hat that I-know the man who it left   on the table

Table I below compares relativization possibilities in Hebrew,
Arabic (colloquial Egyptian), Welsh, Persian, and Batak--all
pronoun retaining languages-- with English, Russian, and Malagasy--
all pronoun deleting languages. The contexts compared are:
co-S: one member of coordinate sentences. co-NP: one member of
coordinate noun phrase. S-cmp-NP: sentence complement of noun
phrase, as in "the rumour that Mary left John".Emb-Q: embedded
question, as in"I don't know who hit John". RelCl: relative clause.
O-Prep: object of a preposition. Conj: occuring in different
grammatical cases in each of two conjuncted sentences, as in
"The boy came early and Mary loves the boy". Poss-NP: possessor
noun phrase as in "John's car". S-cmp-V: occuring in a sentence
complement of a verb, as in "John thought that Mary was reading
a book".

Table I
Relativization is possible into:

	co-S	co-NP	S-cmp-NP	Emb-Q	RelCl	O-Prep	Conj	Poss-NP	S-cmp-V
Hebrew	no	yes	yes	yes	yes	yes	yes	yes	yes
Arabic	no	yes	no	yes	yes	yes	yes	yes	yes
Welsh	no	no	yes	yes	yes	yes	-	yes	-
Persian	no	yes	yes	yes	yes	yes	yes	yes	yes
Batak	no	yes	no	no	no	yes	yes	yes	yes
English	no	no	no	no?	no	yes	yes	yes	yes
Malagasy	no	no	no	no	no	no	no	no	yes
Russian	no	no	no	no	no	yes	yes	yes	no

The data are clear despite a few gaps: Pronoun retention
significantly increases the possibilities of relativization.

B. Second we shall present evidence from transformational grammar
in favor of syntactically deriving natural language sentences
from objects which have the formal properties of our logical
sentences. The basic argument we give is the following:
Many well motivated transformations such as PRONOM, EQUI-NP
DELETION, REFLEXIVIZATION, CONJUNCTION REDUCTION, AND DO-SO
require some noun phrase identity condition to be met in order
to operate. Standard proposals for stating this condition are
inadequate because the resulting transformations become
semantically incoherent. That is, they change meanings in erratic
ways--sometimes the output sentence means the same as the input
one and sometimes it doesn't. For example if PRONOM operates by
replacing full coreferential NP by pronouns, then it would appear
paraphrastic in (13b) below but not in (14b) which has only a
"transparent" reading in distinction to (14a) whose preferred
reading is the opaque one.

(13) a. John came early and John also stayed late
     b. John came early and he also stayed late

(14) a. The man who was drunk was surprised that the man who was
        drunk won
     b. The man who was drunk was surprised that he won

In our approach however the necessary identity condition is
given as identical pronouns bound by the some quantified NP, and
no full NP's need be replaced at all. Thus (13b) is derived
directly from (13b') below:

(13) b'. (John,x)(x came early and x also stayed late)

Analogous arguments can be used in the case of EQUI, REFLEX,
CONJUNCTION REDUCTION, AND DO-SO:

1. EQUI Similarly (15a) and (15b) have logically distinct
   underlying forms and EQUI can operate on strict NP identity--
   i.e. identity of variables bound by the same quantifier.
   Thus EQUI works as is normal, and it is fully paraphrastic,
   for (16a) and (16b) are treated in the same way as (15a) and
   (15b).

   (15) a. The man who was drunk wanted to win
           (d,x)(x want(x win))

    b. The man who was drunk wanted the man who was drunk to win
       (d,x)(x want((d,y)(y win)))

(16) a. Every student wanted to pass
       (A student,x)(x want(x pass))
    b. Every student wanted every student to pass
       (A student,x)(x want((A student,y)(y pass)))

2. REFLEXIVIZATION can operate on the usual quantified NP just as
                on definite NP. It simply marks the commanded
                occurrence of the bound variable as reflexive.

(17) a. Every student hurt himself
       (A student,x)(x hurt x)
    b. Every student hurt every student
       (A student,x)(A student,y)(x hurt y)

(18) a. John hurt himself   b. John hurt John
       (John,x)(x hurt x)   (John,x)(John,y)(x hurt y)

Notice that the logical forms of (18a) and (18b) are distinct, but
given our definition of truth in an interpretation they turn out to
have the same truth conditions. Similarly (19a) and (19b) have the
same truth conditions as do (20a) and (20b). But (21a) and (21b)
are different in truth conditions.

(19) a. Every student cried and applauded
       (A student,x)(x cried and x applauded)
    b. Every student cried and every student applauded
       (A student,x)(x cried) and (A student,y)(y applauded))

(20) a. John cried and applauded
       (John,x)(x cried and x applauded)
    b. John cried and John applauded
       (John,x)(x cried) and (John,y)(y applauded))

(21) a. Some student cried and applauded
       (E student,x)(x cried and x applauded)
    b. Some student cried and some student applauded
       ((E student,x)(x cried) and (E student,y)(y applauded))

3. CONJ-REDUCTION can operate as usually formulated, but the NP's
                which are identical are subject pronouns
                (variables) bound by the same quantified NP. Thus
                CONJ-RED applies to the logical structure under-

lying (19a), (20a), and (21ε) but not to the corresponding
b-sentences.

4. A uniform solution to DO-SO can be achieved using a suitable
   definition of "subject of". Roughly it is as follows:

   DO-SO (S&T) = S & so do **subj**(T) if and only if S and T have
   distinct subjects but are
   otherwise identical.

We might roughly define a subject function, subj, as follows:

   (i) subj(S) is arbitrarily specified if the sentential functor
   generating S is a non-logical (lexical) predicate
   symbol (e.g. 'kiss', 'think', etc.)

   (ii) subj(Neg-S) = subj(S)

   (iii) subj(S C T) = ∅ (where ∅ is the null symbol, which by
   convention will mean having no subject)

   (iv) subj((NP,x)S) = (NP,x) if (NP,x) fully quantifies into the
   the subject of S
   = subj(S) if (NP,x) does not partially
   quantify into the subject of S
   ∅ otherwise

   DEF: Let S be a conjunction of sentences (S_1 C S_2 C ... S_n)
   for n greater than 0.

   We say that (NP,x) fully quantifies into S iff each of the
   S_i has a free occurrence of x as its subject. We say that
   (NP,x) partially quantifies into S iff some of the S_i have
   free occurrences of x as their subjects.

Notice then that the ambiguity in (22) can be represented by
applying the same DO-SO transformation to the logically distinct
sources (23a) and (23b).

(22) John thought he was drunk and so did Bill

(23) a. (John,x)(Bill,y)(x think(x drunk))&(y think(x drunk)
     b. ((John,x)(x think(x drunk)) & (Bill,x)(x think(x drunk)))

Notice that (23a) is the result of quantifying twice into a
conjunction of sentences and it is the conjunction that DO-SO
applies to, before quantifier incorporation. In (23b) the entire
sentence is a conjunction of two quantified sentences. The subject
of the first is '(John,x)' and of the second '(Bill,x)' and

otherwise they are identical, so DO-SO applies.

JOSHI[+]:

FACTORIZATION OF VERBS[*]

Summary

This paper is a review and a critique of the major methodological
considerations involved in justifying factorizations of vocabulary,
in particular verbs. The results of a detailed analysis of some
verbs of seeing (Joshi (1972)) have been very briefly described in
an appendix.

1. Introduction:

One current issue in linguistics is factorization of vocabulary, in particular, verbs. Factorizations of individual verbs or verbs belonging to certain classes have been proposed recently by several linguists, not necessarily of the same persuasion. Some examples are (see Appendix B for notations and conventions): V_{act}: $\underline{do}(V_{act}())$ where V_{act} is an action verb, $\underline{kill}$: $\underline{cause}(x,\underline{become}(\underline{not}(\underline{alive}(y))))$, $\underline{remind}$: $\underline{perceive}(x\ \underline{similar}(y,z))$, $\underline{give}$: $\underline{cause}(x,\ \underline{have}(y,z))$, $\underline{attribute}$: $\underline{claim}(x,\underline{make}(y,z))$,etc. (Bierwisch, Harris, Lakoff, McCawley, Postal, Ross, and others). The motivation of a linguist is roughly as follows: To arrive at representations which, on the other hand, have immediate semantic interpretation and, on the other hand, also form the basis for ultimately deriving the surface forms. Thus the system of primitives (and their organization) which he arrives at has to be both semantically and syntactically relevant. This determines the kind of evidence needed (or the methodological considerations involved) in justifying these factorizations. Recently, Miller (1972 a,b) has made an analysis of the verbs of motion with a view towards setting up a framework for the study of the organization of lexical memory. Some of the evidence used in his study is similar to that of a linguist, reflecting the hypothesis that the linguists' system of primitives has some relevance to the psychological work. Miller also provides some independent support for the psychological validity of his analysis.

This paper is a review and a critique of the major methodological considerations involved in justifying such factorizations. These, certainly,are not all of equal weight and also not necessarily independent of each other. But they do characterize the kinds of arguments that have been used. In Section 3, we give some examples of factorization which have appeared in the literature in order to illustrate some of these arguments.

In Appendix A we will describe very briefly the results of a detailed analysis of some verbs of seeing which was carried out in Joshi (1972). Notations and conventions appear in Appendix B.

2. Some methodological considerations:

2.1 Syntactic and semantic representations:

The choice of a particular scheme of representation will certainly influence the kind of components we will recognize as well as their organization. A priori, there is no reason to require that

the same sort of formal object be used for the syntactic
representations as well as for the semantic representations.
However, if we want to map the semantic representations onto the
syntactic representations i.e., ultimately onto actual sentences,
then it is certainly convenient to have the same type of formal
object used for both the representations. The generative
semanticists make this a basic requirement of the linguistic theory.
Thus if the formal object is a phrase structure tree,then both the
syntactic and semantic representations will be in terms of such
trees. Only a single kind of mapping will connect semantic
representations and syntactic representations. For example, in the
case of phrase structure trees this mapping will be the kind of
mapping effected by a transformational rule. Thus the surface
syntactic trees will be deformations of the semantic trees; to be
sure, only certain kinds of deformations will be allowed.
Alternative representations are dependency trees or the closely
related operator-operand representation, both of which can be
formally related to the phrase structure tree representation
although there are certain advantages or disadvantages with each one
of these representations. It is possible to have even a combination
of these representations. In this paper, we will adopt the operator-
operand representation (see Appendix B).
If we are interested only in the semantic representations, then it is
certainly not necessary to restrict ourselves to phrase structure
trees or dependency trees. Even when we are concerned with mappings
of semantic representations onto syntactic representations, we should
not rule out the possibility of having more than one type of
mapping; however, this opens up the question of what other kinds of
mappings besides transformations (trees onto trees or structured
strings onto structured strings, in general) should be allowed.
Very little can be said about this matter at present. It is
interesting to note in this context that Fillmore (1971) considers
dependency trees with branches also labelled (by case labels, in
particular) as suitable objects for semantic representations but
then laments the fact that these representations lend themselves
least to the view that the semantic and syntactic representations
belong to the same species.
For our present purpose,we will assume that we have only one type of
formal object for the syntactic and semantic representations and
therefore only one type of mapping connecting them. The main point

here is not that we are making this assumption but rather its
implication. That is, this assumption limits our choice of
representations,and as we said in the beginning,the kind of
representation we adopt affects considerably the kind of
factorization we arrive at.

2.2 Syntactic evidence:

While attempting to formulate (syntactic) rules for wellformedness of strings of morphemes, sometimes, one has to postulate
elements in the underlying representation which are not phonetically
manifested. These elements often turn out to be semantically
relevant. A well known example is the underlying you in the
representation for imperative sentences. Another example is the
underlying do in the analysis of action verbs (Ross 1971). Syntactic
evidence pertains only to the distrubution of formal syntactic
elements i.e.,grammatical morphemes. Only such evidence is
permissible in establishing the wellformedness (syntactic) rules.
A purely syntactic argument would not use evidence pertaining to
paraphrase, ambiguity, etc.

In a purely syntactic argument there is an implied assumption that a
sharp distinction can be made between wellformed and illformed
strings. As is well known, this distinction is far from being sharp.
Much of the recent linguistic research depends heavily on looking at
rather marginal sentences (perhaps not so marginal for the authors).
It is as if many deeper aspects of the structure of language are
revealed by considerable stretching of the language. Often one
permits a rather marginal sentence (S_1) as acceptable (and therefore
as an evidence for the argument) by exhibiting another sentence (S_2)
which is more readily acceptable and which is a near paraphrase of S_1,
thus relying not entirely on syntactic evidence.

If elements (i.e. components in the factorization) are postulated in
the underlying representation (and which are not phonetically
manifested) using syntactic evidence and also relying on some
particular semantic relationships (paraphrase and incomplete
definition, in particular) then we will say that the factorization
has been justified by a syntactic-semantic argument.

2.3 Syntactic-semantic evidence:

Paraphrase relationships are certainly the major source for
identifying components in the underlying representations. However,
it is rarely the case that for a sentence (S_1) containing some

lexical item (V) there is a sentence (S_2) containing items
(say, X_1 and X_2) which are potential factors of V and which is a
paraphrase of S_1 i.e. the composite item (say, $X_1(X_2( ))$,
(see Appendix B for notations)) is rarely synonymous with V.
In other words, $X_1(X_2( ))$ is not a definition of V. A fruitful
approach is to look for only 'incomplete definitions'(Miller,1972)
i.e. V implies $X_1(X_2( ))$ but not necessarily vice versa.
The definition of V in terms of $\lambda_1(X_2( ))$ is generally broader
because V may have many other components narrowing its meaning.
Miller (1972) has made extensive use of incomplete definitions in
his analysis of the verbs of motion (see also Sections 2.8 and 3.4).

Arguments based on paraphrases and incomplete definitions combined
with some syntactic evidence (to be called syntactic-semantic
arguments) are the ones most popular with the linguists for obvious
reasons (see Sections 2.1 and 2.7). We want some syntactic evidence
to go along with the factorization arrived at by using paraphrases
and incomplete definitions not only because we are interested
ultimately in mapping the semantic representations onto the
syntactic representations but also because it provides some control
over the kind of paraphrases and incomplete definitions to be
allowed (e.g. for move, we may allow change location (Miller,1972)
but possibly not acquire acceleration; for see, perceive by sight
may be allowed but not receives visual stimulus from, etc.).

A particularly strong syntactic-semantic argument (not always easy
to find) runs as follows. A factorization of a lexical item (V) into
a composite item (say, $\lambda_1(X_2( ))$) which is first suggested by a
paraphrase or an incomplete definition is then justified as follows:
We try to find a transformational rule (out of the bag of already
well established rules) which,in general, would apply only to
sentences whose representation contains $\lambda_1(X_2( ))$ and would also
apply to sentences containing V. If there is such a rule then this
would require that sentences containing V should be given a
representation containing $X_1(X_2( ))$ which reflects the meaning of
such sentences. Otherwise, two such rules would be necessary, one
for sentences whose representation contains $X_1(X_2( ))$ and one for
sentences containing V (Lakoff, 1971). This is the kind of argument
used by Postal (1970) in representing remind (in one of its senses)
as perceive $(x, similar(y,z))$ (see also Section 3.3).

2.4 <u>Possible lexical items</u>:

　　Given a factorization and its representation according to a
certain scheme (e.g. phrase structure trees, dependency trees,
operator operand representation, etc.) we need some rule(s) for
determining how two or more components can be'merged'. We will call
such rules 'predicate merging rules'. The merged components can then
be replaced by a lexical item (lexical insertion), if possible. In
the phrase structure formulation we have the predicate raising rule
of McCawley. In the dependency formulation as well as in the
operator-operand representation an analoguous rule can be formulated.
Fillmore (1971) and Anderson (1971) using dependency representation
adopt a rule (not precisely formulated) which seems to be more
powerful than the predicate raising rule. They call it 'conflation
rule'. Given one of these predicate merging rules, if we can show
that the nature of the rule is such that it will automatically
prevent merging of components for which there cannot be possible
lexical items and the mergings permitted by the rule are the only
possibilities for lexical insertion, then it may be possible to
explain lexical gaps by classifying them as accidental or systematic.
An accidental gap corresponds to the case when a composite predicate
whose composition is permitted by the merging rules but for which
there is no corresponding lexical item. A systematic gap, on the
other hand, corresponds to the case of a composite predicate whose
composition is not permitted by the merging rules. Thus, given a
factorization and some predicate merging rule(s), the factorization
can be justified by our ability to explain lexical gaps in a
particular semantic domain. We should note,however, that an argument
in favour of a particular predicate merging rule is not an argument
supporting a particular factorization but rather it is an argument
in favour of factorization itself and its particular representation
i.e.,in favour of a particular derivational system of formatives.

Sometimes a rather roundabout argument is given for justifying a
particular factorization as follows: First a factorization is
justified in terms of some ad-hoc rule and then it is shown that this
ad-hoc rule can be got rid of by adopting a predicate merging rule
which is needed anyway (e.g. in the <u>do</u> analysis of Ross (1971), the
<u>do deletion</u> rule can be dispensed with; see Section 3.2).

Let us examine the predicate raising rule. It allows one to move an
embedded predicate and adjoin it to the left of the higher predicate

in which it was previously embedded. Thus

(2.4.1)

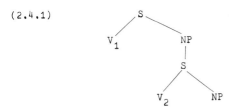

becomes

(2.4.2)

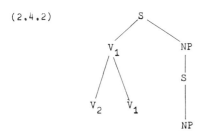

If V_1 and V_2 are called <u>adjacent</u> predicates, then the rule says, roughly, that only adjacent predicates can be merged. Hence, for example:

(2.4.3)

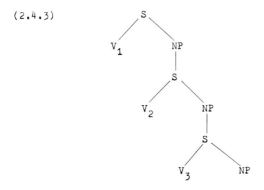

will not become

(2.4.4)

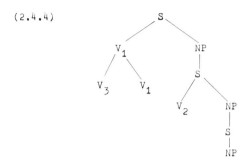

We can generalize this rule to two adjacent predicates on the <u>same</u>
level. This generalization will then be the analog of the conflation
rule described later. Let V_2 and V_3 be two predicates <u>adjacent</u> to V_1
on the same level i.e. we have, for example

(2.4.5)

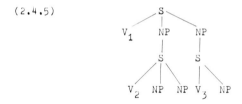

We then can merge V_1, V_2, and V_3 as follows:

(2.4.6)

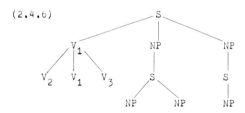

i.e. V_2 is adjoined to the left of V_1 and V_3 to the right. In the
dependency (and also in the operator-operand) representation,
(2.4.7) below which is the analog of (2.4.5)

(2.4.7)

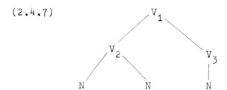

becomes by conflation (Fillmore, 1971)

(2.4.8) V_2 - V_1 - V_3

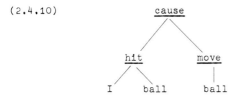

Thus (following Fillmore, 1971)

(2.4.9) I hit the ball.

which has an underlying representation

(2.4.10)

```
                     cause
                    /     \
                  hit      move
                 /   \       |
                I    ball    ball
```

corresponding roughly to

(2.4.11) My hitting the ball caused it to move (go over).

will become by conflation (i.e.,(2.4.10) will become).

(2.4.12)   hit-cause-move
                    /   \
                   I   ball

Replacing hit-cause-move by the lexical item hit we get (2.4.9).

Similarly,we can conflate (2.4.13) to (2.4.14)

(2.4.13)

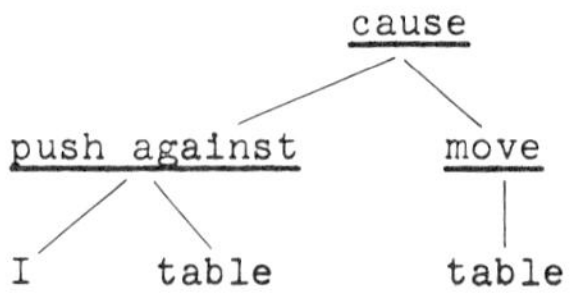

(2.4.14)

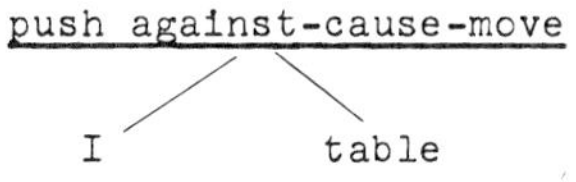

and replacing push against-cause-move by the lexical item push we have

(2.4.15) I pushed the table.

(2.4.13) explains why we have

(2.4.16) I pushed the table into the corner.

but not

*(2.4.17) I leaned the table into the corner.
i.e. the conflated item lean against-cause-move is not replaceable by a lexical item; thus, possibly, indicating an accidental lexical gap (Fillmore, 1971).

Harris (1970) who also adopts the operator-operand notation has a rule which places the operator in the second position i.e., after its first argument (cf. subject raising rule in the phrase structure transformational grammar). Thus given $X(Y_1, Y_2, \ldots Y_k)$ where X is the operator and $Y_1, Y_2, \ldots Y_k$ are the arguments, this rule produces $Y_1 X Y_2 Y_3 \ldots Y_k$. He also allows rules for replacing certain discontinguous composite predicates by a single predicate. These two rules essentially accomplish the same effect as the conflation rule. Thus, for example, (using (2.4.10)), cause(hit(I, ball), move(ball))

will become

hit(I, ball) cause move(ball)

and then the discontiguous composite predicate hit-cause-move
can be replaced by a single predicate hit giving hit(I, ball).
By applying once again the rule which places the operator in the
second position we get I hit the ball. (Note that such a rule is
needed anyway in order to get John ate bread from eat (John, bread).)
Harris seems to consider this rule as well as the rules for
replacing the composite predicates (contiguous as well as
discontiguous) by single predicates as extensions of morpho-
phonemics, perhaps, reflecting his view on the abstractness of the
basic predicates (see also Section 2.9).

2.5 Redundancy:

Given S_1, if S_2 is a paraphrase of S_1 and S_2 is the same as S_1
except for some additional elements (excluding some grammatical
constants) then these extra elements are redundant and provide an
indication for factorization of some element S_1 into two or more
components. For example, let S_1 = he climed the ladder and
S_2 = he climbed up the ladder; then we can say that climb in S_1
'incorporates' up (Gruber, 1965) and hence represent climb possibly
as up(go( )). Similarly, pierce can be represented as through(go( ))
(Gruber, 1965).

This technique is limited because we cannot get all the components
by producing appropriate redundant paraphrases. There is also
another limitation. Sometimes, the putative redundant paraphrase is
clearly unacceptable e.g., he walked→ *he walked on foot (He
travelled on foot is better). This suggests that walk might be
represented as on foot(travel( )).) (Miller, 1971), Anderson,1971).

2.6. Regularization of predicates:

One way predicates are classified is by the number of arguments
required i.e., unary predicates, binary predicates, etc. Unary and
binary predicates are certainly needed. Sometimes, a predicate
requiring more than two arguments, in particular, a ternary
predicate can be represented as a pair of binary predicates where
one predicate is embedded in the other.

Thus give (John, boy, book) (John gave the boy a book) can be
represented as cause (John, have (boy, book))(John caused the boy to
have a book)i.e., by the two predicates cause and have where have is
embedded under cause. The possibility of reducing a ternary
predicate (give, in this case) to two binary predicates and thus
eliminating a ternary predicate can be considered in itself a
justification (not the only one, to be sure) for a factorization
(give(x,y,z) : cause(x, have(y,z))) (Bierwisch, 1971, Harris,1968).
Some other examples of such regularizations are (Harris, 1968):
remove(x,y,z) (he removed the page from the book):
cause(x, lack(z,y)(he caused the book to lack the page),
attribute(x,y,z)(he attributed the plan to her):
claim(x, make(z,y)(he claimed that she made the plan), etc.

It is not claimed here that all predicates requiring more than two
arguments can be regularized in this way. There are some clear
counterexamples such as between. (Bierwisch (1971) suggests the
possibility of representing between as between(x,y) where the second
argument, y, is a set of more than two objects.)

2.7 Semantic evidence:

    Thus far we have considered only the semantic relationship of
paraphrase and incomplete definition. We could, of course, consider
other semantic relationships such as presupposition,* semantic
deviances of various kinds, contradictions, etc. A purely
semantically based representation would indeed use such semantic
relationships and many others. The main objective here is to provide
suitable logical forms so that correct entailments will be
deducible. No syntactic justification be given and in fact it is not
necessary.This is so because although actual sentences of the
language may have been used informally to suggest some components
and their possible organization, there is no obligation to provide
machinery to map the logical forms onto actual sentences. The
adequacy of such a representation could then be justified by appeal
to actual sentences and their interpretation by subjects and there
is no claim here that these representations are the underlying
representations from which the actual sentences would be derived by

---

* Fillmore (1971) has made an analysis of some verbs of judging. His
  arguments are semantic and the semantic relationship of
  presupposition has been exploited extensively.

some transformational rules familiar in linguistics.

The linguist's preoccupation with syntactic (see Section 2.2) or a
syntactic-semantic (see Section 2.3) arguments is fairly easy to
understand. In addition to providing adequate semantic
representations we must also describe the machinery for converting
these semantic representations into actual sentences. This is also
the reason for the assumption that the same sort of formal objects
(e.g., trees) are used for both the syntactic and semantic
representations (see Section 2.1).

Purely semantically based representations, therefore, need not be
restricted to formal objects such as trees. They could be more
complex objects (see Schank (1972)). However, if one examines the
representations which have been justified by purely semantic
criteria one finds that in most cases this freedom of representation
is hardly exploited at all. One reason for this could be the desire
(and not a methodological obligation) to make these representations
as suitable inputs to linguistic transformations. All this is a
reflection of the fact that for natural languages there is no sharp
line between syntax and semantics as is the case for formal or
artificial languages.

Sometimes, for the components based on syntactic or syntactic-
semantic arguments we can find correlates among the components set
up on purely semantical considerations. This can then be regarded as
added support for the factorization (e.g., the do predicate for
action verbs (Ross, 1971) and the intentionality predicate of
Davidson (1970), see Section 3.2).

2.8 Psychological evidence:
    Using incomplete definitions Miller (1972 a,b) has made an
analysis of the verbs of motion. Incomplete definitions (see
Section 2.3) allow us to isolate the shared components of meaning of
a set of lexical items i.e., the components with respect to which
the items are similar in meaning without being necessarily identical
in meaning. Miller depends on his method of incomplete definitions
because it provides him with a characterization of judgements of
similarity in meaning which appears to be confirmed by the results
of his sorting experiments. Judges are asked to sort a set of words
belonging to a particular semantic domain (e.g., motion verbs) into
an unspecified number of piles. The data of such experiments is

processed by some well known techniques leading to "a kind of
composite sorting into word clusters that reflect the commonest
bases of semantic classification that the judges have used". Thus
the components arrived at by using incomplete definitions are
provided some psychological validity. Since the incomplete
definitions are semantic definitions, we can call this kind of
argument semantic with psychological correlates (cf. arguments which
are syntactic (or syntactic-semantic) with semantic correlates,
see Section 2.7).

2.9 Abstractness of the components:

So far we have not said anything about whether or not the
components in the representation for a lexical item are themselves
lexical items (or are to be lexically realized). On the one hand,
we have used lexical items to represent the components and on the
other we have called them predicates i.e., semantic verbs, thus
suggesting that these components need not necessarily correspond to
any lexical items in the language. There are a number of positions
we can take concerning the lexical realizability of the components
(Zwicky, 1971).
1. A component need not be lexically realized, thus allowing the
possibility that none of the components are lexically realized.
2. A component must be lexically realized in some natural language.
3. Most components are lexically realized in the given language
under consideration.
4. All components are lexically realized in the language under
consideration.

The last position (cf. semantic postulates of Carnap) is the
strongest one. It would be unnecessarily restrictive to hold this
position. At the least we want to allow the kind of abstraction
introduced when we set up an arbitrary element which is realized as
one or another lexical item in the appropriate environments which
are mutually exclusive (e.g., occur/do→occur in the context of a
zero object and occur/do→do in the context of a direct object;
see Section 3.1 and 3.2). Also since we are using incomplete
definitions our components are always somewhat abstract because if Y
is a lexical realization of a component X then X is, in general, an
incomplete definition of Y and there need not be (and, in general,
will not be) a lexical item Z such that X is a complete definition
of Z. Confusion arises because we use Y itself as the name of this

component i.e., we use the same expression for X and Y. When we use
a lexical item, say, Y, to represent also a component in a
representation of some lexical item, what we are asserting is that Y
used as a component in some representation is only an incomplete
definition of the lexical item Y. This dual usage of Y is not just a
mnemonic device. It is a reflection of our desire to have the
components, although abstract, 'fairly easily' lexically realizable.
The troublesome part of all this is that we cannot state just how
much incompleteness we would permit in our definitions and still
adopt this double usage. Underlining, capitalizing, using bold face
type, etc. are only notational devices to remind us of this problem
but merely adopting these devices will not help us ignore the
problem. This is what we mean by statements such as strike
(STRIKE) is not the same as 'strike', etc.

Although position 3 appears to be weaker than position 4, there is
really no essential difference between them. Position 2 is quite
attractive; however, it is hard to see (at least at present) how it
can be usefully adopted in practice. Analysis of different and
sufficiently large semantic domains is only beginning (excluding of
course the well known domains of kinship terms and color terms). We
have as yet very little information about how general the components
are (i.e., whether or not they occur in many different semantic
domains) and how the representation in one domain carries over to
some other semantic domains. Hence, setting up components on the
basis of their lexical realization in some language seems to be not
a very useful procedure to follow at this time.
Position 1 would be justified if our aim is to set up
representations such that these (and therefore, the components used
in these representations) need only be justified in terms of their
logical adequacy as the mathematical logicians do. But there is no
reason to suppose that these components would be linguistically
natural (e.g., not both - and - (i.e., Scheffer's stroke) is not
lexically realized in any language (Zwicky, 1971); some other
examples are Goodman's predicate grue, Prior's connective tonk,
etc.). If a component is not lexically realizable in any language,
then representations using such components are not going to be very
useful in the study of natural languages. They may be useful,
however, in the descriptions of artificial languages.

It is interesting to note here an observation of Zwicky (1971) that

in the semantic descriptions which have appeared so far no
components have been proposed which appear to be incapable of
lexical realization.

3. Some examples of factorization:

3.1 Nonstative verbs (occur analysis): It has been suggested that
occur should be one of the components in the underlying
representation of a nonstative verb (Lee, 1969, Ross, 1971). There
is an agentive-nonagentive ambiguity in

(3.1.1) John collapsed.
The proposed underlying representations of (3.1.1) are

(3.1.2) occur (John, collapse(John))

(3.1.3) occur(collapse(John))

The agentive reading is obtained from (3.1.2) by subject formation
and deletion of occur. The nonagentive reading is obtained by
subject raising followed by subject formation and deletion of occur,
i.e., (3.1.4) from (3.1.3) and (3.1.5) from (3.1.4).

(3.1.4) occur(John, collapse(John))
(3.1.5) John collapsed.

Some of the arguments justifying the introduction of occur in the
underlying representation of (3.1.1) are as follows (Lee, 1969).

1. For begin we also have the agentive-nonagentive distinction:

(3.1.6) John began to work.
(3.1.7) The faucet's dripping began.
(3.1.8) The faucet began to drip.

(3.1.6) is only agentive. (3.1.8) is nonagentive and (3.1.7) is a
paraphrase of it. This can be explained by providing the following
representations for (3.1.6) and (3.1.7) respectively.

(3.1.9) begin(John, work(John)
(3.1.10)begin(drip(faucet))

From (3.1.10) by subject raising and subject formation we obtain
(3.1.8). Note that (3.1.7) corresponds to (3.1.10). The reason we
are able to propose such an analysis is that we have a lower

sentence available for begin viz., drip(faucet), i.e., begin is the
higher verb with respect to drip. In the case of collapse we do not
have a lower sentence, i.e., we do not have a higher verb; so we
invent occur. It is not a mere coincidence that we also have a
lexical item 'occur' (in the sense of 'happen')(see Section 2.9).
2. Analogous to (3.1.7) we now have

(3.1.11) John's collapsing occurred·

which corresponds to (3.1.3).

3. (3.1.3) also explains the it in

(3.1.12) John collapsed and I am sorry that it occurred.

4. Harris (1965) uses the occur predicate to explain the ambiguity
in

(3.1.13) John may collapse.

Since we have two components occur and collapse, we may let may
operate on one or the other component. Thus if may operates on
collapse, then from (3.1.2) we get (in the same way as we got
(3.1.5))

(3.1.13) John may collapse.

On the other hand, if may operates on occur in (3.1.3), then we
obtain (analogous to (3.1.11))

(3.1.14) John's collapsing may occur.

From (3.1.14) we once again obtain (3.1.13) in much the same way as
we obtained John collapsed from John's collapsing occurred.

5. Note that occur will not take a stative verb as one of its
arguments.

*(3.1.15) John's being tall occurred.

We have used here syntactic (Section 2.2) as well as syntactic-
semantic (Section 2.3) arguments.

3.2 Nonstative verbs(action verbs,'do' analysis):

In much the same spirit as the occur analysis in Section 3.1,
Ross (1971) has proposed do as one of the components in the underlying representation of an action verb.

The relationship of action verbs and do is clear from the fact that
do (with animate subject) requires an abstract NP object which is
an action nominalization.

(3.2.1) John did a study of earthquakes.

*(3.2.2) John did a knowledge of karate.

We can derive (3.2.1) from

(3.2.3) John studied earthquakes.

by some rule which inserts do in (3.2.3). However, there are several
reasons for incorporating do in the underlying representation itself
and then getting rid of it by some rule which deletes do (a rule
rather similar to the rule for deleting occur in Section 3.1). It
facilitates the derivation of (3.2.4) from (3.2.5) and (3.2.6) from
(3.2.7) (Ross, 1971).

(3.2.4) Driving in the night I have always hated to do.

*(3.2.5) I have always hated to do (driving in the night).

(3.2.6) Solving crossword puzzles is impossible to do.

*(3.2.7) It is impossible to do (solving crossword puzzles).

Since we now have the rule for deleting do,we can also obtain from
(3.2.5) and (3.2.7) the following.

(3.2.8) I have always hated to drive in the night.

(3.2.9) It is impossible to solve crossword puzzles.

Hence, it is proposed that the underlying representation of (3.2.1) should be

(3.2.10) do(study(John, earthquakes))

By subject raising we get (3.2.11) and then by subject formation and do deletion we obtain (3.2.12).

(3.2.11) do(John, study(John, earthquakes))

(3.2.12) John studied earthquakes.

Alternatively, we can dispense with the do deletion rule by using a predicate merging rule (predicate raising or conflation rule, see Section 2.4). Thus from (3.2.10) we will obtain

(3.2.13) do-study(John, earthquakes))

Then a suitable lexical rule will introduce study for do-study. Since the need for a predicate merging rule can be independently justified, if we can explain the derivation of (3.2.12) from (3.2.10) by using a predicate merging rule and not by using the do deletion rule which we just introduced for this purpose, then we have an added justification for the claim that do is a component in the underlying representation of an action verb (see Section 2.3).

Thus far we have used arguments which are either syntactic or syntactic-semantic (see Sections 2.2 and 2.3).

Ross gives yet another justification for the do analysis by suggesting that the do in the underlying representation of an action verb has a semantic correlate viz, the two-place action predicate intentional relating an agent and an event which Davidson (1970) has introduced in his analysis of action sentences. This analysis is purely semantic (see Section 2.7) i.e., based entirely on the suitability of logical forms for deducing correct entailments of action sentences, for being able to refer to action as a singular term, etc.

Finally we can combine the results of Sections 3.1 and 3.2 as follows. Do has the same restrictions with respect to its object complements (viz., it is an action nominalization) as occur has with

respect to its subject complements. In both cases the main verb of
the complement is nonstative (Lee, 1969). Hence, we can set up a
predicate occur/do which is realized as occur in the context of a
zero object and as do in the context of a direct object (see Section
2.9).

3.3 Remind:

Postal (1970) has proposed that the remind (in one of its
senses) should have the components perceive and similar in its
underlying representation. In particular, the proposed incomplete
definition of remind is

(3.3.1) perceive(x, similar(y,z))

From (3.3.1) by suitable transformations (from the set of already
established ones) e.g., subject raising, psych-movement, and
predicate raising, we obtain

(3.3.2) y reminds x of z.

It is possible to give a stronger justification by showing that
there is a rule (viz., deletion of subjects in sentences like
to shave oneself is to torture oneself) which is applicable when the
clause where the deletion takes place is a complement of a verb of
saying, thinking, perceiving, etc. This rule also applies to remind
sentences. If remind is represented as (3.3.1),then this fact
follows automatically because (3.3.1) contains perceive. If remind
is not represented as (3.3.1),we will need two such rules,one for
the sentences containing perceive, etc. and one for sentences
containing remind. (For details of this argument and some other
arguments, see Postal (1970) and Lakoff (1971).)

These arguments also are either syntactic or syntactic-semantic.

3.4 Motion verbs:

Miller (1972a) has made a semantic analysis of a large number
of motion verbs in English (e.g., move, travel, arrive, depart,
walk, run, ride, etc.). His main motivation is to provide a
framework for the study of the organization of lexical memory. The
components are set up by using incomplete definitions. Since these
are semantic relationships,we must classify his arguments as
semantic. However, they must be contrasted with the purely semantic

arguments (Section 2.7) because only one type of semantic relationship is exploited in his analysis (viz., the incomplete definition)
whereas a purely semantic argument is not necessarily restricted to
only this relationship.

The only major syntactic consideration involved in his analysis is
that all the items are of the same syntactic category (verbs). This
is done primarily to keep some control over the context for
comparison. Apparently, there is some psychological evidence for
justifying this restriction.

The main components isolated are change, location, cause, allow,
medium, instrument, etc. This analysis is then further justified by
providing some psychological validity as described in Section 2.8.
It is this kind of justification that forms the basis for the claim
that such analyses are relevant to the study of lexical memory.

In summary, the arguments used are semantic (limited to only one
type of relationship) with psychological correlates, in contrast to
the analyses in Sections 3.1, 3.2, and 3.3.

Appendix A

In Joshi (1972) a detailed analysis of verbs of seeing was carried
out. (This material in a revised form will be published elsewhere).
Here we will give a very short summary of these results.
A.1 There are over 100 <u>seeing</u> verbs satisfying more or less the
criteria in A.2. About 15 of these are clearly <u>seeing</u> verbs and are
also core verbs in the sense that the representations for these are
adequate to account for the remaining. Before a detailed list was
made the expectation was that the number would be over three or four
hundred. Thus it was surprising to find that the number was not very
large (<u>hearing</u> verbs are even fewer).

The analysis is arrived at primarily by using paraphrase relationships and incomplete definitions. Wherever possible it is justified
by providing as much evidence as possible of the kind described in
Sections 2.2 - 2.7. We will not give the detailed analysis here. A
list of some predicates used and a list of some sample
representations is given in Sections A.4 and A.5 respectively. These
two lists and the list of some verbs of seeing in Section A.2 will
give the reader some idea of the detailed analysis.
A.2 <u>Criteria for verbs of seeing</u>:
     By verbs of <u>seeing</u>, we mean verbs which in one of their senses
involve visual **perception** (<u>see</u>, <u>look</u>, <u>appear</u>, <u>gaze</u>, <u>glance</u>, <u>view</u>,
<u>blind</u>, <u>hide</u>, <u>display</u>, <u>expose</u>, etc.). We are concerned here with
verbs which are single lexical items (with a few exceptions such as
<u>look at</u> and <u>look for</u>) and not with frozen expressions which may
serve as <u>seeing</u> verbs (e.g., <u>keep an eye on</u>). Many of these verbs
have both a visual and a nonvisual sense. Unless otherwise stated,
it is only the visual sense that we will be concerned with.

A <u>seeing</u> verb involves visual perception in many different ways:
1. The subject of the verb sees something or the object of the verb
becomes visible (e.g., <u>see</u>: X saw Y). 2. The subject directs sight
in order to see (e.g., <u>look</u>: X looked at Y). 3. The subject becomes
visible to someone (e.g., <u>appear</u>: X appeared). 4. The basic
predicates of <u>see</u>, <u>look</u>, and <u>appear</u> are 'modulated'(modified) by
other predicates such as <u>cause</u>, <u>not</u>, <u>momentary</u>, <u>continual</u>, etc.
yielding a variety of <u>seeing</u> verbs such as <u>hide</u>, <u>expose</u>, <u>glance</u>,
<u>gaze</u>, <u>etc</u>.

There are a number of verbs which pertain to modes of emitting or
reflecting light from an object and do not have any additional sense

of either increasing or decreasing the visibility (e.g. glimmer, glisten, shine, etc.). We do not consider these as seeing verbs. Verbs such as dazzle, darken, etc. are, however, seeing verbs. Verbs such as frown, scowl, etc. involve movement of eyes, eyebrows, or face but not visual perception. Clearly, these are not seeing verbs.

When a verb optionally involves visual perception, it is difficult to give a very sharp criterion for including or excluding it from our list. We include such a verb when it can be essentially represented by see, look, or appear together with one or more additional predicates (such as cause, not, momentary, continual, etc.) which appear in many other semantic domains. If these additional predicates pertain to some specific semantic domain (other than that of seeing verbs) such as, for example, communication verbs, then we will not consider such a verb as seeing verb (e.g., wave, signal, point out, etc.). Verbs such as meet, be at, go to, etc. are also not seeing verbs; however, they are replaceable by see in certain contexts. Verbs such as find, detect, are not seeing verbs; however, they are used in the representation of some seeing verbs.

Finally, visualize is not a seeing verb!

A.3 A list of some verbs of seeing:

appear	gaze	see
behold	glance	search
blind	glare	seek
blur	glimpse	show
conceal	hide	sight
cover	inspect	spot
darken	look	stare
descry	mask	surface
disclose	notice	survey
dazzle	obscure	uncover
display	observe	unmask
disappear	overlook	vanish
discern	peek	view
emerge	peep	watch
espy	peer	witness
examine	reappear	
expose	regard	
exhibit	resemble	

Joshi

eye	reveal
fade	scan
fade-in	scrutinize
fade-out	secrete
flash	screen

The following are not seeing verbs.

point at; wave; signal; meet; be at; go to; detect; find; visualize

brighten; sparkle; glitter; glisten; shimmer; gleam; shine; glow;
light (brighten); twinkle; illuminate

frown; scowl; glower; wink; blink

A.4 List of some predicates used in the analysis:

perceive	momentary
by sight	continual
make sure	intermittent
act	careful(manner)
fact	intent (manner)
state	sly (manner)
aim	distinct(manner)
location	one by one (in sequence)
between	slow
possible	rapid
not	find
cause-intent	
cause-result	
do	
begin	
cease	
resume	
continue	

Out of the two components perceive and by sight, perceive,
of course, would be needed for other verbs of perception; hence, by
sight is the only component specific to the verbs of seeing.Most of
the other components will show up in the analyses of other semantic

domains e.g., motion verbs, communication verbs, etc.

A.5 List of some sample representations:

(1) by sight (perceive(x, (∃ s)P(s)))) P: classifier or identifier
    John saw a cat has the following representation
    by sight (perceive(John, (∃ s) cat(s)))
    This can be roughly paraphrased as John perceived by sight some-
    thing which was (classified or identified as) a cat (or
    possibly as John perceived by sight that something was a cat).
    We have placed (∃ s) inside the scope of perceive. We regard
    see as a verb creating referentially opaque contexts and thus
    treat it like a concept that expresses a propositional attitude.
    Other readings are possible (e.g., by placing (∃ s) outside
    perceive). However, we will be primarily concerned with the
    representation (1) above. For convenience, henceforth we will
    omit (∃ s) in our representations.
(2) by sight (perceive(x, act(Q( )))) Q: action predicate
    (John saw Mary crossing the street)
(3) by sight (perceive(x, fact(Q( ))))
    (John saw that Mary was crossing the street; We saw the
    destruction of the city.)
(4) possible (by sight(perceive(x, P̂(s))))
    (I see now; I can see now.)
(5) cause-intent (by sight(aim(x, loc(y)), possible(by sight
                (perceive(x, P(s)))))
    (He looked at the tree)
(6) become (possible(by sight(perceive(x, P̂(s))))
    (A ship appeared (on the horizon))
(7) cause-intent(cause-result(do(x), between(loc(p), loc(q),
    loc(r))), not(possible(by sight(perceive(x, P̂(s)))))))
    (John hid the jewels behind the mirror)
(8) cause-result(act(Q( ), not(possible(by sight(perceive
    (x, P̂(s)))))))) Q: action or event predicate
    (The storm blinded me)
    etc.

A total of about 30 representations are enough to cover most of the
seeing verbs. These representations show how the components in S
Section A.4 are composed. One could easily write rules for
composition which will generate precisely these representations and

there will be many different ways of writing this grammar. The
particular way in which we choose to write the grammar will affect
the formulation of the rules which allow us to collapse a set of
predicates into a composite predicate which then may or may not be
lexically realized. These rules thus affect the formulation of
possible theories of accidental or systematic lexical gaps.

A.6 Lexical gaps:

There appear to be a number of lexical gaps both in the context
of the verbs of seeing and also in the context of extending the
representations for the verbs of seeing to the verbs of hearing.For
example, in the context of the verbs of seeing there are gaps when
one tries to combine the durative and manner predicates
(e. g., momentary and careful). The more interesting gaps arise when
the seeing representations are carried over to hearing. Many of
these gaps reflect the fact that hearing verbs do not involve the
directional as well as location component explicitly. The inability
of many durative and manner predicates to combine with the basic
representations (i.e., representations for hear and listen) also
leads to gaps just as it does in the case of seeing verbs. The
hearing gaps are much'wider' in this case as compared to the seeing
gaps e.g., no durative predicates at all are allowed on listen.

Whether we should call all these gaps accidental or systematic is
difficult to say. We really do not have at present any theory of
accidental and systematic gaps for the lexicon. We could, of course,
call all these gaps accidental because they correspond to
combinations of components which are permitted by the rules of
composition (not explicitly stated but implicit in the set of
representations in Section A.5) and for which there are no
corresponding lexical items. (We are assuming here that a predicate
merging rule such as predicate raising or conflation is available
for merging only those predicates which are related in a certain way
e.g., a predicate can be merged with other predicates which are its
immediate descendants in a dependency representation. The precise
nature of this rule is not relevant here.) But this is not a very
convincing explanation because it assumes that our representations
and the implied rules of compositions of basic predicates can be
independently justified, which is very doubtful. The situation is
perhaps the other way round. The ability to predict and explain
lexical gaps in terms of a representation should be considered as a
justification for that representation (see also Ross, 1971).

It is clear that similar analyses for _seeing_ and _hearing_ verbs in
several different languages would be most valuable in the study of
lexical gaps in the semantic domain of perception verbs.
A.7 In Joshi (1972) other verbs of perception (nonvisual and non-
aural) have been briefly discussed also.

Appendix B

Notations and conventions:

B.1 Variables: x,y,z ... . These will generally range over concrete
nouns and proper names. P,Q,R, ... are Predicate variables.

B.2 Predicates: Predicates will be either unary or binary (a few
ternary predicates will be needed). The arguments of a predicate may
be variables x,y,z ... or P,Q,R, ... the predicate variables. A
predicate whose argument(s) can be another predicate is sometimes
called an operator. We will often refer to predicates also as
operators.

Examples:

P(x) : run(John) : John ran.

P(x,y) : eat(John, bread) : John ate bread.

P(x,Q( )) : want(I, run(John) : I want John to run.

P(Q( ), y) : surprise(open(John, door), Mary) : John's opening the
                                            door surprised Mary.

P(Q( )) : begin(run(John)) : John began to run.

P(Q( ), R( )) : depend on(leave(Mary), arrive(John) : Mary's leaving
                                        depends on John's arriving.

P(x,y,z) : between(mirror, Mary, jewels) : The mirror is between
                                            Mary and the jewels.

We will not need for our present purpose predicates with no
arguments such as rain( ): it rained.

Unless otherwise stated, we will ignore tense, articles, and number.
We may want to specify for a predicate certain restrictions on its
arguments (i.e., the range of the argument variables will be
restricted).

Examples:

run(x): x may not be inanimate.

ask(x, P( )) : x may not be nonhuman. P cannot be a predicate such
                as want(y, Q( )):* I asked John to want Bill to run.
                But can be predicate such as order(y, Q( )): I asked
                John to order Bill to run.

B.3 'Suppressed' argument: An argument variable with a circumflex
over it i.e., $\hat{x}$, $\hat{y}$, $\hat{z}$, ... or $\hat{P}$, $\hat{Q}$, $\hat{R}$, ... denotes a suppressed
argument. This allows us to interpret, for example, a binary
predicate as a unary predicate by ignoring (or presupposing) the
suppressed argument (Fillmore, 1968). If the suppressed argument has
some restrictions on it, then it is understood that it is specifiable

(recoverable) only <u>upto</u> these restrictions. This convention of a
suppressed argument is the same as that of Fillmore's except that he
allows only the variables x,y,z ... to be suppressed,whereas we
allow here the suppression of predicate variables also. If an
argument is suppressed,then the arguments of that argument, etc. are
also all understood to be suppressed.

+ University of Pennsylvania, Philadelpphia, Pa., 19174. This work
was carried out when the author was on leave of absence at
The Institute For Advanced Study, Princeton, N.J. under a
Guggenheim Fellowship. It was also partially supported by NSF Grant
GS-159 and GS-35125.

I wish to thank Phil Johnson-Laird and George Miller for their
encouragement and many fruitful discussions.

* This paper is based on Sections 1, 2, and 3 of Joshi (1972),
Factorization of verbs: an analysis of verbs of seeing -
unpublished).
The remaining sections of Joshi (1972) contain a detailed analysis
of verbs of seeing. This material in a revised form will be
published elsewhere. In the present paper, we will give a very short
summary of this material in Appendix A.

REFERENCES

1. Anderson, J.M. (1971), The Grammar of Case, Cambridge University
   Press, Cambridge.

2. Ascombe, G.E.M. (1965), The intentionality of perception: a
   grammatical feature, in R.J. Butler (ed.), Analytical Philosophy,
   Second Series, Oxford University Press, Oxford, pp. 158-80.

3. Austin, J. (1962), Sense and Senibilia, Oxford University Press,
   Oxford, (reconstructed from the manuscript notes by G.J.Warnock).

4. Bach, E. (1968), Nouns and nounphrases, in E.Bach and R.T. Harms,
   Universals in Linguistic Theory, Holt, Rinehart and Winston,Inc.,
   New York, pp. 91-124.

5. Bierwisch, M. (1970), Semantics, in J. Lyons (ed.), New Horizons
   in Linguistics, Penguin Books, Harmondsworth, England.

6. Bierwisch, M. (1971), On classifying semantic features, in
   D.D. Steinberg and L.A. Jakobovits (eds.), Semantics,
   Cambridge University Press, Cambridge, pp. 410-435

7. Chisholm, R.M. (1957), Perceiving,Cornell University Press,
   Ithaca.

8. Chomsky, N. (1965), *Aspects of The Theory of Syntax*, M.I.T.Press, Cambridge.

9. Davidson, D. (1967), The logical form of action sentences, in N. Rescher (ed.), *The Logic of Decision and Action*, University of Pittsburgh Press, Pittsburgh, pp. 81-120.

10. Dixon, R.M.W. (1971), A method of semantic description, in D.D. Steinberg and L.A. Jakobovits (eds.), *Semantics*, Cambridge University Press, Cambridge, pp. 436-471.

11. Fraser, B. (1970), Some remarks on the action nominalizations in English, in R.A. Jacobs and P.S. Rosenbaum (eds.), *Readings in English Transformational Grammar*, Ginn and Company, Waltham, Massachussetts, pp. 83-98.

12. Fillmore, C.J. (1968), Lexical entries for verbs, in *Working Papers in Linguistics*, No.2. The Ohio State University,Columbus, pp. 1-29.

13. Fillmore, C.J. (1971), Some problems for case grammar, in *Working Papers in Linguistic*, No.10, The Ohio State University, Columbus, pp. 245-265.

14. Fillmore, C.J. (1971), Verbs of judging: An exercise in semantic description, in E. Bach and R.T. Harms (eds.), *Universals in Linguistic Theory*, Holt, Rinehart and Winston, Inc., New York, pp. 91-124

15. Gruber, J.S. (1965), *Studies in Lexical Relations*, Ph.D. Dissertation, M.I.T., Cambridge, Massachusetts.

16. Gruber, J.S. (1967), Look and See, *Language*, vol. 43, No.4, pp. 937-47

17. Harris, Z.S. (1965), Transformational Theory, *Language*, vol.41, pp. 363-401.

18. Harris, Z.S. (1968), *Mathematical Structures of Language*, John Wiley and Sons (Interscience Publishers), New York.

19. Harris, Z.S. (1970), Two systems of grammar: report and paraphrase, in Z.S. Harris, *Structural and Transformational Linguistics*, D. Reidel Publishing Co., Dordrecht, Holland.

20. Hintikka, J. (1969), *Models and Modalities*, D. Reidel Publishing Co., Dordrecht, Holland.

21. Joshi, A.K. (1972), Factorization of Verbs: An Analysis of Verbs of Seeing, - unpublished.

22. Lakoff, G. (1971), On generative semantics, in D.D. Steinberg and L.A. Jakobovits (eds.), Semantics, Cambridge University Press, Cambridge, pp. 232-296.

23. Lee, P.G. (1969), Do from occur, in Working Papers in Linguistics, No.3, The Ohio State University, Columbus, pp. 1-21.

24. Miller, G.A. (1972a), English verbs of motion: a case study in semantics and lexical memory, in A.W. Melton and E. Martin (eds.), Coding Processes in Human Memory (New York), in press.

25. Miller, G.A. (1972b), Lexical Memory, Proc. American Philosophical Society, vol.116, No.2, pp. 140-144.

26. Palmer, F.R. (1968), A Linguistic Study of English Verbs, University of Miami Press, Coral Gables, Florida.

27. Parsons, T. (1970), Some problems concerning the logic of grammatical modifiers, Synthese, vol.21, pp. 321-334.

28. Pitcher, G. (1971), A Theory of Perception, Princeton University Press, Princeton.

29. Postal, P. (1970), The surface verb remind, Linguistic Inquiry, vol.1, pp. 37-120.

30. Ross, J.R. (1971), Act, unpublished.

31. Ryle, G. (1949), The Concept of Mind, Hutchinson, London.

32. Schank, R.C. (1972), Conceptual dependency: a theory of natural language understanding, Journal of Cognitive Psychology, vol.3, in press.

33. Sibley, F.N. (1955), Seeking, scrutinizing, and seeing, Mind, vol.64, pp. 455-78 (also in Warnock (ed.), The Philosophy of Perception, Oxford University Press, Oxford (1967)).

34. Smith, C. (1964), Determiners and relative clauses in a generative grammar of English, Language, vol.40, pp. 37-52.

35. Vendler, Z. (1957), Verbs and times, The Philosophical Review, vol.66, pp. 143-160 (also in Z. Vendler, Linguistics in Philosophy, Cornell University Press, Ithaca, (1967)).

36. Warnock, G.J. (1967), Introduction, in G.J. Warnock (ed.),
    The Philosophy of Perception, Oxford University Press, Oxford,
    pp. 1-7.

37. Zwicky, A.M. (1971), Linguistics as chemistry: the substance
    theory of semantic primes, Working Papers in Linguistics, No.8,
    The Ohio State University, Columbus, Ohio, pp. 111-135.

SUPPES:
MODEL-THEORETIC SEMANTICS FOR NATURAL LANGUAGE[*]

I would like to present in summary form my ideas about the use of
phrase-structure grammars, in particular context-free grammars,
together with an appropriate model-theoretic semantics to provide
a semantical apparatus for the generation or analysis of utterances
of ordinary language. The machinery described in this paper is
certainly not adequate to all the problems that confront us in
having a complete theory of natural language, but it does provide,
I think, a good basis from which to make additional extensions and
modifications, and it fits in historically very nicely with the
developments of model-theoretic semantics that began with Frege and
received their major impetus from the work of Tarski and his
students, and, on the other hand, the much more recent work on
generative grammars by linguists.
The first part of this paper is drawn from a previous publication
(Suppes, 1970a) and the second part on model-theoretic semantics
from Suppes (1971).[+]

A. PROBABILISTIC GRAMMARS

1. Introduction
Although a fully adequate grammar for a substantial portion of any
natural language does not exist, a vigorous and controversial
discussion of how to choose among several competing grammars has
already developed. On occasion, criteria of simplicity have been
suggested as systematic scientific criteria for selection. The
absence of such systematic criteria of simplicity in other domains
of science inevitably raises doubts about the feasibility of such
criteria for the selection of a grammar. Although some informal and
intuitive discussion of simplicity is often included in the
selection of theories or models in physics or in other branches of
science, there is no serious systematic literature on problems of
measuring simplicity. Nor is there any systematic literature in
which criteria of simplicity are used in a substantive fashion to
select from among several theories. There are many reasons for this,
but perhaps the most pressing one is that the use of more obviously
objective criteria leaves little room for the addition of further
criteria of simplicity. The central thesis of this paper is that
objective probabilistic criteria of a standard scientific sort may

be used to select a grammar.

Certainly the general idea of looking at the distribution of
linguistic types in a given corpus is not new. Everyone is familiar
with the remarkable agreement of Zipf's law with the distribution of
word frequencies in almost any substantial sample of a natural
language. The empirical agreement of these distributions with Zipf's
law is not in dispute, although a large and controversial literature
is concerned with the most appropriate assumptions of a qualitative
and elementary kind from which to derive the law. While there is,
I believe, general agreement about the approximate empirical
adequacy of Zipf's law, no one claims that a probabilistic account
of the frequency distribution of words in a corpus is anything like
an ultimate account of how the words are used or why they are used
when they are. In the same sense, in the discussion here of probabilistic grammars, I do not claim that the frequency distribution
of grammatical types provides an ultimate account of how the
language is used or for what purpose a given utterance is made. Yet,
it does seem correct to claim that the generation of the relative
frequencies of utterances is a proper requirement to place on a
generative grammar for a corpus.

Because of the importance of this last point, let me expand it. It
might be claimed that the relative frequencies of grammatical
utterances are no more pertinent to grammar than the relative
frequency of shapes to geometry. No doubt, in one sense such a claim
is correct. If we are concerned, on one hand, simply with the
mathematical relation between formal languages and the types of
automata that can generate these languages, then there is a full set
of mathematical questions for which relative frequencies are not
appropriate. In the same way, in standard axiomatizations of
geometry, we are concerned only with the representations of the
geometry and its invariants, not with questions of actual
frequency of distribution of figures in nature. In fact, we all
recognize that such questions are foreign to the spirit of either
classical or modern geometry. On the other hand, when we deal with
the physics of objects in nature there are many aspects of shapes
and their frequencies of fundamental importance, ranging from the
discussion of the shape of clouds and the reason for their shape
to the spatial configuration of large and complex organic molecules
like proteins.

From the standpoint of empirical application, one of the more dis-

satisfying aspects of the purely formal theory of grammars is that
no distinction is made between utterances of ordinary length and
utterances that are arbitrarily long, for example, of more than 10^{50}
words. One of the most obvious and fundamental features of actual
spoken speech or written text is the distribution of length of
utterance, and the relatively sharp bounds on the complexity of
utterances, because of the highly restricted use of embedding or
other recursive devices. Not to take account of these facts of
utterance length and the limitations on complexity is to ignore two
major aspects of actual speech and writing. As we shall see, one of
the virtues of a probabilistic grammar is to deal directly with
these central features of language.
Still another way of putting the matter is this. In any application
of concepts to a complex empirical domain, there is always a degree
of uncertainty as to the level of abstraction we should reach for.
In mechanics, for example, we do not take account of the color of
objects, and it is not taken as a responsibility of mechanics to
predict the color of objects. (I refer here to classical mechanics
- it could be taken as a responsibility of quantum mechanics.)
But ignoring major features of empirical phenomena is in all cases
surely a defect and not a virtue. We ignore major features because
it is difficult to account for them, not because they are
uninteresting or improper subjects for investigation. In the case of
grammars, the features of utterance length and utterance complexity
seem central; the distribution of these features is of primary
importance in understanding the character of actual language use.
A different kind of objection to considering probabilistic grammars
at the present stage of inquiry might be the following. It is agreed
on all sides that an adequate grammar, in the sense of simply
accounting for the grammatical structure of sentences, does not
exist for any substantial portion of any natural language. In view
of the absence of even one grammar in terms of this criterion, what
is the point of imposing a stricter criterion to also account for
the relative frequency of utterances? It might be asserted that
until at least one adequate grammar exists, there is no need to be
concerned with a probabilistic criterion of choice. My answer to
such a claim is this. The probabilistic program described in this
paper is meant to be supplementary rather than competitive with
traditional investigations of grammatical structure. The large and
subtle linguistic literature on important features of natural

language syntax constitutes an important and permanent body of
material. To draw an analogy from meteorology, a probabilistic
measure of a grammar's adequacy stands to ordinary linguistic
analysis of particular features, such as verb nominalization or
negative constructions, in the same relation that dynamical meteorology stands to classical observation of the clouds. While
dynamical meteorology can predict the macroscopic movement of
fronts, it cannot predict the exact shape of fair-weather cumulus or
storm-generated cumulonimbus. Put differently, one objective of a
probabilistic grammar is to account for a high percentage of a
corpus with a relatively simple grammar and to isolate the deviant
cases that need additional analysis and explanation. At the present
time, the main tendency in linguistics is to look at the deviant
cases and to ignore trying to give a quantitative account of that
part of a corpus that can be analyzed in relatively simple terms.
Another feature of probabilistic grammars worth noting is that such
a grammar can permit the generation of grammatical types that do not
occur in a given corpus. It is possible to take a tolerant attitude
toward utterances that are on the borderline of grammatical
acceptability, as long as the relative frequency of such utterances
is low. The point is that the objective of the probabilistic model
is not just to give an account of the finite corpus of spoken speech
or written text used as a basis for estimating the parameters of the
model, but to use the finite corpus as a sample to infer parameter
values for a larger, potentially infinite 'population' in the
standard probabilistic fashion. On occasion, there seems to have
been some confusion on this point. It has been seriously suggested
more than once that for a finite corpus one could write a grammar by
simply having a separate rewrite rule for each terminal sentence.
Once a probabilistic grammar is sought, such a proposal is easily
ruled out as acceptable. One method of so doing is to apply a
standard probabilistic test as to whether genuine probabilities have
been observed in a sample. We run a split-half analysis, and it is
required that within sampling variation the same estimates be obtained from two randomly selected halves of the corpus.
Another point of confusion among some linguists and philosophers
with whom I have discussed the methodology of fitting probabilistic
grammars to data is this. It is felt that some sort of legerdemain
is involved in estimating the parameters of a probabilistic grammar
from the data which it is supposed to predict. At a casual glance

it may seem that the predictions should always be good and not too
interesting because the parameters are estimated from the very data
they are used to predict. But this is to misunderstand the many
different ways the game of prediction may be played. Certainly, if
the number of parameters equals the number of predictions the
results are not very interesting. On the other hand, the more the
number of predictions exceeds the number of parameters the greater
the interest in the predictions of the theory. To convince one
linguist of the wide applicability of techniques of estimating
parameters from data they predict and also persuade him that such
estimation is not an intellectually dishonest form of science, I
pointed out that in studying the motion of the simple mechanical
system consisting of the Earth, Moon and Sun, at least nine position
parameters and nine velocity or momentum parameters as well as mass
parameters must be estimated from the data (the actual situation is
much more complicated), and everyone agrees that this is 'honest'
science.

It is hardly possible in this paper to enter into a full-scale
analysis and defense of the role of probabilistic and statistical
methodology in science. What I have said briefly here can easily be
expanded; I have tried to deal with some of the issues in a
monograph on causality (Suppes, 1970b). My own conviction is that at
present the quantitative study of language must almost always be
probabilistic in nature. The data simply cannot be handled quanti-
tatively by a deterministic theory. A third confusion of some linguists needs to be mentioned in this connection. The use of a probabilistic grammar in no ways entails a commitment to finite Markovian
dependencies in the temporal sequence of spoken speech. Two aspects
of such grammars make this clear. First, in general such grammars
generate a stochastic process that is a chain of infinite order in
the terminal vocabulary, not a finite Markov process. Second, the
probabilistic parameters are attached directly to the generation of
non-terminal strings of syntactic categories. Both of these observations are easy to check in the more technical details of later
sections.

The purpose of this part is to define the framework within which
empirical investigations of probabilistic grammars can take place
and to sketch how this attack can be made. The full presentation
of empirical results will be left to other papers. In the detailed
empirical work I have depended on the collaboration of younger

colleagues, especially Elizabeth Gammon and Arlene Moskowitz. I draw
on our joint work for examples in subsequent sections of this paper.
In the next section I give a simple example, indeed, a simple-
minded example, of a probabilistic grammar, to illustrate the
methodology without complications. In the third section I indicate
how such ideas may be applied to the spoken speech of a young child.
In the fourth section I consider briefly the representation problem
for probabilistic languages. I emphasize that the results of an
empirical sort in this paper are all preliminary in nature. The
detailed development of the empirical applications is a complicated
and involved affair and goes beyond the scope of the work presented
here.

2. A Simple Example:I

A simple example that illustrates the methodology of constructing
and testing probabilistic grammars is described in detail in this
section. It is not meant to be complex enough to fit any actual
corpus.

The example is a context-free grammar that can easily be rewritten
as a regular grammar. The five syntactic or semantic categories
are just V_1, V_2, Adj, PN and N, where V_1 is the class of intransitive
verbs, V_2 the class of transitive verbs or two-place predicates,
Adj the class of adjectives, PN the class of proper nouns and N the
class of common nouns. Additional non-terminal vocabulary consists
of the symbols S, NP, VP and AdjP. The set of production rules
consists of the following seven rules, plus the rewrite rules for
terminal vocabulary that belong to one of the five categories. The
probability of using one of the rules is shown on the right. Thus,
since Rule 1 is obligatory, the probability of using it is 1. In
the generation of any sentence, either Rule 2 or Rule 3 must be
used. Thus the probabilities α and $1 - \alpha$, which sum to 1, and so
forth for the other rules.

Production Rule	Probability
1. S → NP + VP	1
2. VP → V_1	$1 - \alpha$
3. VP → V_2 + NP	α
4. NP → PN	$1 - \beta$
5. NP → AdjP + N	β

6. AdjP → AdjP + Aaj   1 - γ
7. AdjP → Adj   γ

This probabilistic grammar has three parameters, α, β, and γ, and
the probability of each grammatical type of sentence can be expressed as a monomial function of the parameters. In particular, if
Adj^n is understood to denote a string of n adjectives, then the
possible grammatical types (infinite in number) all fall under one
of the corresponding schemes, with the indicated probability.

Grammatical Type   Probability

1. PN + V_1 $(1 - α)(1 - β)$

2. PN + V_2 + PN $α(1 - β)^2$

3. Adj^n + N + V_1 $(1 - α)β(1 - γ)^{n-1}γ$

4. PN + V_2 + Adj^n + N $αβ(1 - β)(1 - γ)^{n-1}γ$

5. Adj^n + N + V_2 + PN $αβ(1 - β)(1 - γ)^{n-1}γ$

6. Adj^m + N + V_2 + Adj^n + N $αβ^2(1 - γ)^{m+n-2}γ^2$

On the hypothesis that this grammar is adequate for the corpus we
are studying, each utterance will exemplify one of the grammatical
types falling under the six schemes. The empirical relative
frequency of each type in the corpus can be used to find a maximum-
likelihood estimate of each of the three parameters. Let $x_1,\ldots, x_n$
be the finite sequence of actual utterances. The likelihood function
$L(x_1,\ldots,x_n; α,β,γ)$ is the function that has as its value the
probability of obtaining or generating sequence $x_1,\ldots, x_n$ of
utterances given parameters α, β, γ. The computation of L assumes
the correctness of the probabilistic grammar, and this implies
among other things the statistical independence of the grammatical
type of utterances, an assumption that is violated in any actual
corpus, but probably not too excessively. The maximum-likelihood
estimates of α, β, and γ are just those values â, β̂, and γ̂ that
maximize the probability of the observed or generated sequence
$x_1,\ldots, x_n$. Let y_1 be the number of occurrences of grammatical type
1, i.e., PN + V_1, as given in the above table, let y_2 be the number
of occurrences of type 2, i.e., PN + V_2 + PN, let $y_{3,n}$ be the number
of occurrences of type 3 with a string of n adjectives, and let

similar definitions apply for $y_{4,n}$, $y_{5,n}$ and $y_{6,m,n}$. Then on the assumption of statistical independence, the likelihood function can be expressed as:

$$(1) \quad L(x_1,\ldots, x_n; \ \alpha,\beta,\gamma) = \left[(1-\alpha)(1-\beta)\right]^{y_1} \left[\alpha(1-\beta)^2\right]^{y_2}$$

$$\prod_{n=1}^{\infty} \left[(1-\alpha)\beta(1-\gamma)^{n-1}\gamma\right]^{y_{3,n}} \cdots \prod_{n=1}^{\infty} \prod_{m=1}^{\infty} \left[\alpha\beta^2(1-\gamma)^{m+n-2}\gamma^2\right]^{y_{6,m,n}}.$$

Of course, in any finite corpus the infinite products will always have only a finite number of terms not equal to one. To find $\hat{\alpha}$, $\hat{\beta}$ and $\hat{\gamma}$ as functions of the observed frequencies $y_1,\ldots, y_{6,m,n}$, the standard approach is to take the logarithm of both sides of (1), in order to convert products into sums, and then to take partial derivatives with respect to α, β and γ to find the values that maximize L. The maximum is not changed by taking the log of L, because log is a strictly monotonic increasing function. Letting $\mathcal{L} = \log L$, $y_3 = \sum y_{3,n}$, $y_4 = \sum y_{4,n}$, $y_5 = \sum y_{5,n}$, and $y_6 = \sum\sum y_{6,m,n}$, we have

$$\frac{\partial \mathcal{L}}{\partial \alpha} = -\frac{y_1 + y_3}{1-\alpha} + \frac{y_2 + y_4 + y_5 + y_6}{\alpha} = 0$$

$$\frac{\partial \mathcal{L}}{\partial \beta} = -\frac{y_1}{1-\beta} - \frac{2y_2}{1-\beta} + \frac{y_3}{\beta} + \frac{y_4 + y_5}{\beta} - \frac{y_4 + y_5}{1-\beta} + \frac{2y_6}{\beta} = 0$$

$$\frac{\partial \mathcal{L}}{\partial \gamma} = \frac{y_3 + y_4 + y_5 + y_6}{\gamma} - \left[\frac{y_{3,2} + y_{4,2} + y_{5,2}}{1-\gamma}\right.$$

$$\left. + \cdots + \frac{(n-1)(y_{3,n} + y_{4,n} + y_{5,n})}{1-\gamma} + \cdots \right]$$

$$- \left[\frac{y_{6,1,1}}{1-\gamma} + \cdots + \frac{(m-n-2)y_{6,m,n}}{1-\gamma} + \cdots \right] = 0.$$

If we let

$$z_{6,n} = \sum_{m'+n'=n+1} \sum y_{6,m',n'},$$

then after solving the above three equations we have as maximum-likelihood estimates:

$$\hat{\alpha} = \frac{y_2 + y_4 + y_5 + y_6}{y_1 + y_2 + y_3 + y_4 + y_5 + y_6}$$

$$\hat{\beta} = \frac{y_3 + y_4 + y_5 + 2y_6}{y_1 + 2y_2 + y_3 + 2y_4 + 2y_5 + 2y_6}$$

$$\hat{\gamma} = \frac{y_3 + y_4 + y_5 + z_6}{\sum n(y_{3,n} + y_{4,n} + y_{5,n} + z_{6,n})}$$

As would be expected from the role of γ as a stopping parameter for the addition of adjectives, the maximum-likelihood estimate of γ is just the standard one for the mean of a geometrical distribution. Having estimated α, β and γ from utterance frequency data, we can then test the goodness of fit of the probabilistic grammar in some standard statistical fashion, using a chi-square or some comparable statistical test. Some numerical results of such tests are reported later in the paper. The criterion for acceptance of the grammar is then just a standard statistical one. To say this is not to imply that standard statistical methods or criteria of testing are without their own conceptual problems. Rather the intention is to emphasize that the selection of a grammar can follow a standard scientific methodology of great power and wide applicability, and methodological arguments meant to be special to linguistics - like the discussion of simplicity - can be dispensed with.

3. Grammar For Adam I

Because of the relative syntactic simplicity and brevity of the spoken utterances of very young children, it is natural to begin attempts to write probabilistic grammars by examining such speech.

This section presents some preliminary results for Adam I, a well-known corpus collected by Roger Brown and his associates at Harvard.[1] Adam was a young boy of about 26 months at the time the speech was recorded. The corpus analyzed by Arlene Moskowitz and me consists of eight hours of recordings extending over a period of some weeks. Our work has been based on the written transcript of the tapes made at Harvard. Accepting for the most part the word and utterance boundaries established in the Harvard transcript, we found that the corpus consists of 6109 word occurrences with a vocabulary of 673 different words and 3497 utterances.

Even though the mean utterance length of Adam I is somewhat less than 2.0, there are difficulties in writing a completely adequate probabilistic grammar for the full corpus. An example is considered below.

To provide, however, a sample of what can be done on a more restricted basis, and in a framework that is fairly close to the simple artificial example considered in the preceding section, I restrict my attention to the noun phrases of Adam I. Noun phrases dominate Adam I, if for no other reason than because the most common single utterance is the single noun. Of the 3497 utterances, we have classified 936 as single occurrences of nouns. Another 192 are occurrences of two nouns in sequence, 147 adjective followed by noun, and 138 adjectives alone. In a number of other cases, the whole utterance is a simple noun phrase preceded or followed by a one-word rejoinder, vocative or locative.

The following phrase-structure grammar was written for noun phrases of Adam I. The seven production rules are given below with the corresponding probabilities shown on the right. This particular probabilistic model has five free parameters; the sum of the a_i's is one, so the a_i's contribute four parameters to be fitted to the data, and in the case of the b_i's there is just one free parameter.

Production Rule	Probability
1. NP → N	a_1
2. NP → AdjP	a_2
3. NP → AdjP + N	a_3
4. NP → Pro	a_4
5. NP → NP + NP	a_5

6. $AdjP \rightarrow AdjP + Adj$ b_1
7. $AdjP \rightarrow Adj$ b_2

What is pleasing about these rules, and perhaps surprising, is that
six of them are completely standard. (The one new symbol introduced
here is Pro for pronoun; inflection of pronouns has been ignored in
the present grammar.) The only slightly non-standard rule is Rule 5.
The main application of this rule is in the production of the noun
phrases consisting of a noun followed by a noun, with the first
noun being an uninflected possessive modifying the second noun.
Examples from the corpus are <u>Adam horn</u>, <u>Adam hat</u>, <u>Daddy racket</u> and
<u>Doctordan circus</u>.

To give a better approximation to statistical independence in the
occurrences of utterances, I deleted successive occurrences of the
same noun phrase in the frequency count, and only first occurrences
in a run of occurrences were considered in analyzing the data. The
maximum-likelihood estimates of the parameters were obtained from
the resulting 2434 occurrences of noun phrases in the corpus.

Estimated Parameter Values

a_1 = .6391 b_1 = .0581
a_2 = .0529 b_2 = .9419
a_3 = .0497
a_4 = .1439
a_5 = .1144

On the basis of remarks already made, the high value of a_1 is not
surprising because of the high frequency of occurrences of single
nouns in the corpus. It should be noted that the value of a_1 is even
higher than the relative frequency of single occurrences of nouns,
because the noun-phrase grammar has been written to fit all noun
phrases, including those occurring in full sentence context or in
conjunction with verbs, etc. Thus in a count of single nouns as
noun phrases every occurrence of a single noun as a noun phrase was
counted, and as can be seen from Table I, there are 1445 such single
nouns without immediate repetition. The high value of b_2 indicates
that there are very few occurrences of successive adjectives, and
therefore in almost all cases the adjective phrase was rewritten
simply as an adjective (Rule 7).

Comparison of the theoretical frequencies of the probabilistic grammar with the observed frequencies is given in Table I.

TABLE I

Probabilistic Noun-Phrase Grammar for Adam I

Noun phrase	Observed frequency	Theoretical frequency
N	1445	1555.6
P	388	350 1
NN	231	113 7
AN	135	114 0
A	114	121.3
PN	31	25.6
NA	19	8.9
NNN	12	8.3
AA	10	7.1
NAN	8	8.3
AP	6	2.0
PPN	6	.4
ANN	5	8.3
AAN	4	6.6
PA	4	2.0
ANA	3	.7
APN	3	.1
AAA	2	.4
APA	2	.0
NPP	2	.4
PAA	2	.1
PAN	2	1.9

Some fairly transparent abbreviations are used in the table to reduce its size; as before, N stands for noun, A for adjective, and P for pronoun. From the standpoint of a statistical goodness-of-fit test, the chi-square is still enormous; its value is 309.4 and there are only seven net degrees of freedom. Thus by ordinary statistical standards we must reject the fit of the model, but at this stage of the investigation the qualitative comparison of the observed and theoretical frequencies is encouraging. The rank order of the theoretical frequencies for the more frequent types of noun phrases closely matches that of the observed frequencies. The only really

serious discrepancy is in the case of the phrases consisting of two
nouns, for which the theoretical frequency is substantially less
than the observed frequency. It is possible that a different way of
generating the possessives that dominate the occurrences of these
two nouns in sequence would improve the prediction.
Summation of the observed and theoretical frequencies will show a
discrepancy between the two columns. I explicitly note this. It is
expected, because the column of theoretical frequencies should also
include the classes that were not observed actually occurring in the
corpus. The prediction of the sum of these unobserved classes is
that they should have a frequency of 100.0, which is slightly less
than 5% of the total observed frequency of 2434.
Note that the derivation of the probabilities for each grammatical
type of noun phrase used the simplest derivation. For example, in
the case of Adj + N, the theoretical probability was computed from
successive application of Rule 3, followed by Rule 6, followed by
Rule 7. It is also apparent that a quite different derivation of
this noun phrase can be obtained by using Rule 5. Because of the
rather special character of Rule 5, all derivations avoided Rule 5
when possible and only the simplest derivation was used in computing
the probabilities. In other words, no account was taken of the
ambiguity of the noun phrases. A more exact and sensitive analysis
would require a more thorough investigation of this point. It is
probable that there would be no substantial improvement in
theoretical predictions in the present case, if these matters were
taken account of. The reader may also have observed that the
theoretical frequencies reflect certain symmetries in the predictions that do not exist in the observed frequencies. For example,
the type Pro + Pro + N has an observed frequency of six, and the
permutation N + Pro + Pro has an observed frequency of two. This
discrepancy could easily be attributed to sampling. The symmetries
imposed by the theoretical grammar generated from Rules 1 to 7 are
considerable, but they do not introduce symmetries in any strongly
disturbing way. Again let me emphasize that the symmetries that are
somewhat questionable are almost entirely introduced by means of
Rule 5. Finally, note that I have omitted from the list of noun
phrases the occurrence of two pronouns in sequence because all cases
consisted of the question <u>Who that?</u> or <u>What that?</u>, and it seemed
inappropriate to classify these occurrences as single noun phrases.
I hasten to add that remarks of a similar sort can be made about

some of the other classifications.

It is important for the reader to keep in mind the various qualifications that have been made here. I have no intention of conveying the impression that a definitive result has been obtained.
I present the results of Table I as a preliminary indication of what
can be achieved by the methods introduced in this paper.
Appropriate qualifications and refinements will undoubtedly lead to
better and more substantial findings.

4. Representation Problem For Probabilistic Languages

From what has already been said it should be clear enough that the
imposition of a probabilistic generative structure is an additional
constraint on a grammar. It is natural to ask if a probabilistic
grammar can always be found for a language known merely to have a
grammar. Put in this intuitive fashion, it is not clear exactly
what question is being asked.

As a preliminary to a precise formulation of the question, an
explicit formal characterization of probabilistic grammars is
needed. In a fashion familiar from the literature we may define a
grammar as a quadruple (V_N, V_T, R, S), where V_N, V_T and R are finite
sets, S is a member of V_N, V_N and V_T are disjoint, and R is a set
of ordered pairs, whose first members are in V^+, and whose second
members are in V^*, where $V = V_N \cup V_T$, V^* is the set of all finite
sequences whose terms are elements of V, and V^+ is V^* minus the
empty sequence. As usual, it is intended that V_N be the non-terminal
and V_T the terminal vocabulary, R the set of productions and S the
start symbol. The language L generated by G is defined in the
standard manner and will be omitted here.

In the sense of the earlier sections of this paper, a probabilistic
grammar is obtained by adding a conditional distribution on the
set R of productions. Formally we have:

DEFINITION: A quintuple $G = (V_N, V_T, R, S, p)$ is a probabilistic
grammar if and only if $G = (V_N, V_T, R, S)$ is a grammar, and p is
a real-valued function defined on R such that

(i)   for each (σ_1, σ_j) in R, $p(\sigma_1, \sigma_j) \geq 0$,

(ii)   for each σ_1 in the domain of R
$$\sum_{\sigma_j} p(\sigma_1, \sigma_j) = 1,$$

where the summation is over the range of R.

Various generalizations of this definition are easily given: for
example, it is natural in some contexts to replace the fixed start
symbol S by a probability distribution over V_N. But such generalizations will not really affect the essential character of the
representation problem as formulated here.

For explicitness, we also need the concept of a probabilistic
language, which is just a pair (L, p), where L is a language and
p is a probability density defined on L, i.e., for each x in L,
$p(x) \geqslant 0$ and

$$\sum_{x \in L} p(x) = 1.$$

The first formulation of the representation problem is then this.
Let L be a language of type i (i = 0,1,2,3), with probability
density p. Does there always exist a probabilistic grammar G
(of type i) that generates (L, p)?
What is meant by generation is apparent. If $x \in L$, $p(x)$ must be the
sum of the probabilities of all the derivations of x in G. Ellis
(1969) answered this formulation of the representation problem in
the negative for type 2 and type 3 grammars. His example is easy to
describe. Let $V_T = \{a\}$, and let $L = \{a^n | n \geqslant 1\}$. Let $p(a^{n+1}) = 1/\sqrt{t_n}$,
$n > 0$, where $t_1 = 4$, and t_i = smallest prime such that
$t_i > \max(t_{i-1}, 2^{2i})$ for $i > 1$. In addition, set

$$p(a) = 1 - \sum_{n=1}^{\infty} p(a^{n+1}).$$

The argument depends upon showing that the probabilities assigned
to the strings of L by the above characterization cannot all lie in
the extensions of the field of rational numbers generated by the
finite set of conditional probabilities attached to the finite set
of production rules of any context-free grammar.

From the empirically-oriented standpoint of this paper, Ellis'
example, while perfectly correct mathematically, is conceptually
unsatisfactory, because any finite sample of L drawn according to
the density p could be described also by a density taking only
rational values. Put another way, algebraic examples of Ellis' sort
do not settle the representation problem when it is given a clearly
statistical formulation. Here is one such formulation. (As a matter
of notation, if p is a density on L, p_s is the sample density of
a finite random sample drawn from (L, p).)

Let L be a language of type 1 with probability density p. Does there
always exist a probabilistic grammar G (of type 1) that generates
a density p' on L such that for every sample s of L of size less
than N and with density p_s the null hypothesis that s is drawn from
(L, p') would not be rejected?

I have deliberately imposed a limit N on the size of the sample in
order directly to block asymptotic arguments that yield negative
results. In referring to the null hypothesis' not being rejected
I have in mind using some standard test such as Kolmogorov's and
some standard level of significance. The details on this point do
not matter here, although a precise solution must be explicit on
these matters and also on problems of repeated sampling, fixing
the power of the test, etc. My own conjecture is that the statistical formulation of the problem has an affirmative solution for
every N, but the positive solutions will often not be conceptually
interesting.

A final remark about the density p on L is perhaps needed. Some may
be concerned about the single occurrence of many individual
utterances even in a large corpus. The entire discussion of the
representation problem is easily shifted to the category
descriptions of terminal strings as exemplified in earlier sections
of this paper, and at this level, certainly many grammatical types
occur repeatedly.[2]

B. MODEL-THEORETIC SEMANTICS

1. Introduction

The search for a rigorous and explicit semantics of any
significant portion of a natural language is now intensive and far-
flung--far-flung in the sense that wide varieties of approaches are
being taken. Yet almost everyone agrees that at the present time the
semantics of natural languages are less satisfactorily formulated
than the grammars, even though a complete grammar for any
significant fragment of natural language is yet to be written.

A line of thought especially popular in the last couple of years is
that the semantics of a natural language can be reduced to the
semantics of first order logic. One way of fitting this scheme into
the general approach of generative grammars is to think of the deep
structure as being essentially identical with the structure of
first-order logic. The central difficulty with this approach is that
now as before how the semantics of the surface grammar is to be
formulated is still unclear. In other words, how can explicit formal
relations be established between first-order logic and the structure
of natural languages? Without the outlines of a formal theory, this
line of approach has moved no further than the classical stance of
introductory teaching in logic, which for many years has concentrate
concentrated on the translation of English sentences into first-
order logical notation. The method of translation, of course, is
left at an intuitive and ill-defined level.

The strength of the first-order logic approach is that it represents
essentially the only semantical theory with any systematic or deep
development, namely, model-theoretic semantics as developed in
mathematical logic since the early 1930's, especially since the
appearence of Tarski (1935). The semantical approaches developed by
linguists or others whose viewpoint is that of generative grammar
have been lacking in the formal precision and depth of model-
theoretic semantics. Indeed, some of the most important and
significant results in the foundations of mathematics belong to the
general theory of models. I shall not attempt to review the
approaches to semantics that start from a generative-grammar viewpoint, but I have in mind the work of Fodor, Katz, Lakoff, Mc Cawley,
and others.

My objective is to combine the viewpoint of model-theoretic semantics and generative grammar, to define semantics for context-free
languages and to apply the results to some fragments of natural
language. The ideas contained in this paper were developed while I
was working with hélène Bestougeff on the semantical theory of
question-answering systems. Later I came across some earlier
similar work by Knuth (1968). My developments are rather different
from those of Knuth, especially because my objective is to provide
tools for the analysis of fragments of natural languages, whereas
Knuth was concerned with programming languages.

Although on the surface the viewpoint seems different, I also bene-
fited from a study of Montague's interesting and important work
(1970) on the analysis of English as a formal language. My purely
extensional line of attack is simpler than Montague's. I adopted it
for reasons of expediency, not correctness. I wanted an apparatus
that could be applied in a fairly direct way to empirical analysis
of a corpus. As in part A. on probabilistic grammars, I began with
the speech of a young child, but without doubt, many of the semantical problems that are the center of Montague's concern must be
dealt with in analyzing slightly more complex speech. Indeed, some
of these problems already arise in the corpus studied here. As in
the case of my earlier work on probabilistic grammars, I have found
a full-scale analytic attack on a corpus of speech a humbling and
bedeviling experience. The results reported here hopefully chart
one possible course; in no sense are they more than preliminary.

This part is organized in the following fashion. In Section 2, I
describe a simple artificial example to illustrate how a semantic
valuation function is added to the generative mechanisms of a
context-free grammar. The relevant formal definitions are given in
Section 3. The reader who wants a quick survey of what can be done
with the methods, but who is not really interested in formal
matters, may skip ahead to Section 4, which contains a part of the
detailed empirical results. On the other hand, it will probably be
somewhat difficult to comprehend fully the machinery used in the
empirical analysis without some perusal of Section 3, unless the
reader is already quite familiar with model-theoretic semantics.

2. A Simple Example: II

To illustrate the semantic methods described formally below, I
use as an example the same single language I used in part A. As
remarked there, this example is not meant to be complex enough to
fit any actual corpus.

Production Rule	Semantic Function
1. $S \rightarrow NP + VP$	Truth-function
2. $VP \rightarrow V_1$	Identity
3. $VP \rightarrow V_2 + NP$	Image under the converse relation
4. $NP \rightarrow PN$	Identity
5. $NP \rightarrow AdjP + N$	Intersection
6. $AdjP \rightarrow AdjP + Adj$	Intersection
7. $AdjP \rightarrow Adj$	Identity

The grammatical types are the same as in A.2.

What needs explaining are the semantic functions to the right of
each production rule. For this purpose it is desirable to look at
an example of a sentence generated by this grammar. The intuitive
idea is that we define a valuation function v over the terminal
vocabulary, and as is standard in model-theoretic semantics, v takes
values in some relational structure.

Suppose a speaker wants to say 'John hit Mary'. The valuation
function needs to be defined for the three terminal words 'John',
'hit', and 'Mary'. We then recursively define the denotation of each
labeled node of the derivation tree of the sentence. In this
example, I number the nodes so that the denotation function ψ is
defined for pairs (n,α), where n is a node of the tree and α is a
word in the vocabulary. The tree looks like this.

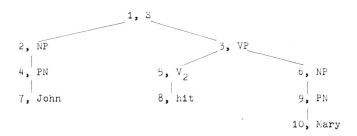

Let I be the identity function, Ǎ the converse of A, i.e.,

$$Ǎ = \{ <x,y>:<y,x> \; ε \; A \} \; ,$$

and f"A the image of A under f, i.e., the range of f restricted to
the domain A, and let T be truth and F falsity. Then the denotation
of each labeled node of the tree is found by working from the bottom
up:[3]

$\psi(10, \; Mary) = v(Mary)$

$\quad \psi(9, \; PN) = I(v(Mary))$

$\quad \psi(8, \; hit) = v(hit)$

$\psi(7, \; John) = v(John)$

$\quad \psi(6, \; NP) = II(v(Mary))$

$\quad \psi(5, \; V_2) = I(v(hit))$

$\quad \psi(4, \; PN) = I(v(John))$

$\psi(3, \; VP) = \overline{I(v(hit))} \; "II(v(Mary))$

$\psi(2, \; NP) = II(v(John))$

$\psi(1, \; S) \; = f(\psi(2, \; NP), \psi(3, \; VP)) = \begin{cases} T \; if \; \psi(2, \; NP) \subseteq \psi(3, VP) \\ F \; otherwise \end{cases}$

Clearly, the functions used above are just the semantic functions
associated with the productions. In particular, the production rules
for the direct descendants of nodes 2, 4, 5, 6, and 9 all have the
identity function as their semantic function.

One point should be emphasized. I do not claim that the set-theoretical semantic functions of actual speech are as simple as those
associated with the production rules given in this section. Consider
Rule 5, for instance. Intersection is fine for old dictators, but
not for alleged dictators. One standard mathematical approach to
this kind of difficulty is to generalize the semantic function to
cover the meaning of both sorts of cases. In the present case of

adjectives, we could require that the semantic function be one that
maps sets of objects into sets of objects. In this vein, Rule 5
would now be represented by

$$\psi(n_1, NP) = \psi(n_2, AdjP)"\psi(n_3, N).$$

Fortunately, generalizations that rule out the familiar simple
functions as semantic functions do not often occur early in
children's speech. Some tentative empirical evidence on this point
is presented in Section 4.

3. Denoting Grammars

I turn now to formal developments. Some standard grammatical
concepts are defined in the interest of completeness. First, if V is
a set, V^* is the set of all finite sequences whose elements are
members of V. I shall often refer to these finite sequences as
strings. The empty sequence, 0, is in V^*; we define $V^+ = V^* - \{0\}$.
A structure $G = \langle V,V_N,P,S \rangle$ is a <u>phrase-structure</u> grammar if and
only if V and P are finite, nonempty sets, V_N is a subset of V, S
is in V_N and $P \subseteq V_N^* \times V^+$. Following the usual terminology, V_N is the
nonterminal vocabulary and $V_T = V - V_N$ the terminal vocabulary.
S is the start symbol of the single axiom from which we derive
strings or words in the language generated by G. The set P is the
set of production or rewrite rules. If $\langle \alpha,\beta \rangle \epsilon$ P, we write $\alpha \rightarrow \beta$,
which we read: from α we may produce or derive β (immediately).

A phrase-structure grammar $G = \langle V,V_N,P,S \rangle$ is <u>context-free</u> if and
only if $P \subseteq V_N \times V^+$, i.e., if $\alpha \rightarrow \beta$ is in P then $\alpha \epsilon V_N$ and $\beta \epsilon V^+$.[4]
These ideas may be illustrated by considering the simple language
of the previous section. Although it is intended that N, PN, Adj,
V_1, and V_2 be nonterminals in any application, we can treat them
as terminals for purposes of illustration, for they do not occur
on the left of any of the seven production rules. With this understanding

$$V_N = \{S,NP,VP,AdjP\}$$

$$V_T = \{N,PN,Adj,V_1,V_2\}$$

and P is defined by the production rules already given. It is
obvious from looking at the production rules that the grammar is
context-free, for only elements of V_N appear on the left-hand side
of any of the seven production rules.

The standard definition of derivations is as follows.
Let $G = \langle V, V_N, P, S \rangle$ be a phrase-structure grammar. First, if $\alpha \to \beta$
is a production of P, and γ and δ are strings in V^*, then
$\gamma\alpha\delta \underset{G}{\Rightarrow} \gamma\beta\delta$. We say that β is d e r i v a b l e from α in G, in
symbols, $\alpha \underset{G}{\overset{*}{\Rightarrow}} \beta$ if there are strings $\alpha_1, \ldots, \alpha_n$ in V^* such that $\alpha = \alpha_1$
$\alpha_1 \underset{G}{\Rightarrow} \alpha_2, \ldots, \alpha_{n-1} \underset{G}{\Rightarrow} \alpha_n, \alpha_n = \beta$. The sequence $\Delta = \langle \alpha_1, \ldots, \alpha_n \rangle$ is a
d e r i v a t i o n in G. The language L(G) generated by G is
$\{\alpha : \alpha \in V_T^* \ \& \ S \underset{G}{\overset{*}{\Rightarrow}} \alpha\}$. In other words, L(G) is the set of all strings
made up of terminal vocabulary and derived from S.

The semantic concepts developed also require use of the concept of
a derivation tree of a grammar. The relevant notions are set forth
in a series of definitions. Certain familiar set-theoretical notions
about relations are also needed. To begin with, a binary structure
is an ordered pair $\langle T, R \rangle$ such that T is a nonempty set and R is a
binary relation on T, i.e., $R \subseteq T \times T$. R is a partial ordering of T
if and only if R is reflexive, antisymmetric and transitive on T.
R is a strict simple ordering of T if and only if R is asymmetric,
transitive, and connected on T. We also need the concept of
R-immediate predecessor. For x and y in T, xJy if and only if xRy,
not yRx and for every z if $z \neq y$ and zRy then zRx. In the language
of formal grammars, we say that if xJy, then x directly dominates y,
or y is the direct descendant of x.

Using these notions, we define in succession tree, ordered tree, and
labeled ordered tree. A binary structure $\langle T, R \rangle$ is a tree if and only
if (i) T is finite, (ii) R is a partial ordering of T, (iii) there
is an R-first element of T, i.e., there is an x such that for every
y, xRy, and (iv) if xJz and yJz, then x = y. If xRy in a tree, we say
that y is a descendant of x. Also the R-first element of a tree is
called the root of the tree, and an element of T that has no
descendants is called a leaf. We call any element of T a node, and
we shall sometimes refer to leaves as terminal nodes.
A ternary structure $\langle T, R, L \rangle$ is an ordered tree if and only if (i) L
is a binary relation on T, (ii) $\langle T, R \rangle$ is a tree, (iii) for each x
in T, L is a strict simple ordering of $\{y : xJy\}$, (iv) if xLy and
yRz then xLz, and (v) if xLy and xRz, then zLy. It is customary to
read xLy as "x is to the left of y." having this ordering is

fundamental to generating terminal strings and not just sets of
terminal words. The <u>terminal</u> <u>string</u> of an ordered labeled tree is
just the sequence of labels $\langle f(x_1),\ldots,f(x_n)\rangle$ of the leaves of the
tree as ordered by L. Formally, a quinary structure $\langle T,V,R,L,f\rangle$ is
a <u>labeled</u> <u>ordered</u> <u>tree</u> if and only if (i) V is a nonempty set,
(ii) $\langle T,R,L\rangle$ is an ordered tree, and (iii) f is a function from T
into V. The function f is the labeling function and f(x) is the
<u>label</u> of node x.

The definition of a derivation tree is relative to a given context-
free grammar.

<u>Definition 1</u>. <u>Let</u> G = $\langle V,V_N,P,S\rangle$ <u>be a</u> <u>context-free</u> <u>grammar</u> <u>and</u> <u>let</u>
τ = $\langle T,V,R,L,f\rangle$ <u>be a</u> <u>labeled</u> <u>ordered</u> <u>tree</u>. τ <u>is a</u> derivation tree
<u>of</u> G <u>if</u> <u>and</u> <u>only</u> <u>if</u>

    (i) <u>If</u> **x** <u>is</u> <u>the</u> <u>root</u> <u>of</u> τ, f(x) = S;
    (ii) <u>If</u> xRy <u>and</u> x $\neq$ y, <u>then</u> f(x) <u>is</u> <u>in</u> V_N;
    (iii) <u>If</u> $y_1,\ldots,y_n$ <u>are</u> <u>all</u> <u>the</u> <u>direct</u> <u>descendants</u> <u>of</u> x, <u>i.e.,</u>

$$\bigcup_{i=1}^{n}\{y_i\} = \{y : xJy\} \neq \emptyset,\ \underline{and}\ y_iLy_j\ \underline{if}\ i < j,\ \underline{then}$$

$$\langle f(x),\langle f(y_1),\ldots,f(y_n)\rangle\rangle$$

<u>is</u> <u>a</u> <u>production</u> <u>in</u> P.

We now turn to semantics proper by introducing the set ϕ of set-
theoretical functions. We shall let the domains of these functions
be n-tuples of any sets (with some appropriate restriction understood to avoid set-theoretical paradoxes).

<u>Definition 2</u>. <u>Let</u> $\langle V,V_N,P,S\rangle$ <u>be a</u> <u>context-free</u> <u>grammar</u>. <u>Let</u> ϕ <u>be a</u>
<u>function</u> <u>defined</u> <u>on</u> P <u>which</u> <u>assigns to</u> <u>each</u> <u>production</u> p <u>in</u> P <u>a</u>
<u>finite</u>, <u>possibly</u> <u>empty</u> <u>set</u> <u>of</u> <u>set-theoretical</u> <u>functions</u> <u>subject to</u>
<u>the</u> <u>restriction</u> <u>that</u> <u>if</u> <u>the</u> <u>right</u> <u>member</u> <u>of</u> <u>production</u> p <u>has</u> n <u>terms</u>
<u>of</u> V, <u>then</u> <u>any</u> <u>function</u> <u>of</u> ϕ(p) <u>has</u> n <u>arguments</u>. <u>Then</u>
G = $\langle V,V_N,P,S,\phi\rangle$ <u>is a</u> potentially denoting context-free grammar.
<u>If</u> <u>for</u> <u>each</u> p <u>in</u> P, ϕ(p) <u>has</u> <u>exactly</u> <u>one</u> <u>member</u>, <u>then</u> G <u>is</u> <u>said to be</u>
simple.

The simplicity and abstractness of the definition may be misleading.
In the case of a formal language, e.g., a context-free programming

language, the creators of the language specify the semantics by
defining ⊄. Matters are more complicated in applying the same idea
of capturing the semantics by such a function for fragments of a
natural language. Perhaps the most difficult problem is that of
giving a straightforward set-theoretical interpretation of intensional contexts, especially to those generated by the expression
of propositional attitudes of believing, wanting, seeking and so
forth. I shall not attempt to deal with these matters in the present
paper.

How the set-theoretical functions in ⊄(p) work was illustrated in
the preceding section; some empirical examples follow in the next
section. The problems of identifying and verifying ⊄ even in the
simplest sort of context are discussed there. In one sense the
definition should be strengthened to permit only one function in
φ(p) of a given number of arguments. The intuitive idea behind the
restriction is clear. In a given application we try first to assign
denotations at the individual word level, and we proceed to two- and
three-word phrases only when necessary. The concept of such hierarchical parsing is familiar in computer programming, and a detailed
example in the context of a question-answering program is worked out
in a joint paper with Hélène Bestougeff. However, as the examples in
the next section show, this restriction seems to be too severe for
natural languages.

A clear separation of the generality of ⊄ and an evaluation function
v is intended. The functions in ⊄ should be constant over many
different uses of a word, phrase or statement. The valuation v, on
the other hand, can change sharply from one occasion of use to the
next. To provide for any finite composition of functions, or other
ascensions in the natural hierarchy of sets and functions built up
from a domain of individuals, the family ℋ'(D) of sets with closure
properties stronger than needed in any particular application is
defined. The abstract objects T (for truth) and F (for falsity) are
excluded as elements of ℋ'(D). In this definition $\mathcal{P}$A is the power
set of A, i.e., the set of all subjects of A.

Definition 3. Let D be a nonempty set. Then ℋ'(D) is the smallest
family of sets such that
  (i) D ε ℋ'(D),
  (ii) if A, B ε ℋ'(D) then A ∪ B ε ℋ'(D),

(iii) if $A \in \mathcal{H}'(D)$ then $\mathcal{P}A \in \mathcal{H}'(D)$,

(iv) if $A \in \mathcal{H}'(D)$ and $B \subseteq A$ then $B \in \mathcal{H}'(D)$.

We define $\mathcal{H}(D) = \mathcal{H}'(D) \cup \{T,F\}$, with $T \notin \mathcal{H}'(D)$, $F \notin \mathcal{H}'(D)$ and $T \neq F$.

A model structure for G is defined just for terminal words and phrases. The meaning or denotation of nonterminal symbols changes from one derivation or derivation tree to another.

Definition 4. Let D be a nonempty set, let $G = \langle V, V_N, P, S \rangle$ be a phrase-structure grammar, and let v be a partial function on V_T^+ to $\mathcal{H}(D)$ such that if v is defined for α in V_T^+ and if γ is a subsequence of α, then v is not defined for γ. Then $\mathcal{M} = \langle D, v \rangle$ is a model structure for G. If the domain of v is exactly V_T, then $\mathcal{M}$ is simple.

We also refer to v as a _valuation function_ for G.

I now define semantic trees that assign denotations to nonterminal symbols in a derivation tree. The definition is for simple potential potentially denoting grammars and for simple model structures. In other words, there is a unique semantic function for each production, and the valuation function is defined just on V_T, and not on phrases of V_T^+.

Definition 5. Let $G = \langle V, V_N, P, S, \phi \rangle$ be a simple, potentially denoting context-free grammar, let $\mathcal{M} = \langle D, v \rangle$ be a simple model structure for G, let $\tau' = \langle T, V, R, L, f \rangle$ be a derivation tree of $\langle V, V_N, P, S \rangle$ such that if x is a terminal node, then $f(x) \in V_T$ and let ψ be a function from f to $\mathcal{H}(D)$ such that

(i) if $\langle x, f(x) \rangle \in$ f and $f(x) \in V_T$, then
$$\psi(x, f(x)) = v(f(x)),$$

(ii) if $\langle x, f(x) \rangle \in$ f, $f(x) \in V_N$, and $y_1, \ldots, y_n$ are all the direct descendants of x with $y_i L y_j$ if $i < j$, then

$$\psi(x, f(x)) = \phi(\psi(y_1, f(y_1)), \ldots, \psi(y_n, f(y_n))),$$

where $\phi = \phi(p)$ and p is the production
$$\langle f(x), \langle f(y_1), \ldots, f(y_n) \rangle \rangle.$$

Then $\tau = \langle T, V, R, L, f, \psi \rangle$ is a simple semantic tree of G and $\mathcal{M}$.

The extension of Definition 5 to semantic trees that are not simple is relatively straightforward, but is not given explicitly here in

the interest of restricting the formal parts of the paper.
The empirical examples considered in the next section implicitly
assume this extension, but the simplicity of the corpus makes the
several set-theoretical functions ϕ attached to a given production
easy to interpret.

The function ψ assigns a denotation to each node of a semantic tree.
The resulting structural analysis can be used to define a concept
of meaning or sense for each node. Perhaps the most natural intuiti
intuitive idea is this. Extend the concept of a model structure by
introducing a set of <u>situations</u>. For each situation $\sigma\langle D_\sigma, v_\sigma\rangle$ is a
model structure. The meaning or sense of an utterance is then the
function ψ of the root of the tree of the utterance. For example,
using the analysis of <u>John hit Mary</u> from Section 3, dropping the
redundant notation for the identity function and using the ordinary
lambda notation for function abstraction, we obtain as the meaning
of the sentence

$$\psi(1,S) = (\lambda\sigma)f(v_\sigma(\underline{John}), v_\sigma(\underline{hit})"v_\sigma(\underline{Mary})),$$

but this idea will not be developed further here. Its affinity to
Kripke-type semantics is clear.

4. Noun-Phrase Semantics of <u>Adam</u> <u>I</u>

In part A, I proposed and tested a probabilistic noun-phrase
grammar for Adam I. The context-free grammar for the noun phrases
of Adam I is as in A.3. To the right of the production rules,
are also shown the main set-theoretical functions that make the
grammar potentially denoting. These semantic functions, as it is
convenient to call them in the present context, are subsequently
discussed extensively. I especially call attention to the semantic
function for Rule 5, which is formally defined.

Noun-Phrase Grammar for Adam I

Production Rule	Semantic Function
1. NP → N	Identity
2. NP → AdjP	Identity
3. NP → AdjP + N	Intersection
4. NP → Pro	Identity
5. NP → NP + NP	Choice function
6. AdjP → AdjP + Adj	Intersection

7. AdjP → Adj   Identity

Table II lists in the fourth column the observed frequency with
which the "standard" semantic function shown as above seems to
provide the correct interpretation for the five most frequent types
(compare Table I). Of course, in the case of the identity function,
there is not much to dispute, and so I concentrate entirely on the
other two cases. First of all, if the derivation uses more than one
rule, then by standard interpretation.

Table II
Probabilistic Noun-Phrase Grammar for Adam I

Noun phrase	Observed frequency	Theoretical frequency	Stand. semantic function
N	1445	1555.6	1445
P	388	350.1	388
NN	231	113.7	154
AN	135	114.0	91
A	114	121.3	114

I mean the derivation that only uses Rule 5 if it is necessary and
that interprets each production rule used in terms of its standard
semantic function. Since none of the derivations is very complex,
I shall not spend much time on this point.

The fundamental ideas of denoting grammars as defined in the preceding section come naturally into play when a detailed analysis is
undertaken of the data summarized in Table I. The most important
step is to identify the additional semantic functions if any in $\Phi(p)$
for each of the seven production rules. A simple way to look at this
is to examine the various types of utterances listed in Table I,
summarize the production rules and semantic functions used for each
type, and then collect all of this evidence in a new summary table
for the production rules.

Therefore I now discuss the types of noun phrases listed in Table I
and consider in detail the data for the five most frequently listed.

Types N and P, the first two, need little comment. The identity
function, and no other function, serves for them. It should be

clearly understood, of course, that the nouns and pronouns listed in
these first two lines--a total of 1833 without immediate repetition-
-do not occur as parts of a larger noun-phrase. The derivation of N
uses only P1 (Production Rule 1), and the derivation of P uses only
P4.

The data on type NN are much richer and more complex. The derivation
is unique; it uses P5 then P1 twice, as shown in the tree. As before,
the semantic function for P1 is just the identity function, so all
the analysis of type NN centers around the interpretation of P5.
To begin with, I must explain what I mean by the choice function
shown above as

the standard semantic function of P5. This is a set-theoretical
function of A and B that for each A is a function selecting an
element of B when B is the argument of f. Thus

$$\phi(A,B) = f_A(B) \ \epsilon \ B.$$

I used 'A' rather than an individual variable to make the notation
general, but in all standard cases, A is a unit set. (I emphasize
again, I do not distinguish unit sets from their members.) A standard
set-theoretical choice function, i.e., a function f such that if B
is in the domain of f and B is nonempty, then $f(B) \ \epsilon \ B$ is a natural
device for expressing possession. Intuitively, each of the
possessors named by Adam has such a function and the function
selects his (or hers or its) object from the class of like objects.
Thus <u>Daddy</u> <u>chair</u> denotes that chair in the class of chairs within
Adam's purview that belongs to or is used especially by Daddy. If we
restrict our possessors to individuals, then in terms of the model
structure $\mathfrak{D} = \langle D,v \rangle$, $\phi(A,B)$ is just a partial function from D X $\mathcal{P}(D)$
to D, where $\mathcal{P}(D)$ is the power set of D.[5]

The choice function is justly labeled the standard semantic function
for P5, but at least four other semantic functions belong in $\Phi(P5)$.
One of these is the converse of $\phi(A,B)$ as defined above, i.e.,

$$\breve{\phi}(A,B) = f_B(A),$$

which means the possessor is named after the thing possessed. Here
are examples from Adam I for which this interpretation seems correct:
part trailer (meaning part of trailer), part towtruck, book boy,
name man, ladder firetruck, taperecorder Ursula.

The third semantic function is a choice function on the Cartesian
product of two sets, often the sets' being unit sets as in the case
of Mommy Daddy. Formally, we have

$$\phi(A,B) = f(A \times B),$$

and $f(A \times B) \in A \times B$. Other examples are Daddy Adam and pencil
paper. The frequency of use of this function is low.
The fourth semantic function proposed for $\phi(P5)$ is the intersection
function,

$$\phi(A,B) = A \cap B.$$

Examples are lady elephant and lady Ursula. Here the first noun is
functioning like an adjective.

The fifth semantic function, following in frequency the choice
function and its converse, is the identity function. It seems clear
from the transcription that some pairs of nouns are used as a proper
name or a simple description, even though each noun is used in other
combinations. (By a simple description I mean a phrase such that no
subsequence of it denotes (see Definition 4). Some examples are pin
game and Daddy Cromer.

I do not consider in the same detail the next two most frequent
types shown in Table I, namely, AN and A. The latter, as in the case
of N and P, is served without complications by the identity
function. As would be expected, the picture is more complicated for
the type AN. Column 4 of Table I indicates that 91 of the 135 in-
stances of AN can be interpreted as using intersection as the
semantic function. Typical examples are these: big drum, big horn,
my shadow, my paper, my tea, my comb, oldtime train, that knee,
green rug, that man, poor doggie, pretty flower. The main exceptions
to the intersection rule are found in the use of numerical or comparative adjectives like two or more. Among the 116 AN phrases
standing alone, i.e., not occurring as part of a lower utterance,
19 have two as the adjective; for example, two checkers, two lights,
two socks, two men, two boots, two rugs. No numerical adjective
other than two is used in the 116 phrases.

I terminate at this point the detailed analysis of the Adam I
corpus, but it should be evident that this is only a beginning.
For extensive analyses along the same lines, I refer to Smith (1972)
and Suppes, Smith and Léveillé (1972).

BIBLIOGRAPHY

Ellis, C., Probabilistic Languages and Automata, Doctoral Dissertation, University of Illinois at Urbana-Champaign, 1969.

Harwood,, F.W., Quantatitative Study of the Speech of Australian
Children, Language and Speech 2 (1959) 236-271.

Knuth, D.E., Semantics of Context-Free Languages, Mathematical
Systems Theory 2 (1968) 127-131.

Montague, R., English as a Formal Language in B. Visentini et al.
(Eds.) Linguaggi Nella Società e Nella Tecnica,Milan, 1970,
pp. 189-224.

Smith, R.L., Jr., The Syntax and Semantics of ERICA, Technical
Report No. 185, Institute for Mathematical Studies in the Social
Sciences, Stanford, 1972.

Suppes, P., Probabilistic Grammars for Natural Languages,
Synthese 22 (1970) 95-116. (a)

Suppes, P., A Probabilistic Theory of Causality, Acta Philosophica
Fennica 24 (1970), North-Holland Publishing Company, Amsterdam. (b)

Suppes, P., Semantics of Context-Free Fragments of Natural
Languages, Technical Report No. 171, Institute for Mathematical
Studies in the Social Sciences, Stanford, 1971. Reprinted in
K.J.J. Hintikka, J.M.E. Moravcsik, and P. Suppes (Eds.),
Approaches to Natural Language, Reidel, Dordrecht, 1973.

Suppes, P., Smith, R., and Léveillé, M., The French Syntax and
Semantics of PHILIPPE, Part 1: Noun Phrases, Technical Report
No. 195, Institute for Mathematical Studies in the Social Sciences,
Stanford, 1972.

Tarski, A., 'Der Wahrheitsbegriff in den Formalisierten Sprachen',
Studia Philosophica 1 (1935) 261-405.

REFERENCES

*This research has been supported by the National Science Foundation under grant NSFGJ-443X. I am indebted to Pentti Kanerva for help in the computer analysis and organization of the data presented in Part B, Section 4, and I am indebted to Dr. Elizabeth Gammon for several useful ideas in connection with the analysis in Section 4. D.M. Gabbay and George Huff have made a number of penetrating comments on Part B, Section 3, and Richard Montague trenchantly criticized an unsatisfactory preliminary version.

+ I am indebted to D. Reidel Publishing Company for the permission to draw part of the material from the two publications.

1 Roger Brown has generously made the transcribed records available and given us permission to publish any of our analyses.

2 W.C. Watt has called my attention to an article by Harwood(1959), which reports some frequency data for the speech of Australian Children, but no probabilistic grammar or other sort of model is proposed or tested. As far as I know, the explicit statistical test of probabilistic grammars, including estimation of parameters, has not been reported prior to the present paper, but given the scattered character of the possibly relevant literature I could just just be ignorant of important predecessors to my own work.

3 I have let the words of V serve as names of themselves to simplify the notation.

4 As Richard Montague pointed out to me, to make context-free grammars a special case of phrase-structure grammars, as defined here, the first members of P should be not elements of V_N, but one-place sequences whose terms are elements of V_N. This same problem arises later in referring to elements of V^*, but treating elements of V as belonging to V^*. Consequently, to avoid notational complexities, I treat elements, their unit sets and one-place sequences whose terms are the elements, as identical.

5 Other possibilities exist for the set-theoretical characterization of possession. In fact, there is an undesirable asymmetry between the choice function for Adam hat and the intersection function for my hat, but it is also clear that v(my) can in a straightforward sense be the set of Adam's possessions but v(Adam) is Adam, not the set of Adam's possessions.

DISCUSSION:

Potts:

Thank you very much.

I think that we might do well to spend just a minute or two before
beginning substantive discussion in identifying the topics which the
members of the panel would like to discuss so that we can do so in
a fairly orderly way. From hearing the papers it struck me that
there are at least three overlapping topics which the panelists may
wish to discuss. First, as between Dr. Keenan and Professor Suppes,
the question whether or not predicate logic should be used in
semantics or, more generally, in grammatical analysis.

Second, can the type of componential analysis proposed by Professor
Joshi be integrated with Dr. Keenan's logical method? And can it
also be integrated with the set-theoretical method outlined by
Professor Suppes?

The third topic is that of levels in Frege's sense. In Professor
Suppes' account we have a hierarchical system and a method of
generating new sets in a hierarchy, whereas the functors used
both by Professor Joshi and Dr. Keenan are all first-level ones.

It might also help members of the audience if the panelists would
care to put to each other some simple questions on the more technical notions which have been employed in the three papers and which
may not have been fully assimilated. Some examples from Professor
Suppes' paper are his notion of congruence, of'the same
proposition', and his procedure for the creation of new sets.

May I now ask each member of the panel if there are further topics,
which he would like to add to this list?

Keenan:

We could discuss the general adequacy of using a context-free
grammar to represent natural language sentences and the possibility
of defining important semantic relations on the structures generated
by such a grammar.

Potts:

Professor Joshi?

Joshi:

Well, I would like to have some discussion about the types of
semantic representations that are selected and the extent to which
the person, or the persons, proposing such semantic representation
feel as their obligation to show how these are eventually mapped

onto actual sentences or the extent to which they think that this
is not their immediate concern.

Potts:

Professor Suppes?

Suppes:

Yes, I would like to have some discussion of Professor Joshi's
interesting analysis of perceptual verbs. When you try to
systematize this analysis, do you find in various languages a kind
of saturation property? I mean do you find something like the
introduction of categories in traditional philosophy so that the
verbs saturate the possibilities in different ways, of course, in
different languages.

Potts:

Good. Well, I suggest that we begin with Professor Joshi's question
about types of semantic representation. This would lead us fairly
naturally into the question about the context-free grammars and that
in turn to the controversy about the use of predicate logic.
So, Professor Joshi?

Joshi:

Psychologists appear to be interested in such factorizations (e.g.,
move - cause to change location etc.) They will be interested in
such an enterprise only if the factors turn out to be
psychologically relevant. They are not necessarily obligated to
show how one might go from these semantic representations to the
sentences. Within linguistics, whatever representation one may
adopt, it is generally understood that it is the linguist's business
to show how these representations can be mapped onto sentences.
Unfortunately, if you look at some recent linguistics papers, one
gets the feeling that even some linguists do not consider this as
their responsibility either. The question then is: whose job is it?

Potts:

Do you see what either Dr. Keenan or Professor Suppes has said as
producing a difficulty here?

Joshi:

I would say that if you are starting with the phrase structure tree
or other closely related representations, you are closer to
realizing that goal because one can see how the surface syntax
could also be represented by similar structures. If the formal
objects you choose for the semantic representations are also useful
in characterizing the surface structures, then you are much better

off; if not, you have problems.

Suppes:

I think it relates to the topic about predicate logic because part
of my criticism of the representation of the semantics of ordinary
language in predicate logic, whether it is the more powerful version
Dr. Keenan presented or traditional first-order predicate logic, is
without explicit rules as to how to go from the logic to the
ordinary language, to the natural language sentence, then one has a
major gap in the analysis. And I think it is a gap in the same way
as you are talking about for the componential type analysis. It is
characteristic for example, it seems to me, of Fillmore's analyses
to have the same weakness. He does not give in many ways very good
analyses of verbs, he does not give enough structure to show how in
a systematic way you get to the actual order of words in the surface
of natural language.

Keenan:

I take the point that we would like to have fully explicit rules,
that we would like completely adequate grammars for all languages;
I feel that that is an enormous task that is the subject-matter for
an entire field, and it is just unreasonable to impose that requirement
before we begin. In fact with respect to the logic I have proposed
the reasons these structures have the form they do is because they
look a lot like surface structures. I have one major problem: I have
lots of pronouns kicking around and I have tried to justify that;
in fact, they are extremely useful, and we consider a wide range of
languages. I have in fact proposed a format for writing down a
relative clause transformation which is independent of the syntax
of any language. Of course, it is wrong, but I mean I have actually
written down such a procedure and tried to indicate where different
categories of languages, so to speak, follow different subroutines
in their realization of the relative clause. Some of them delete
the pronoun, some of them do not, some of them have the head noun
on the right, some on the left, some have a relative pronoun, some
do not, and so on. I would submit that this system here is basically
very amenable to this treatment, but I do not have a completely
worked-out analysis. In the second part of this paper I do argue
that the major noun-phrase transformations that linguists have
worked with, conjunction, reduction, Equi-NP deletion,
pronominalization and so on, work very nicely on this system if the
identity condition used is "being bound by the same quantified noun-

phrase". To this extent, I think there is a lot of syntactic
motivation for doing it this way, (but the) you know completely
detailed analysis we may never have them, that is true.
Suppes:
I think we are not really in a disagreement about that, and I want
to come back to it, but I would contrast your attitude with the
example of Quine, for instance, especially as presented in his book
"Word and Object". Many philosophers have not analysed actual usage
in ordinary language, but want to eliminate it. There are, of
course, proper uses for such a reductive analysis. One can be
interested in what is the minimal apparatus to be used to have a
given expressive power, but I do feel that much analysis that has
been given by philosophers is opposed to what you are really after,
and does not recognize the importance of trying to bridge that gap.
Now my second remark is this. It does seem to me there are two kinds
of strategies and I am not suggesting for a moment that both should
not be explored, but there is a strategy different from yours. The
strategy I am advocating is to deal with a smaller fragment of the
natural language, but then to do the semantics directly on that
structure and it is obviously too early in the game to see which
strategy can be pushed further. But that is an alternative to what
you are proposing.
Keenan:
It is an alternative, but I submit it is inadequate on the grounds
that the only adequacy criterion that I know which will allow us to
choose among various analyses I find hard to apply directly to surface structures. If we claim to represent the meaning of a sentence,
let us say, we surely have to show that it has the semantic
properties that native speakers judge it to have. If it implies
some other sentence, we have to show that; if it presupposes some
other sentence, we have to show that; if it is independent of
another, if it answers a question, all of this has to be shown -
which means that these semantic relations must be defined on the
meaning representations; you simply cannot define consequence on
sentences that are semantically ambiguous. The definition of consequence and all the other logical relations is stated in terms of
relative truth conditions. Now if a sentence could be assigned more
than one truth value in a fixed interpretation, you could argue both
that it does imply this and does not imply that depending on how
you select the truth value that is convenient for your purpose.

It seems to me then that in defining the semantic relations above,
on which we get quite reliable intuitions from native speakers, we
have to define them on objects which at least factor out the
ambiguity of natural language sentences. And to this extent we are
moving away from surface structures. Note that any context-free
grammar of a natural language is essentially ambiguous.

Suppes:

I agree about the ambiguity problem, but I disagree about the
significance of it because the exact point is that in defining
consequence one will use the semantic trees of a sentence. You must
deal with the ambiguities,but to look at them in my terminology is
to deal with the set of semantic trees that represent the meanings,
the possible meanings of a sentence. Now it is quite true that the
move to the semantic trees is a move away from the surface
structure, but, and this is an important but, as far as I am concerned, those trees reflect directly the structure, which is not the
case when you do use a seperate logic. There is a difference in the
intimacy of the connection.

Keenan:

There is no inherent reason why the trees determined by the strings
in the logical language could not be exactly the trees we want to
make up. Thus, the logic I have made up, determines a set of trees
which are in most important respects the trees we need to represent
the few properties of natural language that we can say something
about at all; I mean there are lots of things I simply do not know.
On the other hand, I found in your discussion the representation of
meaning similarity was one which ignored the labels on trees. And I
find this surprising. Linguists at least are concerned with what the
labels are, and it is not hard to find examples of sentences which
have exactly the same tree except for different labels and which are
judged semantically ambiguous for those reasons.

Suppes:

What is the example?

Keenan:

I will give some, yes. The problem comes up precisely with the
consideration of the sort of semantic property that it is not
natural to represent in a context-free grammar, namely the binding
properties of quantifier phrases. The example I have in mind will
be something like this: "John thought that he was sick" let us say.
Somewhat grudgingly we have come to regard the sentence as ambiguous

because most linguists found it is; on the one hand "the" can be
considered as bound by "John" and on the other hand, it can be
considered as referring differently. Now in English that sentence is
ambiguous, in my logic it is not. We have got "John x is such that
x thought that x was drunk" on one reading and we get "John x
x thought that y was sick" on the other reading. And it comes out
that these differ only with respect to label now. That is the only
difference; otherwise their structure is similar. Many languages in
fact preserve this label distinction. In Yoruba we get two different
pronouns in surface depending on whether "he" is bound by "John" or
not. In a slightly different context we will get different pronouns
in Malay; we get different possessive adjectives of the same sort
in Swedish. In fact in simplex sentences the distinction is present
between reflexives and non-reflexives. O.K. But this one here is
ambiguous and as far as I can see the only thing that represents it
is a difference in label.

Suppes:

Oh no, that is a complete misunderstanding of my set-up.The two
readings have distinct semantic trees, which reflect the semantic
ambiguity.

Keenan:

. . . different reference?

Suppes:

Yes, they have a different reference and therefore they have
different semantic trees, and thus you have exactly the two trees
you want, the two semantic trees.

Joshi:

I just want to make sure that some of my earlier comments are not
misunderstood. To the extent Dr. Keenan's representations are
motivated by syntactical considerations, he would have an easier
time going from these representations to the surface syntax. The
contrast I want to draw is between those representations which have
a syntactic-semantic basis and those which have a purely semantic
basis (or conceptual basis). Both Dr. Keenan's and Dr. Suppes'
representations essentially belong to the former category and therefore, from my point of view the contrast between them is not really
very sharp. They both are interested in eventually mapping their
structures onto the surface structures.

Suppes:

I do not know how many people here are familiar with Winograd's

work. This is a recent disrootation written at MIT, on the
processing of natural language in a computer. The disrootation will
be published in the "Journal of Cognitive Psychology". It is a much
discussed example of the presumed successful attempt to process
natural language in a computer. Winograd is concerned to deal with
a simple perceptual situation and to process commands or questions
about this situation.

Now I agree very much with your remarks about that, but there is a
theoretical point that I would like to amplify, and we may want to
get on to this afternoon with our chairman who is unfortunately
somewhat muzzled this morning. The point is the following: Winograd
makes a very big point that the semantics is in terms of procedures
and it is part of his approach not to make a sharp separation of
procedures and data. It is natural to ask of such procedures how
they can fit in with the purely set-theoretic semantics that I have
described here. There are some direct remarks to be made on this
topic, for example, in the case of arithmetic. In many cases the
denotation of a terminal is not the set but a procedure, where we
have procedures we will want to make the set-theoretical operations
combine with procedures in a natural way. So, for example, we might
replace intersection by conjunction. In terms of how we want to
represent semantically the facts of life, the point is not a
philosophical commitment to set-theory but the fact that the
techniques of set-theory are simply the most familiar and the
simplest techniques of computation of this kind. If we have a very
firm grip on the situation, the kind of thing Winograd has
attempted, we can replace a set-theoretical version by a much more
algorithmic or procedure-orientated version and conceptually for my
standpoint that is not a major change.

Keenan:

I would just like to make one remark about the lexical
decomposition of the sort that Professor Joshi was discussing in
this respect. I think probably linguists have been simply very unclear about exactly what properties of surface sentences are
supposed to be determined by their underlying structures and which
of these properties then are supposed to be either preserved or
modified in a fixed way by the transformation. In almost all the
cases of proposed lexical decomposition in the literature it is not
difficult to find cases where plausibly the underlying structures
have distinct semantic and syntactic properties from the things you

derived from them. Even the people who advocate this sort of thing
have provided the arguments. Postal's article on anaphoric islands
will sometimes give sentences like Mary is an orphan as suggested
coming from something like Mary is a young person whose parents are
dead. But obviously that thing provides many noun-phrases that can
be referenced by pronouns and so on which cannot be referenced once
we have replaced that sub-tree by a single lexical item like
orphan . Similarly the other cases, the "kill" being paraphrased by
cause to become dead and so on. Everybody has counterexamples to
the full paraphrase of those two surface structures, and I think
before we can therefore propose this sort of decomposition,we simply
have to stipulate exactly which properties we are considering, which
properties of the surface sentences we are considering determined by
these underlying structures and only then can we really make a convincing case.

Potts:
Well, should we move on now to another topic? Dr. Keenan, perhaps
you would like to pursue your point about context-free grammars?

Keenan:
It is not natural in a context-free grammar to represent the sort of
structures you get with a variable binding operators of any sort;
what you normally have to do in a context-free grammar is generate
some sort of quantified phrase irrespected of whether anything in
the sentence quantified into matches it so that in a context-free
grammar you cannot generate only sentences like Every man is mortal,
but you also necessarily generate things like Every man John loves
Mary where the subordinate sentence quantified into in no way talks
about the phrase announced in the quantifier phrase. From the point
of view of natural language this is surely one of the most unnatural
things I have ever heard of. You never find in natural language
relative clauses like The man that John loves Mary or The man that
all girls are mortal. If you announce this in a head noun-phrase,
the man that, the next thing that comes along has to talk about it.
Now of course you can always fiddle; you can generate the wrong
thing to begin with and then put a filter on the end and get rid of
the garbage. I submit that is a completely unintuitive way to represent the meanings of natural languages. What we should do is
generate what we want to begin with because that is the most
explicit and direct way to describe what the natural language
structures are.

Suppes:

I think we agree on the point about the variable binding; we could
disagree about its use. Still, I can take your point and not quarrel
with this as a feature of context-free languages that we would like
not to have in order to match as closely as
possible the sentences that occur in natural languages. Fortunately
I am not really disturbed by your remark, because we can use indexed
grammars which are slightly richer than context-free grammars. They
introduce indices to keep track of exactly the variable binding
problems you raise,and yet it is known that such indexed grammars
do not go far into the hierarchy of context-sensitive languages.For
example, we can still draw trees. I feel that trees constitute a
certain kind of paradise; there is a great naturalness to the use
of trees in the analysis of the structure of sentences and I am
very reluctant to give up trees. I am not unwilling to give up the
more severe restriction to context-free grammars.
I will make another point. I do accept transformations that map
trees into trees, using a context-free base. But I think
independent of the transformation issue I agree with your remarks
about variable binding and in fact we have found in our own
empirical work that it is desirable to carry along a rather substantial set of indices along the lines we have been talking.

Keenan:

If you were to modify the grammar in that way, that would be a
significant departure from a context-free grammar. The structures
determined by these sentences in a standard logic or any of the
usual extensions can also be represented as trees. One very slight
inexplicitness, namely the sameness of label relation among the
different nodes, is only indicated by writing the same label down.
There is nothing in the actual tree structure that tells you that
and you have to have a clear idea what the vocabulary of labels **is**
so that you know that these two things are not, so to speak,
graphemic variants, but they are different occurrences of the same
symbol. Basically the tree seems to represent most explicitly the
constituent structure properties of the sentence and it leaves
slightly inexplicit, I think, the identity of label functions. And
if we look at transformations that only changed labels but did not
change constituent structure, in a sense the tree structure does
not change that much, but other than that I think the proposals we
had been making then would be very similar. I mean surely the

grammar of the standard logic cannot be written as an indexed
context-free grammar because it is no longer context-free anymore;
it generates a bigger class than that.

Suppes:

Yes, certainly.If we exclude vacuous quantification, logical
notation, then so you cannot say for every x there is a y such
that P(y). In this case it is exactly the indexed grammar that we
are talking about. Concerning the problem about the labels that you
mentioned, it is a question of what you want to buy. If we require
as we do in a phrase-structure grammar, and we do our logic that
way, that we have a fixed finite set of non-terminals,then of
course we must necessarily have this problem of, in my terms, the
denotations in a given tree. For example, the same label occurring
in various places in a tree will be at nodes that have different
denotations. That is an obvious necessary consequence of the fixed
finite nature of the set and of course in traditional logic, by
traditional I mean say, Hilbert-Ackermann,syntax is not discussed
in terms of a phrase-structure grammar, but the difference is not
important.

Keenan:

If you limit yourself to finite indices, surely there will be
semantically essentially ambiguous sentences, cases where the
possible antecedants of the pronouns are more in number than the
number of indices you have got to discriminate among them - something which is admittedly natural; that is the way natural
languages are. The discriminating powers of pronouns can only
distinguish masculine and feminine, singular, plural, a few things
like that, and if you have more noun-phrases than that, essentially
the sentence is ambiguous. This does mean that the only well-under-
stood semantic relation, logical consequence, can, as I see it, not
be really defined on these things. I cannot quite get away from
that. I think you answered that once but I perhaps did not
completely understand the answer. The point is if the structures
are essentially ambiguous, we do not have a consequence relation.

Suppes:

What I have said is that I agree with your remark about the surface
structure being ambiguous, so it means that logical consequence
must be defined for the semantic trees, and, exactly as in the
pronoun case, you will have very different tree structures and
those tree structures will tell you what the different possible

denotations of the pronouns are. So the response is that the dis-
ambiguation occurs at the level of the set of semantic trees of the
surface structure.

Keenan:

I see where the issue is. Usually in a standard logic bound
variables are not considered as having denotation at all, I mean
consider a well-formed sentence like Every barber who shaved just
those barbers who do not shave themselves cut himself. Now what is
the denotation of the last himself? Well, there is not any, because
if it is co-referential with its antecedent which it has to be,
there cannot be one. So there is not any object here that you are
referring to.The sole function of that pronoun is to be anaphoric,
but it does not denote, it cannot be treated as a constituent independent of the noun phrase that binds it. Maybe that gets into a
bit more of, I think, of the kind of important difference between
the intuition of a context-free grammar and the added power you get
with variable binding operators.

Suppes:

Well, I think the following is the case. It is true that we can give,
let us say, in first order logic a characterization of satisfaction
that does not require the bound variables to denote. An even better
example perhaps is this. We do not require that syntential
connective denote, for example, we do not in the ordinary definition
of satisfaction or truth for a first order theory have a denotation
for the connective "and". On the other hand in the case of the
variables we must discuss their denotations very explicitly because
we talk about the values of the variables which must lie in the
domain of the model. I completely agree that in a standard classical
formulation we have things that do not denote, but that in terms of
what I am saying do denote. But I do not see that as a major
problem. I also think if I say John went to the store and he bought
a new shirt, in ordinary intuitive ideas he denotes John, and it is
quite nice to have pronouns denote.

Keenan:

Even if . . .

Suppes:

You do not think that he denotes John?

Keenan:

I did not say that pronouns never denote. I am saying that there are
many uses of pronouns whose purpose is simply to indicate cross-

reference in a sense which is captured at least minimally by the use
of variable binding operators in logic, where they do not denote.
Even if you formulate a semantics of a standard logic in such a way
that variables always denote, the denotations are ignored in the
truth conditions of a sentence like For all except x . . . It does
not matter what x denotes when we look at the truth of that because
we require always that we can look at, we have to look at, all the
things. It does not matter what x refers to; if you make up your
semantics your way, it refers to something. I think it is essential
for your point that these things do denote because otherwise I do
not understand how you will discriminate the trees for sentences
which have deictic pronouns in them which are supposed to denote,
and ones that have these others in them. I mean originally you said
you did it because they denote different things, but in the cases I
gave it is quite clear that the pronoun does not denote; in the case
you gave it does, o.k., but in the one I gave, The barber who shaved
himself etc. etc. the last himself does not denote because there is
not any such individual. And it is not really understood as a
referring expression in that sense.

Suppes:
In that particular example I do not agree with you. In the phrase
The barber who shaved himself, the reflexive pronoun himself has as
a denotation the barber.

Keenan:
Sorry about the whole example, it was one of those tricky ones.
Would you consider Every student shaved himself, what is the denotation of himself then? It does not denote, it is not understood
to refer to an entity in the same way as Every student shaved him
is. There him has to denote; we do not know what its referent is,
but it denotes. But you are telling me the only way the semantic
trees are different is that the him and himself in this case denote
different things, but I think that is intuitively incorrect because
the occurrence of himself is not understood as a denoting
expression.

Suppes:
Yes, I think I agree that I must be careful in how I would formulate
Every man loves himself, as an expression of the same type that is
where there is a quantification binding on the himself. I will
reflect on what I would say about the denotation, I quite agree with
you that it is a good case distinguished from the others.

Potts:

The discussion is now open to the floor. Various people have already
asked to speak and I shall ask them to speak in order, so as to keep
the discussion on one topic for a period and then move to another
topic.

I begin by asking Professor Schnelle to raise a point concerning
presupposition, which is, of course, directed to Dr. Keenan.

Schnelle:

This is not really a question, the question is behind my critical
remark. The notion of presupposition and all the definitions which
were introduced by Keenan are an example of what is usually called
a transposed mode of speech which should not be allowed in
theoretical linguistics. The result is that some reading of what is
presented gives rather odd examples. For instance, in the hand-out
of Mr. Keenan's paper we have the example The fact that Fred left
early really surprised John, and he said that if the other sentence,
Fred left early, is not true then the first one is understood to be
vacuous. I find this quite strange. I can very well imagine a
situation where Fred left early is in fact false, but still the
situation where people communicate the fact that Fred left early
really surprised me is not at all understood as being vacuous. Such
a situation may be that the communicating people do not know that
Fred left early. The others are the examples The man who won won and
Every student who left early left early and so on, then it is said
their natural denials can never be true. Whatever this may mean, if
somebody utters the sentence The man who won did not win, he may
present a proposition which may be true, or false, or whatever. Now
keenan says: this is contradictory on literal reading. I think presupposition, and that is my main point, should be introduced as
being primarily a pragmatic concept. I could give an example of such
a definition as I would imagine it: Speaker x presupposes presupposition q in uttering sentence α if and only if whenever speaker
x utters sentence α with proposition p as its meaning, proposition
p contains q, then during the act of uttering x does not question
the truth of q. The linguist very often does not wish to bother
about all these pragmatical problems and he could make the following
statement: a description for the pragmatic concept of presupposition
is usable if it is a basic one in situations which are standard
relative to the grammatical analysis I propose. he assumes, of
course, that there are such standard situations. Now my definition

reads: If S is a standard situation for a sentence α relative to my
standard grammatical analysis, then x presupposes q ..., as above,
and if and only if the structural presuppositional notion, which
Keenan for instance has given, is true.
But this reduces everything to a literal meaning.
Keenan:
With regard to the sentences I claimed under my definitions presupposed themselves, The man who won won and so on, I would
certainly agree that a sentence like The man who won did not win
could be used in a meaningful way on many occasions. One of the
things I could produce to help us analyze what its meaning was would
be that if we had understood it in my literal sense, it would be obviously untrue; so the speaker must be getting at something else.
This sort of thing happens all the time. Suppose someone says John
is a good father and John is not a good father. On the face of it
is an obvious contradiction, but we give a normal speaker enough
credit for not being so simple-minded as to say an"obvious" contradiction. So we think a , "he must mean something slightly different
from what it literally means", so we reinterpret good perhaps to be
slightly different in meaning in the second case; so we have not
exactly denied what we just asserted. That I think is the kind of
thing we are doing here: If we adopt the relatively literal-minded
analysis I am proposing, we have a basis for saying what this
extended usage is. I have in no wise described the extended usage,
I have no pretence of doing so, but it does give us a basis for
saying why it is not meant in exactly the literal way. Your alternative is a more pragmatically based notion of presupposition, my
initial feeling is that it replaces a clear but very narrow-minded
notion, mine, a very useful notion, by one that covers a lot more
ground but is much less clear and therefore, I think,much less useful.
I do not easily see how I can use your notion to discuss particular
speech of speakers. I imagine I would always be having recourse to
a d h o c criteria. You have to refer to things like The speaker
means q. Well, what does that mean? If we talk about speech acts,
we have to consider all the ways of uttering it. If I say John
thinks that all men are mortal, well, I have just uttered the
sentence All men are mortal, but do I mean it or not? And in many
funny cases like this, all the accidental uses, you have to have
recourse to further sort of a d h o c non-sociological analysis

to get out what you mean by <u>speaker means q</u> and so on.
Admittedly the notion I have got is an abstract notion, it has
nothing whatever to do with speaker's beliefs or intents. I give
it as a property of a sentence in the same way that logical
consequence or logical implication is defined in terms of truth
relations of sentences quite independently of whether anyone utters
them or believes them. The question is whether the world is the way
the sentence says it is. It is an abstraction, we in a sense
abstract away from a speech-situation. My argument is that it is a
useful one; it allows me to distinguish without recourse to vague
things about, you know, what it means to say that p contains q and x
means p and so on, it allows me to distinguish similarities and
differences in meanings between sentences of the sort that I
mentioned. So I give you a pragmatic answer: I can use it to say
interesting things about language.

Potts:
Do you want to pursue on that, Professor Schnelle?

Schnelle:
Just one sentence: You should have said that it is an abstract.

Keenan:
In part II I give a complete definition. It might have been useful
to point that out. I take your point.

Potts:
Dr. Posner also has a question on presupposition.

Posner:
If you take the sentence <u>I thought that he was sick</u>, there is a
difference between the information in <u>I thought that</u>, whatever this
information may be and the information in <u>he was sick</u>. You
describe the difference by saying the one is a presupposition and
the other is an assertion. Perhaps the whole sentence is asserted
the presupposition being a part of it. But take sentences like
<u>That he was sick is possible</u> where <u>he was sick</u> is not presupposed
in the sense it follows from the sentence <u>That he was sick.</u> So you
must have a concept to describe the difference between the
information <u>he was sick</u> and <u>it is possible that</u>, which is very
similar to the difference between the two informations contained in
<u>he was sick</u> and <u>I thought that.</u>

Keenan:
A small point concerning your examples which I am a little unclear
about: In none of those cases <u>I thought that he was sick</u>, he was

sick is possible did I say that the embedded sentence was
presupposed. I discussed, admittedly, with one example a class of
predicates of the surprise sort which take factive embeddings;they
can accept the paraphrase the fact that Fred left surprised John.
Your examples are simply not the cases I am discussing; I admit,
however, your point that there is a distinction in these sentences
between the more dominant and the less dominant information,
although I think it is actually a much less clear distinction than
in the case of the predicates I come to say something about. In very
many languages the locutions for I thought that he was sick are
almost indifferent as to where the negation is placed: I thought
that he was not sick, I did not think that he was sick. The
distinction between the levels on which the information is presented
there is almost non-existent. You can get other examples where it
is not, and I admit that the distinction, the logical distinction
I am making between assertion and presupposition does not capture
completely the distinction between, so to speak, most dominant and
less dominant. It covers several very interesting cases. This
amounts to saying that there is more than one way that information
can be subordinate in a sentence - which any linguist would agree
with, surely. I think I leave my answer at that if that satisfies
you.

Posner:

Just one remark: You said that this distinction between the
different dominances, high, less, low, is unclear. I think it can
easily be made clear if you take a concept of protest and if you
make a test by protesting partial information of the sentence.

Keenan:

If we take the examples you gave, say I think that John is sick.
If I respond,"Do you?" as a weak protest, it means "Do you think
that John is sick?"Well, there is a difference between "Do you?"
and "Is he?" If you could represent in some sort of formally clear
way what you meant by natural protest,you know, I could certainly
consider using that notion. The advantage of the one I have got, is
that it abstracts from this sort of intuition what a natural denial
is. We extend the notion to many sentences that do not have any
natural denials; conjunctions, for example, make presuppositions
here, but there is no natural negation. Disjunctions of sentences
in this system make presuppositions, but there is no natural
negation of such sentences and so on. That is what I define in

terms of falsehood conditions. The basic cases I made this system
up to handle do have natural negations and that works out right.
Well, I leave it at that.

Posner:

I think one can define a situation of protesting which is clearly
enough and which is restricted enough to get a test for
differentiating relevance.

Keenan:

The advantages of the approach I have is that it is all done
formally. I know what sorts of things in models look like and what
truth values look like and I know how to reason clearly with them.
But the more pragmatic notion of a natural protest is something
that needs formalizing before we can work with it. But I accept the
intuition and we will close the discussion on that.

Potts:

We have quite a number of other questions addressed to Dr. Keenan,
but I think we must give him a breather at this point. So I shall
ask Herr Wett to put a question to Professor Joshi on componential
analysis.

Wett:

I have some remarks on your system of componential analysis. When
you have analyzed push, you found at least two elements: move and
cause to. I do not see the reason why you stopped there because
"cause" can be decomposed again and you find lots of components and
you can continue further on. To be honest, I do not think that the
two elements are really in the meaning of "push" because you can
imagine sentences like I pushed the table, and I pushed it again,
but I could not move it.
My question is: why do we do componential analysis?

Joshi:

First of all, the analysis I presented was only an example (as a
matter of fact the example is Fillmore's) and some other analysis
could also be justified. The purpose of my talk was not to justify
one or another factorization but to present the kinds of arguments
that are given for justifying factorization. Of course, this does
not yet answer your question.
Your question really is: Where do you stop? From a linguist's
point of view the main purpose is to establish closer syntactic-
semantic correspondences. The idea is that such decompositions
would help establish these correspondences better than the

undecomposed items. For example, the <u>do</u> in the analysis of action
verbs helps one to relate the question <u>what did he do?</u> to the
sentence <u>He studied</u>. One also looks for independent justification.
For example, in this case one can claim (as Ross appears to do) that
this <u>do</u> is really the phonetic representation of the intentionality
predicate that you may want to set up for all action verbs.
Whatever other justifications one might give, one always wants to
make sure that such decompositions aid in setting up better
syntactic-semantic correspondences. A psychologist would like to see
these components related to the conceptual categories he may have
set up.
Of course, there are the usual considerations which also appear
elsewhere in linguistics, viz., we would like to see to what extent
the components reappear in other semantic domains, to what extent
they group together, to what extent you can compose them to describe
lexical items other than those you started out with, etc.
Within these guidelines there is room for variation and clearly to
that extent the factorizations arrived at are arbitrary.
Potts:
Would you like to pursue that?
Wett:
You can continue the decomposition until you get an infinite description of a sentence like"I push the table".
Joshi:
Oh no, that is not quite the case.
Wett:
Maybe it is an extreme case.
Joshi:
Aside from the considerations that I outlined in my previous answer
to you, we have yet another important consideration. Although our
components are abstract in the sense that they are not the lexical
items themselves, we are clearly interested in having these com-
ponents or their compositions lexically realized. This constrains
us significally. In fact, if one looks at the components that have
been proposed for various verbs, one notices that most of the
components are fairly easily lexically realizable. In my talk, I
outlined the various positions one can take in this respect.
Potts:
Well, we will come back now to Dr. Keenan. There are questions on
two aspects of his formal language, his atomic sentences and his

noun phrases. Although it seems the wrong way round, I am going to
take a question on the noun phrases first because that on the
atomic sentences will lead us into questions about the reference of
pronouns which will invoke Professor Suppes as well. So I am going
to ask Mrs. Barth to speak next.

Barth:

I would like to propose the following questions to Mr. Keenan:
How can in your logic a negation sign which is a first prefix of a
noun phrase be moved beyond the quantified noun phrase,or are they
not moved but absorbed by these noun phrases? Can you in your logic
avoid a conclusion that One cat has two tails starting from the
truth premise that No cat has two tails?

Keenan:

First as regards how negation works in these sentences, it behaves
in a completely standard way. Let me just illustrate in one phrase
what the actual rule in the syntax of the logic is. It says roughly
that if S is a sentence and this thing NP is a noun phrase, a
quantified noun phrase, and x is a variable pronoun, then (NP_x,S)
is a sentence, and we require that x occur free in S and so on.
If S is a negative sentence, well, we get Every student was not
drunk. Quantified noun phrase addition is the same rule if S is an
affirmitive sentence or S is a negative sentence. In other words,
the noun phrases make sentences out of sentences, we can negate
them or we can operate on negative sentences. So there are two
completely natural representations for All mathematicians are not
smart. Let us try your sentence One cat has two tails, I did not
explicitly put in number quantifiers but we can treat them that
way, i.e. as quantifiers, let us say: (a cat x)(2 tails y)(x has y)
I can represent here in a perfectly standard way, a sound way, the
usual quantifier ambiguities in, Every boy loves a girl, Some girl
loves every boy and so on. I take it that that basic way would
handle your No cat has two tails or whatever it is. I do not know
how to handle the essential possession of has,and it seems to me
pretty silly to think of it like a two-plan predicate for the two
tails that the cat has are something that does not exist
independent of the cat.

So I am not bothered by that particular syntax, but the basic
relative scope ambiguities of the quantifiers come out exactly
right in this system. Regarding the specific problems on
existential instantiation I have a complete definition of truth in

a model, but I have not written down a deductive system. So off the
top of my head I do not know what a rule of existential
instantiation would look like; so I will not try and make it up on
the spur of the moment.

Potts:

There are now two questions on the atomic formulas which we can
best take together, the first is from Dr. Posner.

Posner:

Could you please make some more remarks on the status of your noun
phrase representations?

Potts:

The second question is from Dr. Stachowitz on the reference of
pronouns.

Stachowitz:

I do have some questions about representations of quantifiers.
Could you try and show me how you represent "All my friends, who
are in Italy now, are wise,"and the same sentence beginning with
"Almost ...". And then the same sentences without commas, and also
these sentences beginning with "All my friends but one ...".

Keenan:

The justification for treating complex noun phrases in the way that
I am doing is that if I do it this way, I can show that certain
sentences are logically independent, have certain topical consequences, and that certain sentences make certain presuppositions.
There is no guarantee whatever that it could not be done in some
other way; this just happens to be a way I have proposed because it
gets me the comest results for the class of sentences I was looking
at. Let me give just one or two examples. My rule says I get a
quantified noun phrase as follows: Step one: Put any determiner
"some", "every" or "the" in front of a common noun followed by a
pronominal index. O.K. Determiner, noun, x, that is a simple
quantified noun phrase, this gets put into quantified sentences by
a rule that says: Take any sentence S with x is free, then put a
quantified noun phrase in x in front of the sentence. That is a
quantified sentence. We have a second definition of a quantified
noun phrase: Take any quantified noun phrase, and here is a lot of
freedom, convert it, sorry, take any quantified sentence, convert
it into a noun phrase, and here all we really need to do is give
that sentence a pronominal index because we are going to use that
for quantifying into further sentences; so I take simply this

thing, call it x for the moment, and write an index after it and
call the whole thing a quantified noun phrase. You can do much more,
you can put a relativization marker after it, here, if you wanted
to, but you do not actually have to make the distinction between a
head noun and a subordinate sentence because it is already marked
here, by the parentheses. Now the motivation for distinguishing that
structure in the sentence is that in order to practically state the
truth conditions and falsehood conditions which determine the consequences and presuppositions of the sentence, it is natural to be
able to reference this noun phrase; for example, suppose I want to
show that each student in Philadelphia likes horses. I want to show
that presupposes there exist students in Philadelphia; that is if it
is false, we still understand it there are students in Philadelphia
but there is at least one who does not like horses. Well, since I
have this whole thing as a noun phrase, it looks very roughly like,
something like, you know, Every student x is such that x in Philadelphia..., the whole thing is a noun phrase, x likes cheese. Now,
this is the thing that I have to stipulate the truth-in-the-model
conditions for, and I stipulate it as true, roughly, just in case
the set which this noun phrase is interpreted as is not empty and
this sentence x likes cheese holds of every member of the set. This
sentence is false in an arbitrary interpretation; just in case this
set is not empty and this sentence fails for one of its members;
otherwise it gets the third value, in particular if the set is
empty or if this sentence quantified into had more complexively and
made presuppositions that did not have anything to do with this
noun phrase.
The reasons then for discriminating this structure is that I find
it natural to refer to the sets specified by these noun phrases in
the truth conditions. The second reason I indicated briefly in the
presentation, namely if I represent them in this way, I get natural
representations for transparent and opaque readings. An illustration
of this would probably introduce more formalism than is useful at
this moment, but it is not very complicated; the entire semantics
I have given in about two or three pages in part II of this hand-
out.
Concerning the second question on the representations of the various
sorts of relative clauses you suggested the answer is that I do not
have any answer. I have no explicit representation in this system
of non-restrictive relative clauses. The only relative clauses of

complex noun phrases I even attempt to say anything about are
restrictive ones, and I have no way to represent quantifier
modifiers like "almost". O.K. I do not know how to write the
semantics for that. I can represent these things like "all but one"
as long as it is specific I can in effect - in fact in an article
in "Foundations of Language" I worked that out slightly informally,
so I will not go into it further here.-

Stachowitz:
Is it identical to "only one is not in Italy"?

Keenan:
"Only one of my friends is not in Italy". No! I defined it in terms
of "only". What I defined was an"only"-quantifier and then the "all
but x" was stated as a function of that. I do not actually remember
what the function was. But that one could be handled with a certain
minimal degree of adequacy here and then it would be the case that
the whole thing had the category noun phrase or that "one of my
friends" would be a constituent in an underlying structure in that
representation.

Stachowitz:
Now since that"only"assumes that " all my friends but one are in
Italy" is equivalent to"only one of my friends is not in Italy",
I would like to know what your semantic representation of these
sentences is. Is it identical or can we derive it from the other?

Keenan:
What I have proposed in that article in fact was - it was in a sort
of logical framework -   to derive the "all but one" from "only...
not". I introduced it by definition - a transformational. You could
say that we derived that by a transformation, and so they will have
the same underlying representation, yes.

Potts:
While we have this last example, I shall take a question from
Professor Staal on Dr. Keenan's notion of 'making more explicit'.

Staal:
I think that is an interesting notion, but I do not know exactly
what you need it for. The way in which you define it is all right,
in the way you talk about it, it seems to me, you have something in
mind that may not be all right. In your examples you indicated that
it is not the case that the King of France is bald if it is not the
case that there exist, a King of France. In fact it seems to be that
one wants to make these presuppositions e x p l i c i t   and that

is what I am interested in in your definition,that those presuppositions also have to be constructed, they cannot just be enumerated.
Keenan:
Within this system we can ask the following and interesting
question for a given sentence S: Is it possible to find another
sentence whose assertions in this logical sense are the
consequences of the other one? In other words, a sentence which
makes fully explicit all the things that the other sentence
implies, its assertions as well as its presuppositions. And the
answer is: No, it cannot be done.
The claim here is that I have defined a notion of explicitness and
I am not saying that we cannot find a sentence S whose consequences
equal the presuppositions of some other sentence. We can do that,
and that is a theorem in the system. What I am saying is that it is
not the case that for every sentence S there is another sentence T
such that the assertions of T, the things it implies without presupposing them - are equal to the non-trivial consequences of the
original; in other words, the non-trivial ones are ones that can be
false in some state of affairs; they exclude the logically true
ones. That fails in this system for several reasons which you might
argue are shortcomings of the system. I do not want to argue that
one, I will just give the examples. Thus consider proper names in
this system: a sentence with a proper name like John left, i.e.
John is such that he left, presupposes John exists. We can say that
John x is such that x exists. This is one of the sentences that
presuppose themselves. It cannot be false; it can be third valued
if the name John is not interpreted as an individual of the
universal discourse; that is if a non-refering name, and so the
sentence can be untrue, but it cannot be false in this system; that
is a fact of life of this system. But there is no way in this
system to assert the presuppositions of the proper names because
any sentence that appears to assert it is one of those that pre-
supposethemselvesit does not then logically assert it. You can also
not make fully explicit the presuppositions of the factive
predicates because the only way I can say that"Fred's leaving
surprised John" is to put it in a position where it is presupposed
in this system. Maybe I should augment the syntax; I am not
claiming otherwise; I can of course take this sentence and look at
that as a presupposition in the metalanguage. I can take it up and
say this is a presupposition, in fact all its consequences are

presuppositions of the original. In that sense I can make it
explicit; what I simply cannot do is fully paraphrase every sentence
in this system by another in this system which does not make any
presuppositions other than the trivial class of logically true sentences - which under these definitions are presuppositions of every
sentence, - something which is sort of natural actually. Note that
it is impossible in this system to a s s e r t a logically true
sentence, and furthermore they never assert anything - which I look
upon as a small but positive property of this system.
The conjuncted sentences I have proposed were paraphrases,
admittedly in a weak sense; but they are not complete paraphrases
because they do not make the same presuppositions and assertions.
However, it is a common practice in Linguistics and Philosophy to
attempt to explain the meaning of a sentence by pulling out each
of its individual ideas and saying them separately. To some extent
that process can be justified in this system by showing that if we
have two sentences, let us say roughly one of them complex without
conjunctions, the other a conjunction of somewhat simpler
sentences, there is a theorem here that says roughly that the
simple one will assert some of what the complex one presupposes,
given that they have the same truth conditions to begin with. And
this justifies that conjuncting makes some of the original information more explicit. Admittedly, the result is not a complete
paraphrase because you have lost the presupposition structure.
Staal:
And what you want to make explicit also by some methods is exactly
the presupposition structure.
Keenan:
I can do that, but you will not like it. Note that we can rephrase
your question as:
"Is it a case where for every sentence S I can find another
sentence T, such that the consequences of T are equal to the presuppositions of S?"This sentence T then would in a sense tell us
what all the presuppositions of S were because they would be T and
everything that follows from T and that is all. That answer is yes.
Consider: For every sentence S consider the sentence "S or not S",
and then that will do it. But it somehow does not seem insightful.
But still the presuppositions of S are exactly the consequences of
"S or not S".
But the answer to the other question is "no". If you consider

roughly for each sentence S we can sort of compute, let us say as a
function of the structure of S, a finite set of sentences which is
such that all the presuppositions of S are assertions of this set
of sentences.
We simply cannot make all these presuppositions explicit; that is
what we have to show we cannot do in the system - which may be a
shortcoming of the system, maybe we want to make it a requirement
of logic that it should make everything explicit, but I do not think
so because I have tried it out in natural language and it is very
difficult to make explicit the presuppositions of proper names
without getting completely meta-linguistic and saying the name
John denotes. And it is also very difficult to find a sentence
which makes explicit, asserts, the presuppositions of a factive
sentence. You can make up a conjunction: Fred left early and that
fact surprised John, but if we imagine a case where Fred did not
leave early, it still seems that the sentence that fact surprised
John must have the third value because the fact referred to does not
exist. And so it is hard to make that explicit. And that may just
be a fact of natural language, it seems it is natural to presuppose
this, in a logical sense, and so it cannot be made fully explicit.
Hiz:
I am very interested in Professor Suppes' way of doing semantics;
it is familiar, it is intuitive, it is transparent, we know how to
work with it. However, the question is whether it is applicable to
a natural language. To test it let us take some difficult examples.
For instance, when you have a discontinuous morpheme, for instance
the familiar "if,...then" which occurs in different places of a
sentence. Of course artificially you can say I represent it as one
node, but that is not how it appears in the sentence. You rather
would like to attribute to two nodes, to two different words, one
semantic concept presumably of implication, and this is not
provided by the normal tree,and assigning to each node a semantic
quality. Similarly I was not yet quite satisfied with your answer
to the enquiry about pronouns and their relation to referentials.
You may take another discontinuous morpheme: comparative suppose
I say This discussion is of a higher quality than most. Then
usually linguists will take that -er of higher and than, and
higher-than should be really one morpheme which occurs in a discontinuous way. However, at the same time higher is a modifier of
quality and must be akin together and be joined together in form

a higher quality as a noun phrase. So you have here a double-
structure; one structure a higher quality which forms a noun phrase,
and another, namely -er with than which forms a connexion. Here
again it is both discontinuous and over-imposed. If you consider
pronouns, an important feature of pronouns is that they are very
sensitive to intonation, in particular stress, which again over-
imposes another structure. Take an example: If you use an epiphoric
pronoun: When he was eighty years old, Bertrand Russel wrote a book.
If you stress he, then you say When h e was eighty years old,
Bertrand Russel wrote a book, then he is no more a referential for
Bertrand Russel. And therefore you have to provide some method for
stress which is another feature, and you have then to assign to a
node not only a grammatical category, but two categories, namely
that it is a pronoun and that it is stress. However, then this is
not enough because if you consider longer texts, you may have: When
h e was eighty years old, Bertrand Russel wrote a book, but when
I will be eighty years old, I will be senile, where he again is a
referential to Bertrand Russel. All this shows that when you are
making semantic interpretation of your nodes, you must have quite a
lot of rules for how to do it. And those rules are in a way the
content of semantic sentence and this is only a representation of
one aspect of the result.

Suppes:

I think the examples you bring up are good problems for my kind of
formulation. I want to make a couple of distinctions before I come
to the pronoun case. Certainly, the discontinuous morphemes are a
problem. I have discussed here only what I call the simple case
where each node denotes. First, for continuous morphemes, let me
give you an example that is n o t a problem. Take a relation like
have diplomatic relations with. For example Does Japan have
diplomatic relations with China? Now in this case, I would use a
single denotation for the verb phrase, not because this is an
ultimate analysis of the phrase, but because it is expedient not to
escalate the type so much, so that in actual applications one will
let phrases rather than single words denote. And so not every node
has a denotation. In the case of discontinuous morphemes, we can
begin in this fashion and then by transformation perhaps deal with
the matter. But I am not sure this is a satisfactory answer, and I
do not want to give a hasty response as to how I would handle discontinuous morphemes.

Now let me turn to pronouns. First on your point that stress or
emphasis can carry some additional meaning. I quite agree with you,
and one may wish to have more than just a simple denotation carried.
So we want to carry at the node some additional information. And
that is a case of elaboration, not a fundamental change of my
approach to semantics.

I would like to return to give a further example of pronouns, to
Keenan's good example of reflexion, and let me indicate how at least
in an imprompt fashion I would want to handle that kind of example,
just to show how I would hope to move a step further. I think (and
maybe this is something that Keenan and I share) that one of the
dispairing things about any attempt to be systematic is almost anyone can produce an example you have difficulty with. Let me take
three sentences, he loves himself, Everyone loves himself and Someone loves himself. I do not want here to go into how I am going to
handle quantification; that is a topic that would take a longer
discussion. But I would want to say that regarding the himself I
would handle it in the quantified cases - I think I perhaps gave a
different impression in the earlier discussion - , as reflexive.I
would handle it in the same way as here, and let me indicate how I
would attempt to do that. So I would roughly have a tree that looks
like this

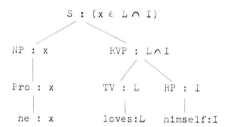

and let me just give on the right-hand side of each node its denotations. So I say a reflexive verb phrase (RVP) goes to the
transitive verb (TV) here and the reflexive noun phrase (RP), and
then TV go to loves and RP to himself. The key is reflexive.
Himself denotes the identity relation (I), and loves the binal
relation L. The root of the tree, which is labelled S, has T or F
as its denotation. Thus $(x \in L \cap F) = T$ if and only if $x \in L \cap F$.
This then is the kind of analysis I would give of himself and I

think this reflects the character of a reflexive pronoun. The
quantification in these two cases takes place on the left side of
the tree and is quite separate from the analysis of himself.
I am under no illusion that what I have said here will necessarily
meet the problems of other pronoun cases. I want to be properly and
more than duly modest about that point. And also, as I have said, I
will need some time to think about discontinuous morphemes. Let me
just close by saying that for my standpoint the effort should be to
push the framework as far as possible and to recognize where it
cannot be made to work.

Potts:

Are you satisfied with that?

Hiz:

Maybe one more example: He who loves himself does not love others
is a universal sentence in normal understanding. Now you have he as
a variable and you want that for a variable he to have a
denotation. however, that would be presumably not quite proper to
do here because it is a universal sentence.

Suppes:

I think in that case, we have an idiosyncracy of quantification,
that is, where the quantifier is understood.The weakness of my
response is that I do not see how to provide an algorithm for
recognizing such cases. For example the key here is the modifying
relative clause, but I am not at all certain that I have any real
clarity on the device that should be used. And by the way,it is
even a problem in ordinary mathematical talk whether the variables
really are bound or not.

Keenan:

The short remark about your rather ingenious way to handle this on
the spur of the moment I think in principle only works where the
anaphoric and deictic pronouns are formally distinct in the
language. So here it will work for himself, but for the example I
originally gave, John thought he was drunk, we do not have an anaphoric and deictic distinction in the system, we have only got a
he. So the thing is ambiguous in that respect and to define your
function you have to discriminate two different things that, I
guess, are in the domaine of the function.

Suppes:

You know I have to draw two different trees, one being different
from the other to do that.

Keenan:

Yes, right.

Potts:

In drawing the symposium to a close, may I say that there will be an opportunity to continue discussion of these topics this afternoon. There are a few questions from the floor which have not been able to take, but I will pass these on to the chairman of this afternoon's session. It only remains then for me to thank the three symposiasts for the excellent papers they have given us this morning and for provoking a very lively discussion. Thank you very much.

GENERAL DISCUSSION

Chairman: C.H.Heidrich, Universität Bonn

February, 19th, afternoon session.

.

Heidrich:

I suggest that we begin this general discussion with some of the
problems that have not been discussed this morning. Dr. Potts
informed me that there are still some questions. Prof. Bar-Hillel
wants to raise a question concerning the extensions of models that
have been proposed this morning.

Bar-Hillel:

My question is a general one advised to almost all speakers of this
morning. But for the purpose of specification I address it to
Prof. Suppes. Professor Suppes has shown us the route to the
paradise. It seems that in this paradise a number of snakes have
remained on the trees. I shall try to play the role of one of those
snakes and my question is the following. The notion that each word
in a sentence should have a denotation is an old and classical one,
but it is also old and classical that it has failed. In the Middle
Ages they knew that you cannot get along with so called
categorematic terms and that you certainly need also syncategorematic terms. It does not seem to be possible to talk about
denotation in general in any serious way. Assume that Suppes has
succeeded in showing how one can give a denotation for such a
classical syncategorematicon like 'the'. I think the question arises
how much one can foresee that the model can be extended. The general
principle that you have to start with little pieces, that you have
to start with "Ausschnitte" from the language in order to continue
is obviously a necessary one. Nevertheless, if you do not see how
you could possibly continue, then it is also a dangerous and a misleading one. My problem is that with regard to t h i s model and to
all the other models I know I most of the time do not see how I
would continue with the next illustration.

I do not see how Professor Suppes could possibly deal with such a
sentence as This book is really red. Just the adverb really, not
just any adverb, because this is, to put it short, a pragmatic
adverb, i.e. one which expresses an attitude of the speaker to this
particular utterance. So my question is: How could this model be
made to work? What does it help to say that this model works for an
infinitely large class of sentences of English, but nevertheless
only for an infinitely minor torso of the English language since
the very next extension, I believe, already breaks down? Though I
ask this question of Professor Suppes, it is meant to everybody in
this room including myself. What good does it do to deal with torsos

of fragments of natural languages if we do not even see how to
expand the treatment of those fragments to enlarge pieces? My
positive claim is, if you do not see how to extend your treatment,
do not give me a treatment of any fragment.

Suppes:

I shall not try to sketch how I would really treat <u>really</u>.I think
it can be done.

The problem here is a kind of contrast: one of the richest
intellectual histories we have is the history of converting what I
like to **call** negative dogma into negative proof. Our problem really
is in terms of your intuition to see how we can decide the issue in
a way that we all can get ashore. That is, either give a positive
construction that shows how the extensions can be made, or give a
negative proof that it cannot be made. And so until we have either
a positive extension or a negative proof, we are left up in the air
regarding the possibilities.

Now just one second remark: I think you raised a very good and
difficult issue, the issue being that if you do not see how to
handle a certain kind of construction whether it is then worth
while to present a fragment. It seems to me that it is easy to argue
both sides of that, you can give many scientific examples of
theories being proposed for which clearly were no intention or hope
of **accounting** for easily stated extensions. But I do say what we
need is the conversion from dogma to proof one way or the other.

Schnelle:

Professor Bar-Hillel's remark was directed towards handling syncategorematic expressions and expressions being pragmatically
described. An example of the first was the treatment of <u>the</u>.
In the Montague treatment at least the tree looks somewhat
different. There is no note for <u>the</u>. So the question does not come
up directly because <u>the</u> is introduced by a special operation. He in
fact has a distinction between syncategorematic and categorematic
terms. This would be a solution to my knowledge.

Suppes:

I would like to make a brief remark on the syncategorematic problem.
I wish to emphasize that it is not so simple for me to have each
note denote. It seems to me that there are two senses how one can
understand the concept 'syncategorematic'. One is that a word occurs
in a phrase and the whole phrase denotes. As an example, we may want
the entire phrase: <u>Bear in mind</u> to denote.

A different sense is where you have a restricted notion of
categorematic, so that if a word denotes a function in the intuitive
sense, you do not want to regard that as categorematic. It is like
somebody's other issues about how you want to handle predicates or
various types of function words, whether we want to treat them as
categorematic, how do we regard the issue of abstract objects. So it
seems to me there are two distinct senses of syncategorematic that
can be used.

Schnelle:

I would like to hear a comment of Professor Hiz on this because I
think it is an example for a model-theoretic approach. And I am not
quite sure whether it would be possible to explain the same thing
in his theory of language description.

Hiz:

You mean in aletheic theory?

Schnelle:

Yes.

Hiz:

I do not see any problem. Why should it not be possible?
Concerning the model-theoretical approach for natural languages in
general, I would therefore like to say the following. It is
presumably unavoidable that the use of language in particular
situations is not quite sharp. As a matter of fact, even in such a
situation one perhaps shouldn't say that it is ambiguous. For
instance, the concept of number as characterized by the concept of
zero, successor, and equality is not sharp enough to distinguish
between different models. It accepts most models, and in that sense
if we are speaking that particular small language, then we never
know which model we are having in mind, whatever it means "to have
in mind". However, for every language of that sort, there is
another language which resolves the obscurity. I can certainly
describe the difference between the two models in a richer language,
in which I will have predecessor for instance and say that in the
first model there is an element without a predecessor but in the
second there is none. By some other means I can describe the
difference between the two models in a richer language. I am fully
aware that not only mathematical language but any language will
always contain some non-sharp concepts in that sense.

Keenan:

I want to respond to Professor Bar-hillel's remark about the

extendability of theories. I take the point that once a theory of a
particular part of the verb has been proposed, a natural and
important requirement is the consideration of what else we can do
with it, how we can extend it to cover more ground. I would like to
defend inextendable theories on the ground that the research
attitudes they generate are more productive in the long run. I think
as a practical guide here, not a theoretical issue, we have to learn
to exclude lots of things that we should like to handle but cannot
in order to make some progress at all. I think there is a counter-
part to this: the sort of approach that tries to represent everything at once in a representation that is so general that its
substantive claims are actually very weak tends to stifle research.
Again I am talking about research attitudes, not about the
theoretical studies of these approaches because the attitude it
generates tends to diminish the interest of finding out what is
actually going on.

Potts:

May I also concern this business of extendability. I think that
there are very reasonable grounds for considering only a fragment
of a natural language. E.g. I think it would be quite reasonable to
say: I am not going to propose now a theory which is going to give
you an account of psychological verbs because these, for the
constructions that follow them, have some kind of propositional
complexity. We have got to understand first of all the kinds of
constructions that follow them and therefore we might leave these
aside for the time being as long as there is nothing in the theory,
which we can say a priori, that it excludes the possibility of
dealing with these.
In fact, the traditional divisions of philosophy give you a very
good idea of what can reasonably be excluded. Namely you could have
a theory which included moral terms but left out political ones,
but would then have to include psychological ones. You could have
a theory which left out the moral and political ones and only went
to suppose the psychological ones. You could have a theory which
included expressions to do with time and place but cut out the
psychological ones. I think there is a very natural progression
here of greater and greater conceptual complexity. This kind of
restriction would be reasonable. But there is another kind which I
think is unreasonable. This is perhaps what Professor Bar-Hillel
was touching on in his example. If we have a theory which includes

adjectives, here one might say,well, adjectives which are in some
way connected with psychological concepts I do exclude. But I
cannot arbitrarily exclude adjectives which are semantically
connected with other types of concepts that my theory does cover,
e.g., if I am going to have a theory which will include tenses,then
I must have temporal adverbs. If I am going to have a theory which
will allow me to talk about places, then I must be prepared to say
something about locative adverbs and locative adjectives. This is
the kind of point which will become unreasonable. The example that
Professor Bar-Hillel has produced is a particularly difficult one
because as J. Austin used to say: "<u>Really</u> is a trousers' word,"
by which he meant, it is a trousers' word in the sense that it
took on its shape from what was wearing it, in other words, that
you understand what <u>really</u> means in a given context by what it is
been contrasted with. It is what you have to look at here , what is
unreal. In the case of <u>The book is really red</u>, well, what would be
some circumstances in which one would say that? When under a sodium
light red colours go also yellow-coloured, you might say: "This is
yellow." You were walking along outside in the street perhaps, and
then you say: "No, it is really red." Then we might be testing
somebody for colour-blindness and we show him the book, and he
says: "It is brown," but you say: "No, it is really red."
Now these are just two of many possible examples.This I think is
going to be a dreadfully difficult case for all linguists. I do not
think we ought to press Professor Suppes to answer questions on
that, but I have tried to suggest here that the kind of answer one
ought to give to Professor Bar-Hillel's question requires quite a
number of careful distinctions to be made. It is not just a very
simple answer.

<u>Bar-Hillel</u>:

I probably did not express myself carefully enough. To take a
torso, to take a fragment and to discuss it, as I said already,this
is the best scientific procedure that has been done since eternity
and will be done until eternity. The point is however: Do I foresee
that this fragment I am dealing with can be incorporated as such
within a larger fragment etc.? I meant that if I foresee that this
fragment will break down at the very next example, then this is
already a difficult strategy. I am only asking for one's attitude
towards a fragment for which the proposer of this fragment probably
sees at the same time that the very next example will already cause

him to change the whole approach. This is "only" a question of
scientific strategy. I do not want to say that I have a privilege
to tell people how to work in science, but I only want to call your
attention to the fact that   particular linguists might become or
will become impatient. Many linguists will no longer stand the fact
that philosophers and logicians will come to them:"Here, you see, I
have a beautiful model for this fragment of language. Let me work
another few hundred years and then I will give you a good part of
the story." Linguists will be satisfied if they are shown the way
how the rest can be handled. Therefore my question is: Should not
model-theoreticians, in the double sense of the word, think ahead of
time and should they not provide models for fragments of which they
already know that they will not stand up to the **very** next counter-
example, which they already can see.
Quine has introduced the concept of the i n d e t e r m i n a c y
o f   t r a n s l a t i o n. Since this term has not been used at all
during this conference, let me please call attention to it, and let
me replace the term 'vague', which Professor Hiż has been using,
by the term 'indeterminate', I am sure Quine will agree with that.
There is a difference between 'vagueness' and 'indeterminacy',and we
need both terms for linguistic considerations. You may find a unique
model,but often there are infinitely many models, and within metalanguage these infinitely many models the unique model remains indeterminate, nothing vague about it, each particular model is
perfectly clear. There is an amount of indeterminacy which cannot be
eradicated and Quine claims that this is a highly important feature
of natural languages. Quine has been refused hundreds of times, but
nevertheless there is a highly interesting idea behind what he has
to say.

Suppes:

I want to continue the dialogue with Professor Bar-Hillel. We can
recognize how powerful it is and has been to look at fragments.
A very nice example is Tarski's decision procedure for elementary
algebra. Now from the standpoint of somebody who wants to work
algebraic problems, it seems ridiculous that we do not know whether
that system is decidable if we add exponentiation. So the viewpoint
affects very much and, I think, Bar-Hillel is too monolythic in his
remarks about the role of fragments. But it depends very much what
the intention is and the kind of insight one hopes to get. So it
would for example be very interesting if we were able to give a

natural definition of fragments and establish within that fragment
what it can do and what it cannot do. The difficulty at present is
that we have a kind of intellectual chaos. We do not have the
apparatus yet established. For example, in spite of the appeal of
the examples that Dr. Potts gives, I do not think that there is a
basis there for serious systematic investigation. There is a basis
for excellent remarks and distinctions, but I cannot see a way to
establish semantically a sharp result about, for example, moral
terms, or moral terms with respect to psychological terms. For I do
not think the distinctions have been formulated sufficiently sharp.
It is not that there is not an intuition there. The difficulty I
have therefore thinking about fragments of natural language is how
to define in an intuitively satisfactory but in a sharp way
fragments in which we can deal.

Schnelle:

Such models as presented by Montague and Suppes are powerful tools
for treating linguistic problems. I want to point to some aspects
of the Montague theory which are not sufficiently known. In
Montague's theory are also at least two levels: one level presenting
his tool, and the other level presenting an analysis of examples for
English. The tool is very powerful, indeed, and the universal
grammar, this is important, does not assume that the structural
description must necessarily be a tree in the sense of immediate
constituent-structure. The system is so powerful as far as I understand it that a transformational grammar is just a specialization
of it. Montague has always been understood as if he only gave a
surface structure analysis, that was because of his examples but not
because of the general theory. We should describe particular
languages with such a framework and, by looking at the structures
in the particular languages, we should find out which kind of
restrictions of this very powerful model are appropriate and which
are not. If many languages, say several hundred, would be described
in this style, we could come back to the universal hypothesis.

Hiż:

I would like to make a few very general comments on the strategy
of linguistics. It will be, of course, illustrated only by a
trivial syntactical problem, but maybe it will show some way of
attacking more than just syntax.

One may consider that the work of several trends in syntax are for
quite a long time under the influence of mathematical logic. And
what we had this morning from Suppes is certainly in that side. But
it is perhaps in a way surprising that one of the fundamental ideas
of mathematical logic is not yet explored well enough by syntax.
It is the idea of a function which was elaborated at such length by
Russell or by so many other mathematicians and logicians from Frege
and Schröder on, namely the idea that every function determines a
class, or various ways of formulating it. What does it mean? It
meant, you can recall in "Principia", if you have a sentence and
you raise one or two phrases from this sentence and replace by
variables, you obtain a class, or a relation, or a triple relation,
etc. And really there was at the beginning of this idea no
restriction of which phrase to raise. This amounts to looking at a
sentence as a function of its components. Just as when you have a
sentence John read a book, you can take this sentence as a
particular substitutional case of the function x read a book, or
you may take it as a substitutional case of John x a book,or as a
substitutional case of John read x. You even can, and with good
profit in linguistics,take it John read a x.

You can say,when you are looking at the sentence John read a book,
it is a substitutional case of the function x read a book and you
can consider this sentence e.g. as an answer to Who read a book?
however,if you consider the very same sentence John read a book as
an answer to What did John read? then you assign a different structure to the sentence.There is perhaps a prejudice among
syntacticians, among all of us, that a sentence should have one
structure on a given level, surface, deep, or whatever. however, it
is perhaps more useful to consider that even such a simple sentence
as John read a book has several structures depending on the context
in which the sentence occurs. I do not mean social context, I mean
linguistic context.

The same phenomenon can be observed in mathematics, and it was very
fruitful. Take the numerical phrase '5+3=8', what I will say is:
here is a sentence, a trivial arithmetical sentence for which it

was historically very important that people gave two different
grammatical analyses. And those two analyses are in a way
incompatible ones. They separately are very clear for this sentence,
and similarly it may be expected - and there is plenty of linguistic
substantiation for it - that even The book is read could have other
useful grammatical analyses, e.g. the definite article which you
have here can also be considered as a referential because it is the
book which was mentioned before, presumably. And therefore I am
making an appeal for plurality of structures for a given text.
Potts:
I would like to speak in support of what Professor Hiz has just
said, I think that he has brought out a most important and vital
principle, one which, Peter Geach has long spoken of as the 'Frege-
principle': that one should be able to analyze many sentences in
more than one way. And this seems to me to be one of the fatal
defects of transformational grammar, that we must start off always
by dividing a sentence into a noun phrase and a verb phrase. One can
take such a simple argument as: Caesar conquered Gaul. Gaul is a
beautiful country. Therefore Caesar conquered a beautiful country,
as an argument in which one needs to take as one constituent of
Caesar conquered Gaul, Caesar conquered x where 'x' marks a gap
for an empty name, a constituent which we are not allowed to have
in transformational grammar because it only allows us to break down
a sentence into noun phrase: Caesar , and verb phrase: conquered
Gaul . There is no node in the tree which dominates the expression
 Caesar conquered . This Frege-principle is of vital importance for
giving an account of even the simplest logical arguments. And although you may be able to provide some kind of definitions with a
transformational grammar which would allow the consequence to go
through, they will be very roundabout and complicated compared with
the simplicity achieved by Frege's alternative analyses. So I would
like to say that this point is highly relevant to the controversy
between categorical grammars on the one hand and transformational
grammar on the other. I will not say phrase structure grammars
because, of course, they are much more general.
Hiz:
Thank you for the support, but I have to oppose your last statement.
I always understood that transformations are exactly to catch the
idea here. The sentence with one structure is transformed into the
very same sentence with another structure. The transformation is

just here. It is a mistake to consider that transformations are in
an essential way connected with any trees. And I do not see why to
go deeper into the woods. On the contrary, transformations are the very
same thing as definitions in mathematics, it is looking at a
sentence from a different point of view. If you say "Here is a
sentence. I will take it now as a function of this and that." That
is exactly what you do when you are writing definitions. Look at
Suppes' "Textbook on Logic" where the theory of definition is at
least outlined contrary to most textbooks on logic.

Montague does not have a theory of definitions in his grammar, and
that is where he does not see the connection between what he is
doing and transformations. It is defintions which are needed and
not trees in order to get transformations.

Potts:

I am sorry I think we are talking across purposes. I cited transformational grammar, but, of course, I meant the base-component of
the transformational grammar. I did not mean anything to do with
transformational rules. Regarding this very simple sentence Caesar
conquered Gaul, you would, I suppose, need transformational rules
for putting the verb in the right tense. But as regards this point
of the alternative Frege analysis, the base-component of the transformational grammar excludes what is needed for this simple argument
in both of the rules given by Chomsky in "Syntactic structures" and
in those given in "Aspects".

Suppes:

I think Potts' and also Hiz's example of analyses raises a subtle
problem. In the case of sentences where we can provide for a set
of analyses, if you take that viewpoint with evidence, then there
are very good counter-examples for that trust in physics or in
geometry. And the important point, historically and conceptually,
has been to escape the particular use of anyone analysis, and has
been to recognize and to discover the i n v a r i a n c e of the
situation independent of the particular analysis in terms of a
given frame of reference. And it seems to me that that is exactly
what is needed in linguistics. That is, we do not in fact want to
be able to go off into several different directions to give
analyses.

Bar-Hillel:

The invariant is there, the invariant is that all those sentences
m e a n the same thing. Nevertheless it is vital to understand

that the same sentence has different structures. Many years ago I
went a step further than that when I insisted that we work with
different grammars for the same language simultaneously. Suppes'
point is almost a kind of immediate consequence of that. Let me ask
the following questions: Why are we able to express the same thing
in natural languages in different ways altogether? Isn't that a
waste of effort? Think about it a few minutes and you will see that
it is important. We shall be able to say the same thing in different
ways that the context shall be expressed by the sentence which can
be analysed in different ways so that we have a multiple analysis.
All these things fulfill a vital communicative function under
different communicative situations and work just because the invariant is kept which is, of course, the major point.
Now a minor correction. I would propose not to use the word
'function' in the sense Hiz was using it. In Germany, since Scholz,
one is used to work with the word 'form', one talks about
'sentential forms' and not about 'sentential functions'. This
is, of course, an unimportant problem.

Hiz:
That is a linguistic problem!

Keenan:
I would like to make one point about the sense in which transformational grammar has always, since "Syntactic Structures",
imposed the multiple analysis on a base-structure or the thing
generated by the phrase-structure component, even where that
generation was formulated in such a way as to assign a unique tree
to the sentence. The reason is that the structural descriptions of
the transformations can describe the structure of the tree in any
way they see it fit, they are stated in a much more powerful
language. And the proof for this is that the same transformation
will apply to the same tree and give you different out-puts.
Passive, e.g. has always been formulated so as to generate from
John gave the book to Mary both Mary was given the book by John
and The book was given to Mary by John. It does this by signalling
out different parts of the structure in its structural description
and assigning the rest maybe not even a category, just giving it
the string-variable. In this sense the transformations have always
imposed a multiple analysis, although they have not always been
formulated so as to impose all possible analysis, to be sure.

Suppes:

I would like to continue the discussion with one remark about the
problem of invariances. Let me give a geometrical analogy. If we
represent geometry, we can do this, as we all know, by numbers. Let
us take some familiar relations: suppose we take e.g. Tarski's axio-
matization for elementary geometry in the terms of 'betweenness'
and 'equal distance'. These notions are invariant in   geometry.
They have a meaning that does not change under analysis. However,
if we look at the numerical assignment, we do not have - in the case
of the particular coordinate system - used the coordinate system to
represent these invariant notions to correspond, I would say, to
the obviously different grammars we can write to express what we
take to be the meaning of a sentence. I do not know how to formulate
an invariant theory, I do not know how to replace our present
conception of grammar where, I think, we all recognize that we can
write down different analyses all of which express in a clear way
the meaning of a sentence. What we need is a deeper theory, corresponding to   geometry, that is based upon concepts that permit us
to formulate in an invariant fashion the meaning of a sentence. And
that simply I do not understand how to do.

Heidrich:

I shall take this as a concluding remark of this part of the
discussion.
The way in which Professor Suppes has just formulated the problem
of meaning suggests to take up, for the rest of the discussion,
some problems that evolve from the title of our colloquium.
Let me say the following in advance: Some questions, I suppose,
will arise from the fact that the possible interpretations of the
German "Kommunikationssemantik" and the English "semantics of
communication" are not equivalent.

Lieb:

I want to raise the following question: Have we really heard anything about 'kommunikationssemantische Analysen', and if so, where
are these analyses? Perhaps it is just a number of individual
points distributed throughout the papers which so far have perhaps
not been connected with the supposed general topic of this
colloquium. I would like to ask Professor Ungeheuer perhaps to give
a short summary from his point of view of what has been said during
this colloquium on this subject.

Ungeheuer:

Mein Eindruck ist folgender: ich habe die drei Tage damit verbracht,
die Diskussionen in den verschiedenen Sitzungen zu beobachten. Darin
stelle ich gewisse Grundstrukturen fest, und ich glaube, man sollte
darüber auch reflektieren können. Eine Denkrichtung, die für uns
natürlich interessant wäre, ist die in Bezug auf die Kommunikationsprozesse, die zwischen menschlichen Individuen sich abspielen oder
das Interaktionsverhalten von menschlichen Individuen als kommunikation. Also das Grundschema, das ich feststelle und das mir natürlich
bekannt ist, vor allen Dingen von linguistischen Diskussionen her
und logischen ist dieses: es gibt eine Kategorie, die man vielleicht
'linguistische Objekte' nennen könnte,(ich könnte auch extensional
sagen: es ist eine Menge solcher Objekte vorhanden).
Linguistische Objekte können Sätze sein, aber auch Texte. Texte sind
in dieser Konstituierung nicht automatisch schon Kommunikationsob-
jekte oder Phänomene, die in irgendeiner Weise mit Kommunikations-
abläufen zu tun haben. Nun gibt es zwei Verhaltensweisen dieser
Menge von linguistischen Objekten gegenüber; die eine Verhaltens-
weise möchte wissenschaftlich versuchen, diese gesamte Menge aufzuzählen: das ist das klassische Enumerationsproblem, das natürlich
zu Beginn der generativen Tradition aufgeworfen worden ist; und zwar
muß ein Apparat entwickelt werden, der dafür sorgt, daß diese Menge
von solchen linguistischen Objekten eben deutlich so gekennzeichnet
wird, daß jedem dieser Objekte eine Strukturbeschreibung zugeordnet
wird, und diese Strukturbeschreibung kann als der Index angesehen
werden, der jeweils diese Objekte voneinander unterscheidet. Nun
kann es passieren, daß der erste Vorschlag, den man gemacht hat,
beispielsweise der syntaktische, und so ist es ja traditionell in
der Geschichte verlaufen, daß der nicht zur Aufzählung ausreicht,
und daß man deswegen gezwungen ist, neue Mittel hinzunehmen, beispielsweise semantische. Das wäre jedenfalls ein Problem, wie man
sich diesen linguistischen Objekten nähern kann, und so hat man es
auch getan. Es taucht in dieser Weise überhaupt nichts auf, was mit
menschlichen Individuen zu tun hat, obgleich merkwürdigerweise ja
in der Gesamtdiskussion Hilfsmittel, Hilfsargumente herbeigezogen
werden, die immer wieder in das faktische der Sprache, in die Kommunikation hineingehen. Aber das Problem selbst besteht darin,
diese Menge von linguistischen Objekten aufzuzählen, seien es
Sätze, seien es Texte. Ich will das hier einmal als Enumerations-
problematik bezeichnen. Der zweite Zugang in der Behandlung dieser

linguistischen Objekte könnte der sein, daß man sagt, jenachdem wie
ich deskriptiv oder vielleicht phänomenologisch die Kategorie lin-
guistisches Objekt abstecke, - aus der Empirie entnehme - , wird es
notwendig sein, diesen linguistischen Objekten Merkmale zuzuordnen,
nicht etwa zum Zwecke der Aufzählung, sondern weil diese Objekte in
der Realität diese Aspekte zeigen. Beispielsweise könnte man sagen,
diese linguistischen Objekte sind in jedem Falle Zeichen, also haben
diese als Zeichen so konzipiert zwei Seiten, zwei Aspekte, und entsprechend müssen diese zwei Aspekte in jeder Weise und auf jedem
Niveau in irgendeiner Weise in Erscheinung treten. Damit haben wir
einen semantischen Aspekt, wir haben dann vielleicht einen syntaktischen Aspekt oder einen morphologischen Aspekt, einen phonolo-
gischen. Dann erinnert man sich, daß es ja schon Theorien gegeben
hat, in denen man nicht nur von zwei Aspekten bei Zeichen gesprochen
hat, sondern von dreien, und die Pragmatik erscheint; die Pragmatik
kann aber auch wichtig werden, wenn man diese Menge von linguistischen Objekten - zwar qua Zeichen - noch anders in ihrer Konstituierung absteckt, indem man nämlich mit hinzunimmt, was menschliche
Individuen mit diesen Zeichen machen, nämlich k o m m u n i -
z i e r e n . Aber diese kommunikativen Merkmale, die treten übli-
cherweise nicht etwa auf, um den Kommunikationsprozess begrifflich
zu analysieren, sondern dienen lediglich dazu, nach wie vor, die
Menge von linguistischen Objekten per se zu konstituieren, was etwas
anderes als Kommunikationsanalyse ist. Das wäre eine Erklärungs-
prozedur, die nicht enumeriert, sondern immerhin analysiert. Das
wäre sozusagen die kognitive Grundhaltung, die kennzeichnend ist
für den größten Teil der Darstellungen, die ich hier gefunden habe.
Wenn ich nun von Kommunikationssemantik oder von Kommunikationstheorie spreche, wie ich es mir vorstelle, dann würde ich meinen,
daß dieser Ausgangspunkt von vornherein zu eng ist, auch wenn bei
diesem approach Kategorien hilfsweise hinzukommen, die weit in die
Pragmatik hineingehen. Ich meine vielmehr, daß von vornherein das
gedankliche, das begriffliche Modell oder der begriffliche Grundan-
satz anders aussehen muß. Es kann sich dann nicht mehr darum handeln, Mengen von reinen Größen von linguistischen Objekten anzu-
setzen, die man behandeln kann, ohne von menschlichen Individuen zu
reden, oder nur charakterisieren kann im Hinblick auf einige Merkmale dieser Individuen, sondern daß als Begriffe selbst menschliche
Individuen in der Theorie auftauchen mit solchen begrifflichen Be-
stimmungsstücken, die ihr Kommunikationsverhalten charakterisieren.

Und dazu gehört nach meiner Einsicht, nach meiner Empirie, die
Beobachtung, daß merkwürdigerweise die Individuen kommunizieren und
annehmen, daß dies funktioniert, und daß sie zu einem Erfolg kommen,
daß sie aber trotzdem bei einiger Reflexion und Beobachtung des
eigenen kommunikativen Verhaltens merkwürdige Dinge tun mit Elementen, aus denen diese linguistischen Objekte einmal abstrahiert worden sind. Sie setzen nämlich ihre Bedeutung und den Sinn zwar im
Verhältnis zu einem Regelsystem, das vorhanden ist, aber trotzdem
nicht nur in strenger Abhängigkeit von irgendwelchen pragmatischen
Bedingungen, sondern sie setzen sie frei aus der Kommunikationssituation heraus, und zwar in einem Maße, das weit über das hinaus-
geht, was man unter dieser Betrachtungsweise auch in der neuesten
Version bereit ist zuzugestehen. Ich kann eine lange Rede halten
und offensichtlich ist es so, daß meine Intention nur die ist, überhaupt ein einziges Wort zu thematisieren, überhaupt nur dies zu
geben, und alles andere läßt sich rein mit der syntaktischen Appara-
tur erklären, die ich natürlich kenne und beherrsche und die ich ab-
laufen lasse, während ich auf der anderen Seite eine von mir stark
intendierte Rede halten kann, voll semantisiert sozusagen, aber ein
Zuhörer da ist, der zwar auch mit mir kommuniziert, jedenfalls sich
anstrengt, es zu tun, aber überhaupt nur das eine oder andere Wort
versteht, d.h. nur dieses mit Sinn belegen kann aufgrund seiner
kommunikativen Setzung und alles andere wieder zwar realisiert als
richtiges Deutsch beispielsweise, aber rein nach der syntaktischen
Maschinerie, die er setzt in der Beherrschung, sonst nichts. D.h.,es
muß in dieser Theorie, die also begrifflich die Individuen berücksichtigt, und zwar so berücksichtigt, wie sie in Kommunikation sich
verhalten, in der Konstruktion, dieses Moment in jedem Fall enthalten sein, daß die Zuordnung von mindestens zwei Aspekten an diesen
linguistischen Objekten, sagen wir Syntax und Semantik,keine feste
und ein für allemal ableitbare ist, sondern daß dies frei im Kommu-
nikationsprozeß im Spiel ist. Sie müssen nur einmal daran denken,
daß wir uns ja nicht nur unterhalten mit solchen Beispielsätzen, die
immer hier gebracht werden, sondern mit solchen Sätzen, die hier
tatsächlich fallen, mit denen beispielsweise, die ich jetzt hier
produziere oder die gestern Herr Apel produziert hat, oder die andere produziert haben. Wenn sie an diese Sätze denken, dann sehen
die doch etwas anders aus. Aber gerade bei diesen schwierigen Fällen
zeigt sich, daß die Semantisierung von syntaktischen Konstruktionen
zwar durch Regeln gesteuert ist, aber diese Regeln von ganz anderen

Bedingungen abhängen, auf ganz andere Art aufgebaut sind als die
linguistischen, die hier in diesem approach bisher genannt worden
sind. Und,was nun mein Argument angeht, ist dies, das eigentlich
kommunikationssemantisch folgendes heißen sollte: in einer möglichen
Kommunikationstheorie dieses viel freiere Verhältnis zwischen einem
Regelsystem, das man beherrschen kann, und nach dem man sinnvolle
oder sinnlose Sätze des Deutschen oder einer beliebigen Sprache produzieren kann, und dem, was eigentlich damit gemeint ist, daß dieses
freiere Spiel eingehen muß in die begriffliche Struktur, und ich
sehe nicht, wie dies bei üblichem linguistischem Zugriff überhaupt
geschehen könnte.

Apel:
Ich möchte eine Bemerkung machen zu dem, was Ungeheuer gesagt hat.
Ich möchte versuchen, sein Anliegen zu verstehen. Ich hatte den Eindruck, daß hier ein Rest geblieben ist, der ihm am Herzen lag, und
den wir offenbar kaum erreicht haben durch das, was bisher diskutiert worden ist. Nun möchte ich aber andererseits den Versuch
machen,doch noch einmal auf dem Wege der Abstraktionen, die hier
dauernd durchgeführt worden sind, mich an diesen Rest heranzutasten.
Ich erinnere in dem Zusammenhang noch mal an die Abstraktionen, die
Schnelle im Panel 1 an die Tafel geschrieben hat. Ich habe den Eindruck, daß wir uns im Bereich von Syntax und Semantik aufgehalten
haben, dann vor allen Dingen in dem Bereich,der festlegt, wie weit
man mit Hilfe der Logik ins Pragmatische hinein semantisieren kann.
Es wurden dann immer Beispiele gebracht, bei denen man fragen muß:
sind sie überhaupt noch semantisierbar, oder wird man sie vielleicht
doch mit verbesserten Mitteln in einer Semantisierung fassen können?
Dann aber ist ein viel radikaleres Problem aufgetreten und durch
Ungeheuer ausgesprochen worden, meine ich, nämlich, daß z.B. die
Deixis hineinkommt mit h i e r und j e t z t, die personale
Deixis mit d u und i c n, außerdem Adverbien und Tenses. Man kann
sich eine gute Vorstellung davon machen, wie abstrakt das immer noch
ist, wenn man an die Arbeit Wunderlichs denkt, der tatsächlich eine
Fülle von Beispielen gebracht hat. Da ist in einer generellen Weise
herausgestellt, was man im Sinne einer generalisierenden Wissenschaft 'Pragmatik' nennen und auch erforschen könnte. Nun habe ich
den Eindruck, was Ungeheuer meinte, würde noch einmal erforderlich
machen, eine Abstraktion zurückzunehmen. Auch diese Art von Abstraktion einer pragmatischen, generalisierenden Wissenschaft, um nämlich zu dem Punkt zu kommen, bei dem in einer konkreten geschicht-

lichen Situation der Mensch aus seiner kommunikativ-metakommunikativen Kompetenz heraus souverän Gebrauch macht von den Mitteln der
Sprachsysteme - , - in einer Weise Gebrauch macht, die Probleme
stellt, die auch nicht eingefangen werden können in einer generalisierenden Pragmatik. Um nun vielleicht eine Brücke zu bauen: es gibt
Sätze, die von dem Standpunkt einer generalisierenden Pragmatik aus
abweichend sind, z.B. der Satz: <u>Ich sage dir hiermit nicht, daß du
mein Freund bist.</u> Der Satz ist, verstanden als performativer Satz,
abweichend, denn ich kann nicht eine negative Performation expli-
zieren. Trotzdem ist der Satz ja offenbar verständlich. Man kann
auch dafür vielleicht wieder generelle Regeln angeben, dann wäre das
immer noch im Bereich der generalisierenden Pragmatik.
Das ist aber nur ein Annäherungsversuch. Ich bin überzeugt, daß die
kommunikativ-metakommunikative Kompetenz des Menschen in der geschichtlichen Situation so souverän ist, daß sie über jede solche
mögliche Generalisierung hinaus Sinn konstruieren könnte.
Es tritt hier ein Problem auf, das in den letzten 50 Jahren Philosophie in der Luft steht. Man hat sich nämlich bemüht, Sinnkriterien
herauszuarbeiten, die ein für allemal klarstellen sollten, was Sinn
und was Unsinn ist. Soweit ich sehe, ist das nicht gelungen. Es ist
nicht gelungen, weil Sinnkriterien auf der Ebene der Logik bereitgestellt sind, auf der Ebene einer Semantik, die an den Sachverhalten orientiert war, das war das zweite, dann auf der Ebene der
Pragmatik, das war schon bei Wittgenstein und Peirce der Fall. Es
gab dann immer noch eine Ebene,wo man sagen konnte, nun, man kann ja
versuchen, in der Situation Kontexte herbeizuschaffen, die den Satz
doch sinnvoll machen würden. Ich würde sagen, das ist eine neue
Ebene, nicht mehr die Ebene der generalisierenden Pragmatik, das
wäre die Ebene der Hermeneutik. Und das hängt meines Erachtens mit
dieser souveränen kommunikativ-metakommunikativen Kompetenz zusammen.
Ich meine, ich habe mit all dem nur einen Versuch gemacht, Unge-
heuers Anliegen zu verbalisieren. Ich weiß nicht, ob mir das gelungen ist.
<u>Ungeheuer:</u>
Das, was ich zuerst gesagt habe, ist sicherlich mein Problem; den
Unterschied von Abstraktion und Konkretheit habe ich nicht gemeint.
Ich frage einfach danach, was brauche ich, um eine Kommunikationstheorie aufzubauen. Ich brauche natürlich eine empirische Basis.
Ich brauche Prädikate, mit denen ich diese empirische Basis beschrei-
be und die ich einführe für meine Theorie. Und darin brauche ich

mindestens Kategorien für menschliche Individuen, aber menschliche
Individuen, die in ganz bestimmter Weise begrifflich berücksichtigt
sind. Dabei ist es mir gleichgültig, ob das, was dabei herauskommt,
Pragmatik oder sonst irgendwie heißt. Ich möchte auch nicht von Kompetenz sprechen; ich gebe ja zu,der Mensch kann das, und dafür daß
er es kann, nochmal. Eine Kategorie einzuführen, halte ich einfach
nicht für notwendig. Was muß ich aber berücksichtigen, d.h. wie muß
ich in dieser Theorie begrifflich ein menschliches Individuum
setzen? Ich setze weiterhin voraus, daß eine Hypothese zu erklären
ist, etwa derart, wie schaffen es die Individuen überhaupt,mit einer
ganz bestimmten Kommunikationsintention zu kommunizieren. Das Wahr-
heitsproblem beispielsweise, das die Logik interessieren muß, ist
dabei völlig in den Hintergrund geraten. Das eigentliche Problem
liegt so: es sind mindestens zwei Individuen da, und die versuchen
sich zu verständigen, und die beiden wissen, was das heißt, "sich
verständigen". Und sie brauchen Kriterien, um zu überprüfen, ob das
Verständigungsziel erreicht worden ist, das Kommunikationsziel.
Haben sie diese Kriterien oder haben sie sie nicht? Welche Strate-
gien verwenden sie, um zu der Hypothese zu gelangen: ich habe den
andern verstanden oder nicht. Welche Taktiken verwenden sie, welche
Hypothesen bauen sie auf? Aufgrund welcher Grundlagen sind solche
Hypothesen überhaupt aufbaubar? Das sind alles Fragen, die in diesem
ersten approach bei diesen zwei Aufteilungen überhaupt nicht auftauchen. Aber das heißt nun nicht, um dies gleich zu sagen, daß
diese ersten beiden Zugänge zu linguistischen Objekten nicht relevant sein könnten. Und das meinten wir ja gerade. Sie sind relevant,
aber möglicherweise nicht so relevant, daß die Theoriebildung dort
direkt übernehmbar ist in eine Kommunikationstheorie. Sie kann
höchstens Anregung geben. Und ich meine auch, daß für die einzelnen
Individuen natürlich die Wahrheitsfrage in ihrer Kommunikationshandlung wichtig ist, aber dies ist eigentlich nicht die kommunikative Problematik. Die kommunikative Problematik ist meinetwegen eine
hermeneutische: wie ist Verständigung, kommunikativ, linguistisch,
sprachlich erreichbar.
Bar-Hillel:
Als ich die Einladung zu dieser Konferenz bekommen habe, habe ich
mich gewundert, daß unter den fünf Themen die Worte "Sprechhandlung", "Sprechakt" nicht einmal vorkamen, obwohl von Kommunikationssemantik die Rede war.

Ungeheuer:

Das hängt damit zusammen, daß Searle vor kurzem hier gewesen ist.

Bar-Hillel:

Auf jeden Fall hat sich wiederum herausgestellt, daß die Brücke von
Syntax, Semantik, Pragmatik zu Sprechhandlungstheorien fehlt.
Die Brücke zwischen diesen beiden Ansätzen, soviel ich weiß, gibt
es bisher noch nicht. Die Sprechhandlungstheoretiker sowie die Syn-
taktiker und Semantiker bearbeiten das ihre, und eventuell wird der
Pragmatik noch Lippendienst geleistet, aber sonst nicht viel mehr.
In den Vorträgen wurde von logischer Semantik, es wurde von linguistischer Semantik gesprochen, sogar das Wort philosophische Semantik tauchte auf, aber es wurde nicht einmal in den fünf Sitzungen,
die wir bisher gehabt haben, der Versuch gemacht zu sehen, wie man
dann weitergehen kann. Wie gesagt, in einer linguistischen Konferenz
wäre das eventuell vollkommen normal gewesen.
Es freut mich, daß in den letzten Minuten noch der Versuch gemacht
wird, einen Ausgleich herzustellen, obwohl mehr als programmatische
Bemerkungen im letzten Augenblick nicht zu machen sind. Jedenfalls
ist klar, wer immer sich mit Semantik oder Syntax beschäftigt, muß
sich jetzt und heute mit Pragmatik beschäftigen, was selbstverständlich auch Montague, Lewis und andere gemacht haben, was aber wiederum in den Sitzungen hier nur hin und wieder erwähnt, aber nicht
einmal ernsthaft behandelt wurde. Das Wort Semantik wurde leider
viel zu ernst genommen. Es hat sich um 'Kommunikationssemantik' gehandelt, und dieses Substantiv 'Kommunikation' wurde sehr schnell
vergessen, es blieb dann nur noch das Wort Semantik übrig.
Im allgemeinen wird jeder Sprecher sowieso darüber sprechen, was er
im Sinne hat und nicht, was von den Leuten, die die Konferenz arran-
gieren, gemeint ist. Aber wenn wir uns in dieser Schlußsitzung nochmal überlegen wollen, was wir uns nach Hause nehmen, dann ist das
Wichtigste: welche neuen Probleme, welche neue Aufgabenstellungen
sind formuliert worden. So würde ich noch einmal auf mein "cetero
censeo" zurückkommen und das Hauptproblem der Sprachphilosophie oder
der Kommunikationsphilosophie oder sogar der Kommunikationstheorie
darin sehen, wie die beiden Richtungen zu einer Konvergenz gebracht
werden können, die eine Richtung, die von Syntax und Semantik zu
Pragmatik hingeht, die andere, die von der Sprechhandlungstheorie
ausgeht.

Ungeneuer:

Ich möchte eigentlich im Anschluß an Bar-Hillels Bemerkung drei

Dinge sagen, aber das eine vorweg: ich sehe die Sache nicht so trau-
rig und tragisch an, was das angeht, daß möglicherweise Intentionen,
die wir gehabt haben, nicht voll erfüllt worden sind. Ich bin
eigentlich schon ganz zufrieden mit dem, was ich gehört und gesehen
habe. Aber einmal mußte einfach der Versuch einer solchen Konfrontation gemacht werden, auch wenn die Konfrontation vielleicht nicht
durchgetragen worden ist, vielleicht auch gar nicht diese Intention
verstanden worden ist; ich meine die Konfrontation von, na sagen wir
mal, Linguistik auf der einen Seite und auch anderen Ansätzen, beispielsweise in Ansätzen, die mehr aus der Psychiatrie oder der
Sozialpsychologie kommen, und den Ansätzen, die wir vielleicht hier
kommunikationstheoretisch oder so etwas nennen. Also, nicht daß der
Eindruck entsteht, Herr Bar-Hillel hätte mir aus dem Herzen gesprochen, was diese pessimistische Bemerkung angeht über den Verlauf
des Kolloquiums. Aber die zweite Bemerkung, das geht die Sprechakte
an. Natürlich hätte man darüber etwas sagen müssen, wie im übrigen
über manches andere mehr im Zusammenhang mit dem Stichwort Kommunikationssemantik. Es hat mehr historisch zufällige Bedingungen gehabt, daß wir nun gerade diese Auswahl getroffen haben. Aber zum
Thema Sprechhandlung, 'speech-acts', Sprechakte muß man doch folgendes hinzufügen: sie sind jedenfalls im Ansatz bei Searle, wenn auch
die Intention auf den Sprechpartner darin enthalten ist, doch immer
noch Kategorien, die jeweils auf ein Individuum bezogen werden.
Wenn überhaupt, müßte man den Sprechakten sozusagen Hörakte gegen-
überstellen, aber das würde immer noch nicht das notwendig machen,
was wir brauchen, nämlich eine Kategorie, die mindestens mehr als
ein Individuum als Bestimmungsstück enthält, und zwar eine solche
Kategorie, die nicht auflösbar ist in Individualkategorien. So wichtig dieser Beitrag ist, so ist er doch nicht das letzte Stück der
Verbindung hin zur Kommunikationstheorie. Was die semantische Seite
angeht: wenn wir Sprechakte vielleicht einmal so auffassen, daß man
generell bei jeder sprachlichen Handlung eine semantische Schichtung
vorfindet, derart, daß man zwei Schichten unterscheiden kann, sagen
wir einmal eine modale Komponente und eine propositionale Komponente, so ist ein Problem bei jeder Kommunikationshandlung darin zu
sehen, daß möglicherweise im Kommunikationsgeschehen selbst die
Grenze zwischen diesen beiden Schichten von den beiden Kommunika-
tionspartnern verschieden gesetzt wird. Eine solche Problematik
taucht in den anderen Zugängen, auch von der linguistischen Seite,
gar nicht auf. Und das Problem ist beispielsweise: wie kann über-

haupt formulatorisch deutlich gemacht werden, wo diese Grenze gesetzt ist? Und was kann geschehen von seiten des Hörers, daß er
durch Inferierung dazu kommt zu entscheiden, wo die Grenze gesetzt
ist? Das sollte nur ein Hinweis sein, wie wenn man von einem kommunikativen Standpunkt ausgeht, man überhaupt den ganzen Bereich des
Semantischen, jetzt mal weiter gedacht als nur linguistische oder
logische Semantik, man auffächern muß, ja schichten muß, komlemen-
tieren muß mit anderen Komponenten, damit man überhaupt die Kategorien gewinnt, in denen nachher die Theorie aufgebaut werden kann.